The Gospel of John

A Reading

Stanley B. Marrow

PAULIST PRESS
New York/Mahwah, N.J.

Also by Stanley B. Marrow published by Paulist Press

PAUL, HIS LETTERS AND HIS THEOLOGY

Cover design by Art Jacobs

Library of Congress Cataloging-in-Publication Data

Marrow, Stanley B.
The Gospel of John: a reading/Stanley B. Marrow.
p. cm.
Includes index.
ISBN 0-8091-3550-7
1. Bible. N.T. John—Commentaries. I. Title.
BS2615.3.M36 1995
226.5′077–dc20 94-44922
CIP

Published by Paulist Press
997 Macarthur Boulevard
Mahwah, NJ 07430

Printed and bound in the
United States of America

Contents

JOHN 3

JOHN 4

JOHN 5

JOHN 6

JOHN 7

JOHN 8

JOHN 9

JOHN 11

JOHN 12

JOHN 13

JOHN 14

JOHN 15

JOHN 16

JOHN 17

JOHN 18

JOHN 19

JOHN 20

JOHN 21

To the memory of

GEORGE W. MACRAE

Proinde in eis qui libenter et humiliter audire noverunt, et vitam quietam in studiis dulcibus et salutaribus agunt, sancta delicietur ecclesia.

Saint Augustine

Introduction

As its title indicates, this is a "reading" of the gospel of John and not, strictly speaking, a commentary on it. There are more and better commentaries on this gospel than on any other. From the earliest times, John has always attracted the finest minds and most sensitive expositors. Our century, moreover, has been blessed with some truly outstanding contributions both to the vast list of commentaries on the fourth gospel and to the endless number of studies of its every aspect. The present work does not even aspire to be counted among them. Its sole aim is to bring a small portion of the accumulated riches of Johannine scholarship to the vast majority of Christian readers, who have neither the leisure nor the opportunity needed to pursue the literature on this or any other New Testament book. It, therefore, reads the gospel from beginning to end, reflecting on its meaning, reveling in its wealth and, above all else, marveling at the mystery it reveals.

The narratives of Jesus' signs and miracles in John compel repeated reading, but require no rereading. They are too clearly and too simply told for that. A proper commentary cannot let their details stand without further ado, as does the present work. On the other hand, the deeds themselves, like the words of Jesus in John, do call for both comment and reflection. The words and deeds of Jesus alike are, to borrow the felicitous phrase of a modern composer, a "dialogue disguised as a sovereign monologue." Should such dialogue with the text prove of some use to the reader, then I owe a great debt of gratitude to all those who, by their writings, instructed me, including the "evangelist."

Where my remarks are scant or absent, then my willingly confessed ignorance is solely to blame. But the reader must be careful not to conclude that, just because I myself have nothing or no more to say on a given part of the gospel, there is nothing or nothing more to be said about it. "If, however, you say: 'That's all there is to know,' you are lost," said Saint Augustine in his *Tractate on John*. Of course, John 21:25 is always there to remind authors and readers alike of the inexhaustible riches of this gospel.

In this work, I call "evangelist" whoever was responsible for the fourth gospel that we have before us. I read his gospel in the order in which it exists and has existed from the time of its appearance among the earliest manuscripts. I refer to him variously as "John" or "the author" without further qualification merely to avoid confusion. I also refer to him in the third person singular masculine simply because I am unwilling and unable either to shrug off twenty centuries of tradition, or to pretend that Caesar, let alone Caesar's wife, is above the grammarians.

The English Bible text used throughout is that of the Revised Standard Version (RSV), which is still the best we have in English. I do not pretend that the New Revised Standard Version (NRSV) is destitute of all merit. On occasion it provides an improved rendering (e.g., John 7:17) and, when it does, I have not hesitated to cite it rather than the RSV. Sometimes I have had recourse to the "marginal" (marg) reading in the RSV or the NRSV text, indicating it either by square brackets [ ] or by "marg" in the reference.

In the text of the RSV, I have made principally three minor alterations: Following the NRSV, I have changed all "thee," "thou," "thine," and the corresponding verb forms, to more modern forms; for reasons given at the proper place (see under 14:16), I have merely transliterated the Greek *parakletos* as "Paraclete" in the farewell discourses (John 14–17), rather than translate it either as "Counselor" (RSV) or as "Advocate" (NRSV); and, finally, I have used "Amen, amen," rather than "Truly, truly," in both RSV and NRSV. The Greek text itself transliterates the Hebrew "amen," which, *pace* the editors of both the RSV and the NRSV, is still current English, "amen" and not "truly" being still the proper response to Christian prayer. Indeed, both the RSV and the NRSV translate 1 Corinthians 14:16, "how can any one in the position of an outsider say the 'Amen' to your thanksgiving when he does not know what you are saying?" Their readers, presumably, can understand all too well what this verse means. If, moreover, the Greek of the New Testament has preserved the Hebrew "amen," then I myself fail to think of a single sound argument for not doing so.

The absence of footnotes and bibliographies makes my burden of gratitude all the heavier. This book itself will, perchance, absolve part of the debt by making accessible to a larger number of readers some small part of the admirable and instructive work of those who, over the years, have taught, informed and enlightened me by their commentaries, studies and reflections on the gospel of John.

The leisure required for writing this book was kindly provided by Weston School of Theology. I have every member of its faculty, student body and staff to thank for responding so wholeheartedly to my plea of "Ignorez-moi passionément!" during a sabbatical leave spent in their midst. I also wish to thank Mr. and Mrs. Z. H. Rassam for the munificent gift which rendered the laborious task of readying the manuscript for publication a pleasure.

Triumph of the Cross, 1993

John 1

The Prologue: the Word in the beginning; the light in darkness; the witness to the light; response to the light; the Word became flesh; the Baptist's witness; law, grace and truth; the invisible God.

The Testimony of John the Baptist: the task of the witness; the Baptist's true greatness.

The First Disciples: call and response; the promise of greater things.

THE PROLOGUE (John 1:1–18)

The Word in the Beginning

In the beginning was the Word, and the Word was with God, and the Word was God (1:1).

Little acquaintance with the Bible is needed to recognize in these opening words of the gospel of John an echo of those that open the book of Genesis, "*In the beginning* God created the heavens and the earth" (Gen 1:1). The fourth gospel begins at a point in time prior to any of the other three. In a sense, it starts at a point that is prior even to the "In the beginning" of Genesis 1:1. For, as the culminating prayer of the farewell discourse of Jesus reminds us, the glory that was given the Son by the Father belonged to the Son even "before the world was made" (Jn 17:5).

In that beginning, "before the world was made," the Word already was (1:1). Even a vague familiarity with the literature on the fourth gospel would suffice to remind us that "the Word," its meaning and provenance, its background and history, have been the constant preoccupation of all those who undertook to comment on the prologue of

John. It is, nevertheless, arguable that, but for an accident of history, the endless proliferation of speculation on the origin and meaning of the *Logos,* "the Word," might have been significantly curtailed, if not altogether avoided. Had the discoveries of manuscripts of the gospel of John in the sands of Egypt been made a century earlier, scholars would not have been so hasty or foolhardy to assign it a date much later than the end of the first century. Had a shepherd stumbled into a cave near the Dead Sea in 1847 rather than in 1947, fewer commentators would have felt the urge to go in search of *Logos* and its origins much beyond the confines of the literature of the Jewish people in the first century of the Christian era.

"In the beginning was the Word" is a statement about the revelatory nature of the God we worship. The rest of John's gospel will, at various points, stress this fact. In doing so, it never again has recourse to the title *Logos*/Word for the very simple reason that this Word "became flesh" (1:14). In this flesh, Jesus Christ carries out the divine revelatory function of the Word, in his words and in his deeds. In him, the process begun with creation–which is itself no less a revelation of God–and carried through the Patriarchs, Moses and the prophets, reaches its culmination, and finds both its appointed end and its fulfilment. What the prophets preached and proclaimed, the "Hear the word of the Lord," is now accomplished and made flesh in the person of Jesus of Nazareth, the Word become flesh, the incarnate *Logos*.

This is why, with the remarkable deftness of his theological touch, John goes on to add, "and the Word was *with* God," before declaring that "the Word was God." We have here one of those Johannine assertions which, in centuries to come, was destined to germinate and eventually blossom into our trinitarian creed. But, even without the benefit of such a "trinitarian" background, the author of the fourth gospel could still say what he said in the midst of his uncompromisingly monotheistic world, and say it with unquestionable fidelity to the given of his faith. Thus, having enunciated that "in the beginning was the Word," i.e., that God is a self-revealer, John does not hesitate to affirm that this Word "was with God," that indeed this Word "was God."

But, to guard against any possible misunderstanding of his statement, John repeats,

He was in the beginning with God (1:2).

We should not, therefore, be too hasty to affirm what John himself is careful to qualify. For, to be sure, "the Word was God." But we have to keep in mind that this identification of the Word with God must preserve the distinction of one from the other: "the Word was with God." So important is this distinction and so necessary to keep in mind that the author of the prologue is compelled to repeat it immediately:

> **all things were made through him, and without him was not anything made that was made. In him was life, and the life was the light of men (1:3–4a).**

However one may choose to punctuate them, each of these two verses makes a distinct affirmation about the Word: (a) "all things were made through him"; and (b) "in him was life." The two verses can also be punctuated to read: "all things were made through him, and without him was not anything made. That which has been made was life in him." But, whichever way one chooses to read them, the verses are there to stress the role of the Word both in creation and in the conferring of life. Both creation and life are, of course, exclusively divine functions. Only God can create; only God can grant life. Thus, by predicating these same functions of the Word, the prologue reiterates its opening statement that "In the beginning was the Word, and the Word was with God, and the Word was God" (1:1).

Like the subsequent themes in the prologue, these statements will be developed at greater length throughout the gospel. What the opening verses of the gospel state so tersely cannot be sufficiently repeated in Christian proclamation throughout the ages. But, alas, nowadays such themes are scarcely accorded much attention in Christian preaching. To confess the role of the Word in creation is first and foremost to acknowledge one's inalterable status as creature. It is at the same time to recall the often forgotten truth that creation itself is a revelation. To recognize that in the Word, in God's revelation, is "life," is to acknowledge that life itself is no less an exclusive gift of God than is the revelation. God who alone can create and reveal is the unique giver of life. Without the recognition and acceptance of this fact, nothing else in the fourth gospel can make sense. Neither the wonder of Jesus' deeds, nor the sublimity of his words could be of value or even of genuine interest to those who refuse to recognize unequivocally their status as creatures, or to acknowledge their life as uniquely the gift of God.

When the evangelist goes on to say,

> **and the life was the light of men (1:4b),**

he calls attention, not just to the themes of life and light that will recur in the gospel, but also to the intimate link that binds the one to the other ("the light of life" 8:12; 3:15 and 12:46; 5:24; 14:6). It is not merely a question of light symbolism, rich and illuminating though this be. The profundity of the statement in 1:4 lies at a deeper level, in the identification of both life and light with the Word. It lies, that is, in the fact that the revelation of God, the Word of God, is life-giving because it illuminates (see 14:6). "And the life was the light of men." The Word illumines and so is the source of life. The revelation is, therefore, the source of both light and life in the world.

The Light in Darkness

But the true meaning of things is in their opposites. So the prologue goes on to say:

> **The light shines in the darkness, and the darkness has not overcome it (1:5).**

This light comes into a darkness and thus accomplishes two things: (a) it enlightens, it sheds light on what was hidden in darkness; and (b) it defines, it sets limits to the darkness itself. This, too, by the way, was the act of primal creation when God said, "Let there be light" (Gen 1:3). The creative word of God did not abolish all darkness, but set its limits–much as a flashlight does in the impenetrable darkness of a cave. The statement in John 1:5 links the act of revelation to that of creation which–as we have already remarked–is itself a revelation.

But the statement, "The light shines in the darkness, and the darkness has not overcome it" (1:5) is also a reminder that the mere fact of the coming of this light into the world does not abolish darkness once for all. Indeed, by adding "and the darkness did not overcome it" (1:5b), the evangelist calls attention to the surrounding darkness which is still there to threaten the light. The struggle between the two is the subject of the entire gospel and, in a way, divides it into two parts: the struggle of the darkness to overcome the light (chapter 2–12), and the coming of light into the world (chapters 13 to the end).

The Witness to the Light

> **There was a man sent from God, whose name was John. He came for testimony, to bear witness to the light, that all might believe through him. He was not the light, but came to bear witness to the light (1:6–8).**

If one were so minded, one could regard these verses as an interruption in the flow of an otherwise seamless prologue. But the verses are a most appropriate insertion here, not only as a link and transition paragraph with what follows, but as a much needed coming down to earth. Far from being an interruption of its even flow, John 1:6–8 is indispensable for the understanding of the prologue as a whole.

Several needed facts about the coming of the "light" into the world are here recalled. The light comes into the world in definable and specified historical circumstances. Verses 6–8 take what looks much like an abstract proposition and root it firmly within human history. In the Johannine prologue, these verses fulfil very much the same function as the verses of the Lukan prologue to Jesus' ministry:

> In the fifteenth year of the reign of Tiberius Caesar, Pontius Pilate being governor of Judea, and Herod being tetrarch of Galilee, and his brother Philip tetrarch of the region of Ituraea and Trachonitis, and Lysanias tetrarch of Abilene, in the high-priesthood of Annas and Caiaphas, the word of God came to John the son of Zechariah in the wilderness (Luke 3:1–2).

Both John's verses and Luke's firmly ground the event of Christ in history. Without such grounding, the statements in John's prologue would tell of just another myth among so many, and the narrative of Luke would be no more than an edifying legend.

John, moreover, makes clear that the mere appearance of the light in the world is no guarantee that it will be either seen or recognized. This is precisely where the Baptist has his indispensable function to perform: "He came for testimony, to bear witness to the light, that all might believe through him" (Jn 1:7). The coming of the revelation into the world, even the coming of the Word in the flesh, does not and cannot dispense with human agency. There always has to be those who are in the world "for testimony, to bear witness to the light" (1:8). There is no other way in which "all might believe" except through others like themselves. The indispensability of human agency remains essential to divine revelation.

Yet, knowing from experience our proclivity to stop short at the witness-bearer, the evangelist adds,

He was not the light, but came to bear witness to the light (1:8).

This is a salutary reminder that not even the gospel itself is "the light," any more than are "the scriptures" themselves: "You search the scriptures, because you think that in them you have eternal life; and it is they that bear witness to me" (5:39). The light is a person, not a book, however sacred; nor a set of propositions, however lofty. It was the function of John the Baptist to identify that person once he appeared on the stage of history.

The true light, which enlightens everyone, was coming into the world (1:9 NRSV).

This, as the NRSV margin indicates, can be read, "He was the true light that enlightens everyone coming into the world." Either way, however, the evangelist affirms the universality of the mission of the Word in "coming into the world." The coming of the Word was all-embracing in its purpose. It excluded no one. It embraced each and every one born into this world, under whatever clime, in whatever state of development or lack thereof, in any stage of civilization or culture. Whatever else will be said in other parts of the gospel about the purpose of this coming of the Word into the world, its universality, its all-embracing purpose, remains inalterable.

To say this is not for one moment to pretend that those who believed "through him" (1:7) always maintain and always act upon this inalterable fact. But, as a description of the "coming into the world" of the true light, the universality of purpose is not merely necessary but constitutive. The light could not have come to enlighten some but not others, any more than God could be said to have created some but not others. It is of the nature of this light as it is of the nature of creation to embrace all creatures in its purpose. God's revelation, no less than God's creation, cannot by definition exclude any one. If, in fact, there be any so excluded, then the explanation of their exclusion will have to be sought elsewhere than in the divine action and its intention. The verses that follow, 1:10–13, will elaborate on this.

Response to the Light

He was in the world, and the world was made through him, yet the world knew him not (1:10).

It is not enough for God to create or to reveal himself as the creator. The creatures must acknowledge themselves to be creatures at the same time that they confess this God as their creator (cf. Rom 1:21). Yet the fact of the matter is that "the world knew him not." Even when the Word is "in the world," the world can persist in rejecting him. This is not a question of natural theology or a theory about the knowability of God. It is a simple statement of fact. God's revelation in the world does not, by its mere presence in the world, compel assent. Even the world made by God can refuse to accept God's revelation, can choose to "know him not," and persist in denying its creaturehood.

So, too, the evangelist can say, of an even more sharply defined segment of this world, of God's own holy people,

He came to his own home, and his own people received him not (1:11).

God not only created the world, but in this world he fashioned a people for himself, made them the repository of his promises and the bearers of his revelation. Nevertheless, when at last those promises found their fulfilment, and that revelation its culmination, "his own people received him not." This statement is in fact more a lament than a judgment or condemnation. But it is a lament that emanated from the very heart of the community from which and for which the Johannine gospel was written. Any member of such a community could not but grieve over those of his own people who "received him not." Their threnody will echo throughout the entire gospel, and find more plangent echoes still in the first epistle of John, "They went out from us, but they were not of us; for if they had been of us, they would have continued with us" (1 Jn 2:19).

The first part of the gospel, up to the end of chapter 12, will play multiple variations on this theme of the rejection of the Word by his own people. The questioning, the controversies, the misunderstandings, all the failures to comprehend and to act upon this comprehension, are demonstrations, not only of what took place in a defined historical situation long ago, but of what continues to take place over the centuries. Among "his own people," whether the Jews of John's time or Christians through the ages, there are those who "receive him not."

But, of course, the rejection was and is no more universal than the acceptance. There were, and are, women and men in every age who did then and do now "receive him":

But to all who received him, who believed in his name, he gave power to become children of God (1:12).

This verse, too, sounds a theme echoed throughout the gospel. This theme finds its highest expression in a compendious summary of the entire life and work of Jesus: "I have manifested your name to those whom you gave me from the world" (17:6 NRSV). It is precisely with them, whom God gave to his Son, that the second part of the gospel (chapters 13–17 and 18–21) will be concerned. Jesus will address the series of his farewell discourses to "his own," to those "who received him, who believed in his name" (1:12). The reader of the gospel must never forget, however, that those who "received him, who believed in his name," were first and foremost none other than individuals from among "his own people."

To all who "received him, who believed in his name," then as now, he "in whom was life" gave "power to become children of God" (1:12). To them he gave and still gives the power to live with the life that is God's gift, the life that only "the Father has...in himself" and has "granted the Son also to have...in himself" (5:26). This is so important a fact, and yet one that is so readily sidestepped or forgotten, that 1 John will take it up and develop it into one of its major themes: "See what love the Father has given us, that we should be called children of God, and *so we are*" (1 Jn 3:1).

To be children of God requires the gift of life from God. Therefore, the prologue goes on to specify how this great gift of "the power to become children of God" is conferred:

> **...who were born, not of blood nor of the will of the flesh nor of the will of man, but of God (1:13).**

The essential quality of life as a God-given gift is integral to its comprehension. The "power to become children of God" belongs solely to those "who were born, not of blood nor of the will of the flesh nor of the will of man, but of God" (1:13). Nothing and no one but the creator-revealer can grant the gift of life or confer the status of being "children of God." Of course, the often forgotten corollary to this truth is that nothing and no one can withhold either the gift of life or the status of being a "child of God." No individual and no institution has it to give to, and therefore none has it to withhold from, anyone. The gift is solely and uniquely "of God."

The Word Became Flesh

> **And the Word became flesh and dwelt among us, full of grace and truth; we have beheld his glory, glory as of the only Son from the Father (1:14).**

This is all too clearly the climax toward which the prologue has been moving. But it is also the foundation upon which the whole gospel rests. It enunciates the core of its message. The Word that was "in the beginning," that was "with God," and that indeed "was God," has become flesh. It has become a man subject to all the limitations of human mortality. The rest of the gospel will demonstrate this in many and varied ways.

But the whole point of John 1:14 will be missed if we do not recognize that—at least for the author of the prologue—its far more important part lies in the statement which follows: "We have beheld his glory, glory as of the only Son from the Father" (1:14b). It is to this all-important fact of beholding the glory of the only Son that the evangelist bears witness; and to this same fact that the author of 1 John comes back to at the very beginning of the letter:

> That which was from the beginning, which we have heard, which we have seen with our eyes, which we have looked upon and touched with our hands, concerning the word of life—the life was made manifest, and we saw it, and testify to it, and proclaim to you the eternal life which was with the Father and was made manifest to us—that which we have seen and heard we proclaim also to you (1 Jn 1:1–3).

The Baptist's Witness

The Word who "became flesh" is identifiable with the Jesus of Nazareth they knew, heard and followed. The whole point at issue is that this Jesus of Nazareth to whom the evangelist and the author of 1 John bear witness is himself the Word which "became flesh," "the only Son of the Father." To this Jesus of Nazareth the evangelist bears witness throughout his gospel. Indeed, to him the whole New Testament bears witness in one form or another. To him, of course, John the Baptist was the first to bear witness. This is why what seems like another interruption (cf. 1:6–8) in the elevated progress of the discourse on the Word is merely an illustration of this fact:

> **John bore witness to him, and cried, "This was he of whom I said, 'He who comes after me ranks before me, for he was before me'" (1:15).**

Such insistence on the identity of the Word become flesh with Jesus of Nazareth, whether in the prologue or in 1 John, might seem excessive, until we remember that—strangely enough—the first difficulty which believers encountered then, and continue to encounter now, was not so much the divinity of the Word as his true humanity. The first hurdle the believers had to overcome was not that "the Word was God" but that this Word did indeed become flesh, the man Jesus of Nazareth. Hence, the remarkable insistence of 1 John on hearing him, seeing him, looking upon and touching him. The author of the fourth gospel himself insists that they indeed did behold the glory of "the only Son from the Father" precisely in the Word become flesh, in Jesus of Nazareth.

It is not cynicism that prompts one to remark that our insistence on the divinity at the cost of the humanity stems not from any excess of love and veneration for the Word that "was God." It stems rather from our inveterate conviction that we do really deserve a first-class revelation, and not one that labors under the impenetrable opacities of the human condition. When the evangelist affirms, "we have beheld his glory," he means with eyes that beheld no more than yours or mine behold when we look at one another. What made his beholding of the "glory as of the only Son" possible was precisely his faith that the Word did indeed "become flesh." This is why the stated purpose of his gospel is very simply "that you may *believe* that Jesus is the Christ, the Son of God" (20:31).

Law, Grace and Truth

That the Word who "became flesh and dwelt among us" is "full of grace and truth" (1:14) is taken up again in

And from his fulness have we all received, grace upon grace (1:16).

The superabundance of that gift of grace is stressed in order to remind those who believe that what they have in Jesus Christ cannot possibly be anything other than pure gift. It is a reminder that this gift is not, and can never be, the result of human ties, social status, personal accomplishments, or any achievement of one's own. The coming of the Word into the world brought us the "fullness" of both "grace and truth" (1:14), of both salvation and revelation. The superabundance of God's gift of salvation and revelation in the Word who became flesh precludes the need of any future addition. In the Word incarnate all is fulfilled, completed, brought to its consummation.

Whatever might have been true prior to the moment when the Word became flesh is henceforth no longer true, at least, no longer true the same way:

> **For the law was given through Moses; grace and truth came from Jesus Christ (1:17).**

To be sure, in John's gospel, the word "grace" appears only in these verses of the prologue. The point, however, is made once and for all. The whole subsequent elaboration of the message of revelation is just that: a witness to the grace of Jesus Christ. This is why we find "grace" coupled here with "truth," a theme that will recur throughout the gospel to climax in Jesus' declaration, "I am the way, and the truth, and the life" (14:6).

Yet we stubbornly forget that the revelation granted us in Jesus Christ is pure grace, sheer and unearned gift. Very little in our religious training and our instruction in what is called "apologetics" has prepared us for the humility needed to recognize in a message like John's the gift of an unmerited and unearnable grace. We are ever reluctant to see the revelation itself as a grace. We prize our intellectual capacities too dearly for the humble acceptance of the revelation as a gift. Therefore, we go about trying to tame the message, reduce it to manageable proportions, to subject it to the criteria of our sciences and translate it into our comprehensible commonplaces. We are forever on the lookout for secondhand slogans and threadbare platitudes to distract us from the "word of life" (1 Jn 1:1). Yet it is the fourth gospel that bears witness to the Word which alone is "full of grace and truth" (Jn 1:14), from whose fulness we have all "received, grace upon grace" (1:16).

The Invisible God

Far from being a jaundiced view of our world, this is precisely the attitude that John illustrates throughout his gospel, in the theological pretensions of Jesus' opponents, the claimed expertise of the religious authorities, the vaunted common sense of his interlocutors, and the invincible "We know" of all those whose minds are already made up. That all these responses ultimately rest on a misunderstanding of one essential fact is made clear in the concluding statement of the prologue:

> **No one has ever seen God; the only Son, who is in the bosom of the Father, he has made him known (1:18).**

The evangelist repeats this incontestable fact over and over again: "No one has ever seen God!" (1:18; 5:37; 6:46; 14:7, 9; and see 1 Jn 4:12). To all who rush to cite as refutation the many examples in the Old Testament, there stands Exodus 33:20 as a stern reminder that "man shall not see me and live." One has only to read this Exodus narrative in its entirety (Ex 33:17–23) to realize what Jacob meant when, only *after* "a man wrestled with him until the breaking of the day" (Gen 32:24), could he say, "For I have seen God face to face, and yet my life is preserved" (Gen 32:30; Dt 5:24; 4:33; see of Moses Ex 33:11; Num 12:6–8; Dt 34:10).

If one were to cite the "visions" of the prophets as a counter argument, then one would only have to read slowly and deliberately the concluding words of Ezekiel's opening vision in order to comprehend that the case of the prophet was no exception. For, after the most elaborate description of his "vision" of God, more elaborate perhaps than even Isaiah's (Is 6), Ezekiel adds, "Such was the *appearance* of the *likeness* of the *glory* of the Lord" (Ezek 1:28; cf. Ex 33:21–22).

The weight of the negative assertion that, "No one has ever seen God" (Jn 1:18), leaves no room for exception. The very absoluteness of the negation finds its confirmation in the one single exception of Jesus Christ, "the only Son, who is in the bosom of the Father, he has made him known" (1:18b). This revelation by the only Son is the abounding grace (1:16–17) which the prologue hymns. It is what the incarnate Word has revealed and has thus made possible: "He who has seen me has seen the Father" (14:9).

In the person of Jesus Christ the absolute, "No one has ever seen God," is abrogated once and for all. Yet the very significance of this momentous abrogation would completely escape us, were we for a moment to forget that all those who "beheld his glory, glory as of the only Son from the Father" (1:14) beheld nothing other than Jesus of Nazareth, a man like them in all things, a man they heard with their ears, saw and looked upon with their eyes, and touched with their hands (1 Jn 1:1).

With the reminder that he who has made the Father known is "in the bosom of the Father" (1:18), the prologue comes full circle to its opening statement about the Word. The Word who became flesh is he who was in the beginning "with God," who indeed "was God" (1:1). It is only he who "is in the bosom of the Father" who could and indeed did make God known. He alone is the Word.

But, before we quit the prologue, it is necessary for the understanding of what follows in the rest of the gospel to keep in mind that, in speaking of "the Word" who was "with God" and who "was God" (v. 1), of "the only Son from the Father" (v. 14), and of "Jesus Christ" (v. 17), the one and same person is meant: Jesus of Nazareth. Henceforth, as the events of his life unfold and his message is preached, whatever is said of this Jesus of Nazareth is true of "the only Son from the Father," "who is in the bosom of the Father," the Word who "was with God," who "was God," who "became flesh and dwelt among us."

THE TESTIMONY OF JOHN THE BAPTIST (John 1:19–37)

The gospel proper begins where all the other gospels do, with the ministry of John the Baptist. That Matthew and Luke have two chapters each prior to that event is no more surprising than John's prologue preceding it. The "beginning from the baptism of John" (Acts 1:22) is, not only the start of the public ministry of Jesus, but also "the beginning of the gospel of Jesus Christ" (Mk 1:1).

> **And this is the testimony of John, when the Jews sent priests and Levites from Jerusalem to ask him, "Who are you?" He confessed, he did not deny, but confessed, "I am not the Christ." And they asked him, "What then? Are you Elijah?" He said, "I am not." "Are you the prophet?" And he answered, "No." They said to him then, "Who are you? Let us have an answer for those who sent us. What do you say about yourself?" He said, "I am the voice of one crying in the wilderness, 'Make straight the way of the Lord,' as the prophet Isaiah said" (1:19–21).**

In this interrogation of John the Baptist by the "priests and Levites from Jerusalem" (1:19), we have a handy compendium of the expectations of the times: the Christ, Elijah, "the prophet" (1:20–21). Whether taken together or singly, these expectations reflect, not just the prevailing mood of the period, but also the diverse forms of the people's hope. Jerusalem's officialdom spoke for what weighed heavily on the minds and hearts of many.

The persistence of the questioners really sets the stage for the Baptist's testimony. His function was to bear witness to the one in whom all those expectations and longings were to be fulfilled. John the Baptist's whole task and mission in the fourth gospel is simply to be witness to him who held the true answer to all the questions of officialdom and the expectations and longings of the populace. The Baptist's chief role in life was to point to the one who was promised, awaited, longed for and expected through the long centuries of God's dealing with his people:

> **Now they had been sent from the Pharisees. They asked him, "Then why are you baptizing, if you are neither the Christ, nor Elijah, nor the prophet?" John answered them, "I baptize with water; but among you stands one whom you do not know, even he who comes after me, the thong of whose sandal I am not worthy to untie." This took place in Bethany beyond the Jordan, where John was baptizing (1:24–28).**

To those who persisted in inquiring about his identity and sought to know the reason behind his activity, John the Baptist had only one answer to give. Both his own person and his work is subordinate to the real purpose of his existence. It was his sole mission in life to point to one who stood among them, "one whom you do not know" (1:26).

This is the whole point. Even when the Word becomes flesh and dwells among us (1:14), he still needs to be pointed out, to have witness borne to him. There is simply no getting around the human mediation in divine revelation, whether in Jesus' own lifetime or thereafter. Despise such human mediation as we might, pretend to have immediate access to the divine if we will, the uncompromising and inalterable fact at the heart of all true religion remains this: "No one has ever seen God" (1:18).

From the account of the ministry of John the Baptist within a Christian context, another point emerges which is much in need of stressing. The one who bears witness, who gives testimony to the Word is, in and of himself, really of no significance. It was not humility that prompted the Baptist to say, "He who comes after me ranks before me, for he was before me" (1:15), "the thong of whose sandal I am not worthy to untie" (1:27). That was merely a perspicacity of the Baptist's self-vision about who he was and what his given task was meant to be. Both his own identity and his mission in the world could only be defined with reference to the one who comes after him. He was to give testimony to the one who comes into the world, the object of the hopes and expectations of that world.

That the Baptist has recourse to Isaiah's prophecy, "I am the voice of one crying in the wilderness" (Is 40:3), to describe his role in the events which were about to unfold, is consistent with the understanding of those events themselves. What is recounted in the fourth or any other gospel derives its intelligibility from God's dealings with his chosen people. Those of us accustomed to see in the person and life of Jesus Christ the key to our understanding of the Old Testament, must never forget that this same Old Testament first has to provide us with the means of comprehending the meaning of the life and person of Jesus Christ. If, as the fathers of the church insist, the Old Testament becomes clear in the pages of the New, it is only because all that takes place in the pages of the New is comprehensible only in the light of the Old. John the Baptist's recourse to the prophecy of Isaiah is thus, not a rhetorical device, but a hermeneutic necessity.

The Task of the Witness

The task of the witness is to bear witness. When therefore the moment came:

> **The next day he saw Jesus coming toward him, and said, "Behold the Lamb of God, who takes away the sin of the world! This is he of whom I said, 'After me comes a man who ranks before me, for he was before me.' I myself did not know him; but for this I came baptizing with water, that he might be revealed to Israel." And John bore witness, "I saw the Spirit descend as a dove from heaven, and it remained on him. I myself did not know him; but he who sent me to baptize with water said to me, 'He on whom you see the Spirit descend and remain, this is he who baptizes with the Holy Spirit.' And I have seen and have borne witness that this is the Son of God" (1:29–34).**

Within this witness of the Baptist, the evangelist crowds all the various details which make up the accounts of Jesus' baptism in the synoptics (Mk 1:9–11; Mt 3:13–17; Lk 3:21–22). The accent in the Baptist's testimony, however, is not so much on the details of the event of the baptism itself as on its significance as revelation. "He on whom you see the Spirit descend and remain, *this is he*" (1:33).

The true identity of Jesus is not the outcome of deductive reasoning, not even by the Baptist himself. It is always the object of divine revelation, "he who sent me to baptize with water *said to me*" (1:33). Only as a result of this divine revelation can the Baptist really say, "This is the Son of God" (1:34). Outwardly, Jesus of Nazareth bore no distinguishing mark. Neither his mien nor his demeanor–even if it was the most distinctive–could have sufficiently set him apart for the Baptist to bear witness to him as "the Son of God," certainly not in any sense intended either by the prologue (1:14, 18) or the conclusion of the fourth gospel (20:31).

Thus, in his description of the testimony of John the Baptist, the evangelist has recourse to the language of prophetic experience. When the Baptist insists, "I myself did not know him; but he who sent me...said to me" (1:33), he echoes "the Lord said" that runs through the whole Old Testament like a constant refrain, from Abraham (Gen 12:1), to Moses (Ex 3:6–7), to Isaiah (Is 6:9), Jeremiah (Jer 1:4) and all the prophets. It is, in their case as in the Baptist's, a reminder to us that God is a revealer, "In the beginning was the Word" (1:1). But the words of the Baptist serve no less as an admonition that this revelation comes only to those who confess, "I myself did not know him" (1:33; cf. 9:41). Revelation can come only to those who need it and know they do.

The Baptist's acknowledgment that the one who sent him said to him, "This is he!" (1:33) affirms the divine origin of his message. It keeps before our eyes that the true identity of Jesus of Nazareth can only be the object of divine revelation. This has to be borne in mind throughout the gospel of John. As divine revelation, therefore, it calls for faith. Without this faith it remains just another unverifiable claim among so many. The subsequent scene will illustrate this:

The Baptist's True Greatness

The next day again John was standing with two of his disciples; and he looked at Jesus as he walked, and said, "Behold, the Lamb of God!" The two disciples heard him say this, and they followed Jesus (1:35–37).

The terse expression of their reaction is an admirable description of the disciples' faith. They required no verification, inquired about no credentials, sought no explanation. Sufficient to have the Baptist point to Jesus for them to follow him. When the evangelist himself declares at the end of his gospel, "These are written that you may believe that Jesus is the Christ, the Son of God" (20:31), he does no more than reiterate the gesture of the Baptist.

Having thus discharged his mission, the Baptist retires. That is all there was to it. Having fulfilled his appointed function, he bows out of the stage. Even the task of bearing witness to Jesus involved the loss of his own disciples to him. There was not so much as a thank-you or a by-your-leave. The two disciples heard John's testimony and "followed Jesus" (1:37).

This–let it not be forgotten–is where the Baptist's true greatness lies. To be sure, others among his disciples would later try to "corner the market" (3:26), as disciples of every master–whether genuine or bogus–in every age are wont to do. But once again John's greatness breaks through. At the appropriate moment, he who was a voice "crying in the wilderness" (1:23) yields fully to him for whom he came to bear witness. Even the disciples who had gathered around the Baptist were provisional. Once he has discharged his mission, they leave him to follow Jesus (1:37).

John the Baptist thus reminds his zealous followers of what they are ever eager to forget: that the very task they are called upon to perform is a gift to which none of them can lay claim as personal property. Not even the Baptist's own divinely appointed task was an exception. "No one can receive anything except what is given him from heaven" (3:27). The realization that the witness-bearer, the proclaimer, the minister, is but the recipient of a gift and not the claimant to a title or the achiever of a distinction, leads the Baptist to betray the secret of his true greatness: "He must increase, but I must decrease" (3:30). This remains the distinctive cachet of all those who bear witness to Jesus.

Of course, this miniature portrait of John the Baptist in the fourth gospel (1:19–37) is not put there merely for our edification. It foreshadows how Jesus himself views his own witness: "I seek not my own will but the will of him who sent me" (5:30); "I do not seek my own glory" (8:50, 54). Of course, it also illustrates the task of witness-bearers in any age.

THE FIRST DISCIPLES (John 1:38–51)

> **Jesus turned and saw them following, and said to them, "What do you seek?" And they said to him, "Rabbi" (which means Teacher), "where are you staying?" He said to them, "Come and see." They came and saw where he was staying; and they stayed with him that day, for it was about the tenth hour (1:38–39).**

It is remarkable that the first words uttered by Jesus in the fourth gospel are a question: "What do you seek?" (1:38). The entire gospel is indeed a reminder, repeated in many ways and in different forms, that anyone of us encountering this message about Jesus must know with clarity what it is we seek when we seek Jesus. In other words, right at the start of the gospel, we must have a clear idea of what it is we are seeking, what it is we ultimately want and desire above all else in this world. The question allows no temporary velleities, makes no room for transient whims, tolerates no current fads or ersatz fashionable anxieties. Ultimately, if the true answer were to emerge, it will have to be the same for every mortal born into the world. It is their mortality that imposes the question. To realize this is to realize that the answer given to, "What do you seek?" necessarily defines the nature of the seeker.

What every one of us desires, seeks, wants and ultimately longs for is, of course, life. It is that without which nothing else matters, neither riches, nor honors, nor friends, nor anything nor anyone else in the world. Without life nothing can be enjoyed. The question put by Jesus to the would-be disciples at the start of the gospel receives its definitive answer in its conclusion, in the concluding statement of its purpose: "These are written that you may believe that Jesus is the Christ, the Son of God, and that believing *you may have life in his name*" (20:31).

Of course, the immediate reaction of the two disciples to Jesus' question is, as it would be in any such conversation, "Rabbi (which means Teacher), where are you staying?" (1:38). The evangelist is not one to sacrifice the dramatic advantage of the scene to theological subtlety. A straightforward question gets a straightforward answer. The theological acumen of the evangelist lies rather in the profundity of meaning that will emerge from the dialogue. At the latter end of the gospel, the same Jesus prays for his disciples, "Father, I desire that they also whom you have given me, may be with me where I am" (17:24). Their question now, however, receives only the invitation to "Come and see" (1:39).

This is an invitation extended to the readers of the gospel as well. The very question of the two disciples, "Rabbi, where are you staying?" (1:38) will, in the course of the gospel, receive a hitherto unsuspected nuance. What started out as an inquiry will end up a petition. "Father," Jesus will pray, "I desire that they also, whom you have given me, may be with me where I am, to behold my glory which you have given me in your love for me before the foundation of the world" (17:24). Even the fact that the first disciples "came and saw where he was staying; and they stayed with him that day" (1:39) will, in the course of the gospel, receive a wealth of meaning that the initial narrative of the calling can barely express.

Thus, the message proclaimed insists, at least in this gospel, that all that any human being can and does desire, seek, long for, try to win, work to possess–all the true and abiding longing of the human heart, in any age and in every generation–finds its only true fulfilment in Jesus Christ.

In explaining this gospel to his congregation, Saint Augustine cites the words of the psalmist:

> One thing have I asked of the Lord, that will I seek after; that I may dwell in the house of the Lord all the days of my life, to behold the beauty of the Lord, and to inquire in his temple (Psalm 27:4).

The saint who knew at first-hand the restlessness of the human heart understood well what the evangelist had in mind when he painted this vignette of the first disciples' encounter with Jesus.

The two disciples "stayed with him that day" (1:39). But staying with him is, of course, never a static thing. So, the first manifest outcome of their encounter with Jesus of Nazareth follows immediately.

Call and Response

> **One of the two who heard John speak, and followed him, was Andrew, Simon Peter's brother. He first found his brother Simon, and said to him, "We have found the Messiah" (which means Christ). He brought him to Jesus, Jesus looked at him, and said, "So you are Simon the Son of John? You shall be called Cephas" (which means Peter) (1:40–42).**

The pattern of call and response is repeated yet again:

> **The next day Jesus decided to go to Galilee. And he found Philip and said to him, "Follow me." Now Philip was from Bethsaida, the city of Andrew and Peter. Philip found Nathanael, and said to him, "We have found him of whom Moses in the law and also the prophets wrote, Jesus of Nazareth, the son of Joseph."**

> **Nathanael said to him, "Can anything good come out of Nazareth?" Philip said to him, "Come and see." Jesus saw Nathanael coming to him, and said to him, "Behold, an Israelite**

indeed, in whom is no guile!" Nathanael said to him, "How do you know me?" Jesus answered him, "Before Philip called you, when you were under the fig tree, I saw you." Nathanael answered him, "Rabbi, you are the Son of God! You are the King of Israel!" (1:43–49).

The immediate result of the encounter with Jesus is an urgency to "evangelize," to bring this good news to others. Thus, Andrew finds his brother, Simon (1:41), and Philip finds Nathanael (1:45), and so it goes to the end of time. In the recognition of the true identity of "Jesus of Nazareth, the son of Joseph" (1:45) there is always a mission. The encounter is always a commission to evangelize, to bring to others the news of "the Messiah" (1:41), the one "of whom Moses in the law and also the prophets wrote" (1:45). In writing his gospel, the evangelist himself does no more than what Andrew and Philip and the rest of Jesus' disciples did.

The quick pace of the narrative, however, cannot be allowed to obscure one of its most striking features. Scholars have commented on the rapid accumulation of christological titles within a very brief space, "the Messiah," the one "of whom Moses in the law and also the prophets wrote," "the Son of God," "the King of Israel." To speak of a "christological title" is really to describe any response to the question, "Who do you say I am?" (Mk 8:29) put by Jesus to his disciples. In John's narrative, Andrew's response is, "'the Messiah' (which means Christ)" (1:41); Philip's, "him of whom Moses in the law and also the prophets wrote" (1:45); and Nathanael's, "the Son of God...the King of Israel" (1:49). Thus, in the encounter with Jesus of Nazareth, a variety of responses to "Who do you say I am?" is given. Though none of them is exhaustive, such responses describe not only who Jesus of Nazareth really is, but also the respondent's relation to him. In our response to "Who do you say I am?" we also disclose our true identity.

There is thus a lesson to be learned from Nathanael's knowing skepticism: "Can anything good come out of Nazareth?" (1:46). Call it prejudice or provincialism if you wish. But, in fact, it is a faithful reflection of our own blasé condescension toward the new in religion, of our smug contentment with what we know, of our reluctance even to consider what we do not know. It is our perennial temptation to think that, just because we have nothing more to say about anything, nothing remains to be said. Here, as perhaps nowhere else in the life of faith, to stand still and barricade oneself in the status quo is, not merely to regress, but to die. Such an attitude would be merely an amusing foible, were it not a genuine obstacle to "follow Jesus" (1:37).

The Promise of Greater Things

> **Jesus answered him, "Because I said to you, I saw you under the fig tree, do you believe? You shall see greater things than these." And he said to him, "Amen, amen, I say to you, you will see heaven opened and the angels of God ascending and descending upon the Son of Man" (1:50–51).**

The dazzle of the miraculous begets faith, but the faith it begets will receive its just assessment at the end of the gospel in Jesus' "Blessed are those who have *not seen* and yet believe" (20:29). The unusual and the extraordinary do not make the miracle. They pass too soon into the usual and the ordinary. The miraculous "makes hungry where most [it] satisfies." Faith alone recognizes the miracle.

This is the reason why Jesus' promise that "You shall see greater things than these" (1:51) is at once a promise and an invitation. It promises all the miracles and wonders that Jesus' disciples will witness, but it directs their attention to a more permanent and enduring reality beyond them. The miracles are but "signs" pointing to him who is "the Son of man."

However one may wish to interpret the addition of "Amen, amen, I say to you, you will see heaven opened, and the angels of God ascending and descending upon the Son of man" (1:51), its immediate reference is to Jacob's vision in Genesis:

> And he dreamed that there was a ladder set up on the earth, and the top of it reached to heaven; and behold, the angels of God were *ascending and descending on it!* (Gen 28:12).

The true meaning of the "Amen, amen" saying, however, lies rather in the verses that follow these in the Genesis narrative. They speak of a revelation and its promise:

> I am the Lord, the God of Abraham your father and the God of Isaac; the land on which you lie I will give to you and to your descendants: and your descendants shall be like the dust of the earth...and by you and your descendants shall all the families of the earth bless themselves. Behold, I am with you and will keep you wherever you go (Gen 28:13–15).

The "greater things" promised Nathanael are the revelation and the promise that will be unfolded in the course of the gospel. There will the disciples of Jesus behold "his glory, glory as of the only Son from the Father" (1:14). This revelation of his glory as "the only Son from the Father" is the principal and ultimate purpose of his coming to dwell among us. "Father, I desire that they also, whom you have given me, may be with me where I am, to behold my glory which you have given me in your love for me before the foundation of the world" (17:24), i.e., "in the beginning."

John 2

The First of his Signs: the miracle account; miracles and signs.

Cleansing the Temple: gospel portraits of Jesus; Johannine misunderstanding; faith and miracles; "he knew what was in man."

THE FIRST OF HIS SIGNS (John 2:1–11)

The miracle at the wedding feast of Cana, one of the best known miracles of Jesus in the New Testament, is the inaugural sign, "the *first* of his signs" (2:11), in a series that will culminate in the raising of Lazarus in chapter 11 of the gospel. In its turn, the raising of Lazarus is the sign *par excellence* of that greatest of all signs, the manifestation of his glory (2:11; 17:1) in the death and resurrection of Jesus of Nazareth. Nevertheless, the narrative which unfolds here in chapter 2 already looks forward precisely to that "hour" of glory when Jesus will pray, "Father, the hour has come; glorify your Son" (17:1).

The Miracle Account

On the third day there was a marriage at Cana in Galilee, and the mother of Jesus was there; Jesus also was invited to the marriage, with his disciples. When the wine gave out, the mother of Jesus said to him, "They have no wine." And Jesus said to her, "O woman, what have you to do with me? My hour has not yet come." His mother said to the servants, "Do whatever he tells you." Now six stone jars were standing there, for the Jewish rites of purification, each holding twenty or thirty gallons. Jesus said to them, "Fill the jars with water." And they

> **filled them up to the brim. He said to them, "Now draw some out, and take it to the steward of the feast." So they took it. When the steward of the feast tasted the water now become wine, and did not know where it came from (though the servants who had drawn the water knew), the steward of the feast called the bridegroom and said to him, "Every man serves the good wine first; and when [they] have drunk freely, then the poor wine; but you have kept the good wine until now." This, the first of his signs, Jesus did at Cana in Galilee, and manifested his glory; and his disciples believed in him (2:1–11).**

The story is too well told to require comment. To elucidate any detail might satisfy curiosity by conjecture, but it cannot improve on the evangelist's narrative. Why the mother of Jesus was there, why his disciples were invited, the functions of the steward of the feast, etc., are all interesting questions, but they cannot enhance the central fact of the miracle, "the first of his signs," which manifested his glory (2:11). To speculate, as some have done, that the groom left the marriage unconsummated and the wedding feast a virgin to become the "beloved disciple" belongs more to the pathology of exegesis than to any classifiable critical inquiry.

Miracles and Signs

What the synoptic gospels call "miracles," John consistently refers to as "signs." One reason for this change in terminology is that, in the gospel of John, as perhaps nowhere else in the New Testament, everything Jesus does, no less than everything he says, speaks to us of the revelation he brings. As Saint Augustine has memorably said, "Even the deed of the Word is a word" (*Tractatus in Joh.* 24.2). The revelation of the Word is thus to be sought as much in what Jesus of Nazareth is and does as in what he says.

The response to this or any other revelation can only be either acceptance or rejection. Indifference, in this context, is tantamount to rejection. Therefore, at the conclusion of the account of the first sign which "Jesus did at Cana in Galilee, and manifested his glory" (2:11a), the evangelist adds, "and his disciples believed in him" (2:11b). Evidently then, faith is the purpose of the sign at Cana, as it is of any other sign recounted in the gospel. Of course, faith is also the aim of every utterance of Jesus recorded there. Indeed, faith is the very purpose of the entire gospel: "these are written that you may believe that Jesus is the Christ, the Son of God" (20:31).

It is, of course, part of the exegete's task to interpret and explain the setting of the miracle, contemporary marriage customs, the role of the mother of Jesus, the dynamics of the dialogue, and the like. But all such explanations, if they are to serve a purpose other than the satisfaction of genuine or pretended curiosity, ought to make the compelling demand for faith clear, and the response to it unavoidable. To balk at Jesus' seeming lack of filial piety, to parlay his mother's response into a treatise on Mariology, to cite Dionysian legends about water changed into wine, can ultimately be distractions from, if not outright evasions of, the demands of faith in Jesus Christ. The sole end of the account of the miracle at Cana is to believe in him: "his disciples believed in him" (2:11).

After this he went down to Capernaum, with his mother and his brothers and his disciples; and there they stayed for a few days (2:12).

CLEANSING THE TEMPLE (John 2:13–25)

The Passover of the Jews was at hand, and Jesus went up to Jerusalem. In the temple he found those who were selling oxen and sheep and pigeons, and the money-changers at their business. And making a whip of cords, he drove them all, with the sheep and oxen, out of the temple; and he poured out the coins of the money-changers and overturned their tables. And he told those who sold the pigeons, "Take these things away; you shall not make my Father's house a house of trade." His disciples remembered that it was written, "Zeal for your house will consume me." The Jews then said to him, "What sign have you to show us for doing this?" Jesus answered them, "Destroy this temple, and in three days I will raise it up." The Jews then said, "It has taken forty-six years to build this temple, and will you raise it up in three days?" But he spoke of the temple of his body (2:13–21).

The scene rapidly shifts from "Cana of Galilee" (2:1) to Capernaum (2:12) and thence to Jerusalem (2:13). Though not a miracle itself, the incident that takes place in the temple in Jerusalem is, nevertheless, a sign and has to be interpreted as such. Its significance lies both in its fulfilment of what "was written" (2:17; see Ps 69:9 "For zeal for your house has consumed me") in the scriptures, and also in the concluding dialogue with those who demanded, "What sign have you to show us for doing this?" (2:18).

Gospel Portraits of Jesus

One incidental and puzzling aspect of the narrative is how generation after generation can read or hear the account itself and yet persist in clinging to their cherished image of Jesus. They cherish an image of a Jesus so "gentle and mild" as to be incapable of "overthrowing" anything, not even the reader's smugness. This is not merely to misread the sign in the incident at the temple, but to reject it outright. The Jesus in the pages of this or any other gospel is not exactly a standard-bearer for bleeding hearts. Those who persist in misreading the gospel message would do well to consult the buyers and sellers and money-changers of the temple in any age for their opinion of Jesus of Nazareth.

The aim of the evangelist is not to provide us with the biography of an inspiring hero, proportioned to the size of our ambitions, conformed to our ideals, and meeting our currently prevailing notions of what constitutes greatness. We have to respect, not only the otherness of Jesus, but also the individual character of the evangelist who portrays him in these pages.

The aim of the narrative in John's gospel is distinct from the accounts of the same incident in the synoptics. Respect for that aim will spare us the futile search for what the gospels do not pretend or intend to give us. Thus, to compare John's account with that in Mark 11:15–17 (Mt 21:12–13; Lk 19:45–46) can be useful for a lot of things, but not for the establishment of a historical fact. In the gospel of John, all the history is in the "became flesh"; and no amount of miracles or triumphs over opponents in controversies, no sublimity of words, nor severity of actions, can remove the stumbling block that it is precisely the Word who was God that has become man and dwelt among us (Jn 1:14). For this, faith is the sole sufficient response.

Thus, while Jesus' disciples, those who accepted him, remembered that it was written, "Zeal for your house will consume me" (2:17), others could only indignantly demand, "What sign have you to show us for doing this?" (2:18). Into one or the other of the two categories, every reader of John must necessarily fall.

Johannine Misunderstanding

In formulating Jesus' reply to the challenge of his opponents, the evangelist puts to use a device he will employ throughout his gospel. To say within the temple precincts itself (2:14), "Destroy this temple, and in three days I will raise it up" (2:18), is to invite misunderstanding from those who knew only too well that it had taken "forty-six years to build this temple" (2:20). But John uses this device of misunderstanding precisely to advance just a step further our own understanding of the revelation of who Jesus really is.

Right at the start of Jesus' public ministry, the evangelist directs the reader's attention from a merely geographical locus like the temple in Jerusalem to the very center of the revelation, to the death and resurrection of Jesus: "But he spoke of the temple of his body" (2:21).

Yet, even to those who might have been able to understand correctly such a statement as, "Destroy this temple, and in three days I will raise it up," it could have made real sense only to their faith: "When therefore he was raised from the dead, his disciples remembered that he had said this" (2:22; 12:16). This "remembering" is, as the evangelist will make clear later, the special function of the Holy Spirit, who will "bring to your remembrance all that I have said to you" (14:26).

When therefore he was raised from the dead, his disciples remembered that he had said this and they believed the scripture and the word which Jesus had spoken (2:22).

As a consequence of this remembering of Jesus' words, the evangelist comments, the disciples "believed the scripture and the word which Jesus had spoken" (2:22). Such a statement is truly remarkable. It puts the word of Jesus on a par with "the scripture," the word of God. Yet, within the context of the fourth gospel, such a statement can astonish us only if we forget the opening words of the prologue. The Word that was "with God," that "was God" (1:1), "became flesh and dwelt among us" (1:14). So the law that was "given through Moses" (1:17), the message proclaimed by the prophets, and the word which Jesus had spoken (2:22) are all the Word of God's revelation. It is precisely this Word that took flesh and "dwelt among us" (1:14).

Now when he was in Jerusalem at the Passover feast, many believed in his name when they saw the signs which he did; but Jesus did not trust himself to them, because he knew all men

and needed no one to bear witness of man; for he himself knew what was in man (2:23–25)

Faith and Miracles

The concluding remarks of chapter 2 make two related points: First, that "many believed in his name when they saw the signs which he did" (2:23). Such a view of the link between faith and miracles differs from the one we find in the synoptic gospels. There we are accustomed to regard faith as the reason for miracles. The last resort of all baffled preachers is, "If you have faith as a grain of mustard seed, you will say to this mountain, 'Move from here to there,' and it will move" (Mt 17:20; cf. Lk 17:6). In passages like "your faith has made you well" (Mt 9:22; Mk 5:34; Lk 8:48), we have come to regard faith as the condition for miracles. The faith that moves mountains is a commonplace of Christian preaching.

In the gospel of John, however, it is the miracle that begets faith (Jn 2:11, 23; 4:48; 6:30; 7:31). This is one reason why John prefers to speak of miracles as "signs." They point, not so much to the action itself, nor to the beneficiary as such (cf. "if you have faith...nothing will be impossible to you" Mt 17:20), but to the identity of him who performs the miracle. The faith that the witness of the sign expresses is a faith in the identity of the person who works the miracle. Eventually, the witness of the signs must come to believe that Jesus is the one sent by the Father (5:36), that he can do nothing of "his own accord" (5:19), that everything he does he does in his "Father's name" (10:25), that the works he does are really the works of the one who sent him (9:4) and "bear witness" (10:25) that he and the Father "are one" (10:30).

In the synoptics, on the other hand, the faith needed for miracles is directed to God, with whom "all things are possible" (Mt 19:26; Mk 10:27; Lk 18:27). If believers only had enough faith, nothing would be impossible to them. When the frustrated disciples ask Jesus why they could not cure the poor tormented boy, Jesus tells them, "Because of your little faith. For truly, I say to you, if you have faith as a grain of mustard seed, you will say to this mountain, 'Move from here to there,' and it will move; and nothing will be impossible to you" (Mt 17:20).

But, from whichever aspect one chooses to view the miracle or understand the sign, there is a great difficulty with this kind of faith. It is John who puts his finger unerringly on the problem when, in his account of the appearance of the risen Jesus, the risen Lord says,

"Blessed are those who have *not seen* and yet believe" (20:29). The difficulty with signs and miracles, even with the greatest of them, is that our appetite for them is insatiable. The recipient of the favor, like the witness of the wonder, keeps coming back for more. We are forever, as it were, testing to see if God is still there, whether our prayers are "getting through." As the whole of John's gospel demonstrates, true faith can ultimately rest only on the Word. The first disciples followed Jesus merely at the Baptist's "Behold, the Lamb of God" (1:36) before they witnessed any signs. Judas Iscariot, Peter and Thomas, even after witnessing so many and such spectacular signs, still betrayed, denied and doubted Jesus.

"He knew what was in man"

This understanding of faith in relation to signs is what prompted John's second remark at the conclusion of this chapter: "but Jesus did not trust himself to them, because he knew all men...for he himself knew what was in man" (2:24–25; and to read here, as does the NRSV, "because he knew all people" is merely silly, even in current demotic American English). Jesus was not duped by the sound of human words, nor misled by the fleeting and fickle enthusiasms of human crowds. He knew too well what was at the heart of anyone who genuinely turned to God. True faith did not call attention to one's piety, but out of despairing need, pleaded for a miracle, any miracle at all.

To be sure, such knowledge of "what was in man" need not have been the exclusive prerogative of Jesus of Nazareth. Any perceptive observer of religious piety or pulpit oratory could reach the same conclusion. By sufficient reflection, any of us could make a similar claim. But the statement in John, as we shall have occasion to see, says a good deal more when it predicates this knowledge "of what was in man" of him who alone could say "I know" the Father (8:55). His knowledge is ultimately the knowledge of him through whom all things were made and in whom was life. It is the knowledge of one who is indeed "the light of men" (1:3–4).

The two concluding statements of this chapter, the one about the many who believed "when they saw the signs which he did" (2:23), and that about Jesus' knowledge of "what was in man" (2:25), make for a good link with and, consequently, a smooth transition to, the dialogue with Nicodemus in the chapter that follows.

John 3

Nicodemus: rebirth from above; flesh and spirit; ascent and descent.

God so loved the world: the work of the evangelist; the world; salvation; eternal life; life; grace and judgment; doing evil; coming to the light.

Jesus and John the Baptist: "who comes from above;" the Spirit; God's wrath.

NICODEMUS (3:1–15)

> **Now there was a man of the Pharisees, named Nicodemus, a ruler of the Jews. This man came to Jesus by night and said to him, "Rabbi, we know that you are a teacher come from God; for no one can do these signs that you do, unless God is with him" (3:1–2).**

This "man of the Pharisees...a ruler of the Jews" (3:1) is a good example of how the signs performed by Jesus can bring one to Jesus and to faith in him. Nicodemus is the one who will try later to bring some reasonableness into the murderous deliberation of Jesus' enemies: "Does our law judge a man without first giving him a hearing and learning what he does?" (7:50–51). His action on that occasion will demonstrate, not only the seriousness of his initial intent in coming to Jesus, but also the sterling quality of his faith. This same faith in the person of Jesus will, moreover, impel him to render to the crucified the piety that ought to have been performed by one of the disciples who had followed the Master from the beginning and witnessed his signs. "Nicodemus also, who had at first come to him by night, came bringing a mixture of myrrh and aloes, about a hundred pounds' weight" (19:39).

"Rabbi, we know that you are a teacher come from God; for no one can do these signs that you do, unless God is with him" (3:2). This opening statement in the dialogue is unexceptionable, even if to speak of "these signs" in the plural might be baffling after only one sign has been narrated thus far in the gospel (2:11). But to be baffled by such a discrepancy is to misunderstand the gospel of John as a history, which it is not; or a biography, which it is never meant to be; or a chronicle, which it gives no hint of being. The author of the fourth gospel is writing a theology, to which he subordinates, and under which he subsumes, all references, whether historical (e.g., 3:1 about Nicodemus; or 4:12 about Jacob's well; or 19:13 about the "place called The Pavement"); or biographical (e.g., "Jesus wept" 11:35, and was "deeply moved" 11:38); or chronological (e.g., the succession of Jewish feasts which structures the evangelist's account, 2:13; 5:1; 6:4; 7:2; 11:55).

Of course, Nicodemus' statement is one which can be made by any good-will witness about any sign performed by Jesus. Recognizing the sign for what it truly is, such a person seeks Jesus out, not as a wonder-worker, but as one "come from God," and with whom God very evidently is. Thus, the coming of Nicodemus to Jesus was not the conclusion to a syllogism. His was not the reasoning which asked, "When the Christ appears will he do more signs than this man has done?" (7:31), or argued, "How can a man who is a sinner do such signs?" (9:16). No, Nicodemus, through the signs, saw the person of Jesus; and, through Jesus himself, the God who was "with him." The eyes of Nicodemus were not arrested at the visible, nor was his reasoning confined to the immediately evident.

Rebirth from Above

Jesus answered him, "Amen, amen, I say to you, unless one is born anew/from above, he cannot see the kingdom of God" (3:3).

Jesus' response immediately sets the stage for a challenge to Nicodemus' faith. After all, Jesus was not the first or indeed the only worker of miracles in the world that Nicodemus had heard of or knew. So Jesus now confronts him with a fact well beyond the merely miraculous.

Whether the double meaning of the Greek word for "anew/from above" was intended by the evangelist or not, it is not what gives rise to the typically Johannine misunderstanding in this dialogue. That misunderstanding stemmed rather from Nicodemus' confounding a purely heavenly reality, which had not crossed his mind, with a corresponding earthly one, with which he was all too familiar. This is what a revelation does. It brings to our attention a heavenly reality, thus opening up infinite vistas before us where hitherto we had expected none.

> **Nicodemus said to him, "How can a man be born when he is old? Can he enter a second time into his mother's womb and be born?" (3:4).**

This is just what the fashioner of this dialogue has in mind. The earthbound reading of Jesus' first statement by Nicodemus is the misunderstanding which occasions the second, more profound revelation. This revelation is then itself elaborated further into a full-blown Johannine discourse on the Word become flesh.

> **Jesus, answered, "Amen, amen, I say to you, unless one is born of water and the Spirit, he cannot enter the kingdom of God (3:5).**

To "see the kingdom of God" (3:3) and to "enter" it (3:5) are alike expressions that belong to "the end," i.e., to the consummation of God's creative plan in the definitive and final establishment of his rule and reign on earth. This is what is technically called "eschatology," *eschaton* being the Greek word for "end," "last." Moreover, the evangelist is aware–as the reader ought to become aware–that the reference to this final and definitive irruption of God's power into the world is actually taking place in him who addresses these words to Nicodemus.

Flesh and Spirit

> **That which is born of the flesh is flesh, and that which is born of the Spirit is spirit (3:6)**

The distinction here between "flesh" and "spirit" is essential both for keeping the heavenly reality distinct from the earthly, and for removing any doubt about the source and origin of the new birth "from above." Such rebirth is not an earthly phenomenon and cannot be subjected to the rules that govern earthly phenomena.

Although commentators are given to disputing the role of the sacraments in the fourth gospel, it is easy enough to see in these verses (3:5–6) a reference to the sacrament of baptism. A new birth "of water and the Spirit" (3:5) can hardly be a reference to anything else. What can mislead us, however, is a misreading of the revelation that "unless one is born of water and the Spirit he cannot enter the kingdom of God" (3:5) as Nicodemus read it, in an "earthly" way. We can so easily be caught up in the mechanisms of an earthly act and forget the revelation's primary reference to the newness of life in the Spirit. Hence, the need for a reminder to keep the realm of the created, "flesh," and the realm of the creator, "spirit," distinct. For we are constantly tempted to blur the distinction between the two, to obliterate the boundaries between the human and the divine, the earthly and the heavenly, created mortal flesh and the Spirit.

> **Do not marvel that I said to you, "You must be born anew." The wind blows where it wills, and you hear the sound of it, but you do not know whence it comes or whither it goes; so it is with every one who is born of the Spirit (3:7–8).**

In this context, another reminder of the distinction between the flesh and the spirit becomes no less necessary. The absolute freedom of the Spirit and the consequent unpredictability of its action are easily lost sight of by the "flesh." Of course, when the evangelist says "the *pneuma* blows where it wills," the Greek term denotes both wind and spirit. But it is not caprice that lies behind this seeming arbitrariness of movement. The statement, "the wind blows where it wills," is rather a corollary to the nature and exercise of divine power in its sovereign freedom from compulsion and coercion. It says about the Spirit here what will be echoed and resumed at the close of the chapter: "It is not by measure that he gives the Spirit" (3:34).

This is the truth on which most hearers of the revelation will stumble. They insist on judging and measuring the action of the Revealer and the content of the revelation by their earthly norms and standards. They insist that the revelation meet their norms, conform to their standards, and be circumscribed by their imagination. They want, in other words, to circumscribe the measure by which God gives the Spirit. The disputes of Jesus with his opponents will amply illustrate this in the pages of the gospel.

> **Nicodemus said to him, "How can this be?" Jesus answered him, "Are you a teacher of Israel, and yet you do not understand this? (3:9–10).**

The dialogue progresses by increasingly concise statements. Nicodemus' "How can this be?" (3:9), like Jesus' "Are you a teacher of Israel, and yet you do not understand this?" (3:10) are only conversational stadia toward the revelation that follows. The whole chapter serves as an admirable demonstration that, for the evangelist, the function of the Word is to reveal, and the function of the Word become flesh is to be the Revealer. Thus, the whole fourth gospel is an elaboration of this theological given. It is "theological" because by means of it God (*theos*) makes himself known to us once and for all in the person of Jesus of Nazareth, who is the Word (*logos*) become flesh.

> **Amen, amen, I say to you, we speak of what we know, and bear witness to what we have seen; but you do not receive our testimony. If I have told you earthly things and you do not believe, how can you believe if I tell you heavenly things? (3:11–12).**

The whole content of the revelation brought by Jesus is based on the fact that he speaks of what he has "seen." This is his unique privilege. For, behind this astonishing claim, lies the incontrovertible fact that "no one has ever seen God" (1:18), which can now be reformulated to say:

Ascent and Descent

> **No one has ascended into heaven but he who descended from heaven, the Son of man (3:13).**

Should the order of these two statements seem inverted, we have to keep in mind the vantage point of their author. You would expect descent from heaven to precede ascent to it. But John, writing *after* the exaltation of the Son of man, knows it is precisely that ascent "into heaven" which revealed and bore definite witness to the Son's descent "from heaven." In other words, the gospel of John, like everything else in the New Testament, was inevitably written in the light of Easter. Everything said about Jesus, and indeed everything said by him had to be understood in that light.

To make the reference to the exaltation clearer, John has recourse to a standard symbol of salvation, the "bronze serpent" of the wilderness in the book of Numbers:

> And the Lord said to Moses, "Make a fiery serpent, and set it on a pole; and every one who is bitten, when he sees it, shall live." So Moses made a bronze serpent, and set it on a pole; and if a ser-

pent bit any man, he would look at the bronze serpent and live (Num 21:8–9).

Taking this literary commonplace of the Exodus event and applying it to the Son of man, the evangelist gives an almost new dimension to the prologue's "For the law was given through Moses; grace and truth came through Jesus Christ" (1:18). So he goes on to explain:

And as Moses lifted up the serpent in the wilderness, so must the Son of man be lifted up (3:14).

As we shall have occasion to see, the lifting up of the Son of man is a reference to the crucifixion which, in the fourth gospel, is an integral part of the whole exaltation-cum-glorification event of Jesus Christ. This event embraces the cross no less than the resurrection, the ascension to the right hand of the Father as well as Pentecost (see 8:28; 12:32). The whole purpose of this descent-ascent movement is

...that whoever believes in him may have eternal life (3:15).

Thus, the intended end of "the Word became flesh," the purpose of all that this involved in the life, death, resurrection and exaltation of Jesus of Nazareth, was simply to give "eternal life" to all those that "believe in him."

Therefore, the "What do you seek?" (1:38) of the opening scene can have for its ultimate response no answer but this eternal life. Whoever seeks Jesus, whoever comes to him, can have only this eternal life in view. Everything else is readily available elsewhere at a discount.

This is why the evangelist now goes on to elucidate in the rest of this chapter what this "eternal life" means. It matters little whether the words that follow are his own or are meant to be the words of Jesus. Where you assign the quotation marks in the discourse is of no importance. The gospel of John is not that kind of a book at all.

GOD SO LOVED THE WORLD (John 3:16–21, 22–30, 31–36)

The Work of the Evangelist

Admittedly, it is difficult to determine whether verses 16–21 are a continuation of Jesus' words to Nicodemus or the evangelist's own comment upon them. But the lack of clarity in the distinction is attributable to the author of the gospel, not to its readers. One can legitimately wonder, moreover, whether this failure in clarity was not intentional. The words in verses 16–21 are just as much the evangelist's as the words that preceded them. John is not the transcriber of a taped interview, but a theologian intent upon giving expression to the significance of the event of our salvation. Whether you accept or reject these words depends, not on their authenticity, but on their content. You do not reject the words because Jesus did not say them, but because you ultimately refuse to believe what they say.

For God so loved the world that he gave his only Son, that whoever believes in him should not perish but have eternal life (3:16).

The World

The "world" in John can be used in a neutral sense to mean the created world or all its inhabitants, as in "He was in the world" (1:10); or it can be used in a negative, pejorative sense to mean everything and everyone opposed to the revelation, as in "*the world* knew him not" (1:10). In "God so loved the world" (3:16), the term is used clearly in the neutral sense. In this sense, the world and all that dwell in it are the objects of God's love and redeeming action. The term thus embraces every mortal on the face of the earth, in every age and in all times.

God, of course, is the creator of this world, "all things were made through him, and without him was not anything that was made" (1:3). The creator further manifests his love for his creation by giving "his only Son" (3:16). We thus find ourselves here at the confines of human language, trying to describe–albeit in vain–the gift of God's most precious possession to "the world" and all who dwell in it.

John views this divine gift as definitive and final. He understands it as the "eschatological" act of God. Because, in giving his only Son, God has no more to give. To those who would object that God's riches are inexhaustible, the evangelist could only say, "If I have told you earthly things and you do not believe, how can you believe if I tell you heavenly things?" (3:12). All too often, those most solicitous to safeguard God's inexhaustible riches forget that "it is not by measure that he gives" (3:34).

Salvation

But what lays immediate claim to our attention is the expressly stated purpose of God's gift of his only Son, "that whoever believes in him should not perish but have eternal life" (3:16b). The first implication of this statement is that everyone born into this world is destined to "perish," and is therefore in need of deliverance. To understand this fact within the framework of the fourth gospel is the indispensable first step toward comprehending "eternal life." Indeed, it is the indispensable first step to understanding the meaning of salvation:

> Our God is a God of salvation; and to God, the Lord, belongs escape from death (Ps 68:20).

Therefore, before all else, we need to remember that, within this gospel, to "perish" is to die, to cease to exist. For, in John, there are no compensatory philosophical consolations to the absoluteness of this death, from the totality of whose dominion no one can escape. What the gospel of John proclaims as the purpose of the coming of the only Son into the world is "eternal life," not exemption from dying, and certainly not immortality, but the overthrow of the power of death itself. This the evangelist calls "eternal life."

Eternal Life

Here two things must be noted: First, to understand "eternal" is not to visualize a life with an infinite succession of time without end. This, in a way, would be relatively easy to do. The difficult–nay, impossible–task is to conceive of a life that does not stand "in the shadow of death." It is this that "eternal life" promises, a life that does not terminate in death nor stands under its sway. Consequently, this divine gift of eternal life, precisely because it does not eliminate the fact of dying nor obviate the need to die, can be grasped only by faith, not by philosophical reasoning. It is the object of the revelation that "whoever believes in him should not perish but have eternal life" (3:16).

Secondly, to understand "eternal life" in this context, it is necessary to reflect that "to perish" and "to have life" are absolutely contradictory and mutually exclusive. Thus, for John, not to believe in the only Son, i.e., not to believe in the revelation, is to die, period. It is not to continue existence in another state, not even in the most horrific of states.

Some Christians, coming upon this, perhaps for the first time, might welcome the statement with glee. If they do, it would be because they imagine that the gospel of John thus gives them licence to do all that they would gladly and willingly do, were it not for the threatened eternal torments in hell. The incomprehensible perversity of such a view lies at the very heart of the problem. If a Christian can even for a moment prefer to perish wholly rather than spend an eternity in hell, it is not because of the fear of hell but out of a disdain for life. Such disdain of life would make the gift of eternal life an irrelevance. It would make the revelation itself incomprehensible.

Life

Moreover, "life" in John, as indeed in its biblical understanding in general, is not continued existence, nor mere survival after death, nor even what is currently called "quality of life." Life is, first and foremost, life *with* someone, life in relation to the other, in relation to God, to those whom we love, and to those who love us. Eternal life is the preservation of these relationships intact, but without the menacing hand of death. Death, on the other hand, is the ineluctable severance of all those relations. In the gospel of John, "to die" is to cease to be, to be "as when I was not yet." To miss this point, would make it well nigh impossible to comprehend why the only answer to Jesus' "What do you seek?" (1:38) can indeed only be "eternal life."

Therefore, to make clear the saving purpose of God, John adds:

> **For God sent the Son into the world, not to condemn the world, but that the world might be saved through him (3:17).**

The sending of God's only Son into the world has for its purpose the salvation of the world. It saves the world, first, from "perishing," from death. To save the world is thus to deliver from the dominion of death all those who are subject to it, not by exempting them from dying, but by granting them life eternal.

Grace and Judgment

Nevertheless, the fact of the matter is that the revelation of this love of God for the world is, of itself, impotent to compel assent. The revelation is, and must continue to be, proclaimed. But, so long as it proclaims a freely and gratuitously offered gift, it can and must be either freely accepted or freely rejected. It is this rejection which is the "condemnation." Such condemnation was not the intention of God in sending his Son into the world. "For God sent the Son into the world, *not to condemn* the world."

> **He who believes in him is not condemned; he who does not believe is condemned already, because he has not believed in the name of the only Son of God (3:18).**

Thus, because this act of God's love is a gift, it always comes, at one and the same time, both as a saving grace and a judgment of condemnation. But whether it is one or the other depends on the free response of the recipient, not on the caprice of the giver. In accepting the gift, the one "who believes" is not condemned, i.e., as the preceding verse makes clear, is "saved," possesses "eternal life." The one who rejects the gift is, by that very fact of the rejection, "condemned *already*." What is at issue here is believing or refusing to believe "in the name of the only Son of God."

Putting it this way would, of course, radically alter the current–then as now–understanding of "judgment." Judgment was and is considered the final crowning act of God's reign. It is, in that sense, "eschatological." Whether you envision it after death or at the "consummation of the ages" is not the point at issue here. What is at issue is what John intends by "condemned *already*," namely, that here and now, in life, before death, this judgment has already taken place. This is indeed a radical shift from the view prevalent in the evangelist's time. Therefore, to remove any doubt about his meaning, John adds his definition of the judgment.

Doing Evil

> **And this is the judgment, that the light has come into the world, and men loved darkness rather than light, because their deeds were evil (3:19).**

This verse is, before all else, a development of a theme in the Prologue: "The true light...was coming into the world...was in the world...yet the world knew him not" (1:9–10). Consequently, it must never be far from one's mind at any point in this discussion that this light is, first and foremost, a gift of life: "the life was the light of men" (1:4). Nevertheless, it remains baffling why, when the light shines, we still prefer darkness and reject the light by refusing to believe "in the name of the only Son of God." In 3:19, John offers one explanation: "because their deeds were evil." The reason we shrink from the revelation and refuse the light is not the sense of shame nor the discomfort of exposure, but our reluctance ever to accept the fact that our deeds are evil.

This explanation is not as farfetched as might appear at first sight. It formulates in a Johannine idiom the "*Repent* and believe in the gospel" of the synoptics (Mk 1:15; 6:12; Mt 3:2; 4:17). Repentance acknowledges one's own evil; and, however unfashionable this may be today, this acknowledgment remains the indispensable first step to accepting the message of salvation.

Even without the benefit of a rudimentary philosophy, however, we can appreciate the fact that no one really chooses to do evil as such. We always choose evil under some aspect of good. Saint Augustine and the medieval scholastics understood this only too well. But, whereas people in the so-called ages of faith might have been a bit too eager to acknowledge the evil they did, in our own age we simply refuse to see any evil in anything we do. The shifting kaleidoscope of our euphemisms for the evil we do should be evidence enough. It is not that we believe that everything we do is good, but that nothing we do is really evil. Evil, if mentioned at all, has come to mean the evil others do.

Yet, even when we recognize evil in others, we shrink instinctively from ascribing it to an individual other. We lay about us with vengeance castigating evil in abstract entities like "society," the "system," the "institution." This is our characteristic way of loving "the darkness rather than the light."

Coming to the Light

Such smug self-sufficiency renders the acceptance of the gift of salvation impossible. Our reluctance to acknowledge the evil that is ours inevitably blinds us to the light:

> **For every one who does evil hates the light, and does not come to the light, lest his deeds should be exposed (3:20).**

Of course, the reverse of this statement is equally valid:

> **But who does what is true comes to the light, that it may be clearly seen that his deeds have been wrought in God (3:21).**

Those who come to the light, who accept the revelation and believe "in the name of the only Son," not only emerge from the darkness and call their own evil by its name, but also have the clarity of vision to perceive that whatever good they do is done "in God," i.e., is the gift of God to them. This, as we shall have occasion to see later, is an ongoing process in the day-to-day life of the believer.

True Christian believers do not enjoy the luxury of muddling as best they can in the expectation of receiving a tabulated and–it is fervently hoped–indulgent tally in the judgment at the last day. Their doing "what is true" and coming "to the light" is a daily repeated task. This is why they need a constant reminder of the revelation, and the gospel of John is just such a reminder.

The light that comes into the world transforms every single action of the believer into a judgment here and now. The light of the revelation that enables believers to see their "deeds as evil" also makes them aware that if they do "what is true," if they live in conformity with and in the light of this revelation, then all their deeds are "done in God," and are therefore God's own gift to them.

In this fact of the revelation lies the supreme freedom of the Christian, a freedom, not merely from all anxiety, but even from the judgment of God, no less than from the opinions of others. In the unshakable conviction that when they do "what is true," when they live according to the Word and their "deeds have been wrought in God" (3:21), the believers realize the supreme freedom of knowing that they "walk in the light" (1 Jn 1:7). It is the task of Christian preaching to remind the believers of this truth, not by providing them with score cards for the final tally, but by proclaiming, as does the gospel of John, that God loved the world (Jn 3:16) and sent his Son into it as the revelation of this love, as light, as the "light of life" (8:12), so that "whoever believes in him should not perish but have eternal life" (3:16).

JESUS AND JOHN THE BAPTIST

After this Jesus and his disciples went into the land of Judea; there he remained with them and baptized. John also was baptizing at Aenon near Salim, because there was much water there; and people came and were baptized. For John had not yet been put in prison.

Now a discussion arose between John's disciples and a Jew over purifying. And they came to John, and said to him, "Rabbi, he

who was with you beyond the Jordan, to whom you bore witness, here he is, baptizing, and all are going to him." John answered, "No one can receive anything except what is given him from heaven. You yourselves bear me witness, that I said, I am not the Christ, but I have been sent before him. He who has the bride is the bridegroom; the friend of the bridegroom, who stands and hears him, rejoices greatly at the bridegroom's voice; therefore this joy of mine is now full. He must increase, but I must decrease" (3:22–24, 25–30).

Even the narrative of the Baptist's activity and the question put to him by his disciples illustrate by a concrete example what has been said about the preceding verses (3:16–21). The Baptist's answer, "No one can receive anything except what is given him from heaven" (3:27), reveals that all John's deeds have been "wrought in God" (3:21). Thus, the narrative in 3:22–30 achieves its climax by disclosing the source of the Baptist's true greatness: "He must increase, but I must decrease" (3:30).

"Who comes from above"

These words are not merely an act of humility on the part of both the Baptist and the author of this gospel. They state, rather, a cardinal theological fact:

He who comes from above is above all; he who is of the earth belongs to the earth, and of the earth he speaks; he who comes from heaven is above all (3:31).

The only reason for the preeminence of Jesus of Nazareth is the truth about his heavenly origin. It forms the object of the revelation. The uniqueness of Jesus of Nazareth derives from the fact that everyone else in creation belongs to the earth, and of the earth only can speak (3:31b). This is so, for the simple reason that "No one has ever seen God" (1:18), but only he who "comes from heaven."

He bears witness to what he has seen and heard, yet no one receives his testimony; he who receives his testimony sets his seal to this, that God is true (3:32–33).

To believe the revelation brought by him who "comes from above" is to acknowledge that God really is "true," and therefore the revealer of the truth. It is not a question here of God's fidelity to his promises, but of what God is in himself. God cannot, as it were, not reveal himself. Indeed, is not this what we really say when we call God "creator"? Every creation is a revelation. Later on, in theological speculations on the Trinity and in reflection on what was before the creation of the world, theologians spoke of God as conceiving the Word from all eternity, i.e., from all eternity God is a revealer. Is not this to say, moreover, that the "revelation" is a self-disclosure of the God who is "true"?

God is "true" precisely because, as Jesus will say in chapter 5, "the testimony which he bears to me is true" (5:32). It is this testimony of God which enables the Son to say in his turn, "my testimony is true" (8:14), and to remind his opponents that "he who sent me is true, and I declare to the world what I have heard from him" (8:26).

The Spirit

For he whom God has sent utters the words of God (3:34a).

This precisely is the task of the only Son whom God sent into the world (3:16–17). His task is to "utter the words of God," to be the Revealer of the Father (3:35). In this gift of his Son, the God who "so loved the world" (3:16) has given us everything,

...for it is not by measure that he gives the Spirit (3:34b).

A brief remark is called for here about the baffling mention of the Spirit in this context. To speak of the Spirit here is only one hint among many to alert the reader that what is written in this gospel is addressed to all those who are "orphaned" (14:18 NRSV) by the departure of the Revealer from this world. Then it becomes the task of this same Spirit, the Spirit-Paraclete, to "teach you all things" (14:26). The gospel of John is very consciously a part of this teaching. It is one means of bringing to remembrance "all that I have said to you." The gift of the Father's love in sending his Son into the world as the Revealer is thus given without any measure, exuberantly (3:34b). This gift is itself also the uninterrupted work of the Spirit. Therefore, it is "without measure" (3:34).

the Father loves the Son, and has given all things into his hand (3:35).

"For God so loved the world that he gave his only Son" (3:16). But that giving of the Son is before all else a gift to the Son himself. The love of the Father for the Son is precisely what is revealed in God's loving the world. The one sent as Revealer into this world cannot carry out the will of the one who sent him if he could not say the "Father has loved me" (15:9). "For the Father loves the Son, and shows him all that he himself is doing" (5:20). Thus, by loving those who are in the world, Jesus reveals the Father's love for himself and thereby bears witness to the love of the Father for them.

God's Wrath

But, in saying all this, we are never far from the judgment inherent in the gift:

> **Whoever believes in the Son has eternal life; whoever disobeys the Son will not see life, but must undergo God's wrath (3:36 NRSV).**

It is important to note the present tense in this statement, "*has* eternal life," and not "will have." Here and now the believers in the Son have eternal life, and out of their faith in this revealed fact must they live. Conversely, "whoever disobeys the Son," whoever refuses to believe the Revealer–for believing is obedience to the revelation–"will not see life." Very clearly, this does not say that the one who rejects the revelation will see a different kind of life, but simply "will not see life," i.e., will "perish" (3:16). This "will not see life" is what damnation is. It is to be "condemned" (3:18), to "come to judgment" (5:24; 3:19), to be under "the wrath of God" (3:36).

For the sake of those who persist in asking the same question in every generation, the "wrath" of God is not the spiteful anger of an arbitrary deity withholding his love from any one of his creatures. The "wrath of God" is rather the judgment that is consequent upon the rejection of God's love. That love is a gift of God in sending his Son into the world. "He who believes in the Son *has* eternal life" (3:36). But who refuses to believe, "who does not obey the Son," who therefore rejects the gift, "shall not see life, but the wrath of God rests upon him" (3:36b RSV).

A gift, even a divine gift, is not a gift unless it is freely accepted. If this gift is eternal life, its rejection can only mean death. The rejection of the free gift is therefore a judgment. This judgment is what the Bible calls the "wrath of God." Before such a rejection by a creature whom God created free, even the creator stands helpless.

John 4

The Woman of Samaria: Johannine misunderstanding; receiving the revelation; Johannine irony; misunderstanding the gift; "our hearts are restless;" worship of the Father; true worship; the revelation; consequences of the revelation; proclaiming and obedience.

Healing the Official's Son: the "evangelist"; the work of salvation.

THE WOMAN OF SAMARIA (John 4:1–42)

Now when the Lord knew that the Pharisees had heard that Jesus was making and baptizing more disciples than John (although Jesus himself did not baptize, but only his disciples), he left Judea and departed again to Galilee. He had to pass through Samaria. So he came to a city of Samaria, called Sychar, near the field that Jacob gave to his son Joseph. Jacob's well was there, and so Jesus, wearied as he was with his journey, sat down beside the well. It was about the sixth hour (4:1–6).

In the economy of the details which lend so much charm to the setting of the narrative that follows, one element in particular echoes the prologue: "wearied as he was with his journey" (4:6). Better than many another mark of the Lord's humanity in this gospel, this weariness is the reminder that the Word "became flesh," heir to all that the human condition is subject to (see, e.g., "Jesus wept" 11:35; "Now is my soul troubled" 12:27). To say this is, of course, not for a moment to suggest that Jesus' life had to be one of unrelieved and intense gloom. Christians did not have to wait for the discovery of Gnostic writings in Nag Hammadi to remind them that joy and laughter are as much part of the life of the flesh as weariness, tears and a "troubled soul."

Johannine Misunderstanding

There came a woman of Samaria to draw water. Jesus said to her, "Give me a drink." For his disciples had gone away into the city to buy food. The Samaritan woman said to him, "How is it that you, a Jew, ask a drink of me, a woman of Samaria?" For Jews have no dealings with Samaritans (4:7–9).

The dialogue between Jesus and the woman of Samaria who came to draw water from the well (4:7) is yet another example of the Johannine technique of "misunderstanding" being put at the service of the revelation. The technique is more elaborately and more tellingly employed here than it was in the dialogue with Nicodemus. The initial request, "Give me a drink," is met by the surprise that "a Jew" should ask a Samaritan for a favor. This remark ought to serve as a reminder that the evangelist never forgot for an instant that Jesus himself was a Jew. By appending the explanatory note, "For Jews have no dealings with Samaritans," John merely underlines this often forgotten fact.

Receiving the Revelation

Jesus answered her, "If you knew the gift of God, and who it is that is saying to you, 'Give me a drink,' you would have asked him, and he would have given you living water" (4:10).

In his response to the woman's astonishment, Jesus lays down two conditions for receiving the revelation he brings into the world. The first is the recognition of one's need for the gift, the revelation, a need that cannot be met elsewhere by anything or anyone: "If you knew the gift of God" (4:10a).

The second condition is the acknowledgment of the giver of the gift: "and who it is that is saying to you, 'Give me a drink.'" Therefore, to recognize the identity of the one bearing the gift is at once to ask for the gift and to receive it: "you would have asked him, and he would have given you living water" (4:10b).

Asking for the gift is a confession of the need for it. Yet it is our deep-seated reluctance to confess our need that impedes our acceptance of the gift even though, in our heart of hearts, we know our absolute longing for it. "Our hearts are restless, O Lord" is a cry, not only of the anguished Augustine (*Confessions* 1.1), but of every mortal on this earth.

Johannine Irony

The woman said to him, "Sir, you have nothing to draw with, and the well is deep; where do you get that living water? Are you greater than our father Jacob, who gave us the well, and drank from it himself, and his sons, and his cattle?" (4:11–12).

As is evident from the woman's reaction, it is not just that the bearer of the gift seems so unlikely a benefactor. It is rather the very extravagance of the gift itself that causes her to wonder. A weary, thirsty traveler offers her what he himself seems to need most. This offers the perfect opportunity for the puzzled woman to temporize, "Sir, you have nothing to draw with, and the well is deep" (4:11).

Into her comprehensible and natural enough misunderstanding, the evangelist insinuates another of his peculiarly effective devices, a Johannine irony: "Are you greater than our father Jacob, who gave us the well?" (4:12). The reader, who knows already what the woman cannot even guess at–that the man who speaks to her is indeed greater than the revered patriarch–can of course appreciate this irony for what it is. In the Johannine narrative, such irony, like the misunderstanding in which it is embedded, is the means the evangelist employs to bring the reader one step closer to the inevitable revelation which is to follow.

Thus the woman's misunderstanding actually sets the stage for Jesus to disclose the meaning of his claim to give her "living water" (4:10).

Misunderstanding the Gift

Jesus said to her, "Every one who drinks of this water will thirst again, but whoever drinks of the water that I shall give him will never thirst; the water that I shall give him will become in him a spring of water welling up to eternal life" (4:13–14).

What Jesus has to offer her will bring an end to her every quest, will satisfy all her needs and longings, and put an end to her lifelong search: She "will *never* thirst." Here again the reader knows what the woman has no means of knowing. Jesus is speaking of the gift which he himself is to this world. Only the "welling up to eternal life" (4:14) could have given the woman some inkling of what Jesus was promising her.

What makes this particular gift so definitive is the fact that what it offers is nothing less than "eternal life." This is why it is indispensable to recognize and acknowledge one's absolute need for it: "If you knew the gift of God" (4:10). It becomes evident here why Jesus speaks of the gift "of God"; for no one but God, the creator, can give "eternal life" (4:14).

Thus our first stumbling block when confronted by this gift is our failure to acknowledge our need for it. Nevertheless, as the gospel will demonstrate, even when we acknowledge our need for the gift, we obstinately seek to satisfy that need everywhere except in the proffered revelation, the only place the gift can really be found.

In our obstinacy we all have a patron in the Samaritan woman. For the moment, she seems satisfied with the gift itself, even though she misunderstands its nature. She imagines that what Jesus is offering her is relief from the drudgery of her daily routine, a deliverance from its discomforts, an exemption from the law of our humanity.

The woman said to him, "Sir, give me this water, that I may not thirst, nor come here to draw" (4:15).

Like her, we all pretend, in one way or another, that the gift of the Word puts an end to all our troubles, resolves the problems of our world and resolves them, moreover, to our own satisfaction.

This is what individuals and institutions in the Christian community understand so well and exploit so readily. They pretend to offer the world a Christianity that can change it, deliver it from its chronic ills, and provide solutions to all its insoluble problems. They cite past, and promise future, miracles. They very conveniently forget two thousand years of mottled history. They try, with persistent and astonishing success, to make us forget that the Word became flesh and came into the world, not to take us out of it, nor to spare us living in it (17:15a), nor to exempt us from the limitations of the flesh which he himself fully underwent (15:18), but to deliver and keep us from evil (17:15b). The gift of the revelation he brings is not a deliverance from toil and discomfort, nor an exemption from the human condition, but "a spring of water welling up to eternal life" (4:15).

"Our hearts are restless"

Jesus said to her, "Go, call your husband, and come here." The woman answered him, "I have no husband." Jesus said to her, "You are right in saying, 'I have no husband'; for you have had five husbands, and he whom you now have is not your husband; this you said truly" (4:16–18).

The woman's misunderstanding, however, advances the revelation yet another step. Jesus invites her to call her husband; she admits she does not have one; and Jesus then discloses his knowledge of her actual situation, as he does the paralytic's in 5:6, and the disciples' in 6:61. This disclosure is itself a sign. It points to the identity of him who said to her, "Give me a drink" (4:10).

Within the context of the narrative and in light of what has been said thus far, it is difficult not to see in "you have had five husbands" (4:18) an indication of the restlessness of the human heart, a restlessness that can find its repose only in him who speaks to her: "If you knew the gift of God" (4:10). She was so apt a pupil because she knew well her great need, even though she fell short of recognizing its true object.

The woman said to him, "Sir, I perceive that you are a prophet (4:19).

She has arrived at last. She confesses him a prophet. This is not, as some believe, a confession of her guilt. It is rather an expression of her astonishment that a total stranger, a Jew in alien Samaria, should know such intimate secrets of her life. Now she perceives, however dimly, who he is that is speaking to her. But she does not stop there.

Our fathers worshiped on this mountain; and you say that in Jerusalem is the place where men ought to worship" (4:20).

Having arrived at the confession of Jesus as a prophet, she does not leave well enough alone. Who of us does? She proceeds to do what all of us are prone to do in the circumstances. She starts a theological discussion: "Our fathers worshiped on this mountain" (4:20). There is nothing like a theological, moral or liturgical puzzle to spare us the need to respond to the revelation. Her question is fair and clear enough, but it has nothing to do with what "a prophet" is trying to tell her. Nevertheless, her misconceived attempt to divert the dialogue into issues more familiar to her, provides the evangelist with the opportunity to take the revelation one step further.

Worship of the Father

Jesus said to her, "Woman, believe me, the hour is coming when neither on this mountain nor in Jerusalem will you worship the Father" (4:21).

Note, first of all, that the way Jesus addresses her, "Woman," is identical to the way he addresses his own mother both at Cana (2:4) and at the foot of the cross (19:26), and also Mary Magdalene at the tomb (20:15). Yet, when one considers the amount of words expended on this small point, particularly in the marriage feast at Cana (2:4), the minor theological sally of the Samaritan woman in 4:20 looks like the paragon of discretion.

The evangelist, of course, could have left "worship" to stand, as it does in the woman's statement in the previous verse, i.e., with an unexpressed, if understood and easily supplied object, "Our fathers worshiped on this mountain" (4:20), since God alone is the object of such worship for Jews, Samaritans and Christians. But he did not. Jesus speaks of "worship of the Father." In so doing he sets the stage for what follows:

> **You worship what you do not know; we worship what we know, for salvation is from the Jews. But the hour is coming, and now is, when the true worshipers will worship the Father in spirit and truth, for such the Father seeks to worship him (4:22–23).**

The only reason why Jesus can say, "You worship what you do *not* know" is, of course, the revelation he himself brings. It is this revelation which makes the knowledge of God wholly other. Henceforth, it is a knowledge of "the Father" and, in the revelation of this fact, the worship is a worship "in spirit and truth." In saying this, however, the evangelist has no intention to dismiss or to discount what had preceded this revelation, nor to disregard what remains inalterably true, that "salvation *is* from the Jews" (4:22).

What the revelation makes possible is the worship of the Father "in spirit and truth," in the power and the light of the revelation brought by him who has just been confessed "prophet," and who will very shortly be revealed and recognized as "the Messiah" (4:26). Salvation is indeed "from the Jews."

True Worship

> **God is spirit, and those who worship him must worship him in spirit and truth (4:24).**

The reason why the Father seeks "true worshipers" who worship him "in spirit and truth" (4:23) is precisely that God himself "is spirit."

Now, there are three such Johannine statements about God, and they are closely allied: "God is spirit" (Jn 4:24); "God is light" (1 Jn 1:5); and "God is love" (1 Jn 4:8, 16). In the final analysis, they all say the same thing. Each statement in its own way says that God is a revealer of himself and is therefore "light"; that he, who is "spirit," cannot not reveal himself precisely because "God is love" and therefore cannot not love.

This is a much needed reminder in a church where God has become a placebo for the self-loathing and self-righteous victims of such as belong only to the earth and of the earth only speak. But to say "God is spirit" is to say all that God really is to this world. It sums up his creative power, his redemptive action, his revelation. That this fact in turn requires worship "in the spirit" is a reminder that the way God is worshiped can only be a response to the God who is spirit, and not to some figment of the imagination of anything that is flesh, however pious and however extravagant. Forgetting the fact that "God is spirit" has turned so much of Christian worship into therapy sessions, and made the God worshiped there merely the ego of the worshipers themselves writ large. The true worshipers of the God who is spirit "must worship in spirit and truth." Thus there can be no true worship of God which is not based on his revelation, "in truth," and grounded in his power to create and give life, "in spirit."

The Revelation

The woman said to him, "I know that Messiah is coming (he who is called Christ); when he comes, he will show us all things" (4:25).

Now she perceives the true tenor of the conversation with this stranger. She gives expression, as did Andrew and Nathanael before her (1:41, 45), to the religious expectations of a people, Jews and Samaritans alike.

It is a temptation to view the whole narrative thus far as a gradual progression in the stages of faith from ignorance to resounding confession, but that would be to miss its point. What we have here is rather a graphic representation, not so much of our progress toward faith, but rather of our reluctance to accept the revelation. The narrative illustrates the ingenious ways we devise to evade it. Our care for social proprieties ("you, a Jew...ask me, a woman of Samaria" 4:9); our down-to-earth common sense ("the well is deep" 4:10); our pride in our tradition ("our father Jacob" 4:12); even our theological savvy ("you say that in Jerusalem is the place...to worship" 4:20). All these form but part of the inexhaustible arsenal of evasions we maintain against the encounter with the revelation. If one is inclined to say that this is all true only of non-believers, then saying it would itself be yet another way of closing one's ear to the revelation.

Jesus said to her, "I who speak to you am he" (4:26).

The forthright response cuts right through the pretended theological expertise, and comes to the essential point of the revelation that "I AM he." Such identification of Jesus of Nazareth with the long-awaited Messiah can only be by means of a revelation. It is not the result of carefully weighing the varied credentials of different claimants to the title, or of sifting through the complex evidence of the messianic expectations of the first century. The disclosure of the true messianic identity of Jesus of Nazareth can only be the object of revelation, because the response to it can only be either faith or unbelief. It is not an opinion or a judgment with which you concur or dissent.

There were many in that first century who claimed to be the Messiah. The times were particularly rife with such expectations. Anyone could then, as anyone can even now, lay claim to this title. What distinguishes the Johannine dialogue in John 4 is precisely the revelation that all the expectations of divine salvation, all the hopes for the final and definitive fulfilment of God's promises to his people, find their object in him who says to the Samaritan woman, "I who speak to you am he."

Of course, scholars continue to dispute what the precise focus of the expectations of first-century Judaism was. Many question the way the term "Messiah" itself was or could have been understood. But, in the gospel of John, the one who is "coming," "the Messiah (he who is called Christ)," who "will *proclaim* all things to us" (as the NRSV better renders 4:25), is unequivocally and definitively identified with Jesus of Nazareth.

We should not allow all the fine erudition about Messiahship–however valuable and necessary–to distract us from the fact that the "I am he" refers to this Jesus of Nazareth precisely as the one who "will proclaim all things." It is he who is the bearer of God's revelation, the Revealer. Understandably enough, this fact is at the very heart of the message of John that "the Word became flesh" (1:14).

No small measure of the evangelist's artistry is displayed in the incidents that follow (4:27–30, 31–38, and 39–42). They show the consequences of this revelation in several of its aspects.

Consequences of the Revelation

> **Just then his disciples came. They marveled that he was talking with a woman, but none said, "What do you wish?" or, "Why are you talking with her?" So the woman left her water jar, and went away into the city, and said to the people, "Come, see a man who told me all that I ever did. Can this be the Christ?" They went out of the city and were coming to him (4:27–30).**

The reaction of the woman to the revelation is portrayed dramatically by the abandonment of what she came to do at the well ("left her water jar" 4:28) in order to go and proclaim the news "to the people": "Come, see a man who told me all that I ever did. Can this be the Christ?" (4:30). The advent of the revelation always relativizes everything else. Whatever form it takes, the revelation never comes for the comfort and complacency of the individual receiving it. When it does come, it inevitably disrupts our routines, overturns the even tenor of our days, and directs our attention away from ourselves to the others who, too, must "come and see" (4:29; 1:39).

> **Meanwhile the disciples besought him, saying, "Rabbi, eat." But he said to them, "I have food to eat of which you do not know." So the disciples said to one another, "Has any one brought him food?" Jesus said to them, "My food is to do the will of him who sent me, and to accomplish his work. Do you not say, 'There are yet four months, then comes the harvest'? I tell you, lift up your eyes, and see how the fields are already white for harvest. He who reaps receives wages, and gathers fruit for eternal life, so that sower and reaper may rejoice together. For here the saying holds true, 'One sows and another reaps.' I sent you to reap that for which you did not labor; others have labored, and you have entered into their labor" (4:31–38).**

Crowded as it is with details, the second incident should not diffuse our concentration on the main point. The Revealer, he who has just proclaimed the revelation, reminds his disciples that he is what he is and does what he does simply and solely in order to accomplish "the work of the one who sent him," the one who is the author of the revelation: "My food is to do the will of him who sent me, and to accomplish his work" (4:34). Without this obedience to the divine will, without the recognition that all the work accomplished by the Revealer is not his but God's alone, that revelation can be no more than a personal opinion and, as such, subject to all the demurs, qualifications and restrictions governing human opinions. Only his obedience to the "will of him who sent me" makes him the Revealer.

But if we are not to be misled into reading the third incident (4:39–42) as some social commentary on the lot of women in the world, it is important to keep this obedience in mind. We note, first of all, that the woman's apostolate was not ineffective:

> **Many Samaritans from that city believed in him because of the woman's testimony, "He told me all that I ever did." So when the Samaritans came to him, they asked him to stay with them; and he stayed there two days (4:39–40).**

This is no small measure of success. But the evangelist goes on to say,

> **And many more believed because of his word (4:41).**

To believe "because of his word," because of the word of the Revealer himself, is the end and purpose of all preaching and proclamation of the message. Those who believe, believe precisely "*because* of *his* word," not because of the charm, intelligence, oratorical skills, or theological acumen of the preacher. The Word is the object of, and the reason for, all the words uttered, whether by the Samaritan woman, by the evangelist, or by any proclaimer of the good news.

Proclaiming and Obedience

> **They said to the woman, "It is no longer because of your words that we believe, for we have heard for ourselves, and we know that this is indeed the Savior of the world" (4:42).**

When, therefore, the Samaritans say this to the woman evangelist, they do no more than remind us, the readers, that what is true of the Revealer himself is no less true of his followers. All that the "Savior of the world" does, he does in order to carry out "the will of him who sent me, and to accomplish his work" (4:34). All that any of his followers does is, consequently, done in obedience to the Revealer and in order to carry out *his* work.

By its very nature, the task of proclaiming the Word never is, nor can it ever be, a solitary task. The interdependence of the laborers on one another, "One sows and another reaps" (4:37), and their dependence on those who preceded them, "I sent you to reap that for which you did not labor; others have labored, and you have entered into their labors" (4:38), are there to remind the readers of the gospel in every generation not to lose sight of the true nature of the revelation and of its transmission. The interdependence of all the proclaimers, including the authors of the gospels, is as much a part of the process of transmitting the revelation as is the ultimate dependence of all the proclaimers on the Revealer himself and on the revelation he brings. The Revealer's own obedience to the will of the one who "sent him" sets the norm and pattern for all who proclaim to every generation that Jesus of Nazareth is "indeed the Savior of the world" (4:42). In the proclamation of the revelation, obedience to the will of the Revealer is all.

HEALING THE OFFICIAL'S SON (John 4:43–54)

> **After the two days he departed to Galilee. For Jesus himself testified that a prophet has no honor in his own country. So when he came to Galilee, the Galileans welcomed him, having seen all that he had done in Jerusalem at the feast, for they too had gone to the feast (4:43–45).**

The transition from the encounter with the Samaritan woman to the "second sign that Jesus did" (4:54) is baffling. It presupposes opposition to Jesus, when we know of none thus far in the gospel. It presumes our knowledge of "all that he had done in Jerusalem at the feast" (4:45), and all we have to fall back on is the concluding remark of chapter 2, "Now when he was in Jerusalem at the Passover feast, many believed in his name when they saw the *signs* which he did" (2:23). Even the great Origen in the third century had to admit failure to find coherence in the sequence. Modern commentators have not been more successful.

The "Evangelist"

The passage, however, can serve as a reminder that the gospel as we have it today underwent redactions at more than one hand. Were the "final redactor," the one we choose to designate as the "evangelist," intent on providing us with a work to meet the standards of unity and composition, whether in the third or the twentieth century, then such a passage as 4:43–45 is only one of many instances of his failure. But the stated purpose of his task, "that you may believe that Jesus is the

Christ, the Son of God, and that believing you may have life in his name" (20:31), is wholly other. Doubtless, there were writers who might well have succeeded where the evangelist failed by providing us with a better and more coherent sequence of events. But it is doubtful whether any author then or later could have better met his own stated purpose, "that you may believe."

The Work of Salvation

> **So he came again to Cana in Galilee, where he had made the water wine. And at Capernaum there was an official whose son was ill. When he heard that Jesus had come from Judea to Galilee, he went and begged him to come down and heal his son, for he was at the point of death. Jesus therefore said to him, "Unless you see signs and wonders you will not believe." The official said to him, "Sir, come down before my child dies." Jesus said to him, "Go, your son will live." The man believed the word that Jesus spoke to him and went his way. As he was going down, his servants met him and told him that his son was living. So he asked them the hour when he began to mend, and they said to him, "Yesterday at the seventh hour the fever left him." The father knew that was the hour when Jesus had said to him, "Your son will live"; and he himself believed, and all his household. This was now the second sign that Jesus did when he had come from Judea to Galilee (4:46–54).**

Jesus' coming "again to Cana in Galilee" (4:46) is the occasion for "the second sign that Jesus did" (4:54). The appropriateness of this particular sign should be gauged by its present position in the text. It follows immediately after the confession that Jesus is "the Savior of the world" (4:42). For the miracle performed by Jesus demonstrates precisely this point: He saves the official's son from death, "Your son will live" (4:53). He is indeed "the Savior."

Whether or not the original language of such assurance possessed a proper term for "mend" (4:52; NRSV "recover"), Jesus' promise of "will live" in 4:50 touches the very heart of salvation. All Jesus' miracles of healing are in a sense a deliverance from death, if only because all illness is an incursion of death upon life. The account of the instantaneous healing by a mere word of Jesus, "that was the hour when Jesus had said to him, 'Your son will live'" (4:53), highlights the element of wonder at the salvation he brings.

But, for all its success as a sign, for all its laudable consequences, the "he himself believed, and all his household" (4:53b), a reminder is still needed to all who read this gospel: "Unless you see signs and wonders you will not believe" (4:48). The whole point in understanding the revelation, which calls for faith, is found precisely in the "Blessed are those who have *not* seen and yet believe" (20:29b). Herein lies the true beatitude of all who read the account of this or any other sign in the fourth gospel.

John 5

The Healing at the Pool: law and revelation; calling God his own Father.

The Father and the Son: resurrection and creation; eschatology; "has life in himself"; the Son of man; hearing and seeing; "the will of him who sent me"; response to the revelation; the Father's witness; universality of salvation; why the missions; searching the scriptures; seeking glory from one another.

THE HEALING AT THE POOL (John 5:1–9, 10–18)

After this there was a feast of the Jews, and Jesus went up to Jerusalem.

Now there is in Jerusalem by the Sheep Gate a pool, in Hebrew called Bethzatha, which has five porticoes. In these lay a multitude of invalids, blind, lame, paralyzed. One man was there, who had been ill for thirty-eight years. When Jesus saw him and knew that he had been lying there a long time, he said to him, "Do you want to be healed?" The sick man answered him, "Sir, I have no man to put me into the pool when the water is troubled, and while I am going another steps down before me." Jesus said to him, "Rise, take up your pallet, and walk." And at once the man was healed, and he took up his pallet and walked. Now that day was the sabbath (5:1–9).

The narrative of the healing itself is straightforward enough: the setting (the "feast of the Jews," the pool by the Sheep Gate in Jerusalem); the description of the situation (one ill for thirty-eight years); Jesus' knowledge of it ("Jesus...knew that he had been lying there a long time"; cf. his similar knowledge of the Samaritan woman in 4:17–18); the command, "Rise, take up your pallet, and walk" (5:8);

and the immediate, miraculous response, "And at once he was healed" (5:9). These require no comment.

The miracle itself, like the healing of the official's son which preceded it (4:46–54), is again an illustration of Jesus' work as "Savior of the world" (4:42). In the words of the Psalmist, he delivers the victims of various illnesses out of "the snares of death" (Ps 18:5; 116:3). Indeed, every healing, whether in John or in the synoptics, is but a partial defeat of the dominion of death, until its final and definitive overthrow in the resurrection of Jesus. As has already been remarked, every malady and every illness, on the other hand, is but an incursion of the power of death on life. Thus, in the final analysis, each of these accounts of Jesus' healings is a demonstration that "in him was life" (1:4).

> **So the Jews said to the man who was cured, "It is the sabbath, it is not lawful for you to carry your pallet." But he answered them, "The man who healed me said to me, 'Take up your pallet, and walk.'" They asked him, "Who is the man who said to you, 'Take up your pallet, and walk'?" Now the man who had been healed did not know who it was, for Jesus had withdrawn, as there was a crowd in the place. Afterward, Jesus found him in the temple, and said to him, "See you are well! Sin no more, that nothing more befall you." The man went away and told the Jews that it was Jesus who had healed him. And this was why the Jews persecuted Jesus, because he did this on the sabbath (5:10–16).**

Unlike similar accounts in the synoptics, John adds at the very end of his account, almost as an afterthought, "Now that day was the sabbath" (5:9b). This is done with the express purpose of setting the stage for the controversy that follows. In the synoptics, the attack of his opponents is directed against Jesus himself (Mk 3:2; Mt 12:10; Lk 6:7). In John, it is directed against the healed man (5:10; 9:13–14).

Such a roundabout way of doing things in John is designed to call our attention to the all-important question: "Who is the man who said to you, 'Take up your pallet, and walk'?" (5:12; cf. "Where is he?" in 9:12). The question about the true identity of Jesus is the only question that matters. It echoes throughout the gospel. "He was in the world... yet the world knew him not" (1:10). The function of all the signs in the fourth gospel is, after all, to reveal the true identity of him who works them.

The controversy that ensues is, therefore, about Jesus' true identity. The question of the sabbath observance merely provides the pretext.

Thus, by means of a seemingly illogical sequence, the evangelist informs us, "And this was why the Jews persecuted Jesus, because he did this on the sabbath" (5:16). In fact, however, this statement merely sets the stage for the discourse that follows (5:17–47), which provides a far truer answer to "Who is the man?" (5:12) than a mere healer on the sabbath.

Law and Revelation

In, "It is the sabbath, it is not lawful for you to carry your pallet" (5:10), we see an infrequently remarked obstacle which the law puts in our way. The law, even God's law, can in fact blind us to the revelation. We have in this account, as indeed also in the healing of the blind man in chapter 9, a useful reminder of this. So sure were Jesus' persecutors (5:16) of their grasp of the demands of the law, that they never paused to ask, let alone to ponder, the reality that was staring them in the face. Those who think that "the Jews" alone are culpable of this blindness are themselves blind.

> **Jesus said to them, "My Father is working still, and I am working" (5:17).**

Jesus' response to his opponents insists on the identification of the work he himself does with the work of the Father. His preliminary, if indirect, response to their question about who the real violator of the sabbath is, lays the ground for the revelation that follows in 5:19–23, 24–30. The work Jesus does is the work of him who gave the law in the first place. His opponents understood the implications of such a claim only too well.

Calling God His Own Father

> **This was why the Jews sought all the more to kill him, because he not only broke the sabbath but also called God his own Father, making himself equal with God (5:18).**

In its way, their reaction to Jesus' claim serves as a compendium of the whole fourth gospel. The violation of the sabbath is by no means incidental. Jesus' action is rightly interpreted both as a demonstration of divine power in the actual healing, and a claim to divine authority by instructing the paralytic to do what is expressly forbidden by God's law. "For the law was given through Moses; grace and truth came through Jesus Christ" (1:17).

In its implications, the incident thus far echoes the question of Jesus in Mark, "Which is easier, to say to the paralytic, 'Your sins are forgiven,' or to say, 'Rise, take up your pallet and walk'?" (Mk 2:9; Mt 9:5; Lk 5:22–23). The miraculous healing and the violation of the sabbath are alike the prerogatives of God.

What, to the mind of Jesus' opponents, was infinitely more outrageous, however, was to claim God as his own Father and, therefore, to claim equality with God, "making himself equal with God" (5:18). The reader needs no particular expertise in comparative religions, and little more than a nodding acquaintance with the Old Testament to realize that God is, by definition, unique, has no one "like" him, let alone anyone "equal" to him (Ps 35:10; 89:6; Is 46:9; Jer 10:6). Yet, as his opponents understood only too well, this was precisely what Jesus claimed, "My Father is working still, and I am working" (5:17).

Moreover, those same opponents knew very well that God is "Father of the fatherless and protector of widows" (Ps 68:5); that David cries to him, "You are my Father, my God, and the Rock of my salvation!" (Ps 89:26); that Isaiah can say, "You, O Lord, are our father, our Redeemer from of old is your name" (Is 63:16); or that God can say, "I have become a father to Israel, and Ephraim is my firstborn" (Jer 31:9). To this way of speaking, all the linguistic ingenuity of philologists, exegetes and historians of religion can be brought to bear, either to elucidate the relationship between God and his people, or to obviate the scandal of "patriarchal" modes of expression. The claim of Jesus in the fourth gospel, however, is not only in a different category altogether, but simply unparalleled elsewhere. It is in this claim that the newness of the revelation (see 1:18) consists. Hence, the outrage at such a claim, then as now!

Jesus' calling "God his own Father" (5:18) makes explicit both the opening affirmation of the prologue that "the Word was *with* God... was in the beginning *with* God" (1:1–2), and its closing statement, "the Son, who is in the bosom of the Father" (1:18). His "making himself equal with God" (5:18), on the other hand, echoes the prologue's "and the Word was God" (1:1). Both assertions are alike necessary. The Word is distinct from God, whom Jesus calls "his own Father," and it is precisely this distinctness which makes the affirmation of his being "*equal* with God" possible.

THE FATHER AND THE SON (John 5:19–30)

These verses begin to explain how the Son's equality with God is to be understood by the believers.

> **Jesus said to them, "Amen, amen, I say to you, the Son can do nothing of his own accord, but only what he sees the Father doing; for whatever he does, that the Son does likewise" (5:19).**

We can be easily misled into reading such a statement to mean the inferiority of the Son, when in fact it discloses his equality with the Father and the intimacy of their relation. The Son "can do nothing," not because he is unable to, but because his whole will is set on doing "nothing of his own accord." Consequently, the Son doing "only what he sees the Father doing" says that everything he does is perfectly attuned to the Father's will. The Son's obedience to the Father in everything he does is such that everything he does is a perfect reflection of the Father's will. Thus, everything the Son does necessarily reveals the Father's will.

Our insurmountable obstacle in comprehending this revealed truth is our almost total inability to see obedience as anything but subservience and subordination. Genuine obedience, such as the obedience of the Son to the Father, far from being the subordination of one to the other, is the manifestation of their union with one another:

> **For the Father loves the Son, and shows him all that he himself is doing; and greater works than these will he show him, that you may marvel (5:20).**

It is this relation of love of the Father for the Son that is the mainspring of the Son's obedience. To slaves, this will seem an insoluble paradox, but to lovers, it is only a truism. Those who truly love can do no other.

Resurrection and Creation

The promise of the "greater works" is a reference to the resurrection, as is made immediately clear in:

> **For as the Father raises the dead and gives them life, so also the Son gives life to whom he will (5:21).**

It is the love of the Father that raises Jesus from the dead. For, whether in creation or in the resurrection, it is God alone who "raises the dead and gives them life." The statement is about as clear as one would wish it to be. To say this about the Father is to say that, in whatever he does, God is always the creator out of nothing. This, in itself, is no more than a reminder of what we confess in the first article of the creed, "I believe in God, the Father Almighty, Creator of heaven and earth."

To add, however, "so also the Son gives life to whom he will" (5:21b) is to affirm, not only the unity of the Father and the Son, which is already stated in verses 19–20, but to make explicit the equality that was enunciated in the prologue by "the Word was with God, and the Word was God." Similarly, the "so also the Son gives life" makes explicit that "in him was life" (1:4a).

Moreover, when the evangelist adds that the Son gives life "to whom he wills," he is reminding us that this life is "the light of men" (1:4b). For the Son to possess what is the exclusive prerogative of God, the power to give life, is to have equality with God. That the Son gives life "to whom he will" (5:21b) calls attention to the fact that "grace and truth came through Jesus Christ" (1:17). As the one who brings "truth," he is the Revealer, "the light of men." The grace he brings, because it is a gift, cannot but come as both grace and judgment. For, just as to accept this grace and truth is to live, so too to reject them is to die. The refusal of the gift of life is, inevitably, a judgment:

> **The Father judges no one, but has given all judgment to the Son, that all may honor the Son, even as they honor the Father. He who does not honor the Son does not honor the Father who sent him (5:22–23).**

To accept the gift of life offered by the Son is to honor him and give him glory. To honor the Son is to honor and give glory to the Father, not mediately, but in the very act and instance of honoring the Son. Henceforth, all judgment is contingent upon the encounter with the Son whom the Father sent into the world. Encounter with the truth of this revelation can be either grace and life, or judgment and death. Between accepting and rejecting the revelation of the Son no middle ground exists.

The judgment is given to the Son precisely because it is he who "became flesh and dwelt among us" (1:14). In the encounter with him, i.e., in the encounter with Jesus of Nazareth, we encounter God himself. This is why the prologue affirms that "grace and truth came through Jesus Christ" (1:17). To reject Jesus Christ is therefore to reject the free gift of eternal life, and hence to die. To refuse to honor the Son is to refuse to honor the Father (5:23b). This is what "judgment" means. To accept him and his offer of life, is not only to "honor the Son even as they honor the Father" (5:23a), but also to have as a consequence eternal life:

> **Amen, amen, I say to you, he who hears my word and believes him who sent me has eternal life, he does not come into judgment, but has passed from death to life (5:24).**

It seems impossible to put it more clearly. To hear his word, to accept the revelation that he brings, is to believe the one who sent him. This faith in Jesus of Nazareth as the one sent by the Father *is* eternal life, a present possession here and now, not just a future promise: "This *is* eternal life, that they know you the only true God, and Jesus Christ whom you have sent" (17:3).

Eschatology

To remove any lingering doubt about the traditional eschatology which expected a judgment only at the end of time, the evangelist adds, "he does *not* come into judgment." The judgment has already taken place in the encounter with this Jesus of Nazareth. So, too, of course, those who believe in him as the one who is sent by the Father, have already "passed from death to life." He will say to Martha, "he who believes in me, *though he die,* yet shall he live, and whoever lives and believes in me *shall never die*" (11:25–26).

Of course, a reminder is called for here. Though this gift of eternal life is a present possession already, it does not exempt its possessor from actually dying. The gift of eternal life, as we shall have occasion to see when we come to chapter 11, is the deliverance from death, not an exemption from dying. The one who brings this revelation is he who himself died and was raised from the dead. Indeed, precisely because the gift of eternal life does not exempt the believer in him from dying, the encounter with this revelation has to be an ongoing process throughout one's life. Consequently, faith in him whom the Father has sent can never be a once-for-all act, but one that needs to be reiterated throughout the believer's mortal life.

This is why the community of believers needs a constant, uninterrupted reminder of the gospel message. The believers, who always face the prospect of dying one day, need always to hear the gospel proclaimed anew. This, in the final analysis, is the reason why the evangelist wrote a gospel at all.

> **Amen, amen, I say to you, the hour is coming, and now is, when the dead will hear the voice of the Son of God, and those who hear will live (5:25).**

That this statement does not exactly square with the preceding affirmation of "has eternal life" and "does not come into judgment, but has passed from death to life" (5:24) is, in the judgment of many commentators, an indication of the complex history of the composition of the fourth gospel. That the gospel of John as we possess it today underwent several stages of editing and redaction, finds confirmation in, among other characteristics, the lingering influence in it of an older, more prevalent eschatology. Thus, the view of the resurrection of the dead in verse 25 is considered by many to be a trace of just such a "future eschatology."

But what is important to note is that even the statement in this verse (5:25) insists on hearing, here and now, "the voice of the Son of God." The judgment, whether envisaged in the present or in the future, in time or out of time, is henceforth always in function of the revelation which the Son of God brings. It is always in function of hearing "the voice of the Son of God" in the present.

"Has life in himself"

The reason for this is made clear in one of those Johannine statements about the Son that can only be described as audacious, and must have seemed like blasphemy to many who encountered it for the first time:

> **For as the Father has life in himself, so he has granted the Son also to have life in himself, and has given him authority to execute judgment, because he is the Son of man (5:26–27).**

This, first of all, makes more explicit the statement that "For as the Father raises the dead and gives them life, so also the Son gives life to whom he will" (5:21). But to appreciate the audacity of such a statement, one has to keep in mind at the outset that God alone "has life in himself." This is the very nature of God. Therefore, he alone can be the giver of genuine life. Life, true life, is therefore the exclusive gift of

God. This needs calling to mind because it lies at the basis of much of the current misunderstanding of the gospel message. Every one other than God, i.e., every creature, has life, not "in himself," but solely as a gift. This is what distinguishes the creature from the creator.

Therefore, when the evangelist says that the Son has life "in himself," he is claiming no less than that "the Word was God" (1:1). But, when he formulates the statement to say that the Father "*granted* the Son also to have life in himself," he is but reminding his readers that "the Word was *with* God" (1:1 and 2), and that this Word in fact "became flesh" (1:14). He is, in other words, keeping the distinction between them clear. It is this sober balance in expression that was to pave the way for future generations in centuries to come to speak of the *one God* even while speaking of *three persons* in the Trinity.

The fact that the Father "has granted the Son also to have life in himself" involves his granting him "authority to execute judgment" (5:27) as well. This, as we have already seen in verses 21–24, is simply because it is the Son who in fact offers the gift of eternal life. Consequently, this gift, in itself and by its very nature as a free gift, can only be eternal life to those who freely accept and receive it. To those who refuse and reject it, it can only be judgment.

The Son of Man

The addition of "because he is the Son of man" (5:27) is both an evocation of the traditional eschatological title of the one who brings the final judgment (see, e.g., Mt 24:37; 25:31; Mk 13:26; Lk 21:27, 36), and a reminder that this judgment is at work here and now (cf. the promise made to Nathanael in 1:51; and see 6:27, 53, 62; 8:28; 9:35; 12:23; 13:31). The point at issue is not that the title "Son of man" is part of the vocabulary stock of traditional eschatology which is so well reflected in 5:28–29, but that the identification of this title with the person of Jesus of Nazareth radically alters our understanding of this eschatology in the fourth gospel.

> **Do not marvel at this; for the hour is coming when all who are in the tombs will hear his voice and come forth, those who have done good, to the resurrection of life, and those who have done evil, to the resurrection of judgment (5:28–29).**

While it is by no means easy to harmonize the "he does not come into judgment, but has passed from death to life" in verse 24 with the "resurrection of life" and the "resurrection of judgment" in verse 29, we have to keep in mind what has just been said about the gift of eternal life. Because, no matter what eschatology one chooses to espouse, the "resurrection" is always in the future, "at the last day" (6:39). The resurrection is necessarily a resurrection from the dead. One has to die before being raised from the dead. But the fact that the gift of eternal life is real and present now does not, and cannot mean, an exemption from dying. In other words, the gift of eternal life here and now does not and cannot obviate the need of the resurrection *from the dead.*

Thus, the necessary corrective–if this be the right word–follows immediately, as though the evangelist feared, not so much a misunderstanding, as a distraction from the principal point.

Hearing and Seeing

> **I can do nothing on my own authority; as I hear I judge; and my judgment is just, because I seek not my own will but the will of him who sent me (5:30).**

We have already had a chance to consider the first of these statements in verse 19. The Son is said there to do "only what he *sees* the Father doing." Here in verse 30, however, he says, "as I *hear,* I judge." But in the fourth gospel, "hearing" (8:26, 40; 15:15) and "seeing" (3:11; 5:19; 6:46; 8:38) are what the Revealer uses to describe his own possession of the revelation: "He bears witness to what he has seen and heard" (3:32; 6:46).

The important thing here, however, is the reason the Revealer gives why his "judgment is just," that is, not merely fair, but right. This reason is not only essential for understanding the revelation, but constitutes a recurrent theme in the gospel: "My food is to do the will of him who sent me" (4:34); "For I have come down from heaven, not to do my own will, but the will of him who sent me" (6:38); "I always do what is pleasing to him [who sent me]" (8:29).

"The will of him who sent me"

He who is sent from the Father as the Word, the Revealer, has no other purpose to accomplish except to carry out the will of the one who sent him. To forget this even for a moment is to misconceive the nature of the revelation. The revelation is not to be sought in the psychology of Jesus, or in his goodness, meekness, gentleness, wisdom, eloquence, or any of the other qualities we search for in our quest of the historical Jesus. The revelation is rather to be found in the totality of his conformity to the will of the Father, i.e., in the perfection of the Son's obedience. In his total obedience to the will of the Father who sent him lies the indisputable justness of the Son's judgment: "My judgment is just, because I seek not my own will but the will of him who sent me" (5:30).

Thus, any seeking of one's "own will" risks falsifying the judgment and calls its verdict into question. So much is awry in human judgment precisely because those who exercise it seek their own will. The hypocrisy of their encomia to "Justice," and of their claims to serve the "Law" or the "cause of Freedom," or whatever else appeals to the fickle fancy of their deluded followers, is only the tribute all lying pays to the truth. So, too, those who wish to evade the judgment of the Son attack, not its justness, but his motive. This is why Jesus insists that it is not his own will that he seeks. He is wholly at the service of the Father who sent him. This is the revelation.

Another ploy we use to evade the responsibility of the encounter with the Revealer is to call his mission into question:

> **If I bear witness to myself, my testimony is not true; there is another who bears witness to me, and I know that the testimony which he bears to me is true (5:31–32).**

This anticipates the objection of the Pharisees, "You are bearing witness to yourself; your testimony is not true" (8:13). The force of Jesus' words lies, not in the dispute about the nature of witness as such, but in the nature of his own relation to the Father. That the "testimony which he bears to me is true," is beyond all question. God's testimony is always true. The real dispute is about who the Jesus who makes such a claim really is. In other words, it is about the nature of his mission, not about the juridical niceties of witness and testimony. Nevertheless, Jesus adds a further reminder:

> **You sent to John, and he has borne witness to the truth. Not that the testimony which I receive is from man; but I say this that you may be saved (5:33–34).**

The appeal Jesus makes to the witness rendered by John the Baptist "to the truth" (1:7, 19–34) is a reminder that the "testimony which I receive" is "not from man" (5:34). He does not belittle the Baptist's testimony or dismiss him as useless. But he does insist that the essential truth lies not in weighing the worth of human witnesses, but in recognizing the source of their mission. The truth of John the Baptist's testimony rests, not in who he was, but in the source of his authority, in the one who sent him. "There was a man sent from God, whose name was John" (1:6).

Response to the Revelation

Precisely at this point we find a common source of misapprehension in our response to the revelation. It is so easy to conceive the revelation as the product of human ingenuity, the consequence of compromise, the outcome of scientific research into the gospels or the scriptures (5:39). We are more intent on the preservation of the witness "from man," on its dogmatic nicety, its literary merit, its partisan appeal. The essence, however, lies elsewhere. It lies in our response to the revelation itself. Only in accepting it do we find our true and only salvation: "I say this that you may be saved" (5:34).

This fact takes nothing away from the one who bears witness. Jesus willingly utters the Baptist's praise. The true greatness of that "burning and shining lamp" lay in his obedient fidelity to the mission of the one who sent him (1:33). He was "a man sent from God" (1:6). His God-given task was to bear witness "that this is the Son of God" (1:34).

He was a burning and shining lamp, and you were willing to rejoice for a while in his light (5:35).

This encomium of the Baptist, however, is not diminished one whit by contrasting it with the "greater" witness of the Revealer:

But the testimony which I have is greater than that of John; for the works which the Father has granted me to accomplish, these very works which I am doing, bear me witness that the Father has sent me (5:36).

The Father's Witness

This appeal to the works "which the Father has granted me to accomplish" is, of course, an appeal primarily–though not exclusively–to the signs which Jesus did in the sight of the people. But again, the important thing to keep in mind is that the accomplishment of these signs is the work of the Father. The signs witness to Jesus' mission, not because they are spectacular, but because they are carried out in perfect obedience to the will of the Father. "The Son can do nothing of his own accord, but only what he sees the Father doing" (5:19). "I can do nothing on my own authority" (5:30). It is in this perfect conformity of his will to the will of the Father that the true value of the signs as witness lies. If the signs he performs do not reveal his true identity as the one sent by the Father, then their witness is in vain. They can rouse admiration but cannot effect salvation: "that you may be saved" (5:34).

"These very works which I am doing" (5:36) refer, of course, both to his deeds and his words as the Revealer. To stop at either is to deny the revelation. Both what Jesus does and what he says bear witness that the Father has sent him (5:36).

And the Father who sent me has himself borne witness to me (5:37a).

It is by means of everything the Son says and does that the Father bears witness to him. But, lest the reader fail to appreciate what an astounding claim this is, he goes on to say:

His voice you have never heard, his form you have never seen (5:37b).

This is a faithful echo of the "No one has ever seen God" in the prologue (1:18). The very God whom no one has ever seen or heard, is the God whom the Revealer has both heard and seen ("he bears witness to what he has seen and heard" 3:32; 5:30; 6:46). Henceforth, the Revealer is the sole access to God: "He who has seen me has seen the Father" (14:9). There is not and there will never be any means of access to the God whose "voice you have never heard" and whose "form you have never seen" (5:37b) other than this Jesus of Nazareth. He alone is the means of our access to God.

Universality of Salvation

Statements like these in John, and they are by no means confined to this chapter, give rise to questions such as "What about the others?" meaning those who are not Christians. What of those who accept neither the exclusivity of salvation in Jesus Christ, nor the impossibility of access to God without him? Any honest response is bound to prove unsatisfactory to those who pose the question, not necessarily because of any inherent defect in the response itself, but because of the tacit presupposition underlying the question itself.

The incontestable datum of the fourth gospel is well summed up in "God so loved the world that he gave his only Son, that whoever believes in him should not perish but have eternal life. For God sent the Son into the world, *not to condemn the world, but that the world might be saved through him*" (3:16–17). We surely know that God's will is not frustrate. We repeat daily in our liturgies that the redemptive work of Christ is "for all men and women," without any exception and with no qualification. What we do not and cannot possibly know is *how* God accomplishes this for those whom we call "non-believers."

Our not knowing how does not serve as an excuse or pretext for evading the consequence of God's loving the whole world and giving his only Son for its salvation. If we truly believe the universality of this statement, then we must realize that the first thing we owe "the world" is love, not an explanation of how God achieves his intended end in the case of those who, for whatever reason, do not believe in "Jesus Christ whom you have sent" (17:3).

Those who devise explanations can ultimately satisfy only those who share their presuppositions. To speak, as is common nowadays, of "anonymous Christians" is an offense to non-Christians and a travesty of the basic premise that "God loved the world." If God loved all those who are in the world, then they are not and cannot in any sense be "anonymous." Anonymous only are the Christians who know this and yet fail to love them. How God's love saves those who do not believe him whom he has sent, is not our business, not even our speculative theological business. The only salutary response to those Christians who persist in posing the question is Jesus' response to Peter, "What is that to you? Follow me!" (21:22).

Why the Missions?

Of course, the question that immediately poses itself is: Why then the Christian missions? The church's missions to non-Christians are a manifestation of the fact that the community of believers cannot not bear witness to the gospel of salvation, cannot cease to proclaim it to every nation and in every age. The results, whether gratifying or disappointing, are not directly attributable to the missionaries, nor ultimately their concern (4:37–38). Their task and principal concern is to bear witness by proclaiming the gospel in a lifetime of genuine loving service to others. What motivates and impels the mission of Christians is the knowledge that God loved the world and gave his only Son for its salvation, for the Christian believers no less than for anyone else on the face of the earth.

This is why the reader of John's gospel must be honest enough to hear Jesus' words in it as addressed, not just to the Jews, or the Pharisees, or any other opponents and enemies of Jesus, but to the Christian community collectively and individually. To discuss whether John's gospel is anti this or that group is ultimately to evade the responsibility staring today's reader in the face:

> **and you do not have his word abiding in you, for you do not believe him whom he has sent (5:38).**

To "believe him whom he has sent" is not to assume a theological stance or to espouse some doctrine or other. It is to live a life informed and fashioned by this belief. This is what it is to have this word of revelation "abide in you" (5:38). My failure to believe the Revealer "whom he has sent" is simply due to the fact that "his word," the revelation, does not "abide in" me, does not shape my whole life and determine all my actions. If I truly believe "him whom he has sent," then my faith in this revelation remains an effective force in the life I live. This life is the only means anybody in the world has of knowing that I am a follower of this Jesus: "By this everyone will know that you are my disciples, if you have love for one another" (13:35 NRSV).

Searching the Scriptures

Of course, it is scarcely ever an out-and-out rejection of the revelation that is in question. We are too subtle by far for this sort of "apostasy"; and those of us with a smattering of theology are subtler still. Even our pursuit of the word of God bears witness to that:

> **You search the scriptures, because you think that in them you have eternal life, and it is they that bear witness to me; yet you refuse to come to me that you may have life (5:39–40).**

No one would want to deny the assiduity of this search of the scriptures down the ages, but especially in our times. Thousands upon thousands of writings, sermons, methodologies and theories of interpretation attest to it. The ultimate reason for this search can only be the quest for "eternal life." Nor does John deny that in these scriptures is life. But that life is there only because the scriptures bear witness to the Word. What many of us search for in the scriptures, however, is not that life at all. Our quest for scriptural slogans, our endless squabbles over interpretation, our mindless opposition to everything old and our unseemly haste to espouse the new in interpretation, and our outrageous claims not just for the infallibility of the text but even the impeccability of its authors, all bear witness to this.

The fact of the matter remains very simply this: for the Christian, the scriptures "bear witness to" Jesus Christ. What life these scriptures possess, they possess because they speak of the Word in every word they speak. All the efforts of exegetes and critics, of theologians, preachers and commentators are, for the Christian, directed to this one end: to proclaim the revelation of the Word which was in the beginning with God, was God, and became flesh and dwelt among us.

This is in no way a plea to abandon the search of the scriptures in all its rich and enriching aspects. It is a needed reminder that to believe that God has spoken to us–however you may wish to describe the subject, the verb and the object–is to believe that, at least within the Johannine context, all the scriptures bear witness to him whom the Father sent, and in whom alone we "have life." Alas, it is also a reminder that the search of the scriptures can itself become a way of refusing to come to him whom the scriptures proclaim in order that we may have life: "You search the scriptures, because you think that in them you have eternal life...yet you refuse to come to me that you may have life" (5:39–40).

What Jesus says to his opponents, to those who refuse to come to him, he can say because:

I do not receive glory from men (5:41).

It is this refusal to receive "glory from men" that sets him apart from all those who, in everything they say or do, in all the causes they espouse and the theories they propound, seek precisely that "glory," the fame, the recognition, the applause, the "bubble reputation."

Because Jesus does not "receive glory from men," he can say boldly:

But I know that you have not the love of God within you (5:42).

How quickly we leap at the absurdity of it all: They do not come to him because they have not the love of God within them; and yet they do not have this love because they have not come to him. It is just this kind of circular illogic in John that provides us with another way to evade the truth of the revelation. The genuine reason for our failure to believe is, of course, neither our fanatical adherence to logic, nor the failure of a particular exegetical method, nor even a pretended aversion to paradox. The true reason is made unavoidably clear in:

> **I have come in my Father's name, and you do not receive me; if another comes in his own name, him you will receive (5:43).**

Nothing is more astonishing in the statement than its second part. Incomprehensible though it is to refuse to receive him who alone brings eternal life, it is far more so to contemplate the scramble after those who offer its counterfeits. We are eager to follow anyone except him who came in the Father's name. The others who come in their own name are received with an avidity and eagerness that is matched only by their transitoriness.

Seeking Glory from One Another

The reason for this brisk traffic in substitutes for the only revelation is:

> **How can you believe, who receive glory from one another and do not seek the glory that comes from the only God? (5:44).**

We so readily flock to others, not because of our love for them, but simply because of our insatiable desire to receive glory from one another. Our search for "glory from one another" is not merely a distraction from the essential purpose of our existence which is to seek "the glory that comes from the only God" (5:44). Were it only that, one might be tempted to dismiss it as just another theological discussion. But it is far more than that. Our search for "glory from one another" is, inevitably, a foredoomed traffic in mutual enslavement. Those who provide me with such transient "glory" are no less aware of my avidity for it than I am of theirs. My dependence on them is no less than theirs on me; and so "deep calls unto deep."

It would be quite nonsensical to read John 5:44 today as addressed to "the Jews." Apart from the fact that to do so would be an injury and insult to any and all non-Christians, it would in fact be an evasion of my responsibility before the text. The glory I seek from others can, of course, be had in shoals. The way to obtaining it is not only broad but well-charted. The elenchus of acceptability in beliefs, slogans, attitudes, religious practices, and moral tenets is all too available to be refused and all too costly to ignore. Embracing it is my surest means of obtaining the "glory" I seek from others. However unpalatable it be, it is in this barter for "glory" that I render myself incapable of believing in him whom the Father sent into the world.

The crisis of the church today is not just that individual believers have set their heart on receiving this "glory from men," but that the whole church has directed its efforts toward it as well. To that end, nothing is too dear and scarcely anything is too sacred to barter or alter, to attenuate or dilute, in order to win the approval of the world, to gain admission to its counsels, and to win the indulgence of its rulers and the complacency of its arbiters of taste.

The concluding verses of the chapter belong, in the original context of the gospel, to the ongoing controversy of Jesus with those of "his own home," his own people who "received him not" (1:10). Indeed, the whole first part of the fourth gospel (chapters 2–12) is a varied descant on this theme. So Jesus' words are, at first blush, clearly addressed within this context to his fellow-Jews:

> **Do not think that I shall accuse you to the Father; it is Moses who accuses you, on whom you set your hope. If you believed Moses, you would believe me, for he wrote of me. But if you do not believe his writings, how will you believe my words? (5:45–47).**

In light of what has been said above, the same Moses who accuses the Jews can as well accuse all of us who "search the scriptures" (5:39). The Moses the Jews sought was in the Torah, on which they set their hope for life. "And now, O Israel, give heed to the statutes and the ordinances which I teach you, and do them; that you may live" (Deut 4:1; 5:33; 30:16–20). He is no less the Moses we seek in our quest for the law by which we hope to gain eternal life (5:39; see 1:17). For us, however, the law and the scriptures are the word of God because they speak of him who is the Word in whom was life (1:4). No one can claim to be the Word "become flesh" who was not also the Word that was "in the beginning" (1:1, 14). So, whoever believes that "grace and truth came through Jesus Christ" must necessarily believe that "the law was given through Moses" (1:17), and that the same law and the same Moses in fact wrote of him (5:46) in whose words they must believe. If you do not believe the writings of Moses, "how will you believe my words?" (5:47).

John 6

Feeding the Five Thousand: the first misunderstanding; temptation.

Walking on the Water.

The Bread of Life: the second misunderstanding; doing the works of God; Moses and Jesus; "I AM"; the gift and its rejection; obedience to the Father; promise of eternal life; the will of the Father.

Response to Jesus' Words: obstacles to the revelation; faith and eternal life; "my flesh for the world"; eucharistic institution.

Eating His Flesh and Drinking His Blood: faith and sacrament; present and future; mutual abiding.

The Words of Eternal Life: the offense of the revelation; the integral revelation; the gift of the Father; the betrayal; "to whom shall we go?"

FEEDING THE FIVE THOUSAND (John 6:1–14, 15)

After this Jesus went to the other side of the Sea of Galilee, which is the Sea of Tiberias. And a multitude followed him, because they saw the signs which he did on those who were diseased. Jesus went up on the mountain, and there sat down with the disciples. Now the Passover, the feast of the Jews, was at hand. Lifting up his eyes, then, and seeing that a multitude was coming to him, Jesus said to Philip, "How are we to buy bread, so that these people may eat?" This he said to test him, for he himself knew what he would do. Philip answered him, "Two hundred denarii would not buy enough bread for each of them to get a little." One of his disciples, Andrew, Simon Peter's brother, said to him, "There is a lad here who has five barley loaves and two fish; but what are these among so many?" Jesus

> **said, "Make the people sit down." Now there was much grass in the place; so the men sat down, in number about five thousand. Jesus then took the loaves, and when he had given thanks, he distributed them to those who were seated; so also the fish, as much as they wanted. And when they had eaten their fill, he told his disciples, "Gather up the fragments left over, that nothing may be lost." So they gathered them up and filled twelve baskets with fragments from the five barley loaves, left by those who had eaten (6:1–13).**

This event, perhaps the most familiar of all the gospel miracles, occurs six times in the four gospels (Mt 14:13–21; Mk 6:32–44; Lk 9:10b–17; Mt 15:32–39; Mk 8:1–10; and here in John 6). You can debate whether the miracle took place once or twice; you can dispute its original form or forms in the tradition; but you cannot overlook its spectacular quality, were it only for the cast of thousands.

As is to be expected, John's account has its peculiarities and its recognizable retouches, like the mention of the Passover feast, the role of Philip, or the aside, "This he said to test him," in verse 6. But the concluding line of the narrative,

> **When the people saw the sign which he had done, they said, "This is indeed the prophet who is to come into the world!" (6:14),**

is what makes it typically Johannine. The multiplication of the loaves in the fourth gospel (6:1–14), moreover, serves as the perfect setting for the long discourse on the bread of life (6:25–71), while the miracle of walking on the water immediately following it (6:16–21) does not.

What gives the peculiarly Johannine cachet to the account, however, is not only the reference to the miracle as a "sign" (6:14; cf. 2:11; 4:54; 6:2, 26), nor the recognition of Jesus as "prophet" (6:14; cf. 4:19; 7:40; 9:17), but the misunderstanding that follows immediately upon this recognition, namely, that "This is indeed the prophet who is to come into the world!" (6:14).

The First Misunderstanding

> **Perceiving then that they were about to come and take him by force to make him king, Jesus withdrew again to the mountain by himself (6:15).**

This is no ordinary misunderstanding within the gospel, nor is it the only one that is occasioned by the miracle. The crowd understands Jesus' identity well enough, but wholly misconceives it: He is indeed a king, indeed the messianic king; but, as he will tell Pilate at his trial, "My kingship is not of this world" (18:36). This is a fact that Jesus' followers, then and now, have been reluctant to grasp.

Later on the crowd will also misunderstand the very nature of the gift Jesus brings in the miracle itself (6:26, 34). Thus, in this dual misunderstanding of his true identity and of the gift he brings, the temptation which is ever there in any encounter with the Revealer is manifested: to understand him solely in this world's terms, and his gifts only in terms of our immediate needs. So Nicodemus understood "rebirth" physiologically (3:4); the Samaritan woman understood "living water" ergonomically (4:15); and now the five thousand understand the multiplication of loaves, first politically (6:15), and then economically (6:26).

Temptation

Such misunderstandings constitute temptations for Jesus himself (cf. the temptation accounts in Mt 4:1–11 and Lk 4:1–13), as they do for all his followers. "Perceiving then that they were about to come and take him by force to make him king" (cf. the devil's offer of "all the kingdoms of the world and the glory of them" in Mt 4:8), and recognizing in their action a "political" temptation, the temptation to power (cf. "To you I will give all this authority and their glory," Lk 4:6), "Jesus withdrew again to the mountain by himself" (Jn 6:15b).

It is remarkable, though by no means comprehensible, why Christian moralists, who urged precisely this strategy of flight before the so-called "temptations of the flesh," where quite evidently "the first eschew is remedy alone," never counselled similar flight from the allure of power. Whether their oversight was intentional or not, and whether it was self-serving or excusable negligence, are intriguing questions but difficult to answer.

WALKING ON THE WATER (John 6:16–21, 22–25)

When evening came, his disciples went down to the sea, got into a boat, and started across the sea to Capernaum. It was now dark, and Jesus had not yet come to them. The sea rose because

> **a strong wind was blowing. When they had rowed about three or four miles, they saw Jesus walking on the sea and drawing near to the boat. They were frightened, but he said to them, "It is I; do not be afraid." Then they were glad to take him into the boat and immediately the boat was at the land to which they were going (6:16–21).**

Though a similar incident is recounted in Matthew 14:22–33 and Mark 6:45–51, and though the incident itself can be confused with the stilling of the storm (Mt 8:23–27; Mk 4:35–41; Lk 8:22–25), the miracle of walking on the water in the fourth gospel is put to an altogether different use. For, whereas in Matthew and Mark, the point of the miracle is in the reassurance of the terrified disciples ("Take heart, it is I; have no fear" Mk 6:50; Mt 14:27) and in calming the wind-tossed sea ("the wind ceased" Mk 6:51; Mt 14:32), the point of the narrative in John is centered on the revelation of Jesus' identity, "I am; do not be afraid" (6:20 NRSV marg.). The similarity of the wording with the synoptics might conceal its significance in John, where, as we shall have occasion to observe shortly, the "I AM" is the revelation formula par excellence.

> **On the next day the people who remained on the other side of the sea saw that there had been only one boat there, and that Jesus had not entered the boat with his disciples, but that his disciples had gone away alone. However, boats from Tiberias came near the place where they ate the bread after the Lord had given thanks. So when the people saw that Jesus was not there, nor his disciples, they themselves got into the boats and went to Capernaum, seeking Jesus (6:22–24).**

The confusing displacement of "the crowd" (6:22 and 24, thus in NRSV, more accurately than "the people" in RSV) on and around "the sea" of Galilee (6:22–24) is the delight of the geographer, cartographer, shipwright and historical realist, which lurk in the bosom of many a biblical interpreter. But the principal interest of these verses is in the fact that "the crowd" is "seeking Jesus" (6:24). It is precisely the motive behind their search for Jesus which constitutes the second misunderstanding of the miracle of the multiplication of the bread. This misunderstanding will in turn provide a most appropriate starting point for the bread of life discourse which follows.

THE BREAD OF LIFE (John 6:25–40, 41–51, 52–59)

The Second Misunderstanding

When they found him on the other side of the sea, they said to him, "Rabbi, when did you come here?" (6:25).

The persistence of the crowd's search for Jesus finally attains its goal. They "found him" whom they sought. But he who "knew what was in man" (2:25) and who, consequently, did not "receive glory from men" (5:41), lost no time in calling their attention to what really lay behind their enthusiasm:

Jesus answered them, "Amen, amen, I say to you, you seek me, not because you saw signs, but because you ate your fill of the loaves" (6:26).

The search after Jesus is, in this instance, a search to satisfy the crowd's present need. The Samaritan woman sought to make life less arduous, to remove from it the sting of drudgery ("that I may not thirst, nor come here to draw" 4:15); the crowd here seeks to make life more secure, to get their "fill of the loaves." There is, of course, nothing reprehensible about either. Nothing is more natural than the quest for life's sustenance. What is reprehensible, however, is the perversion of food and drink into absolute ends in themselves.

Neither the Samaritan woman nor the crowd in Galilee can be regarded as merely past examples of fleeting aberrations. Both examples are alive in our misunderstanding of the Revealer as the solution to the world's ills, or in our misconceiving the role of the community of believers as no more than a world relief organization. Hence, the much needed reminder:

Do not labor for the food which perishes, but for the food which endures to eternal life, which the Son of Man will give to you; for on him has God the Father set his seal (6:27).

The use here of the eschatological title of "Son of man" (see 3:13) is a reminder that we have in him who utters these words God's final and definitive gift to all who hunger, not just for daily bread, but "for the food which endures to eternal life." The gift is such as to end all search, satisfy all desires and end every quest.

The Son of man who gives this bread to the world is he on whom "God the Father has set his seal." This is why he can appeal to all the signs he performs, not only as the work of the Father, but as witnesses to his own true identity as the one whom the Father has in fact sent. "The work which the Father has granted me to accomplish, these very works which I am doing, bear me witness that the Father has sent me" (5:36). In all his words and deeds, the Revealer shows that it is God the Father who has "set his seal" on him as the one he sends into the world, "that the world might be saved through him" (3:17).

Doing the Works of God

Its habitual obtuseness in temporary remission, the crowd asks what it is they must "labor for":

Then they said to him, "What must we do, to be doing the works of God?" (6:28).

Whether intentionally or not, their question, in fact, distinguishes that which all mortals labor for in this world into two categories: the search either for "the food which perishes" or for "the food which endures to eternal life" (6:27). In the response Jesus gives to their question, only the latter can qualify as "doing the works of God." But, of course, it does not necessarily exclude the human endeavor to gain one's livelihood from this category. However, Jesus' response does serve as a salutary reminder that any human striving which terminates in itself or in any other creature as its sole desired end is not and cannot be "the work of God." Consequently, such "food" cannot "endure to life eternal," since this can only be life with "God the Father" (see 6:33).

Jesus answered them, "This is the work of God, that you believe in him whom he has sent" (6:29).

Jesus' unambiguous response here foreshadows the definition of "eternal life" in 17:3, "And this is eternal life, that they know you the only true God, and Jesus Christ whom you have sent," and in 20:31, the stated purpose of the gospel, "that you may believe that Jesus is the Christ, the Son of God, and that believing you may have life in his name." This, though by no means easy, is simple. Yet, when one compares Jesus' response in 6:29 with what Christians have actually made out of the simple "believe in him whom he has sent," one can only marvel at the infinite limits to which human ingenuity would go to evade what alone is needed to do "the works of God." Belief in him who utters these words is all that God requires and everything that we ever need. So far as the evangelist is concerned, all the rest is marginal comment.

Understandably enough, the crowd demands proof of identification from him who claims to be the one whom God has sent. Equally understandable in this context is their appeal to the Exodus miracle of the "bread from heaven":

> **So they said to him, "Then what sign do you do, that we may see, and believe you? What work do you perform? Our fathers ate the manna in the wilderness; as it is written, 'He gave them bread from heaven to eat'" (6:30–31; and see Ps 78:24–25; Ex 16:4, 15).**

Thus, in citing the psalm, the crowd furnishes the appropriate scriptural text for the sermon on the "bread from heaven" which follows. To be sure, they demand a sign and ask Jesus to perform a work. But the only response that he gives them is the revelation which is, in itself, at once the sign and the work of him who is sent by the Father.

Moses and Jesus

> **Jesus then said to them, "Amen, amen, I say to you, it was not Moses who gave you the bread of heaven; my Father gives you the true bread from heaven. For the bread of God is that which comes down from heaven, and gives life to the world" (6:32–33).**

It is not that Moses himself ever claimed to be the giver of the manna in the wilderness, nor that he thought of himself as anything other than a mediator between God and his people. Gerhard von Rad remarked long ago that Moses, as portrayed in the Pentateuch, is remarkably faceless. Everything he is and does holds up the mirror–as it were–to God. He is there to carry out God's will.

Interpreters of John's gospel have long debated the role of Moses in it, whether and in what way Jesus in John is understood as the "New Moses." But–to my knowledge–none has commented on this particular point of contact in their respective missions. Everything Jesus says and does is also a carrying out of the will of the Father (4:34; 5:30; 6:38). Yet, unlike Moses or any other prophet, Jesus not only says what they all could–in a sense–say, "he who receives me receives him who sent me" (13:20), but he alone could and did say, "He who has seen me has seen the Father" (14:9).

Furthermore, what identifies the "true bread" in Jesus' revelatory discourse is both its origin and its purpose. The bread "comes down from heaven" and "gives life to the world" (6:33). This mode of identification is possible, of course, only to faith. Only faith can distinguish the "true" bread from all its many substitutes, even the holiest of them. The criterion of the true bread is its origin from heaven; and its verification, the "life to the world" which it gives. All the pretended offers of bread from creatures, even from the mightiest or the holiest among them, are simply not "true," because they are incapable of giving "life to the world."

The life this bread gives is, of course, eternal life, not just daily sustenance and survival. But the crowd misunderstands the gift yet again as a measure of convenience, a solution to their daily problems, a panacea for the world's ills:

> **They said to him, "Lord, give us this bread always" (6:34; cf. 4:15),**

and thus, they implied, spare us all the irksome demands of the human condition.

"I AM"

> **Jesus said to them, "I am the bread of life. Whoever comes to me will never be hungry, and whoever believes in me will never be thirsty" (6:35 NRSV).**

This is one of the very many "I AM" formulas that punctuate the revelation of Jesus throughout the gospel. In most instances, such formulas are, strictly speaking, theological statements about the bearer of the revelation who utters them. When the formulas are so employed (as they are in "I am the bread of life" in 6:35, 41, 48, 51; "the light of the world" in 8:12; "the door" and the "good shepherd" in 10:7, 9, 11, 14; and "the vine" in 15:1, 5), they signal a revelation over and above what we have when, for example, Jesus says to the Samaritan woman, "I who speak to you am he" (4:26); or when he reminds his opponents, "You are from below, I am from above" (8:23); or when he meets the band of soldiers that came to arrest "Jesus of Nazareth" with "I am he" (18:4–5).

"I am the bread of life" as a formula differs from these others, not merely by its theological content, but also in the way it communicates it. In addressing the soldiers, for instance, Jesus says, "I am he," i.e., "I am Jesus of Nazareth," where, evidently, the "I" is the subject and "Jesus of Nazareth" is the predicate. This is true of his words to the Samaritan woman in 4:26, and to his opponents in 8:23. It can also be said to be, in some sense, true—as we shall see when we come to them—of "I am the resurrection and the life" in 11:25, and of "I am the way, and the truth, and the life" in 14:6.

But, in the "I AM the bread of life" type of formula, the order of subject and predicate is inverted. For, in such formula, it is "I" which is the predicate and "the bread of life" which is the subject. That is, "*the* bread of life" you seek and desire is "I." This is the reason why Rudolf Bultmann very aptly called these "recognition formulas." In them the hearers *recognize* that what they have looked for all along is at last here before them. This is the revelation that Jesus of Nazareth brings to the world.

Thus, to the crowd which had asked, "Lord, give us this bread always" (6:34) Jesus, in fact, offers infinitely more. They seek the assurance of their daily sustenance and look for release from the drudgery of gaining it by "the sweat of their face" (Gen 3:19). Jesus offers them all that every hunger and thirst, every desire and longing of their existence on earth seeks. What they are really looking for is the kind of sustenance that abolishes all hunger and all thirst. This can be attained only if they "come to him," believe in him, receive and accept him as the one sent by the Father.

The Gift and Its Rejection

But I said to you that you have seen me and yet you do not believe (6:36).

Evidently, "I am the bread of life," the bread that gives real life and not merely day-to-day sustenance, requires faith. But the whole first part of the gospel has to wrestle with the mystery of those who "do not believe," who "knew him not" and "received him not" (1:10–11). Confronted by this refusal to believe, even the Revealer stands helpless.

It is one of the paradoxes of this revelation, however, that while the refusal is ours to will, the acceptance in faith is really the Father's gift to us. That is to say, not only the gift itself, but its very acceptance is itself also a gift.

All that the Father gives me will come to me; and him who comes to me I will not cast out (6:37).

Two important things must be noted in this statement. First, the whole operation of "coming to me" is the work of the Father. The insistence of the Revealer on this fact might astonish or displease us. But, unless the whole process be about God, and unless we recognize that all the Revealer does is to carry out the will of the Father who sent him, then we cannot really believe in revelation of any sort. It is his total obedience to the Father that makes Jesus the Revealer. So he acknowledges here (6:37) that all those who come to him are, in fact, the gift of the Father to him: "They were yours, and you gave them to me" (17:6b; see 6:39; 10:29; 17:2).

The second important point to be noted here is that, despite the long and tortuous history of the question, this verse (6:37) is not about "predestination." It does not say that God arbitrarily chooses to save whom he wills, and just as arbitrarily condemns whom he does not. Common sense ought to tell us that a God who "so loved the world that he gave his only Son, that whoever believes in him should not perish but have eternal life" (3:16) is not, and can never be, that capricious.

The God who created us as free human beings made us genuinely free, i.e., able both to accept or reject him as our God. God might have created a creature who had no choice but to obey him, a creature who was not free to disobey him. But, whatever else it might have been, such a creature would not have been a human being. Why the human being God actually created ever chooses not to obey its creator, why so many human beings reject the gift of God, remains always a mystery. It is, ultimately, what we call the mystery of evil.

In the context of the fourth gospel, we have to keep in mind that those who accept the revelation of the Son can only do so freely, of their own free will. No one can be compelled to do so, not even by God. In their acceptance of the revelation, they acknowledge the fact that it is a free gift, and recognize that their very acceptance of it is no less a gift. In this sense, when Jesus says, "All that the Father gives me will come to me" (6:37), he is simply acknowledging a fact, not providing a reason for those who do come to the Father either to boast or to feel superior toward those who ostensibly choose not to "come to him." To boast or feel superior to others would itself be a denial of the gratuity of the gift and a pretence that it is our due because of who we are or what we do.

That whoever comes to Jesus will not be "cast out" describes the nature of the gift as genuine and freely given. It also describes it as an irrevocable gift (cf. "For the gifts and the call of God are irrevocable" in Rom 11:29). The giver in this instance never changes his mind. That privilege belongs to the receiver of the gift who, like Milton's Satan, whom God made "just and right / Sufficient to have stood, though free to fall," yet "rather than be less, / Cared not to be at all."

Obedience to the Father

For I have come down from heaven, not to do my own will, but the will of him who sent me; and this is the will of him who sent me, that I should lose nothing of all that he has given me, but raise it up at the last day (6:38–39).

This insists once again on what the Revealer has already said in 4:34, "My food is to do the will of him who sent me, and to accomplish his work"; and in 5:30, "I seek not my own will but the will of him who sent me." Such insistence is necessary because, unless the Revealer comes to do the will of the Father wholly and fully, then he cannot either reveal the Father or be his Son. The conformity of his will with the will of the Father is but the consequence of what the prologue enunciated at the very beginning: "the Word was with God, and the Word was God" (1:1). It is this totality of obedience, this utter conformity to the will of the Father who sent him, that enables him to say, "I and the Father are one" (10:30).

The "will of him who sent me" is "that I should lose nothing of all that he has given me, but raise it up at the last day" (6:39; see 6:37 and cf. 10:29; 17:12; 18:9). This makes explicit two points. First, it reiterates the fact that, "All that the Father gives me will come to me; and him who comes to me I will not cast out" (6:37). Secondly, it elaborates the meaning of the revelation of "I am the bread of life" (6:35).

Promise of Eternal Life

The bread which grants real, eternal life necessarily bears within it the promise of resurrection "at the last day" (see 6:44, 54). This is not so much a mixing of a future eschatology ("at the *last day*" 6:40) with a realized one ("*has* eternal life" 6:47, 54), as a clarification that the gift of eternal life to mortal human beings in the present necessarily implies the gift of resurrection on the last day, for no gift of God exempts mortals from dying. This is what "he will live forever" (6:51) has to mean when applied to any mortal human being.

The promise, "I will raise him up at the last day" (6:40), is also at the same time a reminder of what the gift of eternal life is not. It is not an exemption from having to die. All mortals "owe God a death." The coming of the revelation does not alter this. Even the Revealer himself had to absolve that debt by his own death on the cross.

Painful and hated though it is, death cannot and does not abrogate the gift of eternal life. This is the true content of the revelation of eternal life. Indeed, the life this revelation proclaims is "eternal" because it defeats and abolishes the finality of death precisely by its promise of the resurrection "at the last day." Thus, the following verse puts all this very neatly together.

The Will of the Father

> **For this is the will of my Father, that every one who sees the Son and believes in him should have eternal life; and I will raise him up at the last day (6:40).**

The Son reveals the will of the Father for all the world. The combination of the present "have eternal life" with the future "I will raise him up" is most instructive. It is the Father's will that "*every one* who sees the Son and believes in him should *have* eternal life" here and now. To add "and I *will raise* him up at the last day" is only the corollary to this present gift of eternal life. The Father's will is, therefore, nothing less than the gift of eternal life, not of a life that goes on forever without death, but a life that needs no longer stand under its dominion, and will hereafter never be under its shadow.

Like any genuinely free gift, the gift of eternal life has to be freely accepted. No one can compel you to receive it under threat or by force. Any compulsion to accept it as surely negates the essence of the gift on the part of the giver as does its refusal on the part of the receiver. Therefore, "*every one* who sees the Son and believes in him," every human being on the face of the earth who "sees the Son," who acknowledges Jesus Christ as the Son of the Father, as the Revealer of the Father and the accomplisher of his will, *has* eternal life. The gift is unconditional on the part of the giver, but conditional solely on the part of the receiver, precisely because it is a gift.

This life, as we have seen, would not be "eternal" were it not for the resurrection "at the last day." It is the resurrection that takes life out of the dominion of death (cf. 1 Cor 15:26, 55). The resurrection is what makes the life of the believer, both before and after death, *eternal* life.

RESPONSE TO JESUS' WORDS (John 6:41–51)

> **The Jews then murmured at him, because he said, "I am the bread which came down from heaven" (6:41).**

In this discourse, neither the miracle of the manna, the "bread from heaven," nor the events of the Exodus are very far from the evangelist's mind. In "The Jews thus murmured at him" (6:41a, 43; and cf. 6:61), we hear echoes of "the people murmured against Moses" in Exodus 15:24 (see Ex 16:2, 7, 8, 9, 12). They murmur against Jesus because they object to Jesus' claim, "I am the bread which came down from heaven" (Jn 6:41b), since to them there is only one such bread, the manna of the Exodus (see 6:31 and Ex 16:4, 15; Ps 78:23–25).

Obstacles to the Revelation

To be sure, none of us would reject such a gift outright. We direct our attention elsewhere; we pretend it is not what we want; we argue it is not the right gift; we object to the one who brings it, etc. As the murmuring shows in this instance, we know the bringer of the gift all too well, a certain Jesus of Nazareth:

> **They said, "Is not this Jesus, the son of Joseph, whose father and mother we know? How does he now say, 'I have come down from heaven'?" (6:42).**

How indeed can he or any ordinary human being make such a claim? Their theology prevents them from accepting such a preposterous statement. To them it is merely a claim on the part of someone just like them, whose family and origin were only too well known to them. The whole world would stand up and say with them when they hear Jesus' words, "This is arrant nonsense! Just an ordinary human being, like you and me, simply does not 'come down from heaven,' let alone pretend to be 'the bread of life'" (6:35, 48, 51).

In expressing their amply justifiable reaction, "the Jews" who "murmured at him" illustrate only too well the absurdity of all those who put their trust in philosophical argument and theological reasoning to compel belief in Jesus Christ. For, when all is said and done, there is no argument that cannot be eventually overturned by counter-argument, and no theological reasoning that cannot sooner or later be reduced to absurdity. The only way to accept the Revealer's claim is faith, every other way being ultimately a rejection. You either believe he "came down from heaven" (6:42) or you do not. Knowing his "father and mother" has really nothing to do with accepting the revelation or rejecting it.

Jesus' answer to those who murmured among themselves (6:43) is simply to repeat what he has already said (see 6:37), not to cite corroborative arguments, nor to enter into a biblical discussion, nor to undertake a lengthy theological disputation:

> **Jesus answered them, "Do not murmur among yourselves. No one can come to me unless the Father who sent me draws him; and I will raise him up at the last day" (6:43–44).**

It is certainly open to question whether the promise of the resurrection is more absurd or less acceptable than the claim to have "come down from heaven." But the response to one or the other can only be faith, i.e., the acceptance of the free gift of God in the person of Jesus of Nazareth. This is what "coming to him" means. Of course, anyone who comes to Jesus and accepts the gift he brings recognizes that the very acceptance of the gift is itself a gift. Therefore, Jesus' promise of "I will raise him up at the last day" is prefaced by "No one can come to me unless the Father who sent me draws him."

> **It is written in the prophets, "And they shall be taught by God." Every one who has heard and learned from the Father comes to me (6:45; see Is 54:13; Jer 31:33–34)**

The entire operation, from the mission of the Son to the offer of the gift and its acceptance by the believer, is the work of the Father. The scriptural citation thus only serves to confirm the agency of the Father. Coming to Jesus is always, and can only be, the gift of the Father: "Every one who has heard and learned from the Father comes to me" (6:45). Of course he who utters this in John's gospel knows that the only way anyone can "hear and learn from the Father" is to hear and learn from him whom the Father has sent. The obvious reason for this is:

> **Not that any one has seen the Father except him who is from God; he has seen the Father (6:46).**

This brings us back to the premise of the prologue: "No one has ever seen God" (1:18a). The only access any mortal ever has to God is through "the only Son, who is in the bosom of the Father, he has made him known" (1:18b). The reason for this is that only he "who is from God" has ever "seen the Father." It was in order to give us access to the Father that the Son came down to dwell among us. Yet all that anyone who encountered him ever saw or could have seen was a man like any other, a Jesus "whose father and mother we know" (6:42). There is but one way to attain this longed-for privilege of "seeing the Father," and that by faith.

Faith and Eternal Life

> **Amen, amen, I say to you, he who believes has eternal life (6:47).**

The consequence of this faith in the one "who is from God" (6:46) is, of course, eternal life. The argument, though elliptical, is obvious enough. At the root of our restless quest, and behind the compulsion of our search for God, there is our desire for life. God alone "has life in himself" and it is he who "has granted the Son also to have life in himself" (5:26). So whoever believes in the Son as the one sent by the Father, as the Revealer of the Father, in fact is granted eternal life here and now. This is what the following verse says by taking up once more the "bread of life" motif:

> **I am the bread of life. Your fathers ate the manna in the wilderness, and they died. This is the bread which comes down from heaven, that [one] may eat of it and not die (6:48–50).**

Every other bread, even "the manna in the wilderness" (6:31), confers at most only sustenance from day to day ("I will rain bread from heaven for you...a day's portion every day" Ex 16:4). Whoever eats of anything else but "the bread of life" is sure to die, and there is an end to it. But whoever eats "the bread which comes down from heaven" will simply not die. Yet, since–like everyone else–such a person is bound to die one day, we have to grasp the promise of "not die" (6:50) in the sense in which the promise is made to Martha: "Who believes in me, *though he die,* yet shall he live" (11:25). It is ultimately this firm assurance that death will not be the end of life, will not be the termination of my relation with God and with all those whom I love and those who love me, which makes the gift of eternal life here and now genuine and precious beyond all description (cf. 1 Cor 2:9).

"My flesh for the world"

It is of utmost importance to keep in mind the "he who believes has eternal life" (6:47). The statement is categorical. Whoever *believes* in him whom the Father has sent possesses this eternal life here and now. Therefore, the evangelist has Jesus go on to say:

> **I am the living bread which came down from heaven; if any one eats of this bread, he will live forever; and the bread which I shall give for the life of the world is my flesh (6:51).**

To claim to be "the *living bread* which came down from heaven" is tantamount to saying, "I am the bread of life" (6:48) and identifying it further as "the bread which comes down from heaven" (6:50). In other words, the "living bread" is the "bread of life." It is "living" bread because it is "from God" (6:46; cf. 5:26) who alone gives life. Consequently, only the bread "from God" can give eternal life and hence is truly "the bread of life" (6:35, 48; cf. 6:31).

This identification is made more explicit still by insisting that "the bread which I shall give for the life of the world *is* my flesh" (6:51c). Several observations need to be made here. Note, first, that the bread is to be given "for the life of the world," i.e., for the whole world, for all who dwell on the face of the earth without exception (see above on 5:37).

Secondly, the manner of formulating the giving of the bread "*for* the life of the world" is–to anyone slightly acquainted with the idiom of the New Testament–a reference to the redeeming death on the cross. Commentators have remarked on the rarity of such references to the death of Christ *for us* in John. Here at least is one of them.

Eucharistic Institution

Commentators have also remarked the absence in the fourth gospel of an account of the institution of the eucharist such as we have in all the other gospels (Mt 26:26–29; Mk 14:22–25; Lk 22:15–20) as well as in 1 Cor 11:23–25. Some have even professed to be baffled by such omission, while others have suggested John 6 as a near substitute for it. But, in a gospel whose pivotal assertion is, "And the Word became flesh and dwelt among us" (1:14), there is scarcely need for such an account of the institution. The omission of the institution of the eucharist in John can prove problematic only for those who, apprehensive about the supposed "non-sacramental" character of this gospel, choose to forget or to overlook that there is only one way of proclaiming the salvation in Jesus Christ, and that is by means of the word. The sacraments are but another mode of proclamation by means of this same word.

How then could one find room for an account of the institution of the eucharist in a gospel which proclaims that this Word "became flesh"? The evangelist has Jesus make this point clear: "If any one eats of this bread, he will live forever" (6:51b), i.e., will live a life that is not under the sway of death now, nor will be interrupted by it in the act of dying. Lest there be any doubt left, Jesus adds that "the bread which I shall give for the life of the world is my flesh" (6:51c). The Word became flesh in order to give his life (cf. "lay down his life" in 10:11) "for the life of the world."

EATING HIS FLESH AND DRINKING HIS BLOOD (John 6:52–59)

Such a statement (6:51) seems destined to lead to misunderstanding. In 6:51, Jesus speaks of "eating this bread," then goes on to identify this same bread "for the life of the world" as "my flesh." No wonder that:

> **The Jews then disputed among themselves, saying, "How can this man give us his flesh to eat?" (6:52).**

They drew the obvious conclusion that Jesus was in fact speaking of giving them "his flesh to eat." But Jesus' response goes on to remove all doubt on this score:

> **So Jesus said to them, "Amen, amen, I say to you, unless you eat the flesh of the Son of Man and drink his blood, you have no life in you" (6:53).**

Amidst the confusion of conflicting opinions on these verses (6:52–59), and the debate on whether they be an integral part of the discourse or a later addition, some important points suffer neglect. In verse 53, apart from the obvious offense that can be given by the mere idea of eating his flesh and drinking his blood, the addition of the phrase "drink his blood" makes the passage a clear reference to the redemptive death on the cross. In other words, "and drink his blood" makes explicit the saving significance of "*for* the life of the world" in 6:51.

Furthermore, the fact that the flesh and the blood are "of the Son of man" makes clear the eschatological nature (see above on 3:5 and 5:25), not only of the death on the cross, but also of the entire revelation event. The reference is to the ushering in of the end time into our present. The eating and the drinking are, therefore, the acknowledgment and confession of the fact that the death of the Son of man on the cross is for "the life of the world."

But, lest the eating and the drinking be vaporized away into a mere figure of speech, Jesus adds that

> **he who eats my flesh and drinks my blood has eternal life, and I will raise him up at the last day (6:54).**

The Greek text actually changes the "eat" in verse 53 to "chew/masticate" in this verse. The verses that follow will accentuate the realism further still.

Faith and Sacrament

But, before leaping at opposing conclusions, let us note carefully what the statement does say. It is, first of all, a clear echo of the solemn affirmation in verse 47, "Amen, amen, I say to you, he who believes has eternal life." There is only one way to have this eternal life (see 20:31). Therefore, can "he who eats my flesh and drinks my blood" be other than the concrete expression of this faith? The sacrament of the Lord's supper is an outward sign of the faith we profess. Hence, this sacrament, above all others, is rightly called "the mystery of faith."

Present and Future

What has also occasioned endless debate between scholars is the seeming tension between "*has* eternal life" here and now, and "I *will* raise him up at the last day." Though we have already alluded to this tension above, it bears repeating. The possession of eternal life here and now does not exempt the believer from dying. The "I will raise him up" presupposes this death, since only the dead can be raised.

Thus, Jesus' very promise, "I will raise him up at the last day," acts as a reminder of this inescapable fact of having to die.

Jesus' promise is, moreover, an indirect statement of what he will say to Martha, "I am the resurrection and the life" (11:25). The present possession of this life has its real cause in the resurrection of Jesus himself. It has its firm foundation in the resurrection he promises the believers in him, those who eat his flesh and drink his blood: "I will raise him up" (6:54).

It seems hardly necessary to add that the reference to the resurrection "at the last day" is no more a denial of the fact that the end (the *eschaton*, whence "eschatology") has already come, than that the promise of a future resurrection is a denial of the possession of eternal life here and now. The evangelist had to reckon with all those who pretend to understand the gospel message as denying the inevitability of death or as abrogating the believer's responsibility for existence in time. He had to forestall the argument of all those who would use this gospel as a passport for flight from the world or as a *laissez-passer* for those who would pass unscathed through it. "I do not pray that you should take them out of the world, but that you should keep them from evil" (17:15).

Mutual Abiding

For my flesh is food indeed, and my blood is drink indeed. He who eats my flesh and drinks my blood abides in me, and I in him (6:55–56).

The reiteration of the statements in this discourse can be conceived of as a conic spiral or as concentric circles each greater than the other and each embracing all that the others contain and more. This, by the way, is characteristic of the style of the fourth gospel. It can be noted from the prologue on to the farewell discourse (chs. 13–17).

The insistence on eating and drinking lays the ground here for elaborating what the gift of eternal life consists of. To this end, we are here introduced to a theme that from now on will assume ever greater significance in the gospel: the mutuality of abiding between the believer and the Revealer, the "abides in me, and I in him" (see 14:20; 15:4–7; 17:23; 1 Jn 3:6, 24; and also "his word abiding in you" Jn 5:38; 1 Jn 2:14, 24).

The burden of the assertion here, "He who eats my flesh and drinks my blood *abides* in me, and I in him" (6:56), is twofold: To "believe" in 6:47, just as to "eat the flesh and drink the blood" in 6:53, is not a once and for all act. It is an act reiterated throughout the life of the believer in this world. Thus "abides in me" is a constant clinging to the Revealer whom the Father sent into the world. Consequently, it is the daily living out of his revelation. This, of course, makes the constant preaching of the word in the community of believers indispensable. It is of this revealed word that the believers have to be constantly reminded, with it they need to be unceasingly encouraged and comforted, and to it they have to respond with their entire person throughout their life.

The "I in him," moreover, is a reminder that only in him is life (1:4), that he alone is the life (14:6), that he is the source of the eternal life which the believer possesses (6:47, 54) as well as the reason why any one who believes in him "will live for ever" (6:58). He is all this, of course, because "as the Father has life in himself, so he has granted the Son also to have life in himself" (5:26). Therefore the Son can add:

> **As the living Father sent me, and I live because of the Father, so he who eats me will live because of me (6:57).**

If confirmation were needed for the meaning of verse 56, then this verse surely provides it. Because he is sent by the Father, and therefore lives because of the Father, i.e., because his entire life is one act of uninterrupted obedience to the Father's will, the Son can truly abide in those who believe in him, and thus be the source of their eternal life (6:40, 47, 54; 3:15, 36; 5:24; 10:10, 28; 11:25–26; 20:31; and see 17:2). The Son lives "because of the Father." Therefore he can say that whoever "eats me will live because of me." This brings the discourse on the bread of life full circle to its starting point:

> **This is the bread which came down from heaven, not such as the fathers ate and died, he who eats this bread will live for ever. This he said in the synagogue, as he taught at Capernaum (6:58–59).**

Not only the contrast with all other bread, even with the most miraculous of breads, but also the identity of this bread "which came down from heaven" with him who is sent from the Father, makes it uniquely the bread of life. It is the bread of life, not only because it gives eternal life, but because he who brings it *is* life (11:25; 14:6).

THE WORDS OF ETERNAL LIFE (John 6:60–65, 66–74)

The Offense of the Revelation

Many of his disciples, when they heard it, said, "This is a hard saying; who can listen to it?" (6:60).

Unlike the reaction of Jesus' opponents in verse 52 ("How can this man give us his flesh to eat?"), though no less understandable, his disciples' reaction is bewilderment. Even the well-disposed find the revelation hard to accept. It offends the common sense of some, and the pretended wisdom of others. It goes counter to the ordinary, the approved, the acceptable. If the tone of Jesus' own disciples was more moderate, their "murmuring" was no less real than that of "the Jews" (6:41).

The Integral Revelation

But Jesus, knowing in himself that his disciples murmured at it, said to them, "Do you take offense at this? Then what if you were to see the Son of Man ascending where he was before?" (6:61–62).

The revelation that Jesus brings is integral. One aspect might prove unacceptable to some, another to others. But the whole revelation stands and falls together. You either accept it integrally or reject it totally. The revelation has no "optional parts." The giving of the bread of life is no less credible than the resurrection and ascension of the Son of man to "where he was before" (6:62), and neither one nor the other is any less difficult to accept than that the Word became flesh and came down to dwell among us (1:14). One fact is bound inextricably to the other. That Jesus can say, "I am the bread of life" is only another way of saying "the Word became flesh." That the Son of man ascends "where he was before" is but a reminder that the Word which was in the beginning with God (1:1) came down and "dwelt among us" (1:14).

In every age there are those who seek to pick and choose in the revelation, who try to make it fit their predetermined parameters, who want desperately to make it acceptable to "the modern world," whether the world of the first or of the twentieth century. This is why the fourth gospel does not hesitate to call all such responses to the revelation by their proper name: refusal to believe (6:64–65).

To those who have it, faith is not an accomplishment, either one's own or anyone else's. It is an outright gift of God to the believer:

> **It is the spirit that gives life, the flesh is of no avail; the words I have spoken to you are spirit and life (6:63).**

The reason why faith in the revelation is a gift of God is that God alone gives life. Whoever believes has eternal life (3:15, 16, 36; 6:47). Because the Spirit is the power of God to vivify, it "gives life." All else is, therefore, "flesh" and "of no avail." Everything created is impotent to give what it does not possess in and of itself. Only the Father "has life in himself" and so has "granted the Son also to have life in himself" (5:26). This is why the revelation which this Son brings, all that he utters, is in fact "spirit and life" (6:63).

The Gift of the Father

It all comes back to what Jesus had already said at the beginning of the discourse on the bread of life:

> **And he said, "This is why I told you that no one can come to me unless it is granted him by the Father" (6:65 and see 6:37).**

To come to him is to believe in him as the only Son whom the Father sent into the world. This is why to believe in him is to have eternal life. This life cannot be granted by anyone but God. "Flesh," all that is created, mutable and doomed to pass away, might claim to have this life and might even pretend to give it, but it remains impotent to do so for the simple reason that it cannot give what it does not possess. Only the Father can grant this superlative gift of coming to the Son and so finding life, eternal life.

The Betrayal

Nothing can lay claim to this gift, not even being a disciple. This is why the warning is sounded by Jesus:

> **But there are some of you that do not believe (6:64a).**

Being with Jesus, following him, witnessing the signs, hearing the discourses, can be, and often is in fact, "of no avail." This is one reason at least why the person of Judas Iscariot emerges so early in the gospel:

> **For Jesus knew from the first who those were that did not believe, and who it was that would betray him (6:64b and see 6:70–71).**

No wonder then that even those closest to Jesus decided to withdraw from his company:

> **After this many of his disciples drew back and no longer went about with him (6:66).**

Yet, Judas Iscariot, good as any of them, stayed on–at least so far as anyone could see. What the evangelist says about him in 12:6 is hindsight. Judas remained to the bitter end, not just one of the twelve, but a member of the administration (13:29). It is not often remarked that in these few verses (6:61–71), just as we approach such a high point in one disciple's response to Jesus, we are immediately called to reality by a reminder of Judas' betrayal:

> **"Did I not choose you, the twelve, and one of you is a devil?" He spoke of Judas the son of Simon Iscariot, for he, one of the twelve, was to betray him (6:70–71).**

All this, however, is not just literary ornament or dramatic astuteness on the part of the evangelist. We are so reluctant to identify with those who decided no longer to go about with Jesus. Yet such a decision is an everyday occurrence in the lives of most of us. Even those who knew him in "the days of his flesh" were not exempt. Nor was the choice to no longer go "about with him" (6:66) confined to those of "little faith," those who stick to some putative absolute minimum of belief. More often than not it happens to those who are only too ready to believe too much, until the day they stumble, not on the Word who was with God and indeed "was God," but on the "became flesh." It is an insufficiently noted fact that the first heresy of Christianity was not to deny that Jesus of Nazareth was God, but to refuse to accept that he was really man.

"To whom shall we go?"

The scene that ensues (6:67–71) is remarkable for various reasons. Perhaps the most intriguing among them is that–as commentators on John have suggested–the incident at the end of John 6 parallels in some way or other the account of Peter's confession at Caeserea Philippi in Mark 8:27–30; Matthew 16:13–20; and Luke 9:18–21. If this observation be right—and there is good reason to believe that it is—then we should note how radically the question put to the disciples by Jesus in John differs from the one in the synoptics ("Who do you say I am?" Mk 8:29 par.):

> **Jesus said to the twelve, "Do you also wish to go away?" (6:67).**

This is not a question about Jesus' identity. It is not about *who* he is, but *what* he is. What is required here is not recognition and acknowledgment, "You are the Christ" (Mk 8:29), or "You are the Christ, the Son of the living God" (Mt 16:16), or "The Christ of God" (Lk 9:20); what is required is a clear-cut option between "going away" from Jesus and "coming to" him. From the first encounter with him, the question was, "What do you *seek*?" (Jn 1:38). Those who genuinely seek him must come to him and see (1:39). To no one else could they really go, for no one else can show them the Father (14:8–9). This Jesus alone is the Revealer of the Father.

> **Simon Peter answered him, "Lord to whom shall we go? You have the words of eternal life; and we have believed, and have come to know that you are the Holy One of God" (6:68–69).**

If this Jesus of Nazareth is indeed who he says he is, the bread of life, the one whom God has sent into the world; if faith in him means having eternal life, then there really is no option whatsoever, no available alternative. He and he alone has "the words of eternal life." He alone is the bringer of the revelation that truly confers what every mortal ultimately seeks.

Peter's "we have believed, and have come to know" is a typically Johannine turn of phrase. To the evangelist, believing and knowing are near synonyms and intimately bound together. Indeed, his whole gospel is a sustained effort to make the hearers of the good news grasp intelligently what they confess. It is in that knowing faith and in that believing knowledge that the author shows himself amply deserving the title of "the theologian." It is in elaborating this theology that his gospel is truly, in the words of Clement of Alexandria, the "spiritual gospel."

John 7

Jesus' Brothers: unbelief; the "brothers" of Jesus; the time of Jesus; the world.

The Feast of Tabernacles: the person of Jesus; *krisis*/judgment; academic credentials; the source of Jesus' teaching; the glory of God; doing the will of God; judging by appearances.

The Crowd and the Authorities: origin and mission; the hour of Jesus; the attempt to arrest Jesus.

Rivers of Living Water: the Spirit; "This is the Christ"; division among the crowd; the authorities; Nicodemus.

JESUS' BROTHERS (John 7:1–9)

After this Jesus went about in Galilee; he would not go about in Judea, because the Jews sought to kill him. Now the Jews' feast of Tabernacles [Booths] was at hand. So his brothers said to him, "Leave here and go to Judea, that your disciples may see the works you are doing. For no [one] works in secret if he seeks to be known openly. If you do these things, show yourself to the world" (7:1–4).

Cynicism need not be the sole reason we find the advice given Jesus by his brothers readily comprehensible. Nor need skepticism question the justness of their reasoning. One might even go so far as to regard their unsolicited advice to a member of their family motivated by genuine concern for Jesus' success. Some might even be ready to err on the side of generosity and call such advice disinterested. These and similar judgments are possible, indeed commonplace. All they require is willful ignorance of human nature.

Unbelief

The evangelist is not of their number. He knows only too well what lay behind such an attitude:

For even his brothers did not believe in him (7:5).

They had witnessed the works he was doing and yet did not believe. They had seen him "show himself to the world" and the world still refused to believe. Why would they all of a sudden entertain greater hopes of success elsewhere? If "his own people received him not" (1:11), what reason had they to think the rest of the world more obliging?

However you may wish to judge their solicitude for Jesus' success, you cannot overlook the evangelist's unflinching assessment of it. The mind-set of "his brothers" is that of those who do not believe. It is, as we shall indicate presently, the mind-set of the "world." The brothers of Jesus want to see the world impressed, whether by spectacular miracles or by imposing wisdom. Their norms of judgment and their standards of measurement are, and necessarily have to be, those of the world they wish to impress. This is precisely what the Revealer himself repudiates. His revelation not only rejects the norms and standards of the world but discloses their utter bankruptcy. The Revealer did not come into the world to dazzle and impress it, and so the world was quick to return the compliment: "the world knew him not" (1:10).

The brothers of Jesus died and passed out of history. But their values and judgments are perpetuated from one generation to the next by those who boast of their ties to the Lord and are, in today's world, the community of believers. For, so long as impressing and pleasing the world is their aim, "even his brothers" do not really believe in Jesus.

The "Brothers" of Jesus

Here a remark on "brothers" is called for. There have always been those who, from the earliest times, sought to interpret "brothers" in any but its literal sense. Some have insisted it refers to "cousins," even though the Greek has a specific term for this (see Col 4:10, "Mark the cousin of Barnabas"). Some suggested it refers to his disciples, as it does in Jesus' words to Mary Magdalene, "go to my brothers and say to them" (20:17 NRSV; cf. the RSV "go to my brethren"). Should this be the case, whom then did "his brothers" have in mind when they said,

"Leave here and go to Judea, that *your disciples* may see the works you are doing" (7:3)?

All such well-intentioned attempts to get around the literal meaning of "brothers" are, of course, an effort to preserve the credal article of the virginity of Mary, understood in the sense of virginity *after* the birth of Jesus. Rather than venture into the tortuous paths of that endless debate, the reader of John must ask whether, in this or any other instance, the Word should be made to fit one's confessional or theological opinion–the Greek term for which is "dogma"–or the other way around.

The evangelist certainly does not hesitate to use "brothers" here or in 2:12; nor is he reluctant to describe their attitude to Jesus and his works in terms that are far from flattering: "For even his brothers did not believe in him" (7:5). Naturally, the brothers of Jesus were attached to his person; but they, like so many others, misunderstood his works and misinterpreted the signs. Proximity to Jesus is not a condition for, and can very well be a hindrance to, belief in him.

The Time of Jesus

Jesus said to them, "My time has not yet come, but your time is always here (7:6).

There is a time for doing just what his brothers requested, in a way they did not even suspect. But that time is God's time, not theirs. Jesus' "my time" is not one arrived at by the reckoning of the world. It can hardly be what the world would call "prime time"; and the "show yourself to the world" (7:4) is scarcely what the world wants to see; indeed, it is diametrically opposed to all that the world judges worth seeing.

The time of Jesus is the time ordained by God, the "hour" of his passion. The fourth gospel uses the expression to mark Jesus' progress toward that supreme revelation on the cross: from the "first of his signs" at Cana in Galilee (2:11), when his hour had "not yet come" (2:4), to the moment "when Jesus knew that his hour had come to depart out of this world to the Father" (13:1).

The time of those who do not believe is, on the contrary, "always here" (7:6). They are in perfect synchrony with the world. They strut on its stage when those who preceded them had barely left it; and they quit it well after a world avid for ever newer spectacles has turned its gaze on the newcomer who promises to banish its boredom and flatter its insatiable vanity. The unbelieving "brothers of Jesus" in any age never decline the invitation to show themselves to the world. Their time is "always here." Therefore,

> **The world cannot hate you, but it hates me because I testify of it that its works are evil (7:7).**

The world, of course, loves its own (15:19). It hates only those who belong to him whom it hates above all others. It hates him because it is he who shows the world what it has no wish to see, "that its works are evil" (7:7).

The World

This is not an inappropriate place to add to what was said above (see on 3:16) about the use of "world" in the fourth gospel. Thus far we have seen it used as a neutral term with reference to the created world of women and men. In this sense, the world was "made through him" (1:10). It is the world which God so loved "that he gave his only Son" (3:16) in order to save it "through him" (3:17); into which "the light of the world" has come (8:12; 3:19); to which the "bread from heaven" gives life (6:33, 51). It is even the world to which his brothers urge Jesus to show himself (7:4).

Of course, it is into this world that the incarnate Word comes, not to judge but to save it (12:47). In it he makes the light of his revelation shine, "I am the light of the world" (8:12). To it he reveals the truth about the Father, and to those who dwell in it he grants eternal life. But, as we have already noted above (see on 3:18 and 5:21, 22–23), this free gift of the Revealer to the "world" (6:33, 47), to every woman and man on the face of the earth, can be either accepted as the gift of eternal life (3:15), or rejected, and so become a judgment unto death ("shall not see life" 3:36).

This latter group, those who reject the revelation and will not accept the gift of the Revealer, is also referred to by the evangelist as the "world." Thus the term has a negative meaning, a pejorative sense, in addition to the neutral one. In this pejorative sense, it is the world which "knew him not" (1:10); which hates him that discloses its works as evil (7:7); for whose judgment the Word has come (9:39; 12:31, 47). The world, in this negative sense, cannot receive the "Spirit of truth" (14:17), and will be "convicted of sin" by this same Spirit (16:8). It is the world which hates the true followers of Jesus (15:18), but loves its own (15:19); the world in which his own will have "tribulation" (16:33), and for which he does not pray (17:9).

In its negative acceptation, the "world" thus becomes an expression of all that is opposed to the revelation and rejects it. In this pejorative sense, the "world" conducted a remorseless fight against the Revealer and "sought to kill him" right from the start (5:18; 7:1, 19, 25; 8:37, 40; 11:53).

Moreover, in the fourth gospel, the opposition to Jesus and to his revelation came from "the Jews." Where else could it really have come from in Palestine of the first century? He was a Jew living among his fellow-Jews. It is this that lends particular poignancy to the prologue's "He came to *his own home,* and *his own people* received him not" (1:11).

It took but a few years thereafter for the community of believers, which counted Jews and Gentiles alike among its members, to encounter the opposition and the hatred of what John calls "the world": "Do not wonder, brethren, that the world hates you" (1 Jn 3:13). This, too, was a world of both Jews and Gentiles. Thus far most readers would be willing to go. What we resolutely refuse to face, however, is the fact that, once the church gained acceptance in the world and perhaps even a good many years before that, the "world" held sway right within the community of those who believe. The world is not just somewhere outside the community of believers, among the Jews of Jesus' times, or in Gentile territory. The "world" was–and, alas, remains–securely ensconced within the Christian community.

Of course, we always pretend that the "world" is others, other people, other religions, or even other Christian denominations. But, as a set of values and principles intent upon the rejection of the revelation and the ouster of the Revealer from its midst, the "world" reigns within the church today. The history of this church in past centuries can be seen as one failed attempt after another to come to some accommodation in the world and with it. The lives of its saints, from the first martyrs to those beyond number who lived their hidden lives in obscure corners and lie now in unmarked graves, bear witness to the hatred of the world both within the ecclesiastical establishment and without.

THE FEAST OF TABERNACLES (John 7:8–24, 25–31, 32–36, 37–39, 40–52)

Go to the feast yourselves; I am not going up to this feast, for my time has not yet fully come." So saying, he remained in

Galilee. But after his brothers had gone up to the feast, then he also went up, not publicly but in private. The Jews were looking for him at the feast, and saying, "Where is he?" (7:8–11).

The use of geographic references to mark off the sections of the various narratives (2:12; 4:46; 6:17, 24, 59) is as distinctive a feature of the fourth gospel as are the chronological references to the cycle of Jewish feasts used to mark the passage of time as the hour of Jesus approaches (2:13, 23; 4:45; 6:4; 11:55; 12:1; 13:1; and 5:1; 7:2, 10). Were it not for the as yet insoluble problem of the sequence of chapters in John–and chapter 7 is among them–we might have been better able to chart a surer course among the succeeding events of Jesus' public ministry within the gospel.

The Person of Jesus

What attracts our attention here, however, is not so much the locality and the time of year, as what Jesus says to his brothers, "Go to the feast yourselves; I am not going up to this feast" (7:8), and the fact that almost immediately afterward, "he also went up, not publicly but in private" (7:10). This looks very much like a deliberate deception on Jesus' part. But what calls for remark in the incident is not so much the clear disparity between Jesus' statement and his action, but the ingenious attempts that have been made by scholars to reconcile one with the other.

If these verses record events that actually took place, the simplest thing to say would be that Jesus changed his mind: a perfectly human, quite common, and scarcely reprehensible action of anyone who dwells in time. Why then the reluctance to adopt this solution? Undoubtedly, for some this reluctance stems from what they learned long ago about the different types of knowledge enjoyed by the incarnate Son while on this earth. For others, it is a vestigial trace of an ancient–perhaps Aristotelian–philosophy which associates mutability with imperfection, God being of necessity both immutable and perfect. But, whatever the explanation, the motive behind such reluctance is usually the desire on the part of Christians to boast of a thoroughly consistent Jesus before a world that volubly honors consistency, but only in the breach. For such believers, it would be an intolerable blemish to admit that Jesus was human enough to have changed his mind.

Krisis/*Judgment*

What is even more fundamental to this incident is that the coming of the Son into the world precipitates a "crisis." This term happens to be a transliteration of the Greek word for "judgment." Those who encounter the revelation must choose one way or another. The world–at least the Johannine world–is thus divisible into those who accept the revelation and those who reject it.

Now, the Greek term John uses for judgment, *krisis,* happens to carry the double meaning of judging and separating. This double sense is graphically illustrated in 7:11–13:

> **And there was much muttering about him among the people. While some said, "He is a good man," others said, "No, he is leading the people astray" (7:12).**

The division in the "crowd" (as the NRSV renders more correctly than the RSV "people") is, in fact, a division of opinion about the person of Jesus. While those who disagree do not necessarily deny that he is "good," they reject him because "he is leading the people astray." His being good or not is really not their concern. It is his disruption of their society, his upsetting their established, and hence acceptable, order of things that displeases them. To lead the crowd anywhere but where they are, which is where their leaders want them to remain, is to lead them astray, to deceive them.

Both those who think Jesus "good" and those who judge him a nuisance leave the reader with little to admire. For, despite their conviction and their settled judgment one way or the other about Jesus, theirs is only an intellectual exercise. In the final analysis, their attitude to Jesus does not even possess the courage of its conviction:

> **Yet for fear of the Jews no one spoke openly of him (7:13).**

It is not a particularly indigenous malignity of the establishment that prevents the crowd's freedom of speech. It is rather the lack of courage on the part of the crowd itself that invests the arbiters of opinion, then as now, with their dreaded power. The process is slow, but its results are assured, whether among first-century Jews or twentieth-century Christians. It matters little whether you read the "fear of the Jews" today as fear of established authority, or fear of the fashion-setters, be it in marketable ideas or in current creeds.

Academic Credentials

About the middle of the feast Jesus went up into the temple and taught. The Jews marveled at it, saying, "How is it that this man has learning, when he has never studied?" (7:14–15).

When after all Jesus did show up at the temple and started teaching, his audience wondered about his qualifications for the job. Thus, when one's mind is set upon rejecting him, any reason at all will do. Here the reason happens to be what we call today his "academic credentials." Those who would reject him submit his qualifications and his teaching to their own criteria and, unsurprisingly, find them wanting.

Those who would reject his teaching today do so for much the same reason. The teaching is simply not "scientific" enough. It was addressed to a less sophisticated audience than the modern world. He was addressing a different situation, and so on. But the only remarkable thing in all this is the recurrent pattern. As in the silence of the crowd "for fear of the Jews" in 7:13, so here in the question they ask: "How is it that this man has learning?" (7:15). It is the crowd that transmogrified the authorities of the day into their fearsome eminence. In turn, it is the authorities that decided to set up study and learning as the criteria by which they chose to assess the Revealer. There was nothing in the nature of things to compel such attitudes or demand such criteria, whether on the part of the authorities or the crowd; and yet nothing in the past two thousand years has changed them.

The Source of Jesus' Teaching

By a twist of Johannine irony, the Jews were absolutely right: "he has never studied" (7:15); and Jesus does not hesitate to agree with them:

So Jesus answered them, "My teaching is not mine, but his who sent me" (7:16).

This is his persistent refrain throughout the gospel. Of himself and for himself, Jesus is nothing: all he does and everything he teaches belongs to the one who sent him (3:34; 8:26; 12:49; 14:24). Hence, the ultimate futility of the crowd's opinion of him personally, whether "He is a good man!" or "No!" (7:12). You either believe in him or you do not. Your personal opinion of him is of no account.

Hence the futility of all those purported portraits of Jesus in theology and piety. They are, when all is said and done, magnified projections of what we think we ourselves would like to be. Whereas all that matters, the only thing that counts, is whether or not Jesus of Nazareth's teaching is his own or "his who sent him." The only criterion for assessing the worth of such portraits of Jesus, for valuing or discounting what has been dubbed "the quest of the historical Jesus," for accepting or discarding the research into that other idol in our current pantheon, "the very words of Jesus," is simply this:

> **Anyone who resolves to do the will of God will know whether the teaching is from God or whether I am speaking on my own (7:17 NRSV).**

The doing of the will of God alone matters. It is the sole criterion of your response to Jesus. The entire mission of the one whom God has sent is to make this will of God known. This is why he who came to dwell among us could say with absolute truth, "My food is to do the will of him who sent me, and to accomplish his work" (4:34); "I can do nothing on my own authority.... I seek not my own will but the will of him who sent me" (5:30; 6:38). Those who come to him, those who hear his word, must necessarily have the same disposition and keep the same end in view. They must be intent upon doing the will of God. Only thus can they recognize Jesus of Nazareth for what he really is: the one sent by God, the one whose whole being was bent on seeking "the glory of him who sent him":

The Glory of God

> **He who speaks on his own authority seeks his own glory; but he who seeks the glory of him who sent him is true, and in him there is no falsehood (7:18).**

How easily forgotten this principle is, especially in those quarters most concerned about the "glory of God." What is true of Jesus is also true of everyone who speaks the word of God. When Jesus or anyone else "speaks on his own authority" then, all protestations to the contrary notwithstanding, he but seeks his own glory. You can try to hide the objective under any of its varied synonyms, fame, reputation, éclat, triumph, success, etc. But glory, which belongs solely to God, remains what the creature is forever after.

There follows the remaining verses of this section (7:19–24) about Moses, the law and circumcision. That these verses sound very much like disjointed opinions on sundry matters has convinced scholars that they are not in their right place within the gospel. The reference to Jesus' "one deed" (7:21), his making "a man's whole body well" on the sabbath (7:23), can make better sense if read in a context closer to the healing of the paralytic at the pool (5:1–9a, 9b–18).

Doing the Will of God

Nevertheless, within the actual context of seeking the will and the glory of God, two remarks can very profitably be made. The first is Jesus' accusation:

> **Did not Moses give you the law? Yet none of you keep the law. Why do you seek to kill me? (7:19).**

When once one is resolved not to accept the revelation, once the mind is set on not doing the will of God, then even the express will of God can serve as an excuse. Jesus accuses the crowds, who boasted of the law of Moses and made such a great show of keeping it in every detail, that they in fact did not keep the law at all. The law is the will of God, and the will of God now is clearly this: to know and believe him whom God has sent into the world.

The danger in reading this incident today is to archeologize it. Yet it is as contemporary as today's sunrise. It tells of what we ourselves do day in and day out: refuse to do the will of God in the very act of pretending to carry it out. This is what the leaders of the community do. This is what its humblest subjects love to do. Anything and everything, including the will of God itself, is fair game in our attempt to evade the will of God. Those of us who study theology are only more adept at the ploy than the rest; but no one is wholly free of this pernicious talent. When touched to the quick, all of us, experts and idiots alike, are apt to deny the accusation and attack our accuser:

> **The [crowd] answered, "You have a demon! Who is seeking to kill you?" Jesus answered them, "I did one deed, and you all marvel at it. Moses gave you circumcision (not that it is from Moses, but from the fathers), and you circumcise a man upon the sabbath. If on the sabbath a man receives circumcision, so that the law of Moses may not be broken, are you angry with me because on the sabbath I made a man's whole body well? Do not judge by appearances, but judge with right judgment" (7:20–24).**

The argument from the lesser instance to the greater, from circumcising a man to healing him wholly, is familiar to the experts in the law. But, like all arguments in interpreting the law, it is used only when it serves a purpose other than carrying out the will of God. Respect for "the law of Moses" (7:23) is all good and fine, but it must respect the person for whose sake the law was given. "Are you angry with me because I healed a man's whole body on the sabbath?" (7:23 NRSV).

Judging by Appearances

But it is the final–almost stray–remark which concludes the section that must arrest our attention: "Do not judge by appearances, but judge with right judgment" (7:24). The remark itself would seem like eminent common sense. Judging by appearances (a book by its cover, etc.) is decried by all alike. But the proof that it is exactly what all of us in fact do, is the prevalence of hypocrisy in our world. For, even in the community of those who believe, judging by appearances is a way of life.

Jesus' admonition in John is directed, in all likelihood, at those who will not accept him because they think they know who he is, or who his parents are (6:42), or where he comes from (7:27), or what his educational background is (7:15). Yet is not this precisely what all the accredited purveyors of Jesus do today, transforming him into all that the crowds find acceptable, ridding him of what they deem intolerable "in this day and age," and endowing him with all that will make his teaching palatable and his message inoffensive and, ultimately, negligible? To "judge with right judgment" can be very disturbing. It is always costly. All too often it is a solitary exercise. It is easier by far to judge, with the rest of the world, "by appearances." Hence, the need to be constantly reminded of Jesus' admonition, "Do not judge by appearances, but judge with right judgment."

THE CROWD AND THE AUTHORITIES (John 7:25–31)

Should anyone require proof of just how little has really changed in twenty centuries, this miniature crowd scene ought to suffice. Querulousness has marked culpable rejection through the ages.

Some of the people of Jerusalem therefore said, "Is not this the man whom they seek to kill? And here he is, speaking openly, and they say nothing to him!" (7:25–26a).

So, it was no secret at all. They were indeed trying to kill him even when they indignantly responded to his, "Why do you seek to kill me?" (7:19) with "You have a demon! Who is seeking to kill you?" (7:20). Jesus, after all, was not crazy. His opponents were really not what they pretended to be, and "some of the people of Jerusalem" (7:25) were quick to spot that weakness and exploit it. This is merely a power game whose first and inevitable victim is always the truth.

The worst of this miniature portrait of the conflict between the crowd and the authorities is its hardy survival through history: Midst the prevailing fear to speak frankly and openly (7:13), bluster tries to conceal the fear (7:15); the slightest hint of honesty (7:19) uncovers it (7:20); the crowd spots the opportunity and exploits it (7:25–26). You have no need to call upon your imagination in order to re-create Jerusalem of the first century, or to exercise your ingenuity at historical reconstruction to summon images of the Inquisition, the witch hunts, or the cold arctic night of the anti-Modernist campaign. All you need to do is be alert to the day-to-day life of the church in our time.

The tragedy of course is not that all this continues to happen; but that it happens within the Christian community itself, and under the guise of carrying out the will of God. Those who cry indignantly, "Why doesn't the church do something?" lay a claim to a wisdom they think is exclusively theirs. They are convinced that everyone else, particularly those in authority, lack such wisdom. Moreover, were the authorities to respond to their compelling demands and really do something, they would be the first to refuse to acknowledge their right to do so.

"Can it be that the authorities really know that this is the Christ? Yet we know where this man comes from; and when the Christ appears no one will know where he comes from" (7:26b–27).

The first strategy in the technique is to accuse the authorities of bad will, interpret even their inactivity as sinister. The crowd always "knows." "We know where this man comes from" (7:27). When and if he comes, the Christ has to conform to their expectations, has to meet their interpretations of the divine promises, has to satisfy their demands for the exotic ("when the Christ appears, no one will know where he comes from"—no need, of course, to add, "except us"). Armored in the security of their religious beliefs, secure in the rightness of their way of doing things, no shadow of doubt need ever threaten their certitude. Should the authorities choose to show some reluctance, then they themselves have no hesitation whatsoever. If ever challenged, they are ready to hide behind the mincing humility of their new-found ignorance ("I am, after all, just a simple Christian").

What militates against a transfer of the situation in the fourth gospel to our day is, of course, the question at issue. In John 7, the burning question is the identity of Jesus and the response to his claim. In today's church such a question seems otiose at best, draws no clamor from "the crowds," and scarcely attracts the attention of "the authorities." The spectacle is elsewhere. It is no longer in "the temple." Its present venue is the courts of law where "the moral issues of our times" make up, for all intents and purposes, the substance of the faith. If the Christ has any role at all to play in the matter, then it is his corroborative pronouncements on what we have already made up our mind is true, "Yet we know where this man comes from" (7:27).

Origin and Mission

So Jesus proclaimed, as he taught in the temple, "You know me, and you know where I come from? But I have not come of my own accord; he who sent me is true, and him you do not know" (7:28).

Jesus returns the discussion to its right track. The question is not one of scriptural expertise. Their claim to know when and whence the Christ comes is only the crowd's way of avoiding recognizing the Christ in the Jesus of Nazareth who stands before them. Their vaunted knowledge of the scriptures and their theological learning is no more than an excuse to look everywhere else except at what is staring them squarely in the face.

Jesus reminds them yet again that it is not he that matters, but the one who sent him. He himself has not come "on his own." He is only the one who obeys the will of God fully and carries it out perfectly. He is the only Son. Failure to recognize him comes ultimately from ignorance of the one who sent him: "Him you do not know" (7:28).

I know him, for I come from him, and he sent me (7:29).

The reason Jesus can be who he really is, God's Revealer to them, is twofold: his origin, "I come from him," and his mission, "he sent me."

His dependence on, and his obedience to the Father constitute the uniqueness of his claim. This is why the refusal to accept him is due ultimately to their ignorance and their refusal to know the one who sent him (7:28).

The Hour of Jesus

So they sought to arrest him (7:30a).

Whenever the truth becomes uncomfortable to hear and too inconvenient to bear, brute power is the answer. Whatever form such power assumes, whether in groups or by individuals, it is always the resort of all who close their ears to the truth:

...but no one laid hands on him, because his hour had not yet come (7:30b).

In Jesus' case, as the fourth evangelist views it, everything is subordinate to that "hour," the time foreordained by God for the accomplishment of his redemptive work (see 8:20; 12:23; 13:1). Neither earthly powers nor human machinations can alter, advance or retard its coming.

The tragedy of the refusal to accept Jesus is only highlighted by those who, amid all the hostility to him, have enough courage to cling to a spark of reason. For, appearances to the contrary notwithstanding, no crowd of human beings is homogeneous. A crowd might "cry with one voice," but there are always in it those voices which are no less present for being silent or less vociferous.

Yet many of the people believed in him; they said, "When the Christ appears, will he do more signs than this man has done?" (7:31).

The reaction of the many in "the crowd" (here again, this is the meaning of the Greek word in the text) was not exactly a ringing endorsement, nor did it signify an unwavering commitment to Jesus. It was merely that ordinary, everyday spark of rationality that refuses to be extinguished by the hot air of the majority. It is, often, a silent refusal to be cowed by the cowardly hectoring of the powerful few or the blind tyranny of their sheeplike followers. Readers of John know, of course, that the powers that be will have their way at last, but that–at least in this one instance–the ultimate victory is not and cannot be theirs.

The Attempt to Arrest Jesus

> **The Pharisees heard the crowd thus muttering about him, and the chief priests and Pharisees sent officers to arrest him (7:32).**

You might choose to call the action of "the chief priests and Pharisees" blameworthy; you can deem it senseless and unjust; but you cannot pretend it is incomprehensible. If Jesus' claims be true, then such claims have to mean the end of the world as they knew it. The use of coercive force is the shortest path they know to safeguarding what they judge is rightfully theirs: position, prestige, authority or influence. The imperturbability of Jesus before the menace of their action becomes all the more striking for their misunderstanding of it:

> **Jesus then said, "I shall be with you a little longer, and then I go to him who sent me; you will seek me and you will not find me; where I am you cannot come" (7:33).**

The reader should not forget that he who came down has to go back whence he came (13:1; 16:28). Yet those whom Jesus addresses refuse to hear anything that does not fit into their scheme of things, anything that is not assimilable into their system of thought:

> **The Jews said to one another, "Where does this man intend to go that we shall not find him? Does he intend to go to the Dispersion among the Greeks and teach the Greeks?" (7:35–36).**

Here again, the irony of the question is not meant to escape the reader, who knows that this is indeed what did happen after Jesus had gone back to the one who sent him (7:33). He whom they refuse now to hear will indeed "go to the Dispersion among the Greeks and teach the Greeks" (7:35). Indeed, the very fact that these words are now recorded in Greek and not in Hebrew or Aramaic can constitute part of the irony.

It cannot but be a mystery, not just to the fourth evangelist, but to any Christian whether of Jewish or Gentile origin and background, that "he came to his own home, and his own people received him not" (1:11). Jesus' opponents in John thus play the unwitting prophet. Somewhere in the back of the reader's mind must echo the words of Jesus in Matthew: "Therefore I tell you, the kingdom of God will be taken away from you and given to a nation producing the fruits of it" (Mt 21:43).

RIVERS OF LIVING WATER (John 7:37–39)

The questions of "the Jews" in 7:35–36 go unanswered. They were expressions of puzzlement, not genuine inquiries. So John leaves them posing questions "to one another" (7:35) and takes up the narrative of the celebration of the feast of Tabernacles (7:2) in the temple of Jerusalem (7:14):

> **On the day of the feast, the great day, Jesus stood up and proclaimed, "If any one thirst, let him come to me and drink" (7:37).**

Even without all the specific details of the ceremony of "the great day" of the feast, there can be no mistaking Jesus' claim. He had already revealed to the woman of Samaria that "whoever drinks of the water that I shall give him will never thirst; the water that I shall give him will become in him a spring of water welling up to eternal life" (4:14). He had already told the multitude, "I am the bread of life; he who comes to me shall not hunger, and he who believes in me shall never thirst" (6:35). The implications of the open invitation to come to him and eat and drink, food that will sate all hunger and drink that will slake all thirst, are clear. "Ho, every one who thirsts, come to the waters; and he who has no money, come, buy and eat! Come buy wine and milk without money and without price" (Is 55:1).

But, lest the significance and the solemnity of Jesus' proclamation escape notice, a scriptural citation of uncertain provenance is appended to it:

> **He who believes in me, as the scripture has said, "Out of his heart shall flow rivers of living water" (7:38; cf. Is 43:19–21; Ez 47:1–12).**

The citation is not altogether easy to locate in "the scripture." Whether the evangelist himself is citing from a faulty memory or whether this is merely an error to which all writers—even those with concordances and computers—are liable, is not what really matters here. What is of importance is the image the citation evokes in its present setting within the gospel. The image seems very much like Ezekiel's description of the temple with water gushing out of its cardinal gates (Ez 47:1–2), and wherever those waters go "every living creature which swarms will live" (Ez 47:9).

The Spirit

Moreover, lest the true meaning of Jesus' words elude the reader, John adds his own—as it were—marginal comment:

Now this he said about the Spirit, which those who believed in him were to receive, for as yet the Spirit had not been given, because Jesus was not yet glorified (7:39).

This Spirit is "the spirit that gives life" (6:63). The believers can receive this great gift only after the glorification of Jesus, i.e., only after Jesus' "hour" has come and the work of redemption is accomplished. But this, of course, is the vantage point of any believing reader of the gospel. Such readers hardly need a reminder that all the gifts that are theirs here and now are gifts of the Spirit. They live at a time when Jesus has been glorified and the Spirit, therefore, has already been given.

"This is the Christ"

When they heard these words, some of the people said, "This is really the prophet." Others said, "This is the Christ." But some said, "Is the Christ to come from Galilee? Has not the scripture said that the Christ is descended from David, and comes from Bethlehem, the village where David was?" (7:40–42).

Once again the words of Jesus precipitate a "crisis" in those who hear them (7:12; see 7:43; 9:16; 10:19). The crowd's reactions vary. Some say, "This is really the prophet" (7:40); others, "This is the Christ" (7:41). But still others, those who have already made up their mind to reject him, are—as always—ready with their scriptural arguments. Paradoxical as it sounds, nothing could blind one more to God than the word of God: "Is the Christ to come from Galilee? Has not the scripture said that the Christ is descended from David, and comes from Bethlehem, the village where David was?" (7:42)

One would have thought that those who genuinely look for the redeemer promised by God would be more open to deliverance in whatever form, however unexpected, and no matter how ill-conformed to their scriptural interpretation and theological speculations it might turn out to be. Of course, this is not just the foible of "the Jews" (7:35), nor of "the chief priests and Pharisees" (7:32). Nothing is more intransigent before the gospel message than the Christians who, secure in their knowledge of the scriptures, their mastery of the catechism, or their competence in theology, set up their habits of knowing as the criterion of orthodoxy. There is, when you come right down to it, little to choose between, "Is the Christ to come from Galilee?" and, "Isn't this what the church has always taught?"

Division among the Crowd

So there was a division among the people over him. Some of them wanted to arrest him, but no one laid hands on him (7:43–44).

The division, the "schism," to render the Greek term here literally, caused by Jesus' words is only one aspect of the judgment for which he came into the world (9:39). This is true whenever his message is proclaimed. The message caused division in Jesus' own time; it caused it in the evangelist's own time, indeed within the evangelist's own community; and it has never ceased to cause it in our time.

The Authorities

The officers then went back to the chief priests and Pharisees, who said to them, "Why did you not bring him?" The officers answered, "No man ever spoke like this man!" (7:45–46).

The officers sent out by the "chief priests and Pharisees" (7:45) to apprehend Jesus went back without him. The reason for their failure—a perfectly comprehensible one—was: "Never has anyone spoken like this!" (7:46 NRSV). Even apart from the irony in these words, whose true import not even the officers themselves could have begun to suspect, one cannot but side with those hapless emissaries. One can even admire and emulate them. Their lowly status did not deprive them of their power to judge, nor did fear rob them of their dignity (cf. 7:13).

Those who sent the officers to "arrest him" (7:32), already had their mind set to reject him. Of course, it was their privilege to reject the opinion of their emissaries. They assumed, in the time-honored fashion, that all who were subject to their authority were intellectually inferior to them.

The Pharisees answered them, "Are you led astray, you also? Have any of the authorities or of the Pharisees believed in him? But this crowd, who do not know the law, are accursed" (7:47–49).

It is even pardonable that the authorities expected some loyalty from their emissaries: "Are you led astray, you also?" (7:47). But where those in authority cannot escape blame is in their conformity to the invariable pattern of the exercise of such authority in history.

First, they set themselves up as the standard and norm of right behavior. Their claim to infallible omniscience is indiscerptibly linked to their pretense to impeccable behavior: "Have any of the authorities or of the Pharisees believed in him?" (7:48). They entertained no doubt whatsoever that this behavior was exemplary for and binding on all who were under them. Even when one knows–as the reader does in this case–where the right lies, the spectacle is lamentable. It is all the more so, not for the evident harm it does others, but for the damnation it brings on the authorities themselves (see 7:49).

Secondly, the other, almost predictable, reaction of the authorities is the disdain with which they regard their subordinates: "But this crowd, who do not know the law, are accursed" (7:49). One would have thought that the crowd's ignorance of the law could be laid at the door of its custodians, those who are "teachers in Israel." But, having already decided to damn those who disagree with them, the authorities justify their arrogance by disdaining, not only the crowd of subordinates, but the very law they claim to know.

In these and similar passages, it is easy enough to divert attention from the main point by raising questions about how the term "the Jews" is used by John, and who specifically were meant by "the authorities (the leaders)" or "the Pharisees." But, when the gospel is heard by the Christian community today, its members cannot, for whatever reason, be so blinded to the daily reality of their life as to fail to see this tragicomedy played out over and over again everywhere by them and around them, not by Jews or Pharisees, but by Christians.

Nicodemus

Even when, not just a member of the undifferentiated, ignorant and damned "crowd" (7:49), but a person of recognized good will, acknowledged expertise (3:10) and respected standing within their own group, dares to call the attention of the authorities to the injustice of their proceedings, he is summarily dismissed with an insult. Nicodemus does no more than remind them of the very law to which they have appealed, of whose knowledge they boasted (7:49):

> **Nicodemus, who had gone to him before, and who was one of them, said to them, "Does our law judge a man without first giving him a hearing and learning what he does?" They replied, "Are you from Galilee too? Search and you will see that no prophet is to rise from Galilee" (7:50–52).**

John 8

The Light of the World: the light of the world; judgment according to the flesh.

Who Are You: Johannine dualism; sin; the function of the Word; the eschatological vantage point; the Son's perfect obedience.

Abraham Our Father: to believe and to know; true freedom; appeal to the past; slavery to sin; paternity, mission and obedience; the father of lies; hearing the word of God.

Before Abraham Was: "will never see death"; the glory of the revealer

The last verse of chapter 7 and the first eleven verses of chapter 8, the story of the woman caught in adultery (John 7:53–8:11) do not, properly speaking, belong to the gospel of John. Because not until the tenth century did these verses begin to appear in the Greek manuscripts of the fourth gospel. This is a fact that rests on manuscript evidence. One can well regret the uncertain history of the transmission of the text of such a touching gospel incident. But neither regret nor its present place in the text can make it an integral part of the gospel of John. As a matter of fact it fits more neatly after, e.g., Luke 21:38 than it does between John 7:52 and 8:12, where it merely interrupts Jesus' discourse at the feast of Tabernacles.

THE LIGHT OF THE WORLD (John 8:12–20)

> **Again Jesus spoke to them, saying, "I am the light of the world. Whoever follows me will never walk in darkness but will have the light of life" (8:12 NRSV).**

What was a dispute, even an angry one at times, in chapter 7 becomes in chapter 8 a series of acrimonious attacks and counterattacks more reminiscent of a fight in a rapidly disintegrating family. Like all such squabbles, it is an unpleasant and disconcerting spectacle even for an impartial spectator. But, for a reader of the fourth gospel, no such impartiality is possible. Nothing short of life and death is at issue.

The Light of the World

Jesus' opening statement is an "I AM" saying that sums up all that he is and all that he does in the world and for it. In "I am the light of the world" (see 9:5 and cf. 1:4, 5, 9 "the true light that enlightens every man"; 3:19 "the light has come into the world"; 12:46 "I have come as light into the world") he discloses his identity as the Revealer. He *is* the light because he *brings* the light, and he brings the light precisely because he is the light. This is what the prologue announced, "In him was life, and the life was the light of men" (1:4). This is also what 8:12 means when Jesus goes on to add, "Whoever follows me will never walk in darkness but will have the *light of life*."

It will have been noticed by now that such "I AM" sayings of Jesus are ultimately claims to being the one who both possesses and dispenses true life. All human search for true life must terminate in him. Without him everything lies hidden in the impenetrable darkness of death. The revelation Jesus brings into the world is, therefore, "the light of the world." It echoes the "Let there be light" (Gen 1:3) of the first creation, the light that not only bathed the whole creation with life but also set the confines and limits which hold back the darkness of chaos.

Whoever becomes Jesus' disciple, "whoever follows me," is thus not only delivered from the realm and the power of darkness, but also possesses "the light of life" (Jn 8:12). This only reaffirms what is a constant refrain in the gospel: that the whole reason for the revelation which the Revealer brings into the world is that those who believe in him might "have life and have it abundantly" (10:10; see 1:4; 3:16; 4:14; 5:24; 6:35, 40; 10:28; 17:2; 20:31).

The Pharisees then said to him, "You are bearing witness to yourself; your testimony is not true" (8:13).

The Pharisees thus challenge Jesus' credentials, regardless of the truth or falsehood of his statement. Perverse though it might seem to us, their position is reasonable enough. Jesus himself had expressed this same view: "If I bear witness to myself, my testimony is not true"

(5:31). "True" in 5:31 as in 8:13 refers to the validity of Jesus' claim. The Pharisees question the validity of his claim to be who he claims to be. Their attitude, of course, is not unique.

We ourselves never cease to set up inquiries into the validity of the revelation, forever subjecting it to our judgment, even while we insist that our suspended verdict is not a refusal to believe. The chic thing to do nowadays is to shrug off lightly this or that article of the faith as, for the time being, "in the garage for repair." This, of course, is none too clever a euphemism for rejecting what is currently deemed "politically incorrect."

> **Jesus answered, "Even if I do bear witness to myself, my testimony is true, for I know whence I have come and whither I am going, but you do not know whence I come or whither I am going" (8:14).**

Jesus' response meets the objection of the Pharisees head on. Indeed, Jesus does bear testimony to himself. Nevertheless, his testimony, the revelation he brings, is by its very nature not subject to human judgment and arbitration. Its truth no less than its validity depend, not merely on the technicalities of a judicial process (8:17), but on the true identity of the witness. Jesus knows both the origin and the purpose of his mission. Before his claim to be the Revealer, the one sent by the Father, only unconditional faith can stand. Rejecting the truth of his claim renders you incapable of assessing its validity simply because you refuse to accept his true identity.

Judgment according to the Flesh

> **You judge according to the flesh, I judge no one. Yet even if I do judge, my judgment is true, for it is not I alone that judge, but I and he [the Father] who sent me (8:15–16 marg.).**

The opponents of Jesus judge "according to the flesh," a human judgment. Indeed, what is at the heart of their error is the illusion that human beings can subject both the revelation and the Revealer to their criteria of judgment.

Such an attitude was by no means peculiar to the Pharisees. Christians, too, have managed remarkably well to subject the revelation to their more pliable dogmatic categories. What makes their calamity of even greater import than the Pharisees' is their claim to do so in the name of Christ himself. The Pharisees at least stood in open opposition to him.

"I judge no one," says Jesus. The judgment belongs to God alone. Indeed, God's function in the world he created is precisely to give life and to judge. From these there is no sabbath rest. But the Father, in sending him into the world, "has given all judgment to the Son" (5:22, 27). The reason why Jesus can claim that his judgment is true and valid is his origin from and his mission by the Father. The question, therefore, is far less complicated than either the Pharisees tried to make it, or the Christians have succeeded in making it. The encounter with this Jesus of Nazareth is the judgment: not ours on him, but his on us.

Nevertheless, no reader of John's gospel can forget for a moment the true purpose of the coming of the Son into the world. "For God sent the Son into the world, not to condemn the world, but that the world might be saved through him" (3:17). "I did not come to judge the world but to save the world" (12:47). This is why he now reminds his opponents here, "I judge no one" (8:15).

In your law it is written that the testimony of two men is true. I bear witness to myself, and the Father who sent me bears witness to me (8:17–18).

This is not, as one might conclude, Jesus' acceptance of the common legal premise from Deuteronomy, "only on the witness of two witnesses, or of three witnesses, shall a charge be sustained" (Dt 19:15; 17:6). Jesus merely sets the question aside and, in doing so, dissociates himself from "*your* law." That he and the Father bear witness is in a category which lies well beyond all others, even the holiest. In any event, he and the Father do not make "two witnesses," but "are one" (10:30). "He who seeks the glory of him who sent him is true, and in him there is no falsehood" (7:18b). The witness he bears is necessarily true because all that the Son says and does redounds to the glory of the Father who sent him.

The point, of course, is not entirely lost on his opponents.

They said to him therefore, "Where is your Father?" Jesus answered, "You know neither me nor my Father; if you knew me, you would know my Father also" (8:19).

This is the tragedy of their rejection. All their pretended expertise in the application of the law concerning witness and its validity comes to nothing. Debate and discussion, however legitimate and necessary, cannot be made the excuse to evade the fundamental given of the revelation. The whole point of this revelation is to acknowledge the true identity of Jesus of Nazareth and, acknowledging it, to come to know the Father. Henceforth there is and there can be no other access to the Father.

The refrain of the concluding verse of this section is not unfamiliar:

> **These words he spoke in the treasury, as he taught in the temple; but no one arrested him, because his hour had not yet come (8:20; see 2:11; 4:54; 6:59, and see also 7:30, 32, 44; 10:39).**

"WHO ARE YOU?" (John 8:21–30)

> **Again he said to them, "I go away, and you will seek me and die in your sin; where I am going, you cannot come" (8:21; cf. 13:33).**

The presence of Jesus in their midst is as defined in time as it is in space. He who came into the world does not stay in the world forever. He has to "go away": "I shall be with you a little longer, and then I go to him who sent me" (7:33); "Jesus, knowing that...he had come from God and was going to God" (13:3). As we shall have occasion to see in the farewell discourses (13:33, 36; 14:4, 5, 28; 16:5, 10, 17), it is precisely in his going away that his work as the Revealer becomes manifest. At this point, however, it is sufficient to note that, while he says to those who reject him, "where I am going, you cannot come," he says almost the same thing also to his disciples (13:33). To the disciples, however, he qualifies his statement: "Where I am going you cannot follow me *now;* but you shall follow afterward" (13:36). The difference between the two statements, therefore, is great.

In typical Johannine fashion, Jesus' hearers once again misunderstand his meaning:

> **Then said the Jews, "Will he kill himself, since he says, 'Where I am going you cannot come'?" (8:22).**

But, as is his wont, the evangelist introduces the misunderstanding only to advance the revelation of Jesus one step further.

Johannine Dualism

In Jesus' response to their question, we encounter–though not for the first time–still another characteristic of the fourth gospel, its dualism. This dualism is the dynamic tension between two opposites: light and darkness, life and death, truth and falsehood, above and below. Of course, the link between light, life and truth is no less real than the link between darkness, death and falsehood. They are two different worlds far apart from each other, one "above" and one "below."

> **He said to them, "You are from below, I am from above; you are of this world, I am not of this world" (8:23).**

As we have already had opportunity to remark, origin determines identity. If you are from below, then of the world you are and to it you belong. "He who comes from above is above all; he who is of the earth belongs to the earth, and of the earth he speaks" (3:31). He who "became flesh and dwelt among us" (1:14), however, is not of this world, is not "from below." He is "from above," from where he was in the beginning "with God" (1:1). It is he, therefore, who brings the revelation and "utters the words of God" (3:34).

This, by the way, is the reason why Jesus said to Nicodemus, "unless one is born from above, he cannot see the kingdom of God" (3:3). It is genesis that determines destiny, just as origin determines identity. The only way those "from below" can enter the realm "above," whence the Revealer came, is by a new birth ("of water and the Spirit" 3:5). The sole necessary condition of this rebirth from above is, of course, faith in him whom God has sent.

Sin

> **I told you that you would die in your sins, for you will die in your sins unless you believe that I am he (8:24).**

As faith in him is the condition of life, so rejection of him is death in sin, "you will die in your sins." For those who have grown up with the notion of moral and immoral deeds, this is bound to seem incomprehensible. What John calls "sins" here are sins precisely because they are a refusal to believe "that I am he." This does not deny the fact that human beings are both capable of, and in fact do, evil. But what makes the evil they do "sin" is that it transgresses the express will of God. Henceforth, with the coming of the Son into the world, this unequivocal will of God is that all should believe him whom he sent into the world. "For this is the will of my Father, that every one who sees the Son and believes in him should have eternal life" (6:40). Those who refuse to believe will die in their sins: "For you will die in your sins unless you believe in me" (8:24).

What lies at the heart of all sin is our grasping for life, the refusal to acknowledge it as a gift, and our pretending to obtain it elsewhere than from him who is "the life" (14:6; 11:25; 1:4; 5:26). Within the context of the fourth gospel–indeed, within the context of the whole New Testament–every sin, from Adam's to mine here and now, is fundamentally the creature's grasp for what can only be received and acknowledged as the gratuitous gift of God: life.

So the only way now open to all that seek this life is faith in him whom God has sent: to "believe that I am he," or as the Greek has it, simply "to believe that I am." This is to believe all that Jesus claims to be. "I am he" is therefore the sum of all the other "I am" statements in the gospel. Nevertheless, as we will have come to expect by now, Jesus' hearers again miss the point.

> **They said to him, "Who are you?" Jesus said to them, "Even what I have told you from the beginning" (8:25).**

The Function of the Word

Taken at its face value, his answer simply confirms what Jesus has told them repeatedly "from the beginning." But he goes on:

> **"I have much to say about you and much to judge; but he who sent me is true, and I declare to the world what I have heard from him" (8:26).**

"To say" and "to judge" are what the Revealer's work is all about. He speaks the word, and the word he speaks precipitates the judgment. Revelation and judgment is the purpose of his coming into the world. This is why, in this instance, "to judge" in the RSV seems preferable to "to condemn" in the NRSV, even though the Greek term bears both meanings. For, elsewhere, Jesus says clearly "I did not come to judge (i.e., to condemn) the world" (12:47). The judgment he brings is a condemnation only when the revelation he brings is rejected. The words he utters are "spirit and life" (6:63), if only we would listen to them.

The one who sent him is "true," for God alone is the sole author of the revelation which he brings. The Revealer's task is thus "to declare to the world" what he heard from God who is "true" (3:33; 7:28).

Jesus' hearers again miss the meaning of what he says.

> **They did not understand that he spoke to them of the Father (8:27).**

The one who speaks to them, he who tells them of what he heard, is the Son of the Father who sent him. As the Son, he speaks to them of the Father. No wonder, then, that his audience failed to understand his meaning or to grasp its implications. He claims to tell them only what he heard from him who is true, i.e., only what he as the Son was taught by the Father who sent him. It is "the only Son, who is in the bosom of the Father," who has made the Father known (1:18b).

> **So Jesus said, "When you have lifted up the Son of Man, then you will know that I am [he], and that I do nothing on my own authority but speak as the Father taught me" (8:28).**

Such periodic reminders of the post-Easter vantage point of the evangelist are of course necessary. They keep before us the fact that what Jesus said and did became intelligible only after his exaltation; that whatever the author of the gospel wrote could have only been written from that vantage point.

The Eschatological Vantage Point

The stress in 8:28, nevertheless, is not just on the eschatological nature of the event that was revealed in the lifting up of the Son of man (see 3:14; 12:32, 34). That event, the death and resurrection and exaltation of Jesus, indeed did constitute the end of the old world and the dawn of the new creation. But what the reader of the gospel needs to be reminded of constantly is that, only in the light of that eschatological event, only after the exaltation of the Son of man, did the disciples of Jesus grasp his true identity and the meaning of his words: "*then* you will know that I am" (8:28 and see 2:22; 12:16; cf. 14:26; 20:9). Only from the post-Easter vantage point could this or any other gospel have been composed. This, by the way, is no small reason why "gospel" remains such a unique genre of literature.

The Son's Perfect Obedience

The true nature of the mission and authority of Jesus as the Revealer is another element that must be kept to the fore. Hence, the repeated insistence on, "I do nothing on my own authority" (8:28 and see 5:19, 30; 7:17, 28; 14:10). The one essential element in the Revealer's mission is the totality of his conformity to the will of his Father. It is that perfect obedience that makes him the Son who speaks "as the Father taught" him (8:28). The intimacy of the relationship between the Son and the Father is thus both the content of the revelation and the definition of the true identity of Jesus of Nazareth who brings it:

> **And he who sent me is with me; he has not left me alone, for I always do what is pleasing to him (8:29).**

The relationship between the Revealer and the Father who sent him is not only intimate but also uninterrupted. To be sure, this is the will of the God who sent him and who "is true" (8:26). But this will of the God who reveals himself (see above on 1:1–4; 3:32–33) becomes manifest only in the Son doing always "what is pleasing to him." Those who wish to discern the will of God have only to look upon the Son and hear him.

The corollary to this will become clear in the farewell discourses where we begin to understand that a like obedience to the will of the Father is the requisite condition for our hearing and following the Son whom the Father sent. At this juncture, we are given only a vague hint of that:

> **As he spoke thus, many believed in him (8:30).**

ABRAHAM OUR FATHER (John 8:31–38, 39–47, 48–59)

> **Jesus then said to the Jews who had believed in him, "If you continue in my word, you are truly my disciples, and you will know the truth, and the truth will make you free" (8:31–32).**

To "continue" ("to abide" is another synonym for the Greek term; see 5:38; 6:56; 15:4, 5, 6, 7, 9, 10, 16) in his word is to live out the revelation he brings. It is the sole condition of true discipleship in the community. To abide in his word is to believe the revelation he brings, to be truly his disciple.

To Believe and to Know

As we have noted already (see on 6:69 above), the evangelist uses "to believe" and "to know" almost interchangeably (see, e.g., 6:69; 10:38; 16:30 and cf. 1 Jn 4:16). Of course, you cannot believe what you do not know; and, conversely, you cannot know what you do not believe. Believing and knowing are not stages in the so-called development of faith. Neither can be without the other. Nor can you divide the Christian community into "simple believers" and the *cognoscenti*, those in the know. That we not only do in fact divide and classify the believers, but also act upon such classification, is proof of how deaf we can be to the revelation even while pretending to expound its meaning.

The faith of the Christian is and can only be a faith in the revelation, a faith which John calls the knowledge of "the truth" (8:32; cf. "the Spirit of truth will guide you into all the truth" 16:13). The Word that is "full of grace and truth" did become flesh (1:14). Jesus Christ brings "grace and truth" (1:17). He is the Revealer who "has told you the truth which I heard from God" (8:40). He was born and came into the world "to bear witness to the truth" (18:37). Indeed, he can say very simply, "I am the truth" (14:6).

True Freedom

The whole purpose of his coming as Revealer is, of course, to "save the world" (3:17; 5:34; 10:9; 12:47). This is the reason why the prologue couples "grace and truth" (1:14, 17). The salvation which the Revealer brings is a grace because it confers on those who receive it "eternal life" (1:4; 3:15, 16, 36; 5:24, 40; 6:40, 47, 63, 68; 10:10, 28; 14:6; 17:2, 3; 20:31). In granting them this gift, he sets them free, free not only from the tyranny and bondage of death and darkness, but also from the falsehood that is at the heart of all the counterfeit offers of life under any name.

The freedom which the revelation gives is the salvation that is ours only in our recognition of this revelation as the gift of eternal life. It is the freedom that all who quote this verse on every occasion scarcely ever possess and are themselves never able to confer. It is the freedom that only the Revealer can grant, and only those who believe in and know the revelation can have. That this freedom is something much more than deliverance from the shackles of death, darkness and falsehood will become evident in the farewell discourses.

The Jews seemed to understand what Jesus was saying but in fact missed his point altogether.

They answered him, "We are descendants of Abraham, and have never been in bondage to anyone. How is it that you say, 'You will be made free'?" (8:33).

There is no doubt about their descent from Abraham. But it is the assurance of that privileged possession which prevents them from hearing the revelation. You cannot set free anyone who thinks he is already free. They regarded their physical descent as a stable, inalienable possession of salvation; and, in doing so, forgot the Giver in the proud possession of his gift. Whether or not they have ever been "in bondage" is not really the point at issue. Here and now they are slaves to their past, and that blinds them to the one who is present in their midst.

Appeal to the Past

The Christian reader can easily take sides in the debate here, which is fast degenerating into a vilification contest. But the response of "the Jews" to Jesus is particular only in its reference to Abraham. The Christian's appeal to the past can be infinitely more enslaving and blinding. It is not only the Jews who think that they have in their faith an inalienable possession. Christians are just as ready to regard the grace that is theirs as an indefeasible right. Their stock of dogmas serves equally well to barricade their present against the light of the revelation which is forever breaking in upon them every time they open the gospel. Their secure possession of the past closes them to the future that is only God's to offer.

Slavery to Sin

Jesus answered them, "Amen, amen, I say to you, every one who commits sin is a slave of sin" (8:34).

It has to be admitted, slavery to "sin" in this verse is not what moralists and preachers are usually at pains to call to the attention of their hearers. The slavery to sin in John 8:34 is not a slavery to an immoral act. It is the stubborn refusal to accept the truth of the revelation. From this refusal springs all the evil we do, as well as our inability to do good (15:5 "apart from me you can do nothing"). This is why you cannot remove this verse (8:34) out of its context any more than you can remove its parallel, which proclaims that "the truth will make you free" (8:32), out of its context. The reverse of "you will know the truth, and the truth will make you free" is precisely that "everyone who commits sin is a slave of sin." Ignorance of the truth of revelation is slavery to sin.

The "one who commits sin" is the one who refuses to believe the revelation, refuses to "know the truth," and therefore is not and cannot be free. What sins are committed within that serfdom are only the manifestations of the darkness and death in which, and out of which, the one who is a slave and not a son lives:

> **The slave does not continue in the house for ever; the son continues for ever (8:35).**

From this the evident conclusion is drawn:

> **So if the Son makes you free, you will be free indeed (8:36).**

However obscure the preceding verse (8:35) might seem to be, and no matter how difficult it is to guess its right meaning in the present context, the statement that follows it is, by contrast, pellucid. The Son, and only the Son, as the one sent by the Father, whose sole wish is to carry out the Father's will, he only can set us genuinely free. The ultimate reason for this is that, to him as the only Son, the Father has granted the power "to have life in himself" (5:26). Only the possessor of life in himself can set us mortals genuinely free. The Revealer and only he is the true redeemer of this world.

> **I know that you are descendants of Abraham; yet you seek to kill me, because my word finds no place in you (8:37).**

Jesus knows only too well how right is their claim to be "descendants of Abraham." Yet it is precisely that proud title of theirs that they persist in clinging to as to an exclusive and permanent possession. In their zeal to guard this privilege, they forgot its nature as a gift, and so forgot its Giver. Therefore, they turn a deaf ear to him whom God has sent. They are so certain of their past possession that no present revelation could "find place" in them. Rather than make them open to the Revealer, their privilege begets murderous intentions against him: "You seek to kill me." Thus are the lines drawn. Their deeds and intentions betray their true descent, just as his own origin is the mainspring of all his actions:

I speak of what I have seen with my Father, and you do what you have heard from your father (8:38).

What he has seen with his Father is, of course, what he has seen with him who is the God of Abraham:

They answered him, "Abraham is our father." Jesus said to them, "If you were Abraham's children, you would do what Abraham did, but now you seek to kill me, a man who has told you the truth which I heard from God; this is not what Abraham did. You do what your father did" (8:39–41a).

If the argument seems to us, not so much obscure as unreasonable, it did not seem so to Jesus' hearers. They shared with him the premise that your origin necessarily determines your deeds. This is a good deal more than the scholastic tenet that actions follow the nature of the agent. The point here is that actions reveal the origin of the agent. Jesus' opponents seek to kill him for doing nothing else than telling them "the truth which I heard from God" (8:40). This is certainly not an action that Abraham their father could ever have contemplated. Therefore, Jesus concludes, they must come from someone other than Abraham. The very certainty of their vaunted descent from Abraham is thus called into question. They get the point, and shift their position.

They said to him, "We were not born of fornication; we have one Father, even God" (8:41b).

They see Jesus' statement as casting doubt about the legitimacy of their birth; and they retort by hinting that he is the one who is illegitimate. This might well be an echo of the charge, of which traces are found in the history of early Christianity, that Jesus was a bastard child (cf. Mt 1:18b).

However, the point to note here is that, within the context of John's gospel, Jesus' "You do what your father did" (8:41) is misunderstood by his opponents and leads them to a still higher claim to divine paternity. This time it is not just Abraham but God himself who is their father: "we have one Father, even God." Both the exchange of slurs about origin and the retort to an argument by exaggerating one's initial premise are perfectly human foibles. Any heated argument eventually produces something like one or the other.

In the hands of the evangelist, however, the acrimonious exchange and the resultant misunderstanding open the way—in typically Johannine fashion—to yet another revelation.

Paternity, Mission and Obedience

Jesus said to them, "If God were your Father, you would love me, for I proceeded and came forth from God; I came not of my own accord, but he sent me" (8:42).

Jesus' response makes three interconnected statements. The first, and perhaps the most unexpected, is "If God were your Father, you would love me." The more familiar Johannine refrain is rather in terms of knowledge: "You know neither me nor my Father; if you knew me, you would know my Father also" (8:19, 55; 14:7; 15:21; 16:3; and cf. 7:28). Nevertheless, even without recourse to any metaphysics of love and knowledge, the context here is sufficient to shed light on the statement. They seek to kill Jesus, whose only fault is that he told them "the truth which I heard from God" (8:40). They seek, in other words, to render him extreme evil for supreme good. Instead of the love they ought to show him, they have only hatred. This is clearly not the behavior that becomes the children of God.

If, as they claimed, God were indeed their Father, then they would have readily loved him who "proceeded and came forth from God." This second statement is a reiteration of the truth about Jesus' mission. The key to his true identity is his origin from God and his obedience to the will of the one who sent him. Therefore, he adds the third statement almost as a corollary: "I came not of my own accord, but he sent me."

Now, if this be so, then it is quite incomprehensible how his opponents could possibly claim God for their Father when they hate the one so intimately linked with him, the one so intent on doing nothing other than the will of the Father. But, once we are determined to reject the Revealer, any reason, even the loftiest of theological reasons, will suffice as an excuse. In this particular passage in John, the degree of theological expertise on the part of Jesus' opponents is not at issue. However, it is not idle to recall that one disadvantage attendant upon the study of theology, whether Jewish or Christian, is the dexterity it affords us, not just to evade, but to conceal our evasion of the truth.

Why do you not understand what I say? It is because you cannot bear to hear my word (8:43).

No one would wish to pretend that the word Jesus brings was any easier then than it is now. The revelation is never easy to hear in any generation. Hearing the word not only exposes the lie at the heart of things, but also overturns the laboriously constructed system of our values, and banishes all our cherished ideas. Therefore, far from being the action of those that claim God for their Father, such intransigence before the word demonstrates, rather, allegiance to God's enemy "the devil."

The Father of Lies

You are of your father the devil, and your will is to do your father's desire. He was a murderer from the beginning, and has nothing to do with the truth, because there is no truth in him. When he lies, he speaks according to his own nature, for he is a liar and the father of lies (8:44).

Though the verse reads like a handy compendium of demonology, it enunciates a disquieting truth that we usually prefer to overlook. The life of any free creature, angelic, demonic or human, who rejects the truth of the revelation is, and can only be, a sustained lie from beginning to end. That the devil "has nothing to do with the truth, because there is no truth in him" is not a description exclusive to the fallen angels. Any creature who utters the "I will not serve" lives a lie. Within the more immediate context of the gospel, however, all who reject the Revealer belong to the company of their "father the devil." Like their father, they are averse to the truth and live out one protracted lie their whole life through.

Yet again the reader of John needs a reminder, if only because of the vehemence of these assertions. I can–indeed must–honestly ask myself where I myself stand vis-à-vis such statements of the Revealer. To turn them into a cudgel to castigate those who do not share my religious convictions is merely to evade the implication of the text for me and to pervert its purpose. These and similar utterances of Jesus in the gospel of John are there, not to fire my religious fanaticism, but to question me about my response to the revelation, over and over again, every time I open its pages. They are not a storehouse of arguments to browbeat into subjection those who, for whatever reason, do not share my faith. It is not whether their life is or is not a lie; but whether my own life is a lie, whether or not I myself do really "hear the words of God" (8:47) in the word of Jesus.

But because I tell the truth, you do not believe me (8:45).

The only response to the revelation, "the truth" which Jesus brings, is to believe. But the truth he brings has consequences that are by no means easy to bear. His revelation is always "a hard saying; who can listen to it?" (6:60), especially since listening to it has to be an uninterrupted, lifelong task. Whatever reasons we ingeniously invent for our rejection of the revelation, the only valid one remains our aversion to "the truth."

> **Which of you convicts me of sin? If I tell the truth, why do you not believe me? (8:46).**

It is his origin and mission that attest Jesus' sinlessness. The rhetorical question, "Which of you convicts me of sin?" is not about the moral rectitude of Jesus of Nazareth. It is certainly not about the current favorites among the cherished virtues of bourgeois morality in any age, those virtues with which the portraits of the historical Jesus are larded. The sinlessness of Jesus is the manifestation of the totality of his obedience to the will of the Father. This is why he adds, "Why do you not believe me?" In a sense, his question requires no answer, even though it does get a sharply defined and yet a very simple one.

Hearing the Word of God

> **He who is of God hears the words of God; the reason why you do not hear them is that you are not of God (8:47).**

This, of course, is not new (see above on 8:42 and on 5:23). Their true origin determines their action; and their action similarly betrays their origin. That they reject him who brings the revelation from God, who is intent on doing solely God's will, is the clear proof that their claim to "have one Father, even God" (8:41) is simply not true. It is a lie, and lying is the way of life in the camp of the enemy, who "has nothing to do with the truth, because there is no truth in him. When he lies, he speaks according to his own nature, for he is a liar and the father of lies" (8:44).

Another reflection still needs to be made here. The only way you can believe him whom God has sent is if you already belong to God. But you cannot plead your not belonging to God as your excuse for rejecting the one whom he has sent. You can only know you are "of God" if you believe in Jesus Christ. So, to adapt what Saint Augustine says in a different context, if you really want to be "of God," to have God as Father, then all you have to do is hear "the words of God." But perhaps it is necessary to add: Should you resolve to hear "the words of God," then nothing and no one in heaven or on earth can prevent you from doing so, certainly not the God who "so loved the world that he gave his only Son" (3:16).

BEFORE ABRAHAM WAS (John 8:48–58)

The Jews answered him, "Are we not right in saying that you are a Samaritan and have a demon?" Jesus answered, "I have not a demon; but I honor my Father, and you dishonor me" (8:48–49).

The link between his being a Samaritan and having a demon is not evident. But, at this acrimonious stage in the confrontation, logic is too dear a luxury. Jesus' answer is a simple denial, "I have not a demon." Such denial, of course, resolves nothing. Hatred is not partial to the truth, but it need not always prevent the truth from being told. The very simple fact of the matter is that Jesus "honors" his Father. The only way the Son honors the Father is by his obedience to the will of the Father. Those who refuse to honor him, who indeed "dishonor" him, cannot conceivably claim to have God as their Father.

Yet I do not seek my own glory; there is One who seeks it and he will be the judge (8:50).

What underlay this argument has already been expressed: "He who does not honor the Son does not honor the Father who sent him" (5:23). This should make clear why the Son "honors" the Father precisely in his obedience, by always doing "what is pleasing to him" (8:29). In all he does, the Son seeks only the glory of the Father, who will glorify the Son (12:28), and who alone "will be the judge."

"Will never see death"

Amen, amen, I say to you, if any one keeps my word, he will never see death (8:51).

This, of course, is both the gift and the promise of the revelation that Jesus brings. It is this fact of "never see death," which is no more than the obverse of "have eternal life," that is at the bottom of those accusations of lying in 8:44. To pretend to live other than from him who alone gives life is to live a lie. With the solemnity of the "Amen, amen, I say to you," Jesus reminds his hearers that those who "keep the word," i.e., those who live out of it, allow it to determine both their life and their vision of things, are they who will "never see death." Those who obey the imperative inherent in the word–the imperative contained in every revelation–are they who "will *never* see death."

Both John and his readers know that no mortal is exempt from dying. No mortal will "never see death." This is a periphrastic tautology. But if death is the severance of relationship with all the living, including the living God, then the revelation that Jesus brings, negates precisely this bitter fact of death. It negates the severance by death of the relationship of the mortal creature with the living God, at the same time that it promises the perdurance of all other relationships in the resurrection. Those who keep his words will indeed "never see death."

Nevertheless, such a statement is bound to be misunderstood by any one in any age. So it is by no means surprising that

> **The Jews said to him, "Now we know that you have a demon. Abraham died, as did the prophets; and you say, 'If any one keeps my word, he will never taste death.' Are you greater than our father Abraham, who died? And the prophets died! Who do you claim to be?" (8:52–53).**

The evidence is incontrovertible. Abraham died; the prophets died; and, the reader can add, Jesus himself died. His claim then does sound very like an assertion of superiority even to the great Abraham. "Who do you claim to be?" So, once again, the misunderstanding of his hearers prepares the ground for the revelation that follows.

The Glory of the Revealer

> **Jesus answered, "If I glorify myself, my glory is nothing; it is my Father who glorifies me, of whom you say that he is your God. But you have not known him; I know him. If I said I do not know him, I should be a liar like you; but I do know him and keep his word. Your father Abraham rejoiced that he was to see my day; he saw it and was glad" (8:54–56).**

The whole glory of Jesus as the Revealer of the Father is that, for himself, he is nothing. "If I glorify myself, my glory is nothing," he says repeatedly (5:41; 7:18; 8:50; and cf. 13:32; 16:14; 17:5). The Father, and he alone "of whom you say that he is your God," is the one who glorifies Jesus Christ. He does so, of course, by raising Jesus from the dead: the "One who seeks" "my own glory" (8:50). It is precisely the revelation of this mystery of the resurrection that can ultimately render possible the statement, "If any one keeps my word, he will never see death" (8:51).

This is another instance where a recollection of the post-Easter standpoint from which the gospel is written can be very illuminating. The evangelist writes with the enormous advantage of hindsight.

Jesus cannot pretend to be other than who he truly is, not even to please his angry opponents. Modern preachers of the word would do well to attend to the obvious lesson here, especially those of us so readily prone to hew Jesus down to accommodate the uncertain taste of the crowd, to offer them the comfort of a revelation tailored to their current preferences, and trimmed to accommodate the constricted horizon of their fashionable prejudices.

The reason Jesus "knows" God the Father is that he "keeps his word." It is precisely this obedience to the Father's will that makes Jesus of Nazareth who he really is, the Son who reveals the Father. It is this that makes it impossible for him to be anyone or anything else, and for God to be other than his Father.

However one may wish to interpret the statement about Abraham rejoicing that "he was to see my day; he saw it and was glad" (8:56), it provides at least one instance where the misunderstanding of the Jews is gladly shared by at least one reader. That this misunderstanding leads to one of the most dazzling revelations of the Son is—or ought to be—sufficient consolation for the ambiguity that occasioned it.

> **The Jews then said to him, "You are not yet fifty years old, and have you seen Abraham?" Jesus said to them, "Amen, amen, I say to you, before Abraham was, I am" (8:58).**

Once again a misunderstanding has yielded, as it were, an exorbitation of the revelation. Jesus lays claim, not just to being temporally antecedent to the patriarch Abraham, but to having been "in the beginning" (1:1). Indeed, he is "the only Son, who is in the bosom of the Father," and now makes the Father known (1:18). This "I AM" is even more absolute than the previous one in "you will die in your sins unless you believe that I am" (8:24). It is a claim to have been there even before the unfolding of God's plan for the election of his people and the salvation of the world. He who makes this claim is not only the fulfilment of the promise, but was there before the promise was even given.

Of course, to any Jew, such a claim is blasphemy, plain and simple:

> **So they took up stones to throw at him, but Jesus hid himself, and went out of the temple (8:58).**

John 9

The Healing of a Man Born Blind: illness and sin; the contingency of the revelation.

The First Round of Questions: recourse to the authorities; the division; a prophet.

The Second Round of Questions: the Jews; expulsion from the synagogue.

The Third Round of Questions: "we know"; the stubborn facts; omniscience and unbelief.

Spiritual Blindness: faith and worship; sight and blindness

THE HEALING OF A MAN BORN BLIND (John 9:1–12)

> **As he passed by, he saw a man blind from his birth. And his disciples asked him, "Rabbi, who sinned, this man or his parents, that he was born blind?" (9:1–2).**

Proud of this world's modern scientific achievements, some people will find the disciples' question, if not irrelevant, naive. However, these same people confronted, say, by a sexually transmitted disease, have no difficulty in seeing it, if not as divine judgment, then at least as the vengeance of "mother nature." But whatever the conclusion reached, by whichever group of the healthy, it is bound to be always self-congratulatory, often self-righteous, and sometimes outright condemnatory–what modern timidity dares only call "judgmental."

Illness and Sin

Were these same modern people to discover that they themselves have an incurable disease, many among them would querulously ask,

"Why me? What have I done?" In a world that regarded sickness as a form of punishment, and believed in a God who visits "the iniquity of the fathers upon the children to the third and fourth generation" (Ex 20:5), the question of the disciples need have caused no surprise. The disciples at least did not shrink from calling blindness by its name, nor pretend that the blind possessed compensatory powers as good as the eyes that see the light of the sun. At least Jesus' disciples were not disposed to trivialize the healing by finding a euphemism for the blindness; and they certainly were not like those who nullify the gift of healing by insisting on the "right" of the blind to be healed.

Nevertheless, in this particular instance, Jesus simply denies the presupposition of the disciples' question.

> **Jesus answered, "It was not that this man sinned, or his parents, but that the works of God might be made manifest in him" (9:3).**

The evangelist thus directs the whole incident to the manifestation of God's power at work in Jesus. This, of course, is the reason why, rather than call them "miracles," demonstrations of Jesus's power as a wonder-worker, John insists on calling them "signs." These signs point to the power of God at work in the person of him whom he sent: "for the works which the Father has granted me to accomplish, these very works which I am doing, bear witness that the Father has sent me" (5:36). The works Jesus accomplishes are, in other words, no less "revelation" than the words he utters.

The Contingency of the Revelation

> **We must work the works of him who sent me, while it is day; night comes, when no one works. As long as I am in the world, I am the light of the world (9:4–5).**

Such a statement by the Revealer emphasizes what has been called the "contingency of the revelation." There is a time when the Revealer is "in the world," but there comes a time when he himself will no longer be there. The revelation he brings is not a set of dogmas that is always there, to which we can turn whenever the mood takes us. The initiative is not ours, but always his. The revelation he brings is always a gift, and his gift is always a revelation: "As long as I am in the world, I am the light of the world" (cf. 8:12).

The miracle that follows, though an apt illustration of this declaration, is straightforward enough in the telling. No one asks Jesus to perform a miracle. He simply recognizes a need and takes the initiative:

> **As he said this, he spat on the ground and made clay of the spittle and anointed the man's eyes with the clay, saying to him, "Go, wash in the pool of Siloam" (which means Sent). So he went and washed and came back seeing (9:6–7).**

The blind man, on the other hand, unquestioningly does what he is told to do, without murmur and without hesitation (cf. the story of Naaman the Syrian and Elisha in 2 Kings 5:11–12). The account of the miracle is simplicity itself and can hardly be bettered for conciseness.

At this juncture, however, the readers of John are ready for a good deal more than just another wonder performed by Jesus of Nazareth; and they are not disappointed. The narrative of the people's reaction to this event can scarcely be excelled anywhere else in the fourth, or any other, gospel.

> **The neighbors and those who had seen him before as a beggar, said, "Is not this the man who used to sit and beg?" (9:8).**

The neighbors, presumably, ought to have known that the man was "blind from birth." Those who knew him just in passing, moreover, knew him as a blind beggar. Therefore, their reaction to his sudden fortune was quite predictable.

> **Some said, "It is he"; others said, "No, but he is like him." He said, "I am the man." They said to him, "Then how were your eyes opened?" He answered, "The man called Jesus made clay and anointed my eyes and said to me, 'Go to Siloam and wash'; so I went and washed and received my sight. They said to him, "Where is he?" He said, "I do not know" (9:8–12).**

To doubt the evidence of their own senses before this incredible fact is natural enough. The blind man dispels their doubt. He is indeed the blind beggar they knew: "I am the man." Unlike the paralytic by the pool (see 5:13), this man at least knows that the man who healed him is "called Jesus."

As has been remarked above, "the man called Jesus," unsolicited by his disciples and unasked by the blind man, had taken the initiative to heal him. To Jesus, it was just being who he is: the one sent by God to carry out the divine will to save. To forget this fact and concentrate on the element of the strange and the marvelous in the narrative is to refuse the "sign." Unless you see them as the manifestation of God's power at work in the world, all such spectacular wonders amount to nothing more than temporary diversions for the amusement of the crowd which is always on the lookout for the unusual and the extraordinary.

The beneficiary of this miracle himself can only state the bare fact: "The man called Jesus made clay and anointed my eyes and said to me, 'Go to Siloam and wash'; so I went and washed and received my sight." The healed man has no further explanation to add. He cannot even satisfy the curiosity of those bewildered by the event. He is ignorant even of the whereabouts of the man who restored his sight.

THE FIRST ROUND OF QUESTIONS (John 9:13–17)

It strikes us as odd perhaps that the neighbors and acquaintances of the blind man should, in the circumstances, have done what they did next:

> **They brought to the Pharisees the man who had formerly been blind (9:13).**

Whether or not these are the same Pharisees that were party to the dispute in the temple in the preceding two chapters is not really what matters. They strike us as being every bit as belligerent and hostile. They must have possessed, moreover, some kind of authority; else, why bring the healed man to them? how could they conduct such an imposing inquiry into the matter as mere busybodies?

Recourse to the Authorities

On the other hand, we cannot very well pretend to be altogether surprised by the actions of the neighbors and acquaintances of the blind man. This is what most of us would do if we encountered the inexplicable in our daily life. So few of us ever stop to question, How do the authorities know? Where do they in fact come by such omniscience? Of course, we have heard it said often that knowledge is power; and so we leap to the conclusion that power must therefore be knowledge.

But, whatever the motive of such recourse to the authorities, it requires no great streak of misanthropy in any of us to realize that such an appeal to them seems natural because it is self-serving. Such a view is all the more compelling when we suspect that the authorities' opinion of those under them is not very flattering: "This crowd, who do not know the law, are accursed" (7:49). Thus, by appealing to them, we not only flatter their vanity and render them better disposed to exempt us from their disdainful judgment, but we hope by our recourse to them to distance ourselves from the rest of the "accursed" crowd. We at least–so the monologue of self-justification goes–are not as stupid and "accursed" as the rest.

Notice how quick we are to spot the "irregular," and how prompt and zealous to report it to the rightful authority. We attribute to them the knowledge we ourselves lack; and, in this unholy alliance between the timorous to please and the ignorant to be flattered, lies the source of most of the power exercised in institutions, even the holiest.

Now it was a sabbath day when Jesus made clay and opened his eyes (9:14).

This late bit of information adds a new twist to the situation. But the addition should not surprise us. The Jesus of the gospels seems to have had a decided penchant for doing things on the sabbath (5:9b; 7:23; and see Mt 12:10 par; Lk 13:14; 14:1–4, etc.). But the real reason for introducing this information here in John is, of course, not far to seek.

The Pharisees again asked him how he had received his sight. And he said to them, "He put clay on my eyes, and I washed, and I see" (9:15).

Of course, those who put the question to the healed blind man possessed no evidently greater intelligence or wisdom than the ordinary people who brought the blind man to them after having put to him the identical question, "Then how were your eyes opened?" (9:10). But it will take a far greater wit than Voltaire to convince any of us, that most of the superior intelligence and wisdom enjoyed by those in power exists solely in the minds of their subjects.

In the midst of all this, however, one has to admire the dogged adherence of the healed blind man to the simple, incontestable fact. He might have been blind, but he sees with blinding clarity the one simple truth that all his open-eyed interrogators cannot see, simply because they will not. So, they first question the fact itself; and, failing to budge its immovable mass, turn to attack the one responsible for it.

The Division

Some of the Pharisees said, "This man is not from God, for he does not keep the sabbath." But others said, "How can a man who is a sinner do such signs?" There was a division among them (9:16).

The deeds of Jesus, like the words he speaks, always cause a division ("schism," literally in the Greek), precipitate dissension, and effect a judgment (*krisis* in the Greek). Confronted by one whose whole reason for being is to do the will of God, the Pharisees simply have recourse to the expedient of denying that he is "from God." No further proof is required than their theological expertise. They know, and they have the scriptural texts to back them up, that you simply cannot break the law of the sabbath and be "from God."

"Some of the Pharisees," however, were less precipitous in their judgment. Arguing from the same premise and looking at the identical fact, they failed to reach the same condemnatory conclusion as others in their group. They at least hesitated. Hence, the "division among them" (see 7:43; 10:19). But such division among Jesus' hearers is not confined to outsiders. Even among his own disciples there was bound to come a moment when many "drew back and no longer went about with him" (6:66). It is of the nature of the revelation to precipitate such "division."

Moreover, this division among the Pharisees makes at least some of them do an eminently reasonable thing. They question the only one who ought to have a worthwhile opinion on the matter, the recipient of the great favor himself.

A Prophet

So they again said to the blind man, "What do you say about him, since he opened your eyes?" He said, "He is a prophet" (9:17).

They understand perfectly well what happened. They know, as everyone else around them knows, that the eyes of the blind are not opened by just anyone who happens along. In their question, they admit that the eyes of the man born blind have in fact been opened. Surely, the incident itself could not have been such a common occurrence as to make them completely forget Isaiah 35:5, "Then the eyes of the blind shall be opened"; or Isaiah 42:7, "I have given you as a covenant to the people, a light to the nations, to open the eyes that are blind." Nevertheless, they ask the blind man himself for his opinion, and what he himself thinks of someone who can do such a thing is very simple: "He is a prophet."

It is helpful to recall here that, from the days of "the prophets of old," Israel regarded the miracles of the prophets as authentication of their prophecy. They could readily cite the example of Elijah or Elisha, to say nothing of the great Moses himself. But whether or not the Jews of Jesus' time associated such miracles with the person of the Messiah is a moot question. This is not to say that they did not expect the messianic times themselves to be accompanied by miracles. So, in the circumstances, the response of the healed blind man, admirable though it is, should not be as puzzling as it might seem.

THE SECOND ROUND OF QUESTIONS (John 9:18–23)

It is, moreover, hard to imagine what else "the Pharisees" expected the man born blind to say. The clarity of his statement of facts is matched only by the certainty of his judgment of who his benefactor was: "a prophet." His interrogators, on the other hand, realize that their line of questioning is leading them nowhere, at least nowhere that they themselves have any intention of going. So, naturally enough, they alter their mode of attack.

One might well wonder what happened to the neighbors and acquaintances of the blind man who brought him to the authorities in the first place. Did they at this point recognize their error and withdraw to ponder, if not the senselessness of their action, at least the response of the blind man? Or, unwilling to admit their own error, did they side with the authorities who were equally unwilling to admit theirs? Unanswerable questions like these bring into focus Jesus' words at the beginning of the incident, "We must work the works of him who sent me, while it is day; night comes, when no one can work" (9:4). For those who will not see, it is always "night."

The Jews

The Jews did not believe that he had been blind and had received his sight, until they called the parents of the man who had received his sight, and asked them, "Is this your son, who you say was born blind? How then does he now see?" (9:18–19).

Before we marvel at the stubborn refusal to believe what has already been conceded as fact (see 9:15), or question the rationale of interrogating the parents about their son, there is a knotty problem that comes up again and again in the fourth gospel. Johannine scholars have spared no effort to disentangle and identify such categories as "the Pharisees" (1:24; 3:1; 4:1; 7:32, 47, 48; 8:13; 9:13, etc.), "the chief priests" (7:32, 45; 11:47; 12:10), or, most problematic of all, "the Jews." There is no getting around the fact that the gospel speaks of "the Jews" as the opponents both of Jesus (5:16, 18; 6:41; 7:1; 8:48, 52, etc.) and of those who believed in him (7:13; 9:22; 20:19), with all the acrimony such opposition engenders. In the only chapters where "the Jews" are not mentioned at all, chapters 14–17, the opponents and their opposition are designated as "the world," in the pejorative sense of that term (see above on 3:16).

Thus, "the Jews" in the first part of the gospel and "the world" in the second are they against whom the community of believers in John's gospel defines itself and, inevitably, takes its stand. Of course, this is precisely what Israel did vis-à-vis "the nations," the Gentiles. This is comprehensible enough as a phenomenon, not just in Judaism and Christianity, but in most any other religion.

The phenomenon in the gospel of John, however, must be assessed in the light of allied facts that are equally important, though not sufficiently recalled: Jesus himself is a Jew (4:9; 18:35), and the gospel neither obscures nor denies this. Indeed, the one solid bit of historical information on which all the gospels agree is the inscription on the cross: the king of the Jews (Jn 19:19; Mt 27:37; Mk 15:26; Lk 23:38). Moreover, the first disciples themselves were Jews, including Nicodemus (3:1), Martha and Mary and their brother Lazarus (11:33), and the beloved disciple. Indeed "the Jews" themselves were divided in their opinion of him (10:19) and some "believed in him" (8:31). There is, moreover, every reason to believe that the fourth gospel itself began its existence in a community of Jewish converts to the nascent faith, which remained a Jewish community until such time as a definitive rift took place and they were expelled from what they considered their rightful spiritual home.

You can regret the consequences of that rift, but you cannot very well deny its existence. There came a moment when the followers of Jesus ceased to be just another Jewish sect among so many in that first century. It would be naive to think that the opposition or the bitterness this engendered was one-sided; just as it would be false to imagine that the Jewish converts to Christianity resorted to a language of acrimony and polemic that radically differed from the one they had learned in their mother faith.

To imagine for a moment, however, that any of this translates into a mandate to persecute or hate anyone or any group that does not share the Christian faith is not only a perversion of that faith but also a total misreading of its gospel. The fact of the matter, however, is that no one has ever needed a scripture to justify hatred, even though all of us are prone to seek subsequent scriptural justification for all our misdeeds. We pretend to be serving a God who "so loved the world" by hating those whom he chose and loved first, from the beginning. We so readily forget that when the Son came into the world he came to "his own home" (1:11).

You could, if you choose, maintain that "the Jews" in 9:18 are distinct from "the Pharisees" in 9:13. Of course, though all the Pharisees are Jews, not all the Jews are Pharisees. But, in the progress of the narrative in chapter 9, the same group of opponents, however you may wish to designate them, are resolved not to accept the miracle (see 9:24 "For the *second time* they called the man who had been blind"). Differentiation into and identification of the different categories of opponents does not really get around the conflict and bitterness evident in these pages.

That the opponents of Jesus revert to their initial refusal to believe the simple facts of the case is no more and not very different from what we all do in such circumstances. We cast about for a euphemism to help us deny the fact by refusing to call the blindness by its name. We expect, even demand, a remedy for our ills; and, when it comes, we set about looking for an explanation to relieve us of the burden of gratitude. Failing that, we attack our benefactor. This much is human enough, and no religious group has a monopoly on such perverse behavior.

The opponents of Jesus now seek out the parents of the blind man. But his parents, with all the pliant shrewdness of the lowly, sidestep the question of the authorities by a simple reassertion of the unalterable facts.

> **His parents answered, "We know that this is our son, and that he was born blind; but how he now sees we do not know, nor do we know who opened his eyes. Ask him; he is of age, he will speak for himself" (9:20–21).**

The fact of the matter is that the son has already repeated his simple story twice: "He put clay on my eyes, and I washed, and I see" (9:15;

9:11). The parents are willing enough to furnish the facts they know first-hand, but avoid an opinion on the cure itself. Their reluctance and the prudence they exercise now receive a more telling explanation.

Expulsion from the Synagogue

> **His parents said this because they feared the Jews, for the Jews had already agreed that if any one should confess him to be Christ, he was to be put out of the synagogue. Therefore his parents said, "He is of age, ask him" (9:22–23).**

The explanation of the evangelist is clear enough as it stands. But a moment's thought should suffice to realize that it does not reflect a situation in the life of Jesus himself, but in the life of the community of his followers. To be sure, Jesus proclaimed his message and found among his fellow-Jews some who accepted it and followed him, just as he encountered others who rejected his message and opposed him, even exhibited outright enmity toward him. But to the end of his life and well beyond it, he and his followers found their spiritual home among "the Jews." Indeed, they had no other home. He regarded the temple of Jerusalem as his "Father's house" (2:16). He had "always taught in synagogues and in the temple where all Jews come together" (18:20). He was first tried by his fellow-Jews as a Jew. There is, moreover, no reason whatsoever to believe that at first his disciples regarded themselves as anything but "Jews."

Those early Jewish converts to the nascent faith regarded themselves as good, devout Jews, "day by day attending the temple together" (Acts 2:46). At this distance in time, we can scarcely imagine the wrench it must have been for them, some years later–sometime after the year A.D. 70 and the destruction of Jerusalem–to be expelled from their spiritual home by fellow-Jews who refused to accept the Jesus Christ they themselves confessed as Messiah and Son of God.

Those who were at first "Christian Jews" were now compelled to become "Jewish Christians" and to break away from their original community of faith. However regrettable, the acrimony and bitterness and outright hatred, which marked the rift and the subsequent struggles between the believers in Christ and the Jews, must surely be comprehensible enough. But to pretend for a moment that it was all one-sided, to lay the blame on one side and absolve the other, is the kind of willful blindness to the truth that makes a mockery of the suffering victims on both sides.

Needless to say, the expulsion of those Jewish Christians "from the synagogue" (9:22) rankled. Its effects, both in the long history of the composition of the fourth gospel and in the varied fortunes of the Johannine community, are noticeable both in 9:22 ("if any one should confess him to be Christ, he was to be put out of the synagogue"), and in 12:42 ("Nevertheless many even of the authorities believed in him, but for fear of the Pharisees they did not confess it, lest they should be put out of the synagogue"). The expulsion from the synagogue is even made into a prophecy of things to come in Jesus' farewell discourse: "They will put you out of the synagogues" (16:2). Thus, understandably enough, the evangelist reads the events of Jesus' times through the prism of his own community's life. Can the reader of the gospel in subsequent generations do any less?

THE THIRD ROUND OF QUESTIONS (John 9:24–34)

> **So for the second time they called the man who had been blind, and said to him, "Give God the praise; we know that this man is a sinner" (9:24).**

Even they must have come to realize by now the infuriating stubbornness of facts. There was no use in asking the man himself "how he now sees." This question had been put to him originally by the people who first discovered him (9:10) and then again by the authorities to whom they brought him (9:15). So, failing in that approach, they now have recourse to their theological expertise and all its pious trappings. Of course, it is all being done to "give God the praise." They *know* "this man is a sinner." Those in authority always do. They come to believe overnight, not only in the infallibility of their opinions, but in the inerrancy of their ways and the peccancy of all dissenters. Those who disagree with them are not merely ignoramuses ("This crowd, who do not know the law") but damned "sinners" ("are accursed" 7:49).

"We know"

Nobody is about to question them *how* they know the man who healed the blind is a sinner. The sad aspect of the comedy, of course, is that their knowledge is as much a figment of the crowd's imagination as is their righteousness. Without the credulity of the crowd, neither the assured knowledge of the authorities nor their presumed sanctity could have survived exposure to the light of day. Even the blind man, who must have had sufficient intelligence to say, as did even some of the Pharisees, "How can a man who is a sinner do such signs?" (9:16b, 31–32), chose to sidestep the implications of their statement:

> **He answered, "Whether he is a sinner, I do not know; one thing I know, that though I was blind, now I see" (9:25).**

In this parry and thrust between two unequally matched opponents, even the most innocent of answers assumes an ominous quality. The healed man knows what his opponents stubbornly refuse even to consider: Anyone genuinely in need of deliverance is in no position to question the moral credentials of his deliverer. The man is grateful enough that he is no longer blind and can now see for the first time in his life. If his questioners cannot grasp that much, then their blindness must indeed be far more incurable than his, if only because theirs is deliberately willed (9:41).

The Stubborn Facts

Since this approach advanced their position not one whit, they return once more to attack the fact itself, hoping to alter it. Someone once explained his preference of facts to theories by, "You can change facts more easily." So, too, the authorities here, having made up their minds that Jesus could not possibly be who he claims to be, and whom many believe he is, set about to attack the facts. Yet, "What stubborn things are facts!"

> **They said to him, "What did he do to you? How did he open your eyes?" (9:26).**

The retreat to the first line of attack (9:19) is an implicit admission of their defeat. Of course, the man born blind, realizing this, sees his opportunity and grasps it. Just the right touch of ingenuousness saves him from appearing what he in fact is in this contest, the undeclared winner.

> **He answered them, "I have told you already, and you would not listen. Why do you want to hear it again? Do you want to become his disciples?" (9:27).**

The proof that he scores heavily against them is evident in the loss of their pretended equanimity.

And they reviled him, saying, "You are his disciple, but we are disciples of Moses. We know God has spoken to Moses, but as for this man, we do not know where he comes from" (9:28–29).

Omniscience and Unbelief

Nothing could more effectively block one's ears to the revelation than the assured possession of dogma, "We know." The first two affirmations, "You are his disciple" and "We are disciples of Moses," are equally questionable. First of all, the man is not, at least not yet, a "disciple" of Jesus. Secondly, if they themselves were truly "disciples of Moses," they would have been a little less reluctant to dismiss Jesus so summarily: "If you believed Moses, you would believe me, for he wrote of me" (5:46).

The third statement is not open to question. They "know God has spoken to Moses." This is an article of their faith, as it is of the blind man's. Once the bankruptcy of those in authority has become manifest, there is no need to succumb to the temptation to call into question everything they say. You can argue that they really brought such an attitude on themselves. But, in fact, an error of whatever magnitude never justifies another error in those who expose it.

Finally, even their claim, "but for this man, we do not know where he comes from," might well be true, if it were an admission of ignorance. But, ironically enough, what makes their position incredible is their very claim to know (9:24). They never cease to confuse their power with knowledge. Even though there were some among them who could at least ask, "How can a man who is a sinner do such signs?" (9:16), they themselves had made up their minds, "This man is not from God" (9:16); "We know that this man is a sinner" (9:24). In this secure knowledge lies the tragedy of their dogmatism and of every other dogmatism down the ages. This dogmatism robs them of the possibility of change, leaves them no room for maneuver, and subtracts them from the number of those who deserve pity. Their assured faith in the rightness of their vision blinds them.

The man answered, "Why, this is a marvel! You do not know where he comes from, and yet he opened my eyes. We know that God does not listen to sinners, but if any one is a worshiper of God and does his will, God listens to him. Never since the world began has it been heard that any one opened the eyes

of a man born blind. If this man were not from God, he could do nothing" (9:30–33).

The fact of the miracle clamors for attention. The opening of the eyes of one born blind is not an everyday occurrence. Indeed, in the context of the narrative, it is not humanly possible to open the eyes of such a person. A wonder like this is God's alone to perform, and to perform solely through his own chosen agent. It requires hardly any theological sophistication to come to the conclusion that, "If this man were not from God, he could do nothing" (9:33), even if you are far from willing or able to say, "Without him was not anything made that was made" (1:3).

Alas, their answer to the commonsensical statement of the man born blind is only too predictable.

They answered him, "You were born in utter sin, and would you teach us?" And they cast him out (9:34).

The tragedy of those who think they know is that no one can teach them. Armored in the security of their dogmatic certainty, they regard all who dare to disagree with them, not just as ignorant, but also as sinners. Righteousness is theirs, because knowledge is theirs; and knowledge is theirs because power is in their hands. Thus, the gates of their unassailable citadel are slammed shut against the light.

Should there still be those who are inclined to think that this reflects only the situation of the Jews in the first century, but not of the Christians in any other, they will do well to take up a history of the church and read it.

SPIRITUAL BLINDNESS (John 9:35–41)

Jesus heard that they had cast him out, and having found him he said, "Do you believe in the Son of Man?" (9:35).

The dreaded expulsion has taken place. The blind man who sees is now spiritually homeless. Once again, Jesus takes the initiative. As at first, unasked, he opened the eyes of the blind man, so now he, "the light of the world" (9:5), spontaneously grants him light. The man himself has advanced in his affirmation from "the man called Jesus" (9:11), to "He is a prophet" (9:17), to someone who is "a worshiper of God and does his will" and one to whom "God listens" (9:31). Now Jesus puts to him the question about the Revealer at the end of time, the one who ushers in God's definitive and eschatological reign in the world: "Do you believe in the Son of Man?"

> **He answered, "And who is he, sir, that I may believe in him?" (9:36).**

Notice that his prior opinions of Jesus were–so to speak–rational, even laudably pious, conjectures. That is why his common sense was so telling an argument against the authorities who questioned him, against the official custodians of piety in his community. Now, however, Jesus proposes to reveal to him the identity of him who was promised "from the beginning" and has been awaited for centuries beyond number. To such a revelation, faith is the only answer: "that I may *believe* in him."

> **Jesus said to him, "You have seen him, and it is he who speaks to you" (9:37).**

One might well ponder the irony of "You have *seen* him." The miracle thus assumes a meaning far beyond anything else up to this point. It reminds one of Simeon's effusion of gratitude at the sight of the child Jesus in the temple: "For mine eyes have *seen* your salvation...a light for the revelation to the Gentiles, and for glory to your people Israel" (Lk 2:30, 32).

In the gospel of John, however, the Revealer is "he who *speaks* to you" (Jn 9:37). This is the Word that has become flesh (1:18). Faith is always faith in the word of the revelation. Herein lies the beatitude of those who, as the risen Jesus will tell Thomas, "have *not seen* and yet believe" (20:29), who have no other access to the Word except the word: "It is he who speaks to you."

Faith and Worship

> **He said, "Lord, I believe"; and he worshiped him (9:38).**

This is the response to the revelation of who Jesus is. It is faith in his word and worship of his person. One is not separable from the other, just as one is meaningless without the other. Without worship, faith is an intellectual exercise; and without faith, worship is empty show. The response to the revelation involves the entire person of the believer. It is the act of worship that gives expression to the totality of this involvement.

This entire final episode (9:35–38) illustrates well what Jesus said to the Samaritan woman, "But the hour is coming, and now is, when the true worshipers will worship the Father in spirit and truth" (4:23). The healed blind man, who believed Jesus' claim to be the Son of man and worshiped him, is a true worshiper indeed. His worship is "in spirit and truth."

At this confession of faith the whole debate with the authorities recedes into the background. The faith of the blind man who now sees is not a conclusion to a syllogism; nor is it a gradual ascent from "the man called Jesus" (9:11), to "a prophet" (9:17), to someone from God (9:33), which finally arrives at the full-blown confession of faith. It is very simply the "Lord, I believe" of the blind man who now sees Jesus of Nazareth standing before him and declaring that he is "the Son of Man." Such faith is, of course, a genuine possibility to everyone confronted by the revelation. You can say "I believe" to the declaration that Jesus is "the Son of Man." But its opposite is every bit as possible and real, for you can just as well refuse to believe. This is why

Jesus said, "For judgment I came into this world, that those who do not see may see, and that those who see may become blind" (9:39).

This easily misunderstood sentence is no more than the statement of a fact. So long as the person addressed by the revelation is free, and so long as revelation is a gift that can make sense only if addressed to one genuinely free either to accept or reject it, then the possibility of rejecting it is every bit as real as that of accepting it. This is what "judgment" means. This is what the Revealer necessarily brings about by his coming into the world.

Sight and Blindness

The gift of God which he brings to the world can be a gift of grace only to those who freely choose to accept it as gift. To accept it as a gift is to live: "Who believes in me, though he die, yet shall he live" (11:25). This is grace. To reject it is to die: "For you will die in your sins unless you believe that I am he" (8:24). This is judgment. The concomitant of grace is judgment. This is not divine caprice. It is dictated by the very nature of the gift.

That "those who do not see may see" describes the situation admirably. The blind, those who know they are blind, come to Jesus and see. But they can come to him only if they know and acknowledge their need for light. "Those who are well have no need of a physician" (Mk 2:17 par.). On the other hand, "those who see," those who have no need of a healer, simply "become blind." There is no one more blind than the person who refuses to see, nor more deaf than the one who refuses to hear.

All this faithfully echoes the Isaiah passage which John as well as the synoptics cite:

> Go, and say to this people:
> Hear and hear, but do not understand;
> see and see, but do not perceive.
> Make the heart of this people fat,
> and their ears heavy,
> and shut their eyes:
> lest they see with their eyes,
> and hear with their ears,
> and understand with their hearts,
> and turn and be healed (Is 6:9–10; see Jn 12:40; Mt 13:14–15; Mk 4:12; Lk 8:10; Acts 28:26–27).

The situation today is no different from what it was in Isaiah's time or in John's. We all want a redeemer, but few of us are willing to admit the need for redemption. Only the ignorant need instruction; only sinners need forgiveness; only the blind cry out for the light. In a world where we boast of our knowledge, where "sin" has been banished from our vocabulary, and where we are forever inventing euphemisms for blindness, a redeemer can at best be a redundant nuisance.

It is not the purpose of Jesus' coming into the world to execute this judgment: "I did not come to judge the world but to save the world" (Jn 12:47). He came as "light into the world" (9:5; 8:12; 11:10; 12:35, 46; 1:9); he came that "they may have life, and have it abundantly" (10:10; 1:4). But so long as what he brings this world is a free gift, then those for whom he brings it remain free to accept or reject it. Before their rejection of this gift, the giver himself stands helpless. Their refusal of the gift is the judgment. His coming into the world with the gift inevitably precipitates the segregation of those who accept from those who refuse it.

Some of the Pharisees near him heard this, and they said to him, "Are we also blind?" (9:40).

The point of what they overheard Jesus say is not lost on them. Yet, ironically enough, their very question illustrates the point Jesus is making. They cannot conceive of themselves as in need of light, so convinced are they of the knowledge they possess. Here again, the reader should not make the vulgar error of thinking that these are proud in their knowledge because they are Pharisees. If this be so, then we are all of us Pharisees. Their attitude, indeed the very question they pose, has been and is common to every segment of the Christian church. That it is more in evidence among the hierarchy and the experts in scripture or theology or the law is merely an occupational hazard. It does not in itself distinguish such categories from the most unlettered of Christians. What all share with one another and with the Pharisees is the assurance of "We see!"

> **Jesus said to them, "If you were blind, you would have no sin. But now that you say, 'We see,' your sin remains" (9:41 NRSV).**

The only sin is the rejection of the gift that Jesus brings. To imagine oneself not in need of this gift, to say "We see" when in fact we are blind, is sin. No formula could better encapsulate this entire chapter, where the man born blind, who knew he was blind without pretending he was not, is given sight. Those who are encased within the armor of their right understanding of the law, of scripture and of tradition, those who are secure in their power and the knowledge they possess, have no need of him. Their "sin remains." It is their refusal to come to him, who is "the light of the world" (9:5), that is the judgment.

John 10

The Sheepfold: the image of the shepherd; the shepherd as leader; parable and allegory.

The Good Shepherd: the intolerance of the revelation; thieves and robbers; life abundant; his life for his sheep; the fold and the church; reciprocal knowledge; one flock; the death on the cross.

Division and Dispute: the Christ; belonging to his sheep; "shall never perish"; the unity of the Father and the Son; the blasphemy; the mission of the Son; believe, know, understand.

THE SHEEPFOLD (John 10:1–6)

The transition from chapter 9 to 10 is not smooth, and there is no reason for pretending to find hidden links between blindness and the shepherd. The healing of the man born blind and the dialogue that follows it have all the unities of time, place and action in a classic Greek drama. To this ninth chapter one can return over and over again, always to find light. No one can leave it indifferent. Its concluding line ("If you were blind, you would have no guilt; but now that you say 'We see,' your guilt remains" 9:41) sees to that. By its very nature it questions one's true–not pretended or imagined–stand before the revelation that Jesus brings.

If, as several Johannine scholars have argued, the fourth gospel does bring together and preserve "sermons" preached to a community of believers by a Christian believer in their midst, then chapter 10 might be as good an example of such a "sermon" as any, perhaps better even than the chapter that preceded it. The abruptness of its solemn opening, far from detracting from its homiletic quality, enhances it.

The Image of the Shepherd

Amen, amen, I tell you, anyone who does not enter the sheepfold by the gate but climbs in by another way is a thief and a bandit. The one who enters by the gate is the shepherd of the sheep (10:1–2 NRSV).

What urban existence has deprived many of us, has been, however imperfectly, supplied by the media. That which inspired both sacred and profane authors with poetic imagery, provided the prophets with allegory, fashioned kingly rule, and vested religious hierarchies, is in John 10 put under tribute to furnish the material necessary to paint another facet of the one of whom enough is never said (21:25).

What the evangelist calls a "figure (of speech)" (10:6) is a miniature that might well be titled an allegory of legitimacy. There is only one legitimate way to enter the sheepfold; any other is suspect, to say the least. Any other would be the way of "a thief and a bandit," but certainly not that of "the shepherd of the sheep."

To him the gatekeeper opens; the sheep hear his voice, and he calls his own sheep by name and leads them out (10:3).

To those who can draw on the storehouse of their childhood memory, the image is faithful in all its details. Sheep are not paragons of intelligence in the animal kingdom. They do not belong to our vocabulary of praise. Yet, to anyone who has ever contemplated the sight of a vast flock responding to the calls of the various shepherds at the end of the day, the wonder is lasting. The sight of that sea of wool dividing and splitting into distinct flocks, each following its own shepherd, might still provide a salutary lesson to tourist groups in the museums of the world.

What needs underlining in the evangelist's description, however, is "he calls his own sheep by name." For this phrase stresses, not only a mutuality of knowledge (10:14), but an intimacy which calling by one's name ought to have preserved despite the promiscuous camaraderie of today's crowds.

The Shepherd as Leader

When he has brought out all his own, he goes before them, and the sheep follow him, for they know his voice (10:4).

The shepherd, by definition, is a leader, however inglorious. Nevertheless, obscured though this image might be today by our electronic gadgetry, the shepherd-leader does indeed go before, does precede, those that follow him. "Going before" the flock is the mark of the true shepherd.

That the "sheep follow him, for they know his voice" insists on the bond of mutual knowledge and intimacy which binds the sheep to their shepherd. The shepherd "calls his own sheep by name and leads them out" (10:3). The sheep follow their shepherd because–in the words of that psalm to which preachers and movie directors alike have recourse when the neap inspiration is upon them–he leads them "beside still waters; he restores [their] life" (Ps 23:2–3).

Parable and Allegory

A stranger they will not follow, but they will flee from him, for they do not know the voice of strangers (10:5).

This repeats negatively what the preceding verse (10:4) depicted positively. The sheep follow only the shepherd they know. They fear strangers, and will not follow unknown voices.

This figure Jesus used with them, but they did not understand what he was saying to them (10:6).

These verses (10:1–5) are a typical parable, what the text calls "this figure" of speech. Of course, all parables are figures of speech. That the hearers "did not understand" the figure is the consequence of an ambiguity that belongs to the nature of any parable. A parable, moreover, presents an added difficulty, a difficulty engendered perhaps by its inherent ambiguity. It gives one the impulse to allegorize its content, i.e., to read it in such a way as to discover a one-to-one correspondence between the parable and that to which it refers. Thus, for example, one is inclined to identify who the "gatekeeper" or the "gate" is, or to take it for granted that the "sheepfold" stands for the church (see, however, v. 16, "I have other sheep, that are not of this fold"). Such an impulse to read the parable as an allegory should, however, be resisted, even though the very next verse seems to invite it. But, in fact, the following verse starts a new line of thought.

THE GOOD SHEPHERD (John 10:7–18)

So Jesus again said to them, "Amen, amen, I say to you, I am the door of the sheep" (10:7).

Jesus proceeds to help his hearers understand what he had just told them. He does so by using again the "Amen, amen" formula to introduce another "I AM" saying. As has already been noted (see above on 6:35 and 8:12), such sayings, by their very nature, make a claim to exclusivity. Jesus insists that the only door by which the sheep can enter the sheepfold, the sole mode of access to it, is he who says, "I am the door of the sheep." There is no other way possible to enter the sheepfold, no other access available. The reader can, therefore, readily understand the danger in allegorizing such a figure with all the momentous consequences of arbitrating inclusion in and exclusion from the fold of Christ.

The Intolerance of the Revelation

The claim to exclusivity in the "I AM" sayings has been spoken of as characterizing the "intolerance of the revelation." By the nature of things, any revelation which claims to bring salvation has to be unique and exclusive. Therefore, such a revelation can tolerate no rivals. Such tolerance would make it suspect and even rob it of meaning. Someone who claims to bring salvation does not and cannot pretend to be just another savior among so many. When Jesus says, "I am the door of the sheep," he means the sole access to the redemption is he and he alone. He will repeat this by saying in the farewell discourse, "I am the way" (14:6).

There is, however, a danger in speaking of the "intolerance of the revelation." Those who believe in the Revealer will be easily tempted to leap to the wrong conclusion. They will arrogate to themselves the intolerance that belongs rightly to the revelation itself. They readily forget they are only the undeserving recipients of an unmerited gift, not the appointed arbiters of who can and who cannot receive it. Worse still, they imagine themselves as somehow worthy of the gift, and therefore in a position to fend off those whom they deem unworthy.

Thieves and Robbers

All who came before me are thieves and robbers; but the sheep did not heed them (10:8).

This sweeping condemnation of all who preceded him as "thieves and robbers" only makes explicit the uniqueness of his position. Because he alone is the Revealer, and therefore the sole access to salvation and life, then anyone else who makes such a claim can only be an impostor. This might sit ill with our broad-mindedness and the readiness with which we pretend to welcome all offers of salvation however contradictory. But such illogic–if this be the right word for it–is in us, not in the revelation that Jesus brings. By demanding that the Revealer and the revelation accommodate every claimant to the title, and by pretending that all offers of salvation are equally valid, we void the revelation of its meaning, and the Revealer of his unique mission: "I am the door of the sheep" (10:7, 9).

Moreover, the "all who came before me" has to be understood first in the light of the Johannine community. They regarded all other claimants to the messianic role, to the Sonship, and to the revelation, as false pretenders ("Who is the liar but he who denies that Jesus is the Christ? This is the antichrist, he who denies the Father and the Son," 1 Jn 2:22). The Christian community today, however, is inclined to look outside its own confines for the "thieves and robbers." But, in its completely different position, this community ought rather to look within its own ranks for such "thieves and robbers." They are those who, in its midst, are the purveyors of easier and more alluring means of access to the revelation, those who within it offer more "modern" and more amenable substitutes for the salvation that Jesus Christ alone brings. Only he who has "life in himself" (5:26) can be the bearer of the revelation that gives eternal life (3:16, 36).

I am the door; if any one enters by me, he will be saved, and will go in and out and find pasture (10:9).

This puts it all very clearly. Another "I AM" saying reiterates the preceding verse. Jesus here says explicitly that he is the only available access to salvation.

It should be noted here that, although compared to the other gospels, the verb "to save" is relatively rare in the fourth gospel (see 3:17; 5:34; 11:12; 12:27, 47), this verse is one instance of its use, "he will be saved." Its usage in this context only underlines Jesus' unique role.

That the one saved "will go in and out and find pasture" is a reference, in typically biblical phraseology (Dt 28:6; 1 Sam 29:6; Ps 121:8, etc.; see also Is 49:9; Ez 34:14; Ps 23:2), not only to a stable state of affairs, but also to the whole life of the one saved. Such a life is secure in the knowledge of salvation and the possession of eternal life. It manifests this security in all its dealings, in all its "going out and...coming in" (Ps 121:8).

Life Abundant

> **The thief comes only to steal and kill and destroy; I came that they may have life, and have it abundantly (10:10).**

To be sure, the negative first part of the statement serves to contrast "the thief" with "the good shepherd" (10:11). But it also serves to highlight the sweeping claim of the second part, "I came that they may have life, and have it abundantly." Moreover, the negative statement, "the thief comes only to steal and kill and destroy," sounds a warning. It alerts all those who belong to the community of believers to be on their guard against anyone and everyone who comes making an offer of life. Neither personal piety, nor ecclesiastical dignity, nor academic prominence can mislead us into accepting such alternative offers for what they are not and cannot possibly be. In the final analysis, all the "thieves" can do is "steal and kill and destroy." The history of the church, the chronicles of religious communities, and the contemporary claims and counterclaims to true salvation furnish many sorry illustrations, not just how deadly all such "thieves" can be, but how exclusive the claim of the Revealer to offer life in fact is.

The entire purpose of the coming of the Revealer into the world is that "they may have life, and have it abundantly." To have life "abundantly" is to have it without limit, without the threat of termination and definitive severance by death.

In reading John or any of the other evangelists, we cannot ever allow ourselves to forget that they all wrote out of their resurrection faith. Their mode of reasoning was, inevitably, the reverse of ours. They started with the given of the gospel that the crucified Jesus was raised from the dead, and they worked their way–as it were–back to the life of Jesus of Nazareth and upward to his origin.

The fourth evangelist does just this. The purpose of Jesus' coming into the world is that "they may have life." We know from the rest of the gospel that "life" is not mere survival, nor simple existence without end, but the "eternal life" which all those who believe in him possess. The believers know that, though they must die one day, yet shall they live: "Who believes in me, though he die, yet shall he live" (11:25). They know that in this gift of "eternal life," which must remain as incomprehensible to those who do not believe in him as it is mysterious to those who do, they have the certainty that "whoever lives and believes in me *shall never die*" (11:26). This is what to have life "abundantly" means.

He came into the world for the purpose of giving this life. This life is what he alone can give. No one else could or ever can give it. This is why a few verses ago mention was made of the "intolerance of the revelation" (see on 10:7). It is precisely in the exclusivity of this revelation that we have the freedom which allows us to escape the lure of those who claim to offer us better, more attractive, or more genuine life. The exclusivity of the revelation which Jesus brings releases us from the fear of those who preposterously claim the power to deprive us of what the only Son came to the world to give us, and what only he can give us "more abundantly."

I am the good shepherd. The good shepherd lays down his life for the sheep (10:11).

This is the third successive "I AM" saying: "I am the door of the sheep" (10:7) which is repeated in "I am the door" (10:9). The "I am the good shepherd" here will be reiterated in 10:14. The repetition itself should alert us to the importance of a Johannine theme that is rich in artistic and theological implications.

From the earliest centuries, Christian iconography delighted in this theme of the good shepherd and its representation. In the Roman Empire the image was already there to use. Representations of the god Hermes carrying a sheep abounded, and all Christians had to do to "christianize" them was change the name. But the "I am the good shepherd" cannot be reduced just to the warmth and glow of some mosaic or other amid the vast artistic detritus of the Roman Empire.

Jesus' claim to be the "good shepherd" becomes even more comprehensible by contrast with the prophetic portraits of the bad ones: "For the shepherds are stupid...and all their flock is scattered" (Jer 10:21); "Woe to the shepherds who destroy and scatter the sheep of my pasture! says the Lord" (Jer 23:1). But none can compare with Ezekiel's great indictment of the bad shepherds in one of the most unjustly neglected passages of the Bible:

> Thus says the Lord God: Ho, shepherds of Israel who have been feeding yourselves! Should not shepherds feed the sheep? You eat the fat, you clothe yourselves with the wool, you slaughter the fatlings; but you do not feed the sheep. The weak you have not strengthened, the sick you have not healed, the crippled you have

> not bound up, the strayed you have not brought back, the lost you have not sought, and with force and harshness you have ruled them. So they were scattered, because there was no shepherd; and they became food for all the wild beasts. My sheep were scattered, they wandered over all the mountains and on every high hill; my sheep were scattered over all the face of the earth, with none to search or seek for them (Ez 34:2–6).

Nothing in John's gospel could quite match either the bitterness or the vehemence of this attack on the "shepherds of Israel."

His Life for His Sheep

The whole significance of the "I AM" saying in John 10:11, however, is not that Jesus is the "good shepherd" but the reason why he is "good." He is good because he lays down his life "for his sheep." Even in the gospel of John, it is only from the foot of the cross that Jesus of Nazareth can be comprehensible at all. If what some of the theories proposed to explain the composition of the gospel claim is true, if the Johannine community really was one that clustered around the "beloved disciple" and preserved his recollections and teachings, then his presence at the foot of the cross (19:26) would be the kind of icon that is a most suitable colophon for his gospel.

The reason the good shepherd is the savior of the sheep (10:9), the reason he can give them life in abundance (10:10), is precisely the fact that he laid down his life "*for* the sheep" (10:11). Commentators have often remarked on the absence from the fourth gospel of a soteriology, that is to say, a doctrine of redemption, an elaboration of the meaning of the death of Jesus "for us." This is true as far as it goes. There are very few occurrences in John of such vocabulary of the redemption as can be found elsewhere in the New Testament. There is, nevertheless, repeated reference to the redemptive death of Jesus in the fourth gospel: in John the Baptist's witness to him "who takes away the sins of the world" (1:29); in the identification of the bread of life "which I shall give *for* the world" as "my flesh" (6:51); and here in the good shepherd who "lays down his life *for* the sheep." These instances are few, but quite telling.

The saying in 10:11 in particular, "I am the good shepherd. The good shepherd lays down his life for his sheep," provides the clue for understanding Jesus' function both as savior and the giver of life. Even in the fourth gospel, where sometimes the passion and crucifixion of

Jesus give the impression of being an uninterrupted pageant of triumph, the cross remains the revelation *par excellence*. It makes everything else comprehensible. All the signs and utterances of the Revealer find their intelligibility in it.

The next two verses underline the uniqueness of the good shepherd and his saving function by a contrast:

> **He who is a hireling and not a shepherd, whose own the sheep are not, sees the wolf coming and leaves the sheep and flees; and the wolf snatches them and scatters them. He flees because he is a hireling and cares nothing for the sheep (10:12–13).**

The object of the caring distinguishes the bad shepherds from the good one. The "hirelings" care only for themselves, all their pious protestations to the contrary notwithstanding. They are hirelings because gain, personal gain, whether in material goods or social standing or—most often—both, is their true motive in everything they do. In the final analysis, they care nothing for the sheep. Now, no less than when John 10 was written, institutional abstractions claim the zeal of "the hirelings." They speak ever so volubly of "the nation" (11:50) or "the church," or "the faithful." But such hirelings are ignorant and mindless of all who constitute such abstractions, all the individual members of nation or community or church, except of course those who can further their own careers.

The Fold and the Church

In contrast with this, the good shepherd can say:

> **I am the good shepherd; I know my own and my own know me (10:14).**

This "I AM" saying adds another determinative characteristic to the relationship between the shepherd and his sheep: the mutuality of knowledge between them.

The good shepherd knows his own, he knows them individually, by name ("he calls his own sheep by name" 10:3). It should be recalled here that, since he in fact has "other sheep, that are not of this fold" (10:16), these can by no stretch of the imagination be called "anonymous" (see on 5:37 above). They are certainly not nameless to the shepherd (10:3). That their name appears on no church register is neither here nor there. Evidently, therefore, you cannot identify "the fold" with "the church" without further ado.

The knowledge between the shepherd and his sheep is, moreover, reciprocal. The good shepherd knows his own, and they in turn know him: they "hear his voice" (10:3); they "follow him, for they know his voice" (10:4). Consequently, "a stranger they will not follow" (10:5). The flock of sheep do this naturally, by instinct; and the wonder of it all never palls. The flock of the good shepherd, too, has done this for centuries: they have known his voice and followed him. They have done so throughout the ages with little recognition from the shepherds. A minor corollary on the *sensus fidelium*, the understanding of the believers, appended sometimes to more imposing tomes on the authority and the power of the "shepherds of Israel," is all the acknowledgment they merit.

Reciprocal Knowledge

The assertion of the mutual knowledge between the good shepherd and his sheep is of still greater importance. It is patterned on the mutual and reciprocal knowledge of the Father and the Son which is at the heart of the revelation

> **...as the Father knows me and I know the Father; and I lay down my life for the sheep (10:15).**

It is, of course, this reciprocal knowledge between the Father and the Son that makes the Son the Revealer of the Father (see 5:17, 19, 30, "I seek not my own will but the will of him who sent me"; 7:28; 14:10, "I am in the Father and the Father in me"). The intimate relationship of the Father and the Son, which is described by the mutuality of their knowledge and love (3:35; 5:20; 15:9; 17:23, 24), is made manifest in the obedience of the Son to the will of the Father in everything the Son says and does. This relationship is supremely revealed in the Son's laying down his "life for the sheep," which manifests, not only his, but also the Father's love for them.

It should be obvious, then, that the mutuality of the knowledge between the sheep and the good shepherd is similarly manifested in their obedience to him. "The sheep hear his voice" (10:3). The good shepherd "leads them...goes before them," and "they follow, for they know his voice" (10:4). It is their knowledge of the good shepherd's voice that makes them follow and obey him "to the end" (13:1).

One Flock

And I have other sheep, that are not of this fold; I must bring them also, and they will heed my voice. So there shall be one flock, one shepherd (10:16).

Though not exactly a primary text in the elaboration of ecclesiologies, and though dutifully trotted out annually by ecumenists, this is a sadly neglected element in our understanding of the community of believers in Jesus Christ. The least it ought to have done would have been to dissuade Christians from their smug certitude of who does and who does not belong to "this fold." It should have made exegetes more reluctant to identify "the fold" with "the church." It ought to have given Christians pause in their dealings with non-Christians, if only because their knowledge of who "the sheep" are, is not coterminous with that of the good shepherd.

There is, to be sure, an urgency ("I must") to bring the whole world into the fold, to make the "other sheep" belong formally–as it were–to "the fold." But this is a task of which the evangelist was acutely aware, perhaps even within his own community and in his generation. It is a task that will go on and on long after Jesus had given expression to it in this pastoral homily (see 11:52 "to gather into one the children of God").

In putting these words, "And I have other sheep" (10:16), on Jesus' lips and in formulating the prayer at the farewell discourse for "those who believe in me through their word" (17:20), the evangelist deliberately calls attention to the continuity between Jesus' work and that of his disciples. Indeed, one may rightly wonder if, while writing his gospel, the evangelist himself was not aware of trying to do just that, that is, of continuing the work of Jesus, "So there shall be one flock, one shepherd."

The Death on the Cross

For this reason the Father loves me, because I lay down my life, that I may take it again. No one takes it from me, but I lay it down of my own accord. I have power to lay it down, and I have power to take it again; this [command] I have received from my Father" (10:17–18).

It is important to render the word, which the RSV translates as "charge," by "command" or "commandment," as it does elsewhere

(12:49, 50; 13:34; 14:15; 15:10, 12), and as the NRSV does here in 10:18. For this obedience to the command of the Father is at the root of the Father's love for the Son and the Son's for the Father: "just as I have kept my Father's commandments and abide in his love" (15:10). Laying down his life for the sheep–as the "good shepherd" must (10:11)–does in fact reveal the reason why the Father loves him (10:17). The love of the Father for him is precisely what enables him to add, "that I may take it again," the reference being, of course, to his resurrection from the dead.

This is why Jesus insists, "No one takes [my life] from me, but I lay it down of my own accord" (10:18a). Such a statement denies the reality neither of the humanity nor of the death of Jesus. It merely puts the malignity of those who encompassed his death in its proper perspective. Above all else, Jesus' statement underlines the fact that the intelligibility of his death on the cross is to be sought elsewhere than in the allotment of guilt either to the Jews or to the Romans.

What intelligibility the death of Jesus on the cross does possess should be sought in its revelation of the total conformity of the Son's will to the Father, to the "command I have received from my Father" (10:18). Such revelation is, when all is said and done, not a revelation of subservience, "*I have power* to lay it down, and I have power to take it again" (10:18). It is a revelation of love, "For this reason the Father loves me, because I lay down my life" (10:17).

DIVISION AND DISPUTE (John 10:19–39)

There was again a division among the Jews because of these words. Many of them said, "He has a demon, and he is mad; why listen to him?" Others said, "These are not the sayings of one who has a demon. Can a demon open the eyes of the blind?" (10:19–21).

The "division among the Jews" is, in fact, only a reflection of the division "because of these words," then as now. The revelation always causes such a split. There can be only one of two responses to it: acceptance or rejection. When once one is resolved to reject "these words," any reason whatever will do. Not all the reasons are negative, like judging the Revealer mad or his utterances nonsense. You can well be convinced that his words are "not the saying of one who has a demon," and leave it at that. You can even find them "inspiring" or be moved to set them to music. But unless an answer is given that goes well beyond the "Can a demon open the eyes of the blind?" then you are dealing only with a variation on the theme of rejection. There is only one mode of acceptance and that is to recognize, beyond the wonderful signs and beyond the words, the identity of him who works the signs and utters the words.

A rather awkward shift now occurs, and the scene changes. The place is still Jerusalem, but the time is the feast of Dedication (= Hanukkah; see Ezra 6:16; 1 Kings 8:63; Num 7:10–11) in the "winter" (December).

It was the feast of the Dedication at Jerusalem; it was winter, and Jesus was walking in the temple, in the portico of Solomon (10:22–23).

Could this segment have been a later insertion? Is it somehow misplaced here by accident or by design? Whatever explanation you wish finally to adopt in order to explain this and very many other "out of place" clusters of verses throughout the gospel, you should keep in mind that the gospel of John as we have it today underwent several stages of composition, of editing and redaction before it acquired its present form and structure. But, however you may choose to resolve such genuine problems in the fourth gospel, your focus of attention must not be diverted away from what is its very core: the revelation of Jesus Christ.

The Christ

So the Jews gathered round him and said to him, "How long will you keep us in suspense? If you are the Christ, tell us plainly" (10:24).

One can very readily understand their impatience and appreciate at its true worth their anxiety to find out the answer to their question. Yet you cannot help but wonder how many among them would have reacted to "I who speak to you am he" (4:26) the way the Samaritan woman did (4:28–29).

A word here is necessary about "the Christ." It renders the Greek word *christos*, which is itself a translation of the Hebrew *messiah*, the anointed one. Now, there are only two instances in the entire New Testament where the Hebrew word is itself transliterated into the Greek as *messias*, "messiah." Both instances are in John, in 1:41 and

4:25 "I know that Messiah is coming (he who is called Christ)." The RSV respects this and uses "Messiah" in these two verses, and uses "Christ" everywhere else, following the Greek original.

The NRSV, however, does not. It uses "Messiah" throughout, except at 4:25 where, to avoid a tautology, it is forced to follow the original. As a translation decision this does irreparable damage to the fidelity to the Greek for which the RSV is rightly respected. As an ecumenical gesture, it is dubious, if not suspect. If the NRSV preserved "Christ" in "Jesus Christ" merely as a personal name (1:17; 17:3), then it transgressed the limits of translation. This is an excellent example of ultracrepidarianism, of the cobbler not sticking to his last.

Scholars continue to debate the nature of the so-called "messianic" expectations prevalent in Jesus' world. They agree that such expectations were varied, not just in their specifics, but also in the general categories to which they could be assigned. Some expectations were religious, others political, still others revolutionary, and many a varied mix of these. Some expected a new Moses; others, a returned Elijah; others, a descendant of David to sit on the throne of his father forever; and still others awaited nothing short of the end of the world and the dawn of a new creation. To gather all these varied hopes and longings under the one rubric of "messianic expectation" is simplistic, and can be misleading. But, given the present context, it can be of some service.

Whatever "the Jews" had in mind when they asked, "If you are the Christ, tell us plainly," it was clearly not what Jesus himself had in mind.

Jesus answered them, "I told you, and you do not believe" (10:25a).

They did not believe simply because they could not and did not want to believe. They did not believe because what Jesus told them was not what they wanted to believe, was not what they had been led to expect. They knew what they wanted to see in the Messiah when he came, and nobody was going to change that.

Theirs was not a philosophical theory, but a religious conviction. Such conviction is not susceptible to change by debate and argument. It illustrates yet again the concluding words of John 9: No one is more deaf than they who refuse to hear; and no one is less in need of light than those who think they see. "If you were blind, you would have no guilt; but now that you say, 'We see,' your guilt remains" (9:41). This must be what the poet had in mind when he spoke of "tears at the heart of things."

Belonging to His Sheep

The works I do in my Father's name, they bear witness to me; but you do not believe, because you do not belong to my sheep (10:25b–26).

Everything Jesus says and does testifies to his true identity, to the fact that "the Father has sent me" (5:36), that "the Father is in me and I am in the Father" (10:38; 14:11). The recognition of who he really is, i.e., faith in his person, is the sole condition of belonging to his sheep. They who "do not believe" show that they "do not belong to" his sheep.

Thus, it is your attitude toward him, your response to him and to the revelation he brings, that discloses your true identity. The "because you do not belong to my sheep" cannot, therefore, be regarded as a prior decree of anyone's exclusion from the fold. The freedom to accept or to reject him remains essential to the whole process. A God who arbitrarily excludes some is as incredible as a God who capriciously includes others. A creature that is not free to say no, like the creature who has no choice but to say yes, is little better than a stone. The whole gift of God's revelation makes no sense unless those who hear it have the freedom both to accept and to reject it. If the creator were to tamper with this, the creatures would cease to be the human beings who can "walk before God in the light of life" (Ps 56:13; see Jn 5:40).

"Shall never perish"

My sheep hear my voice, and I know them, and they follow me; and I give them eternal life, and they shall never perish, and no one shall snatch them out of my hand (10:27–28).

The sheep "hear his voice" (10:3), they attend to it, they obey it. This is why they "follow" him. He leads them, and they "go in and out and find pasture" (10:9). What he gives them is "eternal life," the true life for which everything in their innermost being craves. They need only "hear his voice" to have this gift of eternal life.

The gift is not only freely given but securely granted: "They shall *never* perish." As Paul reminds his readers, "The gifts and the call of God are irrevocable" (Rom 11:29; cf. Jn 16:22). They are irrevocable not only because of the nature of any genuine gift, but because of the nature of the giver. Hence, the need to remind all mortals who are granted this gift of eternal life and yet face the necessity of dying that "they shall *never* perish." Only the God who "raises the dead and gives them life" (Jn 5:21a) can accomplish this. The astonishing part of the revelation is that God has granted the Son power to give "life to whom he will" (5:21b; see 17:2). What is true of the Father is true of the Son.

Those who come to the Son that they "may have life" (5:40), those who hear his voice and are therefore part of his flock, are not only rid of the fear of losing this gift, "they shall *never* perish," but also armed against all those who pretend to deprive them of it: "*No one* shall snatch them out of my hands" (10:28). The "no one" is absolute. No institution, no person, no power on earth can separate a sheep from the good shepherd. It is, nevertheless, a source of endless wonderment to see how ready we are to believe otherwise, to forget that the only way to lose the gift is to reject it, to refuse to hear the voice of the shepherd, to refuse to follow him, and to deliberately reject his offer of eternal life.

My Father, who has given them to me, is greater than all, and no one is able to snatch them out of the Father's hand (10:29).

It is admirable how the reader of the gospel is never allowed to forget that the whole life of the Revealer is in obedience to the Father. Lest we forget even for an instant the reason why "no one shall snatch them out of *my* hand" (10:28), we are immediately reminded that those who belong to the flock are in fact the gift of the Father to the Son: "My Father, who has given them to me" (6:37, 39; 17:6, 10). The security and the permanence of the gift rests solely on the fact that the Father "is greater than all."

The Unity of the Father and the Son

Therefore, when Jesus says, "No one shall snatch them out of my hand" (10:28), he is only repeating what the reader must already know. His statement is, in fact, tantamount to saying "no one is able to snatch them out of the Father's hand." The reason for this astonishing statement can only be:

I and the Father are one (10:30; cf. 17:11, 21–23).

To believe this seems to us as natural as the air we breathe. To those who heard it within the monotheism of the first century, it could scarcely have been anything but arrant blasphemy.

But, before we come to the predictable reaction of Jesus' hearers, there is a point to keep in mind, or merely to recall from our catechism. When Jesus makes this astounding claim in the fourth gospel, he maintains the distinction of "I" and "the Father"; else there could be no real talk of unity. Unity is always between two or more. This distinction in unity will, of course, be an important element in the reflection of later centuries on the mystery of the Trinity.

What we are likely to overlook in these words of Jesus, however, is that he does not say, "I and God are one." The whole reason why he makes the claim at all is not to arrogate to himself the divinity, but to make clear that his mission as the Son is to carry out the will of the Father who sent him (see 4:34; 5:30). It is in this obedience to the will of the Father that he witnesses to his true Sonship. By the totality of his obedience he reveals God as his Father. It is because of the total conformity of his will, because of his obedience, to the will of the Father, that he can say, "I and *the Father* are one."

The Jews took up stones again to stone him (10:31).

Their reaction, of course, is comprehensible. For, unlike the readers of the gospel, unlike those who believe in Jesus, they have no way of understanding his words except as blasphemy. If, as seems quite likely, there was a split within the Johannine community which consisted largely of Jewish converts to the faith in Jesus, then the split must have been over just such a statement. Many willingly enough accepted him as Messiah, prophet, King of Israel, and even Son of God. But the claim to be "the Son" of the Father must have been just too much for them.

The Blasphemy

Indeed the ensuing dialogue leaves no doubt where the stumbling block lay:

Jesus answered them, "I have shown you many good works from the Father; for which of these do you stone me?" The Jews answered him, "It is not for a good work that we stone you but for blasphemy; because you, being a man, make yourself God" (10:32–33).

To them, the whole point is the manifest "blasphemy" of such a claim. In the uncompromising monotheism of their faith, what else could it have been? Pascal could say, "Jesus Christ is the true God of men"

(*Pensées* 547). But Pascal was the beneficiary of centuries of reflection on just how Jesus of Nazareth could be who he really is without putting in jeopardy the uniqueness and the unicity of God, which is at the heart of the entire biblical revelation.

A necessary word of caution. John, of course, is giving expression to his own and to his community's faith in Jesus of Nazareth by employing this narrative device of the dialogue between Jesus and the Jews. We must not, with our enormous benefit of hindsight, read Jesus' words in that context to be more than a claim to divinity. We have to keep in mind that there is a vast difference between "I and the Father are one," and a Jew of Jesus' time claiming, "I am God!"

"You, being a man, make yourself God" (10:33). The difficulty cannot be gotten around simply by denying that he was a man. We who speak so readily of the God-man, who recite without hesitation the creed's "true God and true man," are apt to forget how long it took the church to reach this formulation. Nor did the problem vanish even then. Every generation, including ours, tends to tip the balance one way or the other, so hard is it to keep the humanity and the divinity together in the one Jesus of Nazareth.

The Mission of the Son

Jesus answered them, "Is it not written in your law, 'I said you are gods'? If he called them gods to whom the word of God came (and scripture cannot be broken), do you say of him whom the Father consecrated and sent into the world, 'You are blaspheming,' because I said, 'I am the Son of God'?" (10:34–36).

By depicting the discussion of a biblical text (Ps 82:6, "I say you are gods, sons of the Most High, all of you") in a typically rabbinic style of argument, the evangelist tries to right the balance. The reference to "*your* law" should not mislead us. The "scripture," "the word of God," "your law," to which Jesus refers is, of course, what we call the Old Testament. It was the only "scripture" Jesus ever had, and the only "scripture" all who wrote the New Testament ever knew. Self-evident though this fact be, it is all but forgotten by Christians.

The important point to grasp in Jesus' response to his accusers is his insistence on his mission by the Father. That, ultimately, is the heart of the dialogue. You can discuss and debate when and how "the Father consecrated" him whom he sent; but you should not overlook what this "consecration/sanctification" means. A thing or a person is "consecrated" when dedicated wholly to the service of God. It is therefore "holy" by reason of its belonging to God. Now, everything Jesus does and says is the "work of the Father." His entire life is one uninterrupted act of obedience to the will of the Father who "consecrated and sent" him into the world. This and this alone is the reason for believing in him as "the Son of God":

> **If I am not doing the works of my Father, then do not believe in me; but if I do them, even though you do not believe me, believe the works, that you may know and understand that the Father is in me and I am in the Father" (10:37–38).**

This is the significance of everything Jesus does and says throughout the fourth gospel. All his words and all his deeds are "the works of the Father." To see them as such is to believe in the true identity of him whom the Father has sent into the world. To occupy oneself with the wonders and healings and the raisings from the dead is to avert one's gaze from their true reality as "the works of my Father."

Believe, Know, Understand

When you see these "works" for what they truly are, then you "believe" them as the revelation they are meant to be. Note here how the evangelist links "believe" with "know" and "understand." In Johannine usage, the three verbs, together with the verb "to see," are near synonyms. You cannot do one without the other. There is no believing without knowing, and no knowing without understanding. This is why we have a gospel of John. It teaches us to believe what we know and to understand what we believe.

If you attend to the revelation, whether by seeing the deeds or hearing the words, not just as the words and deeds of Jesus of Nazareth, but as the works of the Father who sent him, then and only then will you come to understand that "the Father is in me and I am in the Father" (10:38). The unity of the Father and the Son is real only because all that the Son does is "the works of my Father" (10:37). He always carries out to the full the will of the Father. To him he remains obedient in everything.

But there is only one way of grasping this fact. It is to believe in Jesus of Nazareth and so to obey the will of the Father. "For this is the will of my Father, that every one who sees the Son and believes in him should have eternal life" (6:40). Is it any wonder then that:

> **Again they tried to arrest him, but he escaped from their hands (10:39).**

The picture, nevertheless, is not so bleak. To be sure, there were those who rejected him, but there were also those who believed in him. Had this not been so, there would have been no gospel of John to remind us of all this.

> **He went away again across the Jordan to the place where John at first baptized, and there he remained. And many came to him; and they said, "John did no sign, but everything that John said about this man was true." And many believed in him there (10:40–42).**

If John did no sign, the one single sign he surely did do is that "He came for testimony, to bear witness to the light, that all might believe through him. He was not the light, but came to bear witness to the light (1:6–8). The witness he bore to the light was true. Thus, however bitter and acrimonious the reaction of those who heard Jesus and saw his signs, however stubborn their refusal to believe in him, there were among them many others who "believed in him." To read the gospel of John today is to realize that there still are.

John 11

The Death of Lazarus: "walk in the light"; Thomas.

The Resurrection and the Life: Martha and Mary; the resurrection of the dead; the resurrection and the life; "shall never die"; death; life.

At Lazarus' Tomb: "Jesus wept"; faith and the signs.

The Raising of Lazarus: prayer and thanksgiving.

The Plot to Kill Jesus.

THE DEATH OF LAZARUS (John 11:1–16)

The miracle of the raising of Lazarus, the climax of the signs in the fourth gospel, is also the incident in the public ministry which John uses as directly contributing to the arrest and crucifixion of Jesus (see 12:17–19). As such, it replaces what in the synoptics is the cleansing of the temple (Mt 21:12–13; Mk 11:15–17; Lk 19:45–46) which, as we have already seen, the fourth evangelist transferred to the beginning of Jesus' public ministry (Jn 2:14–22). That the miracle of bringing the dead Lazarus back to life should be chosen to crown the public ministry of Jesus and be the final major event leading to his condemnation and death is, evidently, a most suitable choice in the gospel of "life."

Now a certain man was ill, Lazarus of Bethany, the village of Mary and her sister Martha. It was Mary who anointed the Lord with ointment and wiped his feet with her hair, whose brother was ill (11:1–2).

A straightforward enough introduction of the *dramatis personae* opens the account. The particular event cited to identify this Mary as the one "who anointed the Lord with ointment and wiped his feet with her hair" will be recounted in the next chapter (12:1–8; see Mt 26:6–13; Mk 14:3–9). Yet the evangelist speaks of it as already familiar to the reader.

Though a rather small point, this mode of procedure should serve to remind us–if we need to be reminded–that the evangelist selects elements from within the tradition about Jesus and arranges them so as to offer his readers, not an essay in critical biography, but a message of salvation through the medium of this and other like incidents in the public ministry. His concern, therefore, is other than biographical and chronological accuracy.

So the sisters went to him, saying, "Lord, he whom you love is ill" (11:3).

The very simplicity of the statement can make one overlook what an astonishing act of faith it is. A simple statement of fact suffices, as when the mother of Jesus says, "They have no wine" (2:3); or the official, "Sir, come down before my child dies" (4:49). True faith is never prolix.

In this narrative we meet for the first time the person called Lazarus, "he whom you love" (11:3). He comes on stage, plays his role (see 12:10, 17), and walks out of history; and, despite all the pious efforts to identify him or trace his subsequent fortunes, we know no more about him. Yet Christians, ever reluctant to give up their cherished notion that the evangelist is writing a history of the life and times of Jesus, rather than proclaiming a message about him, are ever on the lookout for Lazarus' later fate.

But when Jesus heard it he said, "This illness is not unto death; it is for the glory of God, so that the Son of God may be glorified by means of it" (11:4).

The ambiguity of Jesus' opening statement cannot very well escape those who already know the story and its outcome. But the finality of his action easily might. The whole incident finds its intelligibility in its true, stated purpose: the glory of God and the glorification of his Son. This is the theme that the prologue announced (1:14) and the rest of the gospel reiterates (2:11; 5:41, 44; 7:18; 8:50, 54; 11:40; 12:43 see NRSV; 13:31; 17:5, 22, 24). Everything that Jesus says and does throughout the gospel has for its end the glory of God in the glorification of the Son: "Now is the Son of man glorified, and in him God is glorified" (13:31).

Now Jesus loved Martha and her sister and Lazarus. So when he learned that he was ill, he stayed two days longer in the place where he was. Then after this he said to the disciples, "Let us go into Judea again." The disciples said to him, "Rabbi, the Jews were but now seeking to stone you, and are you going there again?" (11:6–8).

Jesus' action always baffles. Just when he is expected to rush to the bedside of his friend Lazarus, he lingers "two days longer" (11:6; cf. 7:3–10). You can, of course, use this and other similar bits of information to construct a character sketch of Jesus. But, apart from its utter uselessness, such a character sketch would miss the mark. It merely averts one's gaze from what the evangelist is trying to convey to the reader. A character sketch of Jesus is useless because its components were simply not furnished by the evangelist for that purpose. Moreover, it is not Jesus' phlegmatic temperament that the gospel proclaims. Jesus' response to the reaction of his disciples should make this clear.

"Walk in the light"

Jesus answered, "Are there not twelve hours in the day? If any one walks in the day, he does not stumble, because he sees the light of this world. But if any one walks in the night, he stumbles, because the light is not in him" (11:9–10).

This puts the disciples' question, "Rabbi, the Jews were but now seeking to stone you, and are you going there again?" (11:7), on a wholly different plane. Jesus' action is the action of the Revealer and, as such, is not dictated by the counsels of human prudence, nor subject to the sequence of logically scheduled events. The opportune time for his action is determined by the Revealer, not by the date of a calendar or the hours of a day or the suitability of the occasion (see 7:6).

The very clear point that Jesus makes is that his presence in the world is an invitation to his followers to "walk in the light" in order to avoid stumbling. It is he, of course, who is this light: "I am the light of the world" (8:12; 9:5; 12:46 and cf. 1:4–5; 12:35–36). Those who walk in the night are bound to stumble; and that night, when "the light of this world" will no longer be there, is fast approaching (see 13:30b).

Thus he spoke, and then he said to them, "Our friend Lazarus has fallen asleep, but I go to wake him out of sleep. The disci-

ples said to him, "Lord, if he has fallen asleep, he will recover." Now Jesus had spoken of his death, but they thought that he meant taking rest in sleep (11:11–13).

Because of the disciples' lack of comprehension, Jesus spells out the situation in terms even they could readily grasp. This is again the device of misunderstanding in the fourth gospel, which the evangelist uses to illustrate the great condescension of the Revealer. Not for him the lofty and arcane revelations of bearers of heavenly messages for the select few. The Word speaks in accents intelligible to all, even to the unlettered and the obtuse.

Yet, even when Jesus explains his intent in simple language, his disciples miss the ordinary play on words in "to sleep," from the Greek equivalent of which (*koimao*) we have our word "cemetery." You can argue that the disciples' lack of understanding was only the expression of ordinary human reluctance to believe that their friend is in fact dead. This is the incredulity with which we all greet the death of a loved one: "Our friend Lazarus has fallen asleep" (11:11). Death will always run up against the denial of its inescapable finality.

Then Jesus told them plainly, "Lazarus is dead; and for your sake I am glad that I was not there, so that you may believe. But let us go to him" (11:14–15).

The whole purpose of the narrative is thus summed up in "that you may believe." All other elements in it can be a distraction from, or an evasion of, this clearly stated purpose of the entire gospel (see 20:31; cf. 1:12; 19:35). Thus, the skillfully knitted details, the dramatic pauses, the vivid portrayals are there to serve the one purpose: "that you may believe" (see 11:42 "that they may believe that you have sent me"; cf. 2:11, 23; 6:29).

Thomas

Thomas, called the Twin, said to his fellow disciples, "Let us go, that we may die with him" (11:16).

The literal-minded we always have with us. It seems as though nothing Jesus said to the disciples (11:8–16) really meant anything to Thomas. However laudable his enthusiasm, his deafness is almost laughable. Like all his imitators down the centuries, those who keep insisting against all and everyone, "But it says right here in the good book," Thomas had made up his mind on just what Jesus is all about, and there was an end to it. Even, as in John 11, the words of Jesus himself cannot deflect or budge him from what he "knows" (cf. 9:24, 29; 6:42; 7:27).

We are accustomed to regard Thomas as "doubting Thomas" because of his stubborn behavior in the resurrection appearance, "Unless I see in his hands the print of the nails, and place my fingers in the mark of the nails, and place my hand in his side, I will not believe" (20:25). But, by casting him in that skeptical role, Christian piety lost a model far truer to its life of faith than Thomas' doubt. The truth of the matter is that Thomas was not a victim of doubt. No doubt disturbed his firm, stubborn assurance, either in the present narrative or at the resurrection appearance. No one and nothing could assail the secure stronghold of his knowledge. He is the undeclared patron of the Christians who will not be bothered with anything they don't already "know."

THE RESURRECTION AND THE LIFE (John 11:17–27)

Now when Jesus came, he found that Lazarus had already been in the tomb four days. Bethany was near Jerusalem, about two miles off, and many of the Jews had come to Martha and Mary to console them concerning their brother. When Martha heard that Jesus was coming, she went and met him, while Mary sat at the house. Martha said to Jesus, "Lord, if you had been here, my brother would not have died. And even now I know that whatever you ask from God, God will give you" (11:17–22).

Martha and Mary

Those who have made "spiritual" capital out of the narrative of Martha and Mary in Luke 10:38–42, might do well to reflect upon the inversion of their roles in this chapter. In John 11, it is clearly Martha who is eager to hear the Lord's teaching (Lk 10:39), "while Mary sat at the house" (Jn 11:20; cf. 12:2–3). In John's gospel, Martha is the paragon. Yet, when one considers the endless quantities of pious froth which the Lucan narrative has generated about the ideal of the Christian life, about the "one thing is needful" (Lk 10:42), something akin to despair is bound to supervene in the heart of any interpreter.

Martha's request is, of course, an act of faith in the person of Jesus. She not only confesses her firm belief in his power to work miracles, "Lord, if you had been here, my brother would not have died" (Jn 11:21), but also acknowledges his unique relationship to God. Martha believes that the mere presence of Jesus at her brother's bedside would have sufficed to hold back the rapacious hand of death. But, now that her brother has actually died, she knows, however vaguely, that "whatever you ask from God, God will give you" (11:22). She could not then have known what the reader already knows, viz., that her request was nothing short of asking to have the dead brought back to life.

Martha not only knew the finality and irreversibility of death itself, but also believed God to be the sole and unique origin of life. Nevertheless, her words to Jesus keep that very knowledge of human mortality–as it were–in abeyance. She can thus say with unbounded confidence, "And even now I know that whatever you ask of God, God will give you" (11:22).

The Resurrection of the Dead

Jesus said to her, "Your brother will rise again" (11:23).

His response once again occasions a misunderstanding which will set the stage for a further revelation. Martha, like most of the Jews of her time, believed in the resurrection of the dead, though some other Jews, the "Sadducees...who say there is no resurrection" (Mt 22:23; Acts 23:8) rejected it. Martha believed, that is to say, that at the end of time God will raise the dead to life. So, naturally enough, this is what she took Jesus to mean by his answer:

Martha said to him, "I know that he will rise again in the resurrection of the last day" (11:24).

What she had asked for was some remedy for the loss of her brother, perhaps even by bringing him back to life. She evidently did not have in mind "the resurrection of the last day," when all the dead, her brother included, will be raised to life. That was, at it were, an article of her creed, not the import of her present request, "And even now I know that whatever you ask from God, God will give you" (11:22).

The reason for belaboring this point here is the misunderstanding to which it is implicitly subjected whenever we speak of the "resurrection of Lazarus." What we have to keep in mind is the fundamental difference between a Lazarus who is brought back to life only to have to die some time later, and a Jesus who rises from the dead never to die again. The "resurrection of the dead" belongs to this latter category. Lazarus himself died sometime after the miracle, as he evidently had to; so did the only son of the widow of Nain in Luke 7:11–17, and the daughter of the ruler in Mark 5:35–42 (cf. "the child is not dead but sleeping" in Mk 5:39 with "Our friend Lazarus has fallen asleep" in Jn 11:11).

The Resurrection and the Life

Jesus said to her, "I am the resurrection and the life" (11:25a).

You can read Jesus' statement as a reference to his own resurrection and then the "I AM" formula here would be a straightforward subject-predicate "identification" (see above on 6:35). But it makes better sense at this juncture in the narrative to read it like most of the other "I AM" sayings, the personal pronoun being the predicate in the sentence, not its subject, so that what Jesus says is, "the resurrection of the dead is I." He is not saying, "I am the risen one." What he asserts in this "I AM" saying is that all that Martha and every other believer in the resurrection expected, looked and hoped for, finds its ultimate reality and fulfilment in him. This is why his affirmation links together "the resurrection" and "the life."

The gift of life–and by "life" John always understands eternal life–is a gift to *mortal* human beings. With or without this gift, they all have to die. No one is exempted from this law of mortality, not even the Word become flesh. "Flesh" means subjection to mortality: "All flesh is grass" (Is 40:6). Indeed the subjection to the ineluctable law of death is a primary meaning of this "flesh" which the Word became (1:14).

Now, to him as the only Son of the Father, the Father who "has life in himself" has also granted "to have life in himself" (5:26). This is the fact which is demonstrated and proclaimed by raising the Son from the dead. So, too, to those to whom the Son grants eternal life, he himself is the resurrection. As mortal human beings they face the fact of death; but as believers in the Son who possess his gift of eternal life here and now, they can confidently look forward to their own resurrection from the dead. Of course, you have to die before you can rise from the dead never to die again; else, the resurrection would be merely a resuscitation. This is why the Jesus who died and rose from the dead can say to all who believe in him, "I am the resurrection *and* the life." Therefore, he goes on to say,

He who believes in me, though he die, yet shall he live, and whoever lives and believes in me shall never die (11:25b–26a).

This puts it all quite succinctly. Those who believe in him still have to die, of course. They are no different in this from anyone else on the face of the earth, including Jesus himself. The "though he die" is real. Yet, given the unavoidable fact of death, it is astonishing how Christians could have actually understood Jesus' statement to mean an exemption from dying, a reprieve from the inescapable need to die. The "yet shall he live" would have no meaning if the death itself were not real.

"Shall never die"

Jesus goes on to say, "whoever lives," whoever has the gift of eternal life because she or he "believes in me," shall in fact live, even though one day each has to die like everyone else. This is not an insertion of a so-called future eschatology in a gospel that repeatedly insists on the possession of eternal life here and now (see 3:16, 36; 5:24; 6:40, 47, 54; 10:10, 28; 17:2–3; 20:31). Therefore, to say that Christians do not die because they have eternal life is manifestly false. What Jesus in fact does say here is, "*even though* he die"–which indeed every one of us must–"*yet* shall he live." This is so because of the resurrection. Therefore, he who is "the resurrection and the life" can say that "whoever *lives* and believes in me shall *never* die," that is, the eternal life which the believer possesses here and now cannot and will not be interrupted even by death. This, of course, is a mystery revealed to us as the object of our faith, not a philosophical thesis on the immortality of the soul.

Death

It is essential to keep in mind that the gospel here in John 11 speaks with an understanding of death that Christians do not usually share. In the gospel of John–which is by no means unique in the New Testament in this regard–death, far from being the separation of the immortal soul from the corrupt body, is total. When I die, the whole "I" dies. The question of the immortal soul does not even arise here at all, even though it is clearly a Christian doctrine. So, in order to understand Jesus' words in this chapter and elsewhere in this gospel, you have to keep firmly in mind the totality of death. The "though he die" is absolute. When God raises us to life, he acts as the creator always acts, he creates out of nothing.

Life

This is why the second part of the statement in 11:26 is all the more astonishing. "Whoever lives and believes in me shall never die" (11:26b). Once again we must keep in mind that "to believe" in Jesus Christ is, in the gospel of John, "to live," to have eternal life (3:15, 36; 5:24; 6:40, 47; 10:10, 28; 11:25; 17:3; 20:31). The gift of eternal life, which can only be the object of faith, is inalienable and uninterruptible. But it is this only to those who believe, only to those who accept eternal life as a gift. Of course, the reason why Jesus can say that they "shall never die" is that he himself in whom they believe is "the resurrection and the life" (11:25).

This is an opportune moment to clarify what "life" is in such a biblical context. You can start by saying that death is the absence of life. Life itself, however, is not mere existence. It is, in its biblical understanding, always life *with* someone. Life is first and foremost life in the presence of, before the face of, God ("that I may walk before God in the light of life" Ps 56:13; 27:8–9; 143:7). It is life with all those whom we love and all who love us (Ps 128; Qoheleth 9:9).

Death irrevocably severs all such relations, with God and with all the living. Thus, the dying Christ on the cross could cry out in Mark, "My God, my God, why have you forsaken me?" (Mk 15:34). What God, and only God the creator, has accomplished in Christ strikes precisely at this severance of relationships. To believe in the resurrection is to believe that death cannot and does not sever the one essential relationship with the living God. It is to hold firmly, moreover, that the relationship with those we love and those who love us will be maintained intact at the resurrection "at the last day."

How God bridges the gap between the actual death of the believer and the resurrection of the dead, I do not know, nor can anyone pretend to know. *When* God will bring this to pass, I do not know, and no one has any means of finding out: "But of that day or that hour no one knows, not even the angels in heaven, nor the Son, but only the Father" (Mk 13:32). Yet this revealed fact of our resurrection is integral and allows no exception. Grasping this fact firmly, in the face of all odds and against all arguments to the contrary, is the indispensable condition for understanding what the second part of the gospel of John will say about the command to love one another.

There are, as we shall see in that second part, no casual encounters for the believers. To those who have the gift of eternal life because they believe in him whom God has sent, love is indeed "strong as death" (Song 8:6). It is "strong as death" in a sense that the author of the Canticle could not have begun to imagine or comprehend.

> **"Do you believe this?" She said to him, "Yes, Lord; I believe that you are the Christ, the Son of God, he who is coming into the world" (11:26b–27).**

The question, of course, is addressed to each of us who reads this gospel. Martha's own response to the question is a crescendo. He in whom she believes is "the Christ" (1:41; 4:25, 29; 7:26, 41; 9:22; 17:3; 20:31), the promised and long-awaited Messiah. He is, she confesses, "the Son of God" (1:34, 49; 3:18; 10:36; 11:4; 19:7). But the climax is reached in her confession that the Jesus who speaks to her here and now is "he who is coming into the world" (1:9 and cf. 3:19; see 5:43; 6:14; 12:46).

Of the three, "the one to come" is the title which responds most directly to Jesus' "I am the resurrection and the life" (11:25). For, in eschatological parlance, "he who is coming into the world" is he who has been promised to come at the end of time, to exercise judgment ("For judgment I came into the world" 9:39; see 5:22), and thus to establish definitively God's reign on earth. It is in accomplishing this that he grants the gift of eternal life to all who believe in him.

By his resurrection from the dead, which is the distinguishing event of the end time, Jesus once and for all establishes the fact that he is "the one who is coming into the world." This, therefore, is what he means when he says, "I am the resurrection and the life" (11:25). This, too, by the way, is the reason why his uniqueness as the one risen from the dead has to be maintained at all cost. It can allow no exception.

Faith in him is eternal life now because we possess the pledge that, though we die, yet shall we live (11:26a). We therefore believe in the resurrection of the dead on the last day because we not only possess eternal life here and now, but also believe that he who is already risen from the dead is indeed the one who "is coming into the world."

AT LAZARUS' TOMB (John 11:28–37)

> **When she had said this, she went and called her sister Mary, saying quietly, "The Teacher is here and is calling for you." And when she heard it, she rose quickly and went to him. Now**

Jesus had not yet come to the village, but was still in the place where Martha had met him. When the Jews who were with her in the house, consoling her, saw Mary rise quickly and go out, they followed her, supposing that she was going to the tomb to weep there. Then Mary, when she came where Jesus was and saw him, fell at his feet, saying to him, "Lord, if you had been here, my brother would not have died" (11:28–32).

It is hard to improve on the narrative, here as elsewhere in the gospel. The genius–and the word is not used idly–who composed it knew what he wanted to say and how to say it briefly and tellingly. He managed to write what is undeniably the most sublime of gospels with the smallest vocabulary of all four gospels.

The title "Lord" which Mary uses to address Jesus, as did Martha before her (11:21, 27), is here a title of respect, as it is not, for instance, in Thomas' confession in 20:28, or in Mary Magdalene's in 20:18. There is, to be sure, no doubt of Jesus' love for the sisters and their brother (11:3, 5), nor of the two women for Jesus himself, as is evident from their actions throughout the narrative. But, hard though it be to grasp this truth in our casual world, their love, far from excluding respect, thrives on it. Hence, their addressing him as "Lord."

There is, moreover, nothing remarkable about Mary's words to Jesus. They repeat word for word what her sister had already said. Both are simple statements of faith in Jesus: "Lord, if you had been here, my brother would not have died" (11:32; cf. 11:21). The same confident faith in Jesus' power begets the same unexpressed hope that even now death has not had its final say.

When Jesus saw her weeping, and the Jews who came with her also weeping, he was deeply moved in spirit and troubled (11:33).

It scarcely needs saying that the tears we shed at deathbeds and gravesides are not for the departed but for us, the bereaved. Death severs a relationship with me, the living, and severs it definitively and irrevocably. The "dead know nothing" (Qoheleth 9:5); they do not and cannot weep for themselves or for those they leave behind.

Jesus' being "deeply moved in spirit and troubled" (Jn 11:33) is but the natural and spontaneous sympathy of his love for those who were grieving. It is a measure of his affection for them, just as the tears shed by "the Jews who came with her" were a measure of their love for the bereaved sisters.

"Jesus wept"

...and he said, "Where have you laid him?" They said to him, "Lord, come and see." Jesus wept (11:34–35).

Only a culture that thinks tears "unmanly" can make much fuss about the last two words, "Jesus wept." Martha wept, so did Mary, so did the Jews. Jesus' tears, if anything, are the signature of his humanity in a gospel that all too often is accused of underplaying it. The tears Jesus shed are as much a sign of the reality of the "flesh" as is the death he will undergo.

The argument, dear to so many spiritual writers over the centuries, that we have in the gospels the fact that Jesus wept but not that Jesus laughed is as ridiculous as the conclusions drawn from it. Their descant on this "vale of tears" and on all the sad specimens of flebile humanity with which they populate it, is matter for laughter not for refutation. On the other hand, we did not have to wait for the discovery of a Gnostic tract to tell us of the "laughing savior," any more than we required a philosophical argument to convince us that laughter is a distinguishing mark of human beings within the animal kingdom.

Once again we do need to remind ourselves of the catastrophic consequences of all such attempts to assemble an "identikit" of the historical Jesus. In the final analysis, these portraits are more faithful representations of the authors than of their subject.

So the Jews said, "See how he loved him!" But some of them said, "Could not he who opened the eyes of the blind man have kept this man from dying?" (11:36–37).

One can hardly argue with the conclusion some of the Jews drew from the fact that "Jesus wept." His tears were but an outward manifestation of "how he loved" Lazarus. Similarly, there is no need to take the remark of the other Jews as hostile or polemical. They really say, albeit in a more explicit fashion, what both Martha and Mary have already said, "Lord, if you had been here, my brother would not have died" (11:21, 32). If there was any malice in the remark of "some of them," it is not evident at this stage, but will become so in 11:46 when they go and denounce Jesus to the Pharisees.

Faith and the Signs

What is instructive in the question some of the Jews pose, however, is the way they regard the undoubted wonders of Jesus. We are all prone to treat whatever we regard as miraculous in the same way. This is indeed what is problematic with faith in and because of "the signs." Our appetite for them is insatiable. We are forever going back to test their source. Would not the opening of the eyes of a man born blind suffice to establish Jesus' identity beyond question, even if he were to work no other miracle for the rest of his days? The reason why the sign in and by itself does not suffice is that all of us regard not the miracle worker but the benefit that accrues to us, a healing here, a recovery there, a success in this, an avoided failure in that, etc. Like the Jews, we are forever saying, "Could not he who opened the eyes of the blind man have kept this man from dying?" (11:37). Our tragedy is to pretend that this is faith. But it is nothing of the sort. It believes only the gift and forgets the giver. Jesus, to be sure, did not keep "this man from dying." Nevertheless, he went their expectations one better. He raised the man from the dead. Yet precisely this very act will soon bring him to his own death.

THE RAISING OF LAZARUS (John 11:38–44)

> **Then Jesus, deeply moved again, came to the tomb; it was a cave, and a stone lay upon it. Jesus said, "Take away the stone." Martha, the sister of the dead man, said to him, "Lord, by this time there will be an odor, for he has been dead four days" (11:38–39).**

With all the good will in the world, logic, our particular brand of logic, dies hard. Martha's desire for some miracle, her boundless trust in Jesus' power ("I know that whatever you ask from God, God will give you" 11:22), and her confession of him as "the Christ, the Son of God, he who is coming into the world" (11:27), are all in abeyance to what her reason, her accustomed way of seeing things, tells her. She expects a divine intervention, but one in accordance with the settled tenor of her life. Of course, she is not alone in this. We all want a God comprehensible within the confines of our everyday logic, conformed to our pet theories, respectful of the limits we have set for divine action. Jesus recalls all this to her:

Jesus said to her, "Did I not tell you that if you would believe you would see the glory of God?" (11:40).

Faith in him and in the Father who sent him requires a willingness to abandon, not our intelligence, but the comfort of our accustomed ways of thinking; not our rational powers, but our pet theories, the idols of our mind. It is one thing to confess him as "the Christ, the Son of God, he who is coming into the world" (11:27), quite another to acknowledge all that such confession implies about who and what I myself am. Only such faith as involves the whole person has eyes to truly see "the glory of God," the creative and life-giving power of the creator in the person of Jesus of Nazareth (cf. 2 Cor 4:6).

Everything that Jesus says and does is in order to reveal this glory: "We have beheld his glory, glory as of the only Son from the Father" (1:14b; 2:11; 7:18). Indeed, the whole sequence of events in this chapter is directed firmly to that one ultimate end: "This illness...is for the glory of God, so that the Son of God may be glorified by means of it" (11:4; see 17:4).

Prayer and Thanksgiving

So they took away the stone. And Jesus lifted up his eyes and said, "Father, I thank you that you have heard me. I know that you hear me always, but I have said this on account of the people standing by, that they may believe that you sent me" (11:41–42).

The prayer of Jesus, like any exercise deserving the name of prayer, is first and foremost an act of thanksgiving. The elements in his prayer which, in this particular instance, belong exclusively to his dignity as the Son, should not distract us from the thanksgiving he offers as an essential constituent of prayer. He who prays is Jesus of Nazareth. His prayer is an act of thanksgiving to the Father, pure and simple.

The prayer of his followers, too, can only be that, an act of thanksgiving. In fact, this is what it is. Of course, we commonly refer to it as "eucharist," a Greek word for thanksgiving, even while we persist in our search for ways to pray. The act of thanksgiving is and remains the supreme prayer of all Jesus' followers.

Jesus' prayer to the Father, moreover, is an act of thanksgiving for favors already granted: "Father, I thank you that you have heard me" (11:41). So, too, the prayer of the Christian is always an act of gratitude for gifts already granted, favors already received. What underlies this assured expression of gratitude is the recognition of the gift already given (see 15:7, 16b; 16:24) in the very acknowledgment of its giver, "Father, I thank you!"

This is not to deny for a moment Jesus' special and unique relationship to the Father, nor to minimize the theological implications of the "you hear me always." The Father hears him always because the Son always does his will. Indeed, do we ourselves not always pray, "Thy will be done"? A Christian believer reading these lines in John's gospel hardly needs such a reminder. But, because we have been made to overlook or forget it by the self-appointed "experts" on prayer, what all of us need is a firm and unwavering grasp of the essence of Christian prayer. Scarcely any instruction is necessary to grasp this, because it admits neither grades of prayer nor gradations of proficiency in praying. There are no ladders to scale and no stages and states to differentiate and seek to attain. All that any Christian can pray or need to pray is: "Father, I thank you that you have heard me!" The rest is "literature."

The reason Jesus took the traditional posture of prayer, i.e., "lifted up his eyes," and uttered audibly the prayers he addressed to the Father, was the same reason he did everything else: "That they may believe that you have sent me" (11:42). The Word did not become man to exempt himself from the ordinary ways of humanity.

> **When he had said this, he cried with a loud voice, "Lazarus, come out." The dead man came out, his hands and feet bound with bandages, and his face wrapped with a cloth. Jesus said to them, "Unbind him, and let him go" (11:43–44).**

As in all the miracles, the action is simple, the effect instantaneous, and the results understated. This, the last and the greatest of the signs that Jesus did, is the most cogent argument for the inadequacy of the signs. Of all the other signs, this, which brings a dead and buried man back to life, brings Jesus himself to his death.

In Jesus' world, as indeed in ours, seeing with one's eyes is the principal means of certitude. Yet the whole gospel of John is a demonstration of the beatitude, the blessedness, of "those who *have not seen* and yet believe" (20:29). Seeing with the eyes can even be a hindrance. The first part of the gospel is there to remind us that, despite all the signs that Jesus did before their very eyes, "He came to his own home, and his own people received him not" (1:11). The most secure way to the Word is hearing (cf. Rom 10:17, "So faith comes from what is heard").

THE PLOT TO KILL JESUS (John 11:45–57)

> **Many of the Jews therefore, who had come with Mary and had seen what he did, believed in him; but some of them went to the Pharisees and told them what Jesus had done (11:45–46).**

Once again, Jesus' action causes a division. Many of those who "saw what he did, believed in him." Yet there were others who also "saw what he did" and, far from believing in him, went and denounced him. No amount of good works, even spectacular works, is sufficient; no show of power, even the power to bring the dead to life from the tomb, is suasive; no quantity of reasons and reasoning can compel any one of us to believe.

What faith in the Revealer requires is nothing short of letting go of all that I cherish and hold most dear: my view of myself, my understanding of who I am, my system of values, and all the manufactured props and supports of my restless self. Witness, for instance, the ensuing scenario:

> **So the chief priests and the Pharisees gathered the council, and said, "What are we to do? For this man performs many signs. If we let him go on thus, every one will believe in him, and the Romans will come and destroy both our holy place and our nation" (11:47–48).**

In their world, the obvious answer to someone who "performs many signs" would have been to believe in him as the one sent by God. The authorities no longer deny the "many signs" he performed (see 9:24, 29, 34); they merely persist in refusing to acknowledge their significance. Their own perverse reasoning must have seemed irrefutable to them: "If we let him go on thus, every one will believe in him, and the Romans will come and destroy both our holy place and our nation" (11:48).

The authorities, of course, were not mistaken. That was just what the Romans did to their holy places and nation. But the link between that anticipated catastrophe and the "many signs" which Jesus did existed only in the mind of the "chief priests and the Pharisees" (11:47). We should not, however, judge them singular in their attitude to Jesus of Nazareth and to the revelation he brought. Only a few centuries later, voices in the Roman Empire would blame the "new religion" for all the ills that befell it. One of them described the new religion as "a fabulous and formless darkness mastering the loveliness of the world," which a modern poet would take up and memorably enshrine in:

The Babylonian starlight brought
A fabulous, formless darkness in;
Odour of blood when Christ was slain
Made all Platonic tolerance vain
And vain all Doric discipline.
(W. B. Yeats, "Two Songs for a Play")

Much closer to our time, barely two centuries ago, a Christian historian would similarly blame Christianity for the decline and fall of everything of worth in civilization's finest hour.

But one of them, Caiaphas, who was high priest that year, said to them, "You know nothing at all; you do not understand that it is expedient for you that one man should die for the people, and that the whole nation should not perish" (11:49–50).

Unexceptionable reasoning once again takes hold of the situation. The high priest's knowledge comes to rescue his underlings from their ignorance. His understanding, which–he himself is doubtless convinced–got him to his present eminence, comes to the rescue of the small, timorous minds around him. He knows, almost by natural instinct, what is "expedient." Legitimately constituted authority is a past master in the art of expediency. Caiaphas, in the security of his faultless reasoning, misses the irony of his own words. He is the prophet despite himself.

He did not say this of his own accord, but being high priest that year he prophesied that Jesus should die for the nation, and not for the nation only, but to gather into one the children of God who are scattered abroad (11:51–52).

That the evangelist can at this point intervene to explain the true significance of the high priest's words should suffice to remind us, not only of the evangelist's advantage of hindsight, but of Caiaphas' utter inability to grasp any meaning beyond the secure logic of his clear argument. Caiaphas, the master of "what is expedient," continues to have within the Christian community far better and sometimes even more loyal followers than Jesus managed to win in his lifetime.

So from that day on they took counsel how to put him to death (11:53).

The decision, which up to now has been expressed only hesitantly (5:16, 18; 7:1, 19, 25, 30; 8:37, 40), is now finally taken. In the end, expediency, under whatever name, always triumphs over the revelation. All that remains now are the details and the technicalities which could be safely passed on to the underlings, who will be certain to carry them out with exemplary attention to minutiae. They will have their chance to glory in their imagined self-importance, redoubling their zeal to hide what lingering doubts they might have had and to distract them from any misgivings they might still have.

> **Jesus therefore no longer went about openly among the Jews, but went from there to the country near the wilderness, to a town called Ephraim; and there he stayed with the disciples.**
>
> **Now the Passover of the Jews was at hand, and many were up from the country to Jerusalem before the Passover, to purify themselves. They were looking for Jesus and saying to one another as they stood in the temple, "What do you think? That he will not come to the feast?" Now the chief priests and the Pharisees had given orders that if any one knew where he was, he should let them know, so that they might arrest him (11:54, 55–57).**

The scene for the final act is thus set. Jesus himself "no longer went about openly among the Jews" (11:54; cf. 18:20 "I have spoken openly to the world.... I have said nothing secretly"), but retired with his disciples to "a town called Ephraim" (11:54). The crowds that went up to Jerusalem "before the Passover" (11:55) were left prey to the rumors that were born of the general uncertainty, "What do you think? That he will not come to the feast?" (11:56). Their questionings only strengthened the resolve of the authorities. So, "the chief priests and the Pharisees" issued definite orders "that if any one knew where he was, he should let them know, so that they might arrest him" (11:57).

But, despite all the deadly decision of the authorities and amidst all the questionings of the uncertain crowd, Jesus alone knew that "his hour had come to depart out of this world to the Father" (13:1), and no amount of human decision or calculation could or would delay or deflect him from it.

John 12

The Anointing at Bethany: Mary and Mary; Mary's deed; Judas Iscariot.

The Plot against Lazarus.

The Triumphal Entry into Jerusalem: the fulfilment of the scriptures; the Easter perspective.

Some Greeks Seek Jesus: the hour of the Son of man; the law of life; following Jesus.

The Son of Man Must Be Lifted Up: "now is the judgment"; the Son of man.

The Mystery of Unbelief: refusal to believe; love of praise.

Judgment by Jesus' Word: the revelation; the revealer; all the world; response to the revelation.

THE ANOINTING AT BETHANY (John 12:1–8)

Six days before the Passover, Jesus came to Bethany, where Lazarus was, whom Jesus had raised from the dead. There they made him a supper; Martha served, and Lazarus was one of those at table with him. Mary took a pound of costly ointment of pure nard and anointed the feet of Jesus and wiped his feet with her hair; and the house was filled with the fragrance of the ointment (12:1–4).

The link with the preceding chapter is evident; the transition is smooth. Remarks like these, nevertheless, require a word of caution. The division of the New Testament books into chapters and verses is more recent than we care to note. Properly speaking, the ancient manuscripts of these books had neither chapter divisions nor numbered verses. Indeed, there were no breaks even between the words themselves. The chapter divisions came from the High Middle Ages, and the verse numbering followed later in the Renaissance. To make much of these chapters and verses might delight numerologists, but biblical interpreters must consider rather the significance of the paragraph sequence and the link of the sentences to one another. The principal value of chapter and verse numbers is, first and foremost, the convenience of reference.

Generally speaking, the opening verses of chapter 12 follow very naturally upon the events narrated in chapter 11. The time sequence, "six days before the Passover" (12:1) synchronizes with "the Passover of the Jews was at hand" in 11:55. But the reference to the "six days" does a great deal more than that. It starts–so to speak–the countdown to the passion and, together with the carefully noted sequence of the opening week (1:29, 35, 43; 2:1), serves to bracket the span of the public ministry of Jesus. That ministry in the gospel of John stretches over almost three times the period allotted to it in the synoptics. It begins around Passover of one year (2:13 "The passover of the Jews was at hand"), goes to the second "Passover, the feast of the Jews, was at hand" (6:4) of the multiplication of the loaves, and finally comes to this last Passover (11:55; 12:1).

But even more significant than the mention of the Passover in 12:1 is the reference to Lazarus "whom Jesus had raised from the dead" (see 11:44) and to his sisters Martha and Mary. The supper takes place in Bethany, "the village of Mary and her sister Martha" (11:1), and what takes place at this supper has already been referred to when Mary was introduced in the previous chapter as she "who anointed the Lord with ointment and wiped his feet with her hair" in 11:2.

Mary and Mary

At the supper in Bethany it was Martha who "served" (12:2). This agrees with her description as the one "distracted with much serving" in Luke 10:40. But the same could not as easily be said of Mary. Luke speaks of "a woman of the city, who was a sinner," who came into the house of a Simon the Pharisee with an "alabaster flask of ointment," stood behind Jesus at his feet and "weeping, she began to wet his feet with her tears, and wiped them with the hair of her head, and kissed his feet, and anointed them with the ointment" (Lk 7:37–38). Whether the sinner in Luke 7 and Mary the sister of Lazarus ("their brother," Jn

11:19), who also "anointed the feet of Jesus" (Jn 12:3), are one and the same is, though quite likely, still open to doubt. Whether, on the other hand, Mary the sister of Lazarus in John 11 is to be identified with the Mary Magdalene who "stood weeping outside the tomb" and later clung to the risen Jesus (20:1, 11–18), is matter for conjecture.

Such unresolved questions might prove a problem to novelists and film makers, though their fecund imagination does not seem to be much hindered by them. But, to one intent upon understanding the gospel, they can, at most, provide a distraction. For the central character in this and every other narrative remains always Jesus of Nazareth. The role of Mary "the mother of Jesus" at Cana (2:1–5), or of the sister of Lazarus in John 11 and here (12:3), or of Mary Magdalene in John 20, whom Luke describes as "Mary, called Magdalene, from whom seven demons had gone out" (Lk 8:2), must always be subordinate to the role of Jesus.

Mary's Deed

Nevertheless, Mary's action at the supper in Bethany (cf. Mt 26:6–13 and Mk 14:3–9), which occupies our attention here, is both memorable (see Mt 26:13, "Amen, I say to you, wherever this gospel is preached in the whole world, what she has done will be told in memory of her"; Mk 14:9) and instructive. The reader has a great deal to learn, not just from her genuine love for Jesus but from the way she manifested it. Even in her own home, the unusual service she rendered Jesus would have required extraordinary courage, if not in our day, certainly in hers. She had to love a great deal to be so uninhibited in openly demonstrating her love. All genuine love is, almost by definition, generous. Love of Mary's magnitude is generous with an extravagance in quantity as well as in quality and cost: "a pound of costly ointment of pure nard" (Jn 12:3). The expression of such love recognizes no limits and respects few conventions.

Mary's extravagant generosity is coupled–as indeed such generosity always is–with a profound humility. Loving another is always humbling. Mary gives outward expression to this humility by anointing "the feet of Jesus" and wiping "his feet with her hair" (12:3; cf. Jesus' own action in 13:12–14). Such generosity in loving Jesus, such extravagance and courage in demonstrating her love, and yet such self-effacing humility in expressing it, contrast sharply with the cool reason of Caiaphas' self-absorption in the previous chapter (11:49–52). Mary's love contrasts more sharply still with Judas Iscariot's hypocrisy in what now follows.

Judas Iscariot

But Judas Iscariot, one of his disciples (he who was to betray him), said, "Why was this ointment not sold for three hundred denarii and given to the poor?" This he said, not that he cared for the poor but because he was a thief, and as he had the money box he used to take what was put into it (12:4–6).

Judas Iscariot, "he who was to betray him" (see 6:64, 71; 13:2, 11, 21), provides, in John as well as in the other gospels, a remarkable "role model," as the current jargon would probably not care to call it. His action in this instance is of such enormity as to offer all of us a chance, rarely if ever passed up, to feel superior, to express shock at it, and to feel aggrieved by its manifest injustice. Yet, Judas' hypocrisy is ours. His real misfortune was to have been caught out by the evangelist and exposed so cruelly: "He was a thief" (12:6). Who but a thief knows so accurately the price of things ("three hundred denarii," 12:5), expresses so dramatically his care for the unfortunate others, or talks so zealously of "the poor"? "This he said, not that he cared for the poor but because he was a thief" (12:6; see 13:29).

Nevertheless, we must never forget that this same Judas Iscariot was not only "one of his disciples" (12:4) but also one of "the twelve" (6:70). We do not know, nor have any way of knowing, how he was called by Jesus. But we need not imagine his call to have been very much different from the others described in John 1, whether of Andrew (1:35–40), Simon (1:41–42), Philip (1:43–44) or Nathanael (1:45–51). Nor have we any reason to suppose that Judas Iscariot responded to Jesus' call less wholeheartedly or with any less alacrity than the rest.

The evangelist, of course, portrays Jesus as knowing perfectly what he chose and whom he chose. "Did I not choose you, the twelve, and one of you is a devil?" (6:70). "I know whom I have chosen" (13:18). If Jesus did indeed know, then his choice was not very impressive, and its final outcome not very encouraging. At the foot of the cross, not one of "the twelve" was there; and it is debatable whether Judas Iscariot's betrayal was more reprehensible than Peter's triple denial (13:38; 18:15–18, 25–27). Yet, reflecting upon those whom Jesus chose and continues to choose, we do well to keep in mind that, in the words of the modern poet,

...the faith
Is not exclusive in the fools it chooses
That the vain, the ambitious and the highly sexed

Are the natural prey of the incarnate Christ.
(C. H. Sisson, "A Letter to John Donne," in *In the Trojan Ditch*)

Jesus said, "Let her alone, let her keep it for the day of my burial. The poor you always have with you, but you do not always have me" (12:7–8).

Jesus wards off the criticism of Mary's action, first by a symbolic reminder of his approaching death (see the service that Nicodemus renders the dead Jesus in 19:39–40). But, in doing so, he really demolishes Judas' objection by exposing, albeit indirectly and less cruelly than the fourth evangelist himself, the hypocrisy that is at its very core. Then Jesus adds the reminder that: "The poor you have always with you" (12:8). They are always there to provide us with all the threadbare cloaks of our hypocrisy. They are there to hide our greed, our grasp for power, our desiccated emotions, and our lack of caring. They are our ready excuse for evading the demands of service and the burdens of love.

THE PLOT AGAINST LAZARUS (John 12:9–11)

When the great crowd of the Jews learned that he was there, they came, not only on account of Jesus but also to see Lazarus, whom he had raised from the dead (12:9).

There is a study waiting to be made on just how much mankind's religions owe to curiosity. Such curiosity fuels interest in religious matters, fills once unfrequented shrines, swells pilgrimages to holy places, and keeps miracles and their rumors in the news. This, of course, makes no mention of that other curiosity about the occult, the realm of the dead, or that most irresistible of all curiosities, Satan and the satanic. Lazarus as one "returned from the dead," the object of Jesus' greatest miracle, must have proved an irresistible attraction. It is the miracle, not the miracle-worker we seek. The great crowd came "not only on account of Jesus" (12:9, 18).

When John speaks of "the great crowd of the Jews" here or speaks of "the Jews" far less flatteringly elsewhere, we should never allow ourselves to forget (see above on 9:18–19) that, out of those same Jews, came Jesus and the mother of Jesus, Mary, Martha and Lazarus, Judas and Caiaphas, the chief priests and Peter, the twelve, and, most likely, the "John" to whom we owe this gospel. To recall this inescapable fact, which is never denied or evaded in its pages, is all the more necessary whenever the fourth gospel falls victim to those whose outraged zeal for "the poor" passes all bounds.

> **So the chief priests planned to put Lazarus also to death, because on account of him many of the Jews were going away and believing in Jesus (12:10–11).**

Today, the plan to "put Lazarus also to death" would come under the heading of "destroying the evidence." As with the man born blind in chapter 9, the most natural first reaction of the authorities was to deny the evidence (9:15, 18, 24). In the case of someone raised from the dead, however, the only means to do this is to destroy the evidence altogether.

Jesus and everything he does continue to bring about a division between the people. While some were resolved to do away with Jesus and even to get rid of the Lazarus he brought back to life, others "believed in him" (11:45). Our knowledge of how the story ends in the ignominy of the death on the cross, when not only the many who believed in Jesus but also his own disciples abandoned him, should not make us overlook the fact that there always was and there always will be two reactions to the Revealer: to believe or to refuse to believe in him, to accept the revelation he brings or to reject it. Yet our knowledge of that ignominious end should temper our estimate of the enthusiasm that greeted him, whether after the miracle of the loaves (6:15) or after the raising of Lazarus (11:45).

THE TRIUMPHAL ENTRY INTO JERUSALEM (John 12:12–19)

> **The next day a great crowd who had come to the feast heard that Jesus was coming to Jerusalem. So they took branches of palm trees and went out to meet him, crying, "Hosanna! Blessed is he who comes in the name of the Lord, even the King of Israel!" And Jesus found a young ass and sat upon it; as it is written, "Fear not, daughter of Zion; behold, your king is coming, sitting on an ass's colt!" (12:12–15).**

"King" is the title with which Nathanael confessed his faith in Jesus: "Rabbi, you are the Son of God! You are the King of Israel!" (1:49). "King" is what the uncomprehending crowd wanted to make him "by force" after the multiplication of the loaves (6:15). "So you are a king?"

(18:37) is what the bewildered Pilate said to him. "Hail, King of the Jews!" is the mockery of the soldiers who derided him at his trial (19:2–3). And "Jesus of Nazareth, the King of the Jews" is the title under which he was crucified (19:19). The title of kingship, which meant so many things to so many different people, had only one meaning for him who, knowing that his "kingship is not from the world" (18:36), could say, "For this I was born, and for this I have come into the world" (18:37).

The Fulfilment of the Scriptures

Amid all the noise of the cheering procession, Jesus, who "knew all men...knew what was in man" (2:25), did not trust himself to them (2:24). He who once "withdrew again to the mountain by himself" when the crowd tried to "take him by force to make him king" (6:15), now lets the crowd have its day. His "hour" draws nigh. We can speculate, but without any hope of arriving even at an intelligent guess, what percentage of those who waved palm branches and shouted hosannas would in a few days scream, "Away with him, away with him, crucify him!" (19:15).

But, if there was any lesson to be learned from this, it was quickly forgotten. For, in years to come, the followers of Jesus would not only court the hosannas of the crowds, but use them as the yardstick of their own success in a world that cannot but hate them (15:18).

In this whole scene of momentary triumph, however, there was one facet that could not have been present to the mind of the cheering crowd. The whole triumphal procession was in fact the fulfilment of a prophecy:

> Rejoice greatly, O daughter of Zion!
>   Shout aloud, O daughter of Jerusalem!
> Lo, your king comes to you;
>   triumphant and victorious is he,
> humble and riding on an ass,
>   on a colt the foal of an ass (Zechariah 9:9).

It was with the realization that the word of divine promise found its true fulfilment in him, that believers came to understand the real identity of Jesus of Nazareth. For, in all the many and varied theories about the genesis of faith in Jesus of Nazareth, we should not overlook a simple fact. Some time, very soon after the crucifixion, someone among

Jesus' followers must have come to the realization that "all the scriptures" found their fulfilment and ultimate intelligibility in him. Luke goes so far as to describe the risen Jesus himself as the source of this insight (Lk 24:27, "And beginning with Moses and all the prophets, he interpreted to them in all the scriptures the things concerning himself"). But John is content simply to add:

> **His disciples did not understand this at first, but when Jesus was glorified, then they remembered that this had been written of him and had been done to him (Jn 12:16).**

Of course, this fact has already been noted at the start of the gospel: "When therefore he was raised from the dead, his disciples remembered that he had said this; and they believed the scripture and the word which Jesus had spoken" (2:22; cf. 1:17). For us who read the gospel now, it ought to remind us of what we are likely to forget, viz., that this and the other gospels were all written from a post-Easter perspective. The Jesus they wrote about was the risen Jesus in whom they believed.

The Easter Perspective

All the evangelists, each in his own fashion, used the central fact of the death and the resurrection to illumine the life of Jesus of Nazareth, rather than the other way around. The fourth gospel, moreover, adds a new element to this process. The fact that Jesus' followers, then as now, "remember" (12:16) with so much comprehension is a function which belongs exclusively to "the [Paraclete], the Holy Spirit, whom the Father will send in my name" (14:26). This, in the final analysis, is at the basis of everything we say about "inspiration."

> **The crowd that had been with him when he called Lazarus out of the tomb and raised him from the dead bore witness. The reason why the crowd went to meet him was that they heard he had done this sign. The Pharisees then said to one another, "You see that you can do nothing; look, the world has gone after him" (12:17–19).**

Once again we are made to realize that the great sign of calling Lazarus out of the tomb and raising him from the dead, not only attracted the attention it rightly deserved, but also confirmed and intensified the fear and hostility that will very soon bring Jesus himself to his death.

One is left to speculate whether there is not a hidden irony in the words of the hostile Pharisees. The world, at least the world they knew, did certainly seem to go "after him." What the Pharisees expressed was their alarm and fear. But it was also an unwitting description of what in fact will happen, no matter what they did. The world indeed did go after him.

SOME GREEKS SEEK JESUS (John 12:20–26)

Now among those who went up to worship at the feast were some Greeks. So these came to Philip, who was from Bethsaida in Galilee, and said to him, "Sir, we wish to see Jesus." Philip went and told Andrew; Andrew went with Philip and they told Jesus (12:20–22).

Whatever the reasons that found them among "those who went up to worship at the feast," those "Greeks" were native born Greeks and not Gentile converts to Judaism. The technical term for the latter in the New Testament is "Hellenists" (Acts 6:1). The "Greeks" here in John 12:20 are the first Greeks to come to Jesus in the fourth gospel, and it is this fact that prompts Jesus to say that the "hour has come" (12:23). The scene, in other words, is a miniature of the eventual coming of the Gentiles to the faith.

The circuitous process by which the word finally reaches Jesus is puzzling only to those who insist on discovering the logic of human protocol. But, whatever Andrew and Philip finally managed to convey to Jesus out of the simple and straightforward request of "the Greeks," that request was not actually granted—or so it seems. At least we have no way of finding out from John whether "the Greeks" in fact did "see Jesus." Their role here is to provide, once again, the occasion for Jesus' revelation.

The Hour of the Son of Man

And Jesus answered them, "The hour has come for the Son of man to be glorified" (12:23).

The "hour" which had "not yet come" at Cana (2:4) has at last arrived. It is, of course, the hour of the death and glorification of Jesus, the hour of the accomplishment of the revelation (19:30), the hour that makes all else in the gospel comprehensible (see 12:16).

Once again Jesus employs the title Son of man (1:51; 3:13, 14; 6:27, 53, 62; 9:35; and cf. the "Now is the Son of man glorified" in 13:31). This Son of man is he who "descended from heaven" (3:13), who will be "lifted up" (3:14) and ascend to "where he was before" (6:62), so that "whoever believes in him may have eternal life" (3:15).

Scholars discuss and dispute the extent to which the passion and death of Jesus is operative throughout the fourth gospel. Reading the gospel, one can get the impression that the Word came into the world only to go back again to where he came from. The cross is thus seen as no more than the starting point of the journey upward. Nevertheless, to readers unwilling to dismiss whatever does not fit such a reading of the gospel as "later editorial addition or redaction," there are sufficient references to the death on the cross throughout it to give them reason. The death of Jesus on the cross, even when spoken of as "glorification" and exaltation, the "being lifted up" (12:23, 32), remains the one single fact that lends intelligibility to the whole revelation. Only at the foot of the cross does the revelation make any sense at all.

The Law of Life

Amen, amen, I say to you, unless a grain of wheat falls into the earth and dies, it remains alone; but if it dies, it bears much fruit. He who loves his life loses it, and he who hates his life in this world will keep it for eternal life (12:24–25).

The coming of Jesus into the world overturns all its cherished values. If the "Amen, amen" saying were merely an agricultural truism or only a parable, the statement that follows it transmutes it into a law of life for the Christian. It is, of course, not exclusive to John. Jesus' saying, "He who loves his life loses it, and he who hates his life in this world will keep it for eternal life" is recorded by both Matthew (Mt 16:25; cf. 10:39) and Luke (Lk 17:33).

If this saying finds its place in John's gospel also, it is not merely at the whim of some secondary redactor who decided to include it here. True, the saying itself does enunciate a truth which is difficult for the believer to accept. Yet, in a gospel that insists so much on the gift brought by the Son of God into the world, what other proof could anyone have that the believers in him possess eternal life than the prodigality with which they expend their own lives in the loving service of others? It is in squandering their lives for others–"who hates his life in this world" (Jn 12:25)–that they provide irrefutable proof of their possession of the eternal life he brought them.

The saying, moreover, is a fitting preface to the Revealer's "having loved his own...he loved them to the end" (13:1). The death he will die for his own is both the revelation and the proof of this love, and can therefore be spoken of as Jesus' glorification. What he does, those who follow him, the sharers of his glory (17:22), are also called to do.

Following Jesus

If any one serves me, he must follow me; and where I am, there shall my servant be also; if any one serves me, the Father will honor him (12:26).

To confess Jesus, to believe him as the Son and the Revealer of the Father, is not a mental exercise. It involves the entire being and life of the believer. Anyone who serves the Lord must follow him in his service to his Father by the totality of his obedience, and in his love for us "to the end." Those who serve the Son must follow him both by their obedience to the will of the Father and their love for one another.

The Father "glorified and will glorify" his name (12:28) in all that the Son did. Everything the Son did was in order to fulfil the will of the Father who sent him. In this obedience he laid down his life to be "the Savior of the world" (4:42; 10:11b). So, too, those who serve the Son do so by following him in their obedience to the will of the Father and in their "hatred" of their life (12:25) for the sake of others. Thus the Father will "honor" them, and they shall be where the Son is (12:26).

Where Jesus goes, there shall those who serve him go. He goes to the Father, and so too shall they. These words of Jesus in 12:26, "where I am, there shall my servant be also," radically alter the biblical understanding of death. Death was a descent into Sheol, the dank and dismal habitation of the dead (Ps 6:5; 18:5; 88:3; Is 28:15; 38:18). Henceforth, the death of those who serve and follow the Lord is an ascent to the Father where the Son is.

THE SON OF MAN MUST BE LIFTED UP (John 12:27–36)

Now is my soul troubled. And what shall I say, "Father, save me from this hour?" No, for this purpose I have come to this hour. Father, glorify your name (12:27–28a).

If, unlike the synoptics, the gospel of John has no account of the institution of the eucharist (Mt 26:26–29; Mk 14:22–25; Lk 22:15–20), it has no account of the agony in the garden either (Mt 26:36–46; Mk 14:32–42; Lk 22:40–46). But, while the former is, after a fashion, transposed to John 6 in the discourse on the bread of life; the latter, the agony in the garden, might be said to have its equivalent here in 12:27.

However, as one would expect from the Johannine Christ, the prayer–if it can be described as such here–is unlike that in the synoptics: "Abba, Father, all things are possible to you, remove this cup from me; yet not what I will, but what you will" (Mk 14:36 par.). In John, the prayer is just the opposite. Jesus utters a forthright "No!" to any request like "Father, save me from this hour" (12:27).

Nevertheless, on the one essential point in both instances, John and the synoptics do in fact agree, even if their mode of expression differs. It is the will of God that is supreme in the life of Jesus, whether in the synoptics or in John. If in the synoptics its acceptance is resignedly expressed, "If this cannot pass...your will be done" (Mt 26:42); in John, it is forthrightly embraced as the very *raison d'être* of Jesus' entire life. "For this purpose I have come to this hour" (Jn 12:27). This purpose is the glorification of the Father's name by the Son's total obedience to his will (see 17:4).

Another important incident that is missing from John's account of Jesus' ministry is the transfiguration (Mt 17:1–9; Mk 9:2–10; Lk 9:28–36). A moment's reflection should suffice to see the reason for this omission in the fourth gospel. The Word become flesh is he to whom all the scriptures bear witness, "it is they that bear witness to me" (Jn 5:39). In the gospel of John, Jesus' glorification takes place throughout his life. It shines in every sign he performs. It reaches its climax precisely in his death on the cross and resurrection (2:11; 7:39; 11:4). Here in chapter 12, as in the synoptic accounts of the transfiguration, a voice from heaven bears further witness to it:

Then a voice came from heaven, "I have glorified it, and I will glorify it again" (12:28b; see 8:54 and 17:4).

The whole life of Jesus glorifies God by carrying out his will in everything and, precisely in that glorifying of his heavenly Father, he himself is glorified as the Son: "I have glorified you on earth, having accomplished the work which you gave me to do; and now, Father, glorify me..." (17:4–5).

"Now is the judgment"

The crowd standing by heard it and said that it had thundered. Others said, "An angel has spoken to him." Jesus answered, "This voice has come for your sake, not for mine. Now is the judgment of this world, now shall the ruler of this world be cast out" (12:29–31).

The whole extraordinary event, like all the extraordinary events in Jesus' life, is for "your sake" (12:30), for the sake of the whole world. All that anyone in the world needs is to hearken to "this voice."

It is all good and fine to speak, as some scholars have done, of the Jesus of the fourth gospel as a "God striding the earth," or to describe "the light of the world" as effulgent, "glistening, intensely white," as he was at the transfiguration (Mk 9:3 par.). Of course, had this been true of all the eyes that beheld Jesus of Nazareth, there would have been no problem whatsoever. But only the eyes of faith can truly say, "We have beheld his glory, glory as of the only Son from the Father" (Jn 1:14b), when in fact their gaze fell on no one "but Jesus only" (Mk 9:8), a Jesus who cries out, "Now is my soul troubled" (Jn 12:27).

This fact, incidentally, is what precipitates the judgment. He comes into the world in mortal flesh, subject to all that our mortality is heir to: thirst and weariness (4:6, 7), tears (11:35) and anguish of soul (12:27). Yet, in the encounter with the Jesus of Nazareth, to behold his glory and believe in him as the one sent by the Father, is to have eternal life. On the other hand, to refuse to see who he truly is and to shut our ears to what he says is to be judged already. Indeed, it is to pronounce judgment on our own selves as dead. Therefore, "Now is the judgment of the world" (12:31) by him who did not come "to judge the world but to save the world" (12:47). There is no paradox here. If paradox there is, then it is in the human will that chooses to reject him.

The decision is wholly ours. To believe in him is to have eternal life. That is the gift. To refuse to believe is the judgment. This is our decision, and ours alone. Even "the ruler of this world," Satan, can no longer be used as an excuse. We can no longer say with Eve, "The serpent beguiled me, and I ate" (Gen 3:13), because the "ruler of this world," Milton's "artificer of fraud," has been "cast out."

> **"and I, when I am lifted up from the earth, will draw all to myself." He said this to show by what death he was to die (12:32–33).**

Though it seems hardly necessary to add such an explanatory verse at this juncture, it is nevertheless a needed reminder that Jesus' obedience to the will of the Father brings him to the "hour" for which he came into the world, i.e., brings him to the cross. As early as chapter 3, there has been reference to this fact of the cross, which might perhaps more easily be overlooked in John than in the other evangelists: "And as Moses lifted up the serpent in the wilderness, so must the Son of man be lifted up, that whoever believes in him may have eternal life" (3:14–15; see 8:28).

> **The crowd answered him, "We have heard from the law that the Christ remains for ever. How can you say that the Son of man must be lifted up? Who is this Son of man?" (12:34).**

Once again the word of God, which was meant as "a lamp to my feet and a light to my path" (Ps 119:105), is the stumbling block. Even without the evangelist's aside in 12:33, "He said this to show by what death he was to die," the crowd understood only too well what Jesus was talking about. But their confidence in what they knew, their security in their dogmatic tenets, blinds them to the truth staring them in the face. No one is less receptive to the revelation than the one content with the truth he or she holds dear.

The Son of Man

"Who is this Son of man?" It is good to keep in mind that frequently the phrase "son of man" can be a semitic mode of oblique self-reference. Thus, "the Son of man came eating and drinking" in Matthew 11:19 is a way of saying, "I came eating and drinking." But there are instances when the phrase assumes its very important technical reference to a figure of the last days, i.e., an eschatological figure, the establishment of whose "everlasting dominion" (Dan 7:13–14) signals the final judgment of the world and the dawning of the new age of salvation.

In John, though the title "Son of man" is freighted with all these eschatological connotations, it acquires its own particularly Johannine significânce. It comes to designate the bearer of the final and definitive revelation of God to the world.

"No one has ascended into heaven but he who descended from heaven, the Son of man" (3:13). The Son has been given "authority to execute judgment," which is precisely what the revelation he brings does, "because he is the Son of man" (5:27). This Son of man gives his flesh as food which "endures to eternal life" (6:27, 53). He came into the world for judgment (9:35–39). When the Son of man is lifted up on the cross then the world will know who he really is (8:28; 12:31–34). By his death on the cross, the Son of man glorifies the Father and is himself glorified (12:23). Should there be any doubt about the Son of man's role as the Revealer, the one who brings the revelation of the Father to this world and thus precipitates the judgment, then the following verse should resolve it:

Jesus said to them, "The light is with you for a little longer. Walk while you have the light, lest the darkness overtakes you; he who walks in the darkness does not know where he goes. While you have the light, believe in the light, that you may become sons of light" (12:35–36a).

As the drama draws to a close, this warning is all the more timely. The contingency of the revelation is an aspect of its urgency. "Seek the Lord while he may be found, call upon him while he is near" (Is 55:6). The revelation is not there at our disposal anytime we please to turn to it. We have grown so accustomed to confounding the revelation with a creed or a set of dogmatic assertions that we scarcely comprehend the urgency of the exhortation to "walk while you have the light" for it is "with you for a little longer" (cf. Jn 7:33; 13:33; 14:19; 16:16–19). The coming of the light into the world requires nothing short of the total dedication of our person to the Revealer, who is "the light of the world" (8:12; 9:5; 11:10; cf. 1:4–5, 9).

"While you have the light, believe in the light." We remarked above (see above on 6:69; 8:31–32 and 10:37–38) that "to know" and "to believe" in John are near synonyms. To them must also be added the verb "to see." For to see the light, not to allow oneself to be overtaken by the darkness, is to believe in him who is the light because he brings the light of revelation into this world (see 6:40; 9:39).

When Jesus had said this, he departed and hid himself from them (12:36b).

To the very end, Jesus remains master of his destiny: "I lay down my life.... No one takes it from me, but I lay it down of my own accord" (10:17–18).

THE MYSTERY OF UNBELIEF (John 12:37–43)

> **Though he had done so many signs before them, yet they did not believe in him (12:37).**

This is more the evangelist's lament than a judgment in anger. They had challenged Jesus, "What sign have you to show us?" (2:18). He did "these signs" (2:23; 4:54) and, though many followed him (6:2), still many others who saw the same and as many signs refused to believe. Jesus' appeal to them, "Even though you do not believe me, believe the works, that you may know and understand that the Father is in me and I am in the Father" (10:38; 5:36; 10:25; 14:11), is in vain.

Refusal to Believe

Faith in the Revealer cannot be deduced from the signs he performs, any more than it can be concluded to from the arguments he proposes. The stubborn refusal to believe remains ultimately a mystery. To cite, as does the evangelist here, the scriptures as an explanation of this willful blindness is really to admit defeat before the mystery of the human will:

> **...it was that the word spoken by the prophet Isaiah might be fulfilled: "Lord, who has believed our report, and to whom has the arm of the Lord been revealed?" Therefore they could not believe. For Isaiah again said, "He has blinded their eyes and hardened their heart, lest they should see with their eyes and perceive with their heart, and turn for me to heal them." Isaiah said this because he saw his glory and spoke of him (12:38–41; see Is 53:1; 6:10).**

The piling up of scriptural quotations is in itself a sign of incomprehension before the stubborn refusal to believe. But, in our effort to search out the different meanings of the Isaian citations, we can easily miss the most significant of them all. That Isaiah said all this "because he saw his glory and spoke of him" (Jn 12:41) must not be allowed to slide by as just another aside of the evangelist. If the verse (12:41) is—as it doubtless must be—a reference to the account of the prophet's inaugural vision in Isaiah 6:1–10, then the christological claim of the evangelist at this point is astounding. If Isaiah's saying he saw "the Lord sitting upon a throne" (Is 6:1) is in fact read as a reference to Jesus of Nazareth, then the "Before Abraham was, I am" (8:58) would be merely a corollary.

The claim that "Isaiah said this because he saw his glory and spoke of him" (12:41) might in itself have been some reason for the reluctance of many "to believe in him." But the evangelist knew that the reason for the rejection of Jesus' claim lay much deeper than that, much deeper than the religious scruples of a strictly monotheistic faith.

> **Nevertheless many even of the authorities believed in him, but for fear of the Pharisees they did not confess it, lest they should be put out of the synagogue; for they loved the praise of men more than the praise of God (12:42–43).**

Those in authority are not, by reason of their office or eminence, necessarily blinded by the truth any more than they are—as they are wont to claim—more clear-sighted about it. Their reaction to the revelation is the reaction of all other ordinary mortals: some believing, others refusing to believe. The "authorities" are, in other words, as much the stuff of judgment as anyone else. Their status in the community, in and of itself, creates no exception either in their favor or against it.

The fear of some of those in authority who did believe in him but did not openly confess their faith "lest they should be put out of the synagogue" (12:42) is identical to the fear of the parents of the blind man in 9:22. Such fear of being put out of the synagogue, moreover, would be quite intelligible, though hardly in Jesus' own lifetime. The statement in 12:42 or in 9:22 reflects a quite different situation, the situation in which the Johannine community found itself in the latter part of the first century. The definitive rift between Jews and Christians had already taken place by then and, in all likelihood, the followers of Jesus of Nazareth were already the subject of the daily imprecation by their former coreligionists, their fellow-Jews: "For the apostates let there be no hope.... Let the Nazarenes [Christians] and the Minim [heretics] be destroyed in a moment.... And let them be blotted out of the Book of Life and not be inscribed together with the righteous" (The Benediction Against Heretics).

Love of Praise

If fear can offer an explanation, albeit partial, for the reticence of believers to confess openly their faith in Jesus of Nazareth, something infinitely more pernicious, if only because harder to identify and more subtle in its influence, lies at the heart of the unwillingness to believe. The evangelist's diagnosis minces no words: "They loved the praise of men more than the praise of God" (12:43). It is in this insidious option for the "praise of men" over "the praise of God" that our unbelief, no less than that of the Pharisees, finds its real explanation. Indeed, this very preference of "the praise of men" renders us incapable of believing; for "How can you believe, who receive glory from one another?" (5:44).

The blinding preference of the "praise of men" is not new to Jesus' time nor peculiar to John's gospel. Jeremiah could just as rightly say, "Cursed is the man who trusts in man" (Jer 17:5; Is 2:22; Ps 146:3). It is this trust "in men," this insatiable hunger for their approval, the never-ending quest for their favor, that renders us blind to the Revealer and deaf to the word of the revelation.

This was not a peculiarity of the house of Israel, any more than of the Jews and Pharisees of Jesus' time. It is the principle and norm according to which we live much of our lives in the church today. Seeking "the praise of men" is what determines, not just the proclamation of the gospel, but the gospel itself. Everything we do is designed to win this praise. Anything that risks losing it is studiously avoided. The revelation itself is tailored and trimmed to meet the stringent requirements of its "political correctness," the exacting demands of its current fads and fashions. It is we who love "the praise of men more than the praise of God" (12:43).

JUDGMENT BY JESUS' WORD (John 12:44–50)

And Jesus cried out and said, "He who believes in me, believes not in me but in him who sent me" (12:44).

The saying is familiar enough because it occurs, in one form or another, both in Matthew: "He who receives you receives me, and he who receives me receives him who sent me" (Mt 10:40; cf. 18:5); and in Luke: "He who hears you hears me, and he who rejects me, rejects him who sent me" (Lk 10:16). We have variations on the theme in John: "He who does not honor the Son does not honor the Father who sent him" (Jn 5:23b); "He who hates me hates my Father also" (15:23). But of all these sayings none can compare with the boldness of, "You believe in God, believe also in me" (14:1b) which, though it inverts the direction of the argument, puts on a par, more explicitly than any other saying, faith in God and faith in the person of Jesus.

The Revelation

The statement in 12:44, "He who believes in me, believes not in me but in him who sent me," sums up Jesus' task as the Revealer. In general, commentators are willing enough to concede that Jesus as the Revealer is at the very core of the message of the fourth gospel. But they are justifiably reluctant to admit that all that Jesus in fact does reveal is *that* he is the Revealer of the Father, and yet he never says *what* he reveals. What Jesus does reveal, however, is precisely this: In the encounter with him, in the encounter with a Jew of the first century, Jesus of Nazareth, someone like us in all things, we in fact do encounter God himself. This is the *what* of the revelation.

This surely is not nothing. The prophets of old spoke to the people a message in human words, but what the people in fact heard and believed was "the word of the Lord." None of the prophets ever claimed more than that, not even Moses himself. They could say that whoever heard their message heard the God who sent them; whoever believed their message believed, not in them, but in the Lord who spoke to them, "Go, and say to this people..." (Is 6:9). But none of them ever dreamt that they themselves or anyone else in all creation could ever add:

And he who sees me sees him who sent me (12:45).

No prophet could ever say, "If you knew me, you would know my Father also" (8:19), or respond to a demand like "Lord, show us the Father," with "He who has seen me has seen the Father" (14:9b). The prologue, which asserted that, "No one has ever seen God" (1:18), asserts no less categorically that "the Word became flesh and dwelt among us." It goes on to add, "we have *beheld* his glory, glory as of the only Son of the Father" (1:14), for it is he who has "made him known" (1:18). No such statement could ever be made by or about any prophet of old.

Of course, only the eyes of faith can perceive this. Only those who believe that this Jesus of Nazareth, whose Galilean origin is well known

(7:27, 41; cf. 1:46), whose father and mother are no less well known (6:42), is in fact the Son whom the Father has sent into the world, only they can believe that "he who sees me sees him who sent me" (12:45). Henceforth, anyone who desires to see God, anyone who thereby seeks to have life–for this is the real reason why anyone desires to "see" God–has only to turn to this Galilean Jew. Because this is indeed so, Jesus can go on to say:

> **I have come as light into the world, that whoever believes in me may not remain in darkness (12:46).**

This chapter in John brings to a close the first half of the gospel, the part commonly referred to as "the Book of Signs." This "book" can be read as an extensive commentary on the prologue's "He came to his own home, and his own people received him not" (1:11). Thus, the few verses that conclude chapter 12 resume the major themes of the first part of the gospel, and in 12:46 the theme of light, which is fundamentally the theme of revelation, is taken up once again (1:4, 5, 7–8, 9; 3:19; 8:12; 9:5; 11:10; 12:35–36).

The Revealer

We have had frequent occasion to refer to Jesus as "the Revealer" and to speak of "the revelation" he brings. Yet it could have scarcely escaped anyone's attention that the evangelist never calls Jesus "Revealer" any more than he speaks of the "revelation" except once in 12:38, and even then he is citing Isaiah 53:1. But, though the terms themselves are absent, the reality they express is very much present and operating in every page.

"The Word" (1:1, 14), the light (1:4–5), the truth (1:14), the glory (1:14) and all the corresponding forms of "to hear," "to see," "to believe," "to know," and "to understand" refer to the reality of "revelation" and the identity of the "Revealer." The Word incarnate comes into the world as "light" (1:9; 3:19; 8:12; 9:5), as the bearer of the divine revelation that delivers from darkness, from the realm of death. Jesus' coming into the world as light is the coming of the Revealer who brings the gift of eternal life. He is literally "the light of life" (8:12) because the life he brings is "the light of men" (1:4).

He tells us the truth which he heard from God (8:40), and it is this truth which sets us free (8:32). Indeed he himself is "the truth," the revelation which is the only way to life (14:6). His whole life is the manifestation of the glory of God (1:14; 2:11; 11:40; 12:41). Though we might not think of it as such, "glory" is perhaps the nearest synonym for "revelation" that we can find in the fourth gospel. God's glory is the revelation of his being. This is why it can be spoken of as light and as truth.

All the World

It is necessary to note yet again here that the coming of this revelation "as light into the world" (12:46) is, as often elsewhere in John, a coming into "the world" in its neutral, not its pejorative, sense. The revelation comes into the world, i.e., into the dwelling place of all women and men on the face of the earth. The term "world" here thus allows neither constriction nor specification. The light did not come for some but not for others. Any attempt to limit the all-embracing amplitude of "the world" has its reason in something other than fidelity to the gospel itself.

What the RSV in this verse (12:46) renders as "whoever" and the NRSV as "everyone" can equally well be translated "*all* who believe in me." This all "who believe in me" is similarly unrestricted, either by prior divine decree or by posterior implicit condition. Anyone at all who believes in him does "not remain in darkness" or, put positively, possesses "eternal life" (3:15, 16, 36; 5:24, 40; 6:40). All speculation about prior election or reprobation in this regard is idle, indeed meaningless.

Response to the Revelation

If any one hears my sayings and does not keep them, I do not judge him; for I did not come to judge the world but to save the world (12:47).

What restriction there is can come, not from God nor from the one he sent, but only from the free creature who encounters the revelation. Hearing the word of the revelation is not mere attention to information. It is not just a notional assent to propositions. The revelation that the Revealer brings demands a response, and such response as embraces the totality of the person responding. To hear the words of Jesus is to obey the will of the Father expressed in them. All revelation in the biblical context is an imperative. The Torah is revelation, as is the Decalogue, as are the words of the prophets: "For thus says the Lord to the house of Israel: 'Seek me and live'" (Amos 5:4). Hearing the word must involve keeping it. Failure to keep it is tantamount to rejecting it. Believing the word which the Revealer brings, means both hearing him and keeping his word.

If, however, we choose not to believe, if we refuse to hear and keep the word, then that refusal is itself the "judgment." We ourselves choose to remain in darkness, and so we die. This is not the Revealer's doing: "I do not judge him," for the very simple reason that the purpose of his coming into the world was not to judge "but to save the world" (12:47). His work is salvation. It is his gift, his grace to the world (cf. 1:17). Those who reject his revelation pass judgment on themselves in the very act of their rejection of the salvation which the revelation offers them. This is the mystery of our being free human beings, before whose rejection the Revealer himself stands helpless.

He who rejects me and does not receive my sayings has a judge; the word that I have spoken will be his judge on the last day (12:48).

This judgment is another theme that has run through the first part of the gospel (3:17, 18, 19; 5:22, 24, 27, 29, 30; 7:24; 8:15, 16; 9:39; 12:31). Nevertheless, we have to keep in mind that the purpose of Christ's coming into the world was not to judge it: "I did not come to judge the world but to save the world" (12:47). He did not come to condemn anyone in the world, but to save everyone in it. Yet his very coming into the world cannot but bring about a judgment. He comes into a world of free human beings who can as readily reject as accept him and his gift. The revelation he brings inevitably operates a segregation, a separation and division. Therefore, he says, "For judgment I came into the world" (9:39).

What precipitates this judgment is of course "the word," the revelation which he brings in obedience to the God who "loved the world" (3:16):

For I have not spoken on my own authority, the Father who sent me has himself given me commandment what to say and what to speak (12:49).

This is another frequently reiterated theme of the gospel. The Revealer is, in and for himself, nothing. Whatever he does he does in total obedience to the Father's command (4:34; 5:30; 6:38; 8:28). It is in the totality of his obedience to the will of the one who sent him that Jesus reveals God as his Father, and reveals himself as the Son sent by the

Father to "save the world" (12:47). This obedience is what underlies all the astonishing pronouncements about his relationship to God, which culminate in "I and the Father are one" (10:30 and cf. 1:14, 18; see 3:35; 5:17, 18, 19–24, 26, 27, 36, 37, 43; 6:27, 37, 46, 57; 8:16, 18, 19, 28, 29, 38, 54; 10:15, 17, 18, 25, 29, 36, 37–38; 11:41–42; 12:28).

And I know that his commandment is eternal life. What I say, therefore, I say as the Father has bidden me (12:50).

The express will of the Father is "eternal life." It is the will of a God who "so loved the world that he gave his only Son, that whoever believes in him should not perish but have eternal life" (3:16). Everything God does, he does with this end in view: to give life. He sends his only Son into the world for no other reason except that "they may have *life,* and have it abundantly" (10:10).

The whole mission of the Son is, therefore, summed up in this gift of eternal life. The wonder is that he "came into his own home, and his own people received him not" (1:11), that he came into the world and yet the world persisted and still persists in knowing him not (1:10). That those who desire life above all else in creation, the life without which creation itself would be nothing to them, should reject the eternal life the Revealer brings them, and turn away from him who has "the word of eternal life" (6:68), is the abiding mystery of the first part of the fourth gospel.

John 13

The Book of Glory: the farewell discourses; the evangelist prophet; Augustine's *Tractatus*.

Washing the Disciples' Feet: God's love for the world; "love"; the devil; from God and to God; first interpretation of the foot washing; willingness to be loved; second interpretation of the foot washing; "as I have done"; loving his own; the sent and the sender.

Jesus Foretells His Betrayal: the disciple whom Jesus loved; the fate of Judas.

The New Commandment: glory/glorify; Jesus' departure from the world; the new commandment; "as I have loved"; true discipleship.

Peter's Denial Foretold: following Jesus.

THE BOOK OF GLORY

With this chapter begins the second part of the gospel. As the first part has come to be referred to as the Book of Signs, so the second is called the "Book of Glory." It can equally well be called the "Revelation of the Glory." But, evidently, such a designation can apply equally well to the entire book, and not just to its second part. The second part is, in fact, a series of farewell discourses (chapters 13–17) that are followed by two chapters on the passion (chapters 18–19), and one on the resurrection appearances (chapter 20), to which is added still another chapter on one more resurrection appearance (chapter 21) by way of an epilogue or an appendix to the completed work.

John 21, which circulated as an integral part of the gospel from the earliest times, is a reminder–if any were needed–that the gospel of John underwent several stages of development before it acquired its present shape. Unlike the story of the woman caught in adultery (Jn

7:53–8:11), which is missing from all the early manuscripts, John 21 is found in the earliest among them.

As we have already remarked, the first part of the gospel is, in a sense, a commentary on the prologue's "He came to his own home, and his own people received him not" (1:11). Thus the manifestation of God's love in the sending of his Son into the world became a scandal and a stumbling block to a world that "knew him not" (1:10).

The second part, on the other hand, can be regarded as an extended commentary on the prologue's "But to all who received him, who believed in his name, he gave power to become children of God" (1:12). Nevertheless, it will also show how God's love, now manifested in the community of believers, will still encounter opposition, hatred and persecution.

The peculiar cachet of this community of those who believed in the Word become flesh, the distinguishing mark of its identity in the world, will be that love with which God "loved the world" and "gave his only Son" (3:16). It is therefore only fitting that the farewell discourse of Jesus, which elaborates this theme of love, should culminate in the death on the cross, the point of intersection between the love of God and the hatred of the world. In the cross is the revelation of the Father's love for the world, the manifestation of the Son's love for "his own who were in the world" (13:1), and the gift of the Spirit (19:30) as the assurance of the permanence of both one and the other in a changing world.

The Farewell Discourses

A word about the nature of the farewell discourses is called for here. Of the many and varied ways that describe this series of discourses as the last testament of Jesus to his own, or an exhortation and commissioning of his disciples, or a prolonged leave-taking of those whom he loves and yet must leave behind in a hostile world, the most comprehensive description would seem to be a collection of sermons to the community of the believers in him. Such a description can readily embrace all the other elements hitherto discerned in the discourses: testament, farewell, commission and exhortation.

To designate them as "sermons," however, is by no means exclusive to the farewell discourses. The designation is every bit as suitable to the other short or long discourses we have encountered throughout the first part of the gospel, from "For God so loved the world" in 3:16–21, to "He who believes in me" (12:44–50). As will have been surely noted, it is not always easy to say when Jesus' words cease and where the evangelist's voice takes over. John 3:16 is a very good example: Who in fact does say, "For God so loved the world that he gave his only Son, that whoever believes in him should not perish but have eternal life"? Is it Jesus or the evangelist?

The Evangelist Prophet

Indeed, one can read, not such a discourse, but the whole gospel as a series of sermons by the evangelist. The evangelist would then be seen as assuming the role of the Old Testament prophets who prefaced their preaching to God's people with, "Thus says the Lord." To debate whether the prophet or God utters the words in such passages would be quite meaningless. God always uses human beings to communicate his revelation to his people.

Augustine's Tractatus

But the process does not stop with the prophet or the evangelist. Thus, for example, Saint Augustine, whether or not he adverted to this particular feature in John's gospel, set out to do much the same thing in his famous series of homilies on it. As the evangelist took Jesus' words and deeds as a basis for his sermons to the Johannine community, so Augustine took the evangelist's work and used it as the basis for his daily sermons to his congregation during the Lent of 407. Augustine's *Tractatus in Ioannem* is not, properly speaking, a commentary. But, just as the evangelist used Jesus' words to comfort his community in its trials, joys, sorrows and perplexity, so Saint Augustine took the evangelist's words to preach to his own community in the midst of its trials and hardships, its bewilderment and confusion.

In his homilies on the gospel, the Bishop of Hippo did not stop to explain every word or phrase. He allotted disproportionate space to some–to us–seemingly unimportant matters, many of them only remotely connected with what the gospel actually says. He was selective in what he expounded to his hearers, but only because he never forgot for a moment that he was bringing to his people the word of life on which he himself had fed. Can anyone who, in any age, undertakes to elucidate the gospel for God's people do otherwise?

Indeed, did the author of the fourth gospel do any less? He, too, must have sought to nurture his community on the word of life that was his own daily bread. He, too, had to be selective in choosing to expound this or that tradition about Jesus of Nazareth. In near despair at the infinite possibilities of addition to what he had already written, he concluded, "But there are also many other things which Jesus did; were every one of them to be written, I suppose that the whole world itself could not contain the books that would be written" (21:25).

WASHING THE DISCIPLES' FEET (John 13:1–20)

> **Now before the feast of the Passover, when Jesus knew that his hour had come to depart out of this world to the Father, having loved his own who were in the world, he loved them to the end (13:1).**

This is Jesus' last Passover on earth. It is also his last supper with his own disciples (13:4). The "hour," which he foresaw from the very beginning ("My hour has not yet come" 2:4; 7:30; 8:20), has finally arrived (12:23, 27; 13:1). He now has to depart from the world into which he came. He has to return to the Father from whom he came. The whole gospel of John can thus be summed up in this descending and ascending movement. The "only Son, who is in the bosom of the Father" (1:18) comes into the world only to leave it. For, as we shall have occasion to see, it is only in the contemplation of his departure from the world that the believers in him can come to understand his coming into it. Paradoxical as it sounds, the whole purpose of the coming of the Revealer into the world is to console us for his having to leave it.

God's Love for the World

At the very beginning of the whole movement of descent-ascent stands the love of God for the whole world (3:16). The Father sent the Son he loves (3:35) into a hostile world where "men loved darkness rather than light" (3:19). The love that the Son is about to manifest in his death on the cross is the reason why the Father loves him: "because I lay down my life" (10:17). On the cross, Jesus manifests his loving obedience to the Father in and by the very act of revealing his love for the world.

But we must not allow ourselves to think that this love for the world was in any way abstract or undifferentiated. This love was very unlike that of many of us who love humanity but can't stand any of its members. The love with which Christ loved his own in the world is individual, distinct as well as distinctive: "Now Jesus loved Martha and her sister and Lazarus" (11:5), and the list can be protracted to infinity.

"Love"

Before we proceed any further, however, it is necessary to make one single point clear. But, in order to do this, I have to depart from my resolve to avoid any technical and philological discussion in these pages. I shall, however, be quit of it in one single paragraph.

There is a Hebrew word for "to love," *'ahabh.* It describes God's love for his people ("because the Lord loves you," Dt 7:8), and theirs for God ("You shall therefore love the Lord your God," Dt 11:1); the love of Abraham for Isaac (Gen 22:2) and of Isaac for Rebekah (Gen 24:67); of Jacob for Rachel (Gen 29:18, 30); of Shechem and Dinah (Gen 34:3), Michal and David (1 Sam 18:20), Jonathan and David (2 Sam 1:26); the love of the neighbor (Lev 19:18) and of the stranger (Dt 10:19); the love of Hosea for an adulteress (Hos 3:1) and of Amnon for his sister Tamar whom he raped (2 Sam 13:15). All these instances of the Hebrew term are rendered by *agapan* in the Septuagint, the Greek version of the Old Testament. After varied fortunes had befallen the several other terms which Greek possessed for "to love," *agapan* came to be the current term. Though Greek, unlike Hebrew, possessed at least four different words for "to love," *agapan* is the one used in the Septuagint to translate the Hebrew *'ahabh.*

The explanation is called for at this juncture because the amount of sheer nonsense produced by so-called "spiritual" writers on the subject of love knows no bounds. We have to keep in mind that the "love" of Jesus for his own differs not one whit from the "love" of his own for him and for one another; that the word "love" is the only term we have or ever will have to speak of the love of God for us, or of our love for God. Any distinction we might choose to introduce between one love and another is a distinction that can only arise, not from the love itself, but from the uniqueness of each lover and the corresponding uniqueness of each person who is loved.

Therefore, when John says that Jesus, "having loved his own who were in the world, he loved them to the end" (13:1), he is not creating a new category of love. To ask what *kind* of love, or to insist that this was divine not human love, is not only arrant nonsense, but a heresy that as long ago as the first century denied the reality of Jesus' humanity. What marks Jesus' love for his own is the "unto the end," the very totality of his giving himself to those he loved. But we shall have occasion to reflect later that this very totality of self-donation is what ought to mark all love.

The Devil

> **And during supper, when the devil had already put it into the heart of Judas Iscariot, Simon's son, to betray him, Jesus, knowing that the Father had given all things into his hands, and that he had come from God and was going to God (13:2–3)....**

No matter what one thinks of "the devil" or of the mechanism of temptation, neither Judas Iscariot, nor I, nor anyone of us need go outside ourselves for an explanation of the evil we choose. However out of vogue such an opinion might be today, a moment's reflection should suffice to show us the difference between my betrayal of a friend and a deadly tidal wave. Each of us, though able to stand by the grace of God, is free to fall by himself; and though there is only one way to stand, there are myriad ways each of us can choose to fall. God made us "just and right,/Sufficient to have stood, though free to fall" (*Paradise Lost* 3.98).

Jesus' "knowing that the Father had given all things into his hands" (13:3; see 3:35) echoes what the prologue had already proclaimed: "All things were made through him, and without him was not anything made that was made" (1:3; cf. 5:26–27). In 13:3, the evangelist's remark insists on the fact that all that Jesus has is a gift of the Father (cf. 3:35; 10:29). This is why, standing before the tomb of Lazarus, Jesus could pray, "Father, I thank you that you have heard me. I knew that you hear me always" (11:41–42). His prayer of thanksgiving is a recognition of the fact that all he has is from the Father. It is a permanent disposition because the gift of God is integral and uninterrupted.

From God and to God

Jesus also knew that "he had come from God and was going to God" (13:3; cf. 8:42; 16:5). As has been remarked already, this fact is a summary of the whole mission of the Son. Indeed, it is a summary of the whole gospel. Of course, that he came from God and goes back to God is true of the incarnate Word in a unique way. But we should not lose sight of the fact that the statement can be true of every one of us. We, too, come from God and to God must we also return.

Thee, God, I come from, to thee go,
All day long I like fountain flow
From thy hand out, swayed about
Mote-like in thy mighty glow.

G. M. Hopkins

This is why this movement of coming forth and returning shaped the structure of the great medieval summas of theology. But, come to think of it, this going abroad and returning home was already there in Homer's Iliad, going abroad, and Odyssey, the journey home. In this world, we are all on our journey home. Thus Dante can begin his Divine Comedy with, "In the middle of the road of our life." So, the truth enunciated about Jesus knowing that "he had come from God and was going to God" (Jn 13:3) is but another confirmation of the truth that "the Word became flesh" (1:14).

[Jesus] rose from supper, laid aside his garments, and girded himself with a towel. Then he poured water into a basin, and began to wash the disciples' feet, and to wipe them with the towel with which he was girded (13:4–5).

We need no course in social anthropology to tell us all that is implied in such a gesture. But we do need a moment's reflection on the unostentatiousness of Jesus' action. It was not theater, nor was it meant to be. That, despite the clarity of the words and the natural simplicity of what they describe in the gospel, we persist in thinking of the washing of the feet as grand drama is—one suspects—largely due to the Holy Thursday liturgy. Of course, the Jesus of John was not a prelate, and had no need to stage a show for the benefit of spectators seeking ersatz edification. High drama is ill-suited for imparting lessons in humility. To be sure, the washing of the feet is susceptible of more than one interpretation, but the popular view of the Holy Thursday liturgy can scarcely be one of them.

First Interpretation of the Foot Washing

The evangelist himself offers two successive interpretations of the narrative: one in the dialogue with Peter (13:6–11), and the other in Jesus' exhortation after he had performed the humble service to his disciples (13:12–20):

He came to Simon Peter; and Peter said to him, "Lord, do you wash my feet?" (13:6).

Peter's reaction is quite comprehensible. It is normal enough at the sight of someone we esteem greatly rendering us a humble and humbling service. In itself, such reaction on the part of the recipient is not necessarily one of humility. In Peter's case, it was something else altogether.

Jesus answered, "What I am doing you do not know now, but afterward you will understand." Peter said to him, "You shall never wash my feet" (13:7–8a).

What Peter does "not know now" and will exhibit a remarkable slowness to understand even afterward, is not only Jesus' love for him but also the new order which this love institutes (see, e.g., "If any one would be first, he must be last of all and servant of all" Mk 9:35; "whoever would be great among you must be your servant, and whoever would be first among you must be slave of all" Mk 10:43–44). To be sure, the understanding of all that Jesus says and does can only dawn on his disciples after his death and resurrection (see Jn 2:22; 12:16). But this was not exactly what lay behind Peter's categoric refusal.

Willingness to Be Loved

Peter refuses to accept a gift and, thereby, fails to comprehend the action of the giver even on its most elementary level. His forthright refusal, "You shall never wash my feet," draws from Jesus one of those principles of Christian life to which we hardly ever advert:

Jesus answered him, "If I do not wash you, you have no part in me" (13:8b).

Of course, the most evident meaning of Jesus' words is that, if we are not cleansed of our sins, we cannot be his disciples. But the point of his response lies at a deeper level still. It is a reminder that the sole, indispensable condition for having a part in him is our willingness to accept his gift. Jesus, who "loved his own" (13:1), can only offer this love to them, but cannot compel them to accept it. The gesture of washing the feet is just such an offer of love. You cannot have a part in him, be his disciple, or respond to his command to "love one another"

(13:34), unless you accept the gift of love he offers, unless you allow yourself to be loved.

Astonishing though it is, Peter's rejection is not singular. To accept the gift of love from another is ultimately to confess a need. This is why it is always humbling to be loved, whether by Jesus of Nazareth or by anyone else. Yet, being loved is the indispensable precondition for loving ("We love, because he first loved us" 1 John 4:19). Since this is so, the genuine surprise is in how we have succeeded in secluding Christians from this love, indeed in filling them with self-loathing, while we persisted in exhorting them to love one another.

The first lesson of the washing of the feet is not the humility of Jesus who stoops to render this service, but the pride of Peter that refuses to accept it. The humility of Jesus in this incident is not in the lowliness of the menial task he performs, but in his acknowledging that "the Father had given all things into his hands" (Jn 13:3; 3:35). All that Jesus himself has is a gift. It is his recognition of this fact that sets him free to love his own "to the end" (13:1), and to demonstrate it by washing their feet.

Before Jesus' response, "If I do not wash you, you have no part in me" (13:8), the reaction of Peter typifies his misunderstanding and, after it, demonstrates his misguided zeal.

> **Simon Peter said to him, "Lord, not my feet only but also my hands and my head!" (13:9).**

Here, too, Peter misunderstands the nature of the gift and, in doing so, fails to acknowledge the giver. His suddenly found zeal for ablution is impulsive but, alas, also ill-founded (cf. 13:36–38).

That the opening statement of this chapter, that Jesus "loved his own...to the end" (13:1), did in fact include Judas Iscariot among "his own" can astonish or grieve us; but that it includes the Simon Peter whom Jesus will appoint the shepherd of his flock (21:15, 16, 17) can only console us.

> **Jesus said to him, "He who has bathed does not need to wash, except for his feet, but he is clean all over; and you are clean, but not every one of you." For he knew who was to betray him; that was why he said, "You are not all clean" (13:10–11).**

If there be a meaning beyond the obvious in the first statement, "He who has bathed does not need to wash, except for his feet, but he is clean all over," then it must be subtle indeed. If we remember that the cleanliness in this context is not hygienic but salvific, a cleanliness brought by him who "takes away the sin of the world" (1:29), who has "come to save the world" (12:47); and if this cleanliness can be attained only "by the word which I have spoken to you" (15:3), then we have to ask: Is Jesus in fact telling Peter any more than that the cleanliness he brings is integral and admits no gradation? That being clean in this sense is therefore a total state? In this sense, you can no more be clean in part than you can be partially saved.

What is more important to note, however, is the evangelist's affirmation, "For he knew who was to betray him" (13:11). Right at the start of this second part of the gospel, we are again reminded how resolutely and unhesitatingly Jesus advances to his death on the cross: "I lay down my life.... No one takes it from me, but I lay it down of my own accord" (10:17–18). Yet, with all the foreknowledge with which the evangelist credits him, Jesus goes on loving his own "to the end," Judas Iscariot who betrayed him, Simon Peter who denied him, and the disciple "whom Jesus loved" (13:23). The love is always unqualifiedly the same. What its recipient does with it is, of course, another matter. To accept it is "eternal life"; to refuse it is the "judgment."

Second Interpretation of the Foot Washing

When he had washed their feet, and taken his garments, and resumed his place, he said to them, "Do you know what I have done to you?" (13:12).

This verse initiates another line of interpretation of Jesus' action. The first interpretation (13:6–11) called attention to the absolute need to receive the gift of his love, to accept the service he offers, in order to belong to him (13:8). Its focus of attention was the recipient of the gift. The second interpretation, however, focuses attention on the person of the giver. To say that it proposes Jesus as a model is, of course, true but misleading. This is what Jesus sets out to forestall by posing the question, "Do you know what I have done to you?" But, judging from the subsequent history of the community of those who believe in him, his success in this attempt at clarity was less than remarkable.

"Do you know what I have done to you?" should call attention, not to the external action of washing their feet, but to its true significance. Aping the foot washing is easy and requires no particular virtue beyond the histrionic. Indeed, it can readily serve to mask the very opposite of what it is intended to signify. We are far too well-schooled in hypocrisy not to realize this. The true meaning of Jesus' action is exposed in his words.

"As I have done"

> **You call me Teacher and Lord; and you are right, for so I am. If I then, your Lord and Teacher, have washed your feet, you also ought to wash one another's feet (13:13–14).**

To understand Jesus' action, it is important to keep in mind that he who performs this action is indeed their "Teacher and Lord," not somebody on an equal footing with them, either in position or in dignity. These are not courtesy titles. He is not their Lord and Master by their indulgence. What he is to them, he is by reason of what he does for them; and what he does for them, he does because of who he is for them. He is not a creation of their choice, not the beneficiary of a plebiscite. It was he who chose them to be his disciples, not they who chose him for their "Teacher and Lord" (15:16).

Therefore, "I have given you an example, that you also should do *as I have done* to you" is, evidently, not an argument from parity, as it is often wrongly interpreted. It is rather an argument from the greater to the lesser. If he who is uniquely their Lord and Master renders them this humble service, which is the proper task of a slave and a servant, then all the more reason why they, who are in fact slaves and servants, should render this service to one another.

The incident is thus a perfect illustration of the order of hierarchy in the Christian community. So long as there is a gospel to proclaim, a message to preach, and a truth to teach, this community is and remains necessarily hierarchical. What characterizes this community in the world is not the "democracy" of its members but the nature of its hierarchy. It is a hierarchy stood on its head, where "the great among you must be your servant; and whoever would be first among you must be slave of all" (Mk 10:43–44; see Mk 9:35; Mt 23:11; 20:27; Lk 22:26–27). In the foot washing, the action of Jesus is a demonstration that he who is their leader stands among them as the "one who serves" (Lk 22:26–27). John's narrative of the foot washing is but a graphic demonstration of this gospel truth.

The imperative that follows, "you also should do as I have done to you" (Jn 13:15), derives from the right comprehension of the Lord's action. It is not an invitation to an ostentatious display of theatrical humility, but a reminder to all who belong to the community of the service they owe one another. The imperative is not an opportunity to disguise domination in the habiliments of humility, but a compelling need to understand all hierarchy in the Christian community as humble, self-effacing service.

For I have given you an example, that you also should do as I have done to you (13:15).

Our willful misunderstanding of these words of Jesus in John demonstrates how deaf we can be when once we choose not to hear (cf. 9:39, 41; 12:40). The example is not a prescription for the ceremony of Maundy Thursday, but for the pattern of behavior of the community's ministers every day of the year. You cannot go around every day of the year as the grand high cockalorum of the kingdom of God and hope to draw a discreet veil of humility over your behavior on Holy Thursday.

That "you should do as I have done to you" (13:15) is to do as Jesus has done in showing himself to be the last of all, the slave for all, and the servant of all:

Amen, amen, I say to you, a slave is not greater than his master; nor is he who is sent greater than he who sent him (13:16).

As the marginal note in the RSV indicates, "slave," not "servant," is the term used in the Greek here. But, whichever term you choose, there can be no evading the meaning of this solemn, "Amen, amen, I say to you" pronouncement (see 15:20; cf. Mt 10:24; Lk 6:40). Jesus is undeniably their "Lord and Teacher" (Jn 13:14), yet he renders them the service that befits a slave in their midst.

Though the conclusion to be drawn from the Lord's action is too evident to require explicitation, the evangelist draws it nevertheless:

If you know these things, blessed are you, if you do them (13:17).

The exhortation is formulated as a beatitude, "blessed are you," which belongs to those who comprehend Jesus' words as a way of life. Believing in him is not just an intellectual exercise. It is rather a whole life lived in accordance with the word he utters.

These "things" to which Jesus refers are, of course, the revelation he brings. This revelation can be grasped and apprehended only by "doing," by living out the truth it reveals. This, in fact, is what is meant by "*doing* the truth" (3:21; cf. "live according to the truth" 1 Jn 1:6), living out the revelation and its implications in one's daily life.

Loving His Own

It can all too readily be forgotten that this entire series of sayings of Jesus derive their intelligibility from the opening verse of the chapter: "Having loved his own who were in the world, he loved them to the end" (13:1). Without this love, the washing of the feet would be an empty gesture. Without it, the humility of the act would be a mere pathology. Only when seen in the light of this love for his own, do Jesus' words have any meaning at all. Only because of this love can the beatitude, "Blessed are you if you do them" (13:17), be more than an empty formula.

Moreover, if we remember that when the evangelist uses "his own" in 13:1 rather than "his disciples," he wishes to include all believers down the ages, then we can begin to appreciate the significance of the dual lesson he draws from the washing of the feet. Peter's stubbornness (13:8) is ours whenever we recognize readily enough our service of others as humbling, and yet refuse to acknowledge that to be served by a loving other is more humiliating still. To give can well be "more blessed" than to receive (Acts 20:35), but to receive is infinitely more humbling. We are all too ready to forget that the first lesson to be drawn from the foot washing is that the absolutely indispensable condition for "having a part" in him (Jn 13:8) is the willingness to accept the offer of his love, to receive his service. Of course, Jesus, having left this world and returned to the Father, his love and service can come to us only from the other (13:20).

So, too, in the second interpretation of the foot washing (13:12–17), to grasp the meaning of what their Lord and Master did for his disciples can only come from the realization that all love is, in Simone Weil's words, "creative attention" to the need of the other. As such, it is of course not susceptible of prior organization and planning, where it always risks becoming a hollow exercise in hypocrisy. If Jesus gives his disciples "an example" (13:15) it is the example, not of this specific action of foot washing, nor merely of the humility it requires, but of the total forgetfulness of himself in the service of others. This, and this alone, enables the Teacher and Lord to assume the role of the slave and servant. It is this forgetfulness of self which allows the attention to the other to be truly creative.

Anyone who has accepted this loving service from another can see in it an "example," not of how to love in return the one who rendered it, but rather of how to love one another: "you also ought to wash *one another's* feet" (13:14). What Jesus commands them to do is not to reciprocate his love and service, but to replicate it in their daily life in the community of believers.

> **I am not speaking of you all; I know whom I have chosen; it is that the scripture may be fulfilled, "He who ate my bread has lifted his heel against me." I tell you this now, before it takes place, that when it does take place you may believe that I am [he] (13:18–19).**

The betrayer and the betrayal cannot for very long be far from Jesus' mind while Judas Iscariot is still with them. The event of the foot washing is, in its way, the founding of the community. It not only establishes the community of the disciples with the Lord (13:8, "If I do not wash you, you have no part in me"), but also the community of the disciples among themselves (13:14, "you also ought to wash one another's feet"). In both these instances there is the need to warn the disciples against self-confidence; and, in both, the example of Judas is there to remind them (13:10–11 and 18–19).

In the latter instance (13:18–19), the warning serves the double purpose of minimizing the scandal by situating the betrayal within the purview of prophecy ("Even my bosom friend in whom I trusted, who ate of my bread, has lifted his heel against me," Ps 41:9), and of reinforcing the disciples' own faith in him as the Revealer, "that...you may believe that I am" (Jn 13:19). The disciples ought to realize the truth of his claim, "I know whom I have chosen" (13:18). Even the case of Judas Iscariot should come as no surprise, any more than that of Peter, or indeed of all but the "disciple whom Jesus loved" (19:26). Betrayal, denial and defection are, alas, a constant in the life of the community.

The Sent and the Sender

> **Amen, amen, I say to you, he who receives any one whom I send receives me; and he who receives me receives him who sent me (13:20).**

Jesus' remark at the close of this section is baffling. It seems out of place and without connection with what preceded it. Yet, as a conclusion to the whole event of the foot washing, it admirably serves as a reminder of the lessons contained in it.

The linkage of the one sent with the sender establishes the order of service in the community. First, Peter's demur at the Lord's humble service is a pale reflection of our own refusal to accept the loving service of others. Peter's reluctance to accept the humbling service of his acknowledged Lord and Master is matched by our refusal to accept it from those we deem inadequate, unqualified, lacking credentials, or what have you. We want everything to come from the mouth of the Lord himself; we seek forever to find the definitive words of Jesus on this or that subject; we really want a first-rate redeemer to meet our specific requirements in order to parade him proudly before the world as the avatar of all its current preferences. The more urgent our need for redemption, the more exigent our requirements for a redeemer seem to be.

The second, more elusive, point in this representative substitution, "who receives any one whom I send receives me...," is the very logic, not just of the foot washing, but of the incarnation itself. What the eyes of the disciples beheld was only Jesus of Nazareth, when in fact they were seeing "the Father" (14:9). So, too, the Christians see in those who serve them merely other human beings like themselves, subject to all the limitations and foibles of our humanity, when they ought to see in them the Lord who sent them, "who receives *any one* whom I send receives me; and who receives me receives him who sent me" (13:20).

We balk at this recognition, and so we set about manufacturing idols among those who are "sent," endowing our current favorites among them with "charisma," setting them apart from the–to us–lowly and despicable herd of messengers of the Word.

We go further still. Little by little, we magnify the miraculous and the glorious in the one who sent the messengers of the Word. Thus, we try increasingly to conceal all the genuine traces of Jesus' humanity, save of course those that most flatter our image of ourselves. We want the Word to be an incarnation of our current preferences.

To all such attempts to minimize the truth of "became flesh," there can be but one answer: "Amen, amen, I say to you, he who receives any one whom I send receives me; and who receives me receives him who sent me" (13:20). The nub of this solemn "Amen, amen, I say to you," which establishes the linkage of the messengers with the Lord, and of the Lord with the Father, lies in Jesus' exhortation to "do as I have done to you" (13:15), no less than in his, "If I do not wash you, you have no part in me" (13:8b).

From the perspective of the evangelist, i.e., after Jesus' departure "out of this world to the Father" (13:1), our having a part in the Lord remains always contingent upon our acceptance of loving service from those whom he sends. Of course, we are not particularly inclined to accept such love and service at their hands willingly, any more than was Peter at Jesus' own hands. We even go Peter one better: we think we deserve more, and expect the brightest, the most eloquent, the highly esteemed in the eyes of the world, etc.

It is remarkable how those most in need of love are least willing to undergo the humility of being loved. The most beggarly among us are the most stubborn in our haughty disdain of the love offered us by others. We pretend we have a right to this love and service, but only from those who meet our exacting standards. In so pretending, we blind ourselves to the love all around us. We forget too readily that this is the only place where the love of him whom the Father sent and of the Father who sent him can be had, i.e., in the love of the other for us.

Of course, those in need of this love and service are in no position to dictate how or from whom they receive it. By refusing it from those whom Jesus sends, they really can have "no part" (13:8) in him who sent them. They are therefore incapable of loving Jesus or seeing him in others any more than they are of seeing and loving the Father in him.

This chain of representation and substitution from the one who serves us, to the Lord who served his disciples, to the Father who sent him to serve, is what establishes the community of believers. In this community, the "love one another" is necessarily patterned on the "as I have love you" (13:34).

JESUS FORETELLS HIS BETRAYAL (John 13:21–30)

When Jesus had thus spoken, he was troubled in spirit, and testified, "Amen, amen, I say to you, one of you will betray me" (13:21).

This inner agitation, the being "troubled in spirit," echoes the "he was deeply moved in spirit and troubled" at the death of Lazarus (11:33). The same Greek verb is employed in both instances, as it is also in

"Now my soul is troubled" in 12:27. The verb is also used to describe the stirring of the water in the pool of Bethsaida (5:7). It describes Jesus as deeply troubled and emotionally stirred, as well he might be at the death of a friend, the prospect of betrayal by one of his own, or the approach of his own death. If such a reaction on the part of Jesus poses any problem, then that problem arises, not from the straightforward statements of the evangelist, but from our own unwillingness to grasp the reality of the "became flesh" (1:14) in all its implications.

The statement that "one of you will betray me" (13:21) can similarly be regarded as either a prophecy, an apprehension, or an observation of fact. Jesus not only knew Judas for some time but also loved him as one of "his own" (13:1). He is not the first man in history to experience such misgivings vis-à-vis someone he knew and loved. Moreover, it can be left to the imagination of the reader whether, in the final analysis, Jesus was more "troubled in spirit" by Judas' betrayal or by Peter's denial. After all, on Peter depended the future of the community far more than it did on Judas Iscariot.

The Disciple Whom Jesus Loved

The disciples looked at one another, uncertain of whom he spoke. One of his disciples, whom Jesus loved, was lying close to the breast of Jesus; so Simon Peter beckoned to him and said, "Tell us who it is of whom he speaks" (13:22–24).

This is the first mention of the disciple "whom Jesus loved," the beloved disciple, in the gospel. He alone of all the disciples will be at the foot of the cross (19:26). We shall find him at the tomb on the day of the resurrection (20:2), and in the final appearance of the risen Lord by the Sea of Tiberias (21:7, 20). Beyond these occurrences, his identity remains problematic. Whether he was one of "the twelve" and identifiable with John the son of Zebedee; whether he was the anonymous "other disciple...known to the high priest" (18:15, 16); whether he was a real person or the idealized figure of a Christian believer; whether the community from whence the gospel issued was his and whether he is in fact "the disciple who is bearing witness to these things, and who has written these things" (21:24; 19:35), are all questions which continue to be discussed by scholars. To such questions, interpreters have proposed answers ranging from the fanciful to the probable. Perhaps the more plausible among recent hypotheses is that the beloved disciple did indeed belong to the community from which the fourth gospel emanated, and that it is likely his recollections and reflections lay at its roots.

Peter's recourse to the beloved disciple to satisfy his curiosity about the identity of the betrayer is at best ambivalent. It could be merely a sample of Peter's timidity, which would eventually prove so tragic in the courtyard of the high priest at the trial of Jesus (18:17, 25, 27). If this were the case, we might regard it as an ironic instance of Jesus' knowing only too well "whom he has chosen" (13:18). On the other hand, Peter's action might have been dictated by nothing more than the reclining arrangement and the convenience of the beloved disciple's proximity to Jesus at the supper, "close to the breast of Jesus" (13:23, 25). This is what the text suggests:

> **So lying thus, close to the breast of Jesus, he said to him, "Lord, who is it?" Jesus answered, "It is he to whom I shall give the morsel when I have dipped it." So when he had dipped the morsel, he gave it to Judas, the son of Simon Iscariot. Then after the morsel, Satan entered into him. Jesus said to him, "What you are going to do, do quickly" (13:25–27).**

The entry of Satan into Judas, "the son of Simon Iscariot," is neither an excuse nor an exculpation of the betrayer's deed. Though it belongs to the same category as Eve's "The serpent beguiled me, and I ate" (Gen 3:13), the statement in John 13:27 (cf. 13:2) avails as little to minimize Judas' guilt or to extenuate his responsibility.

To insist on this point here, as in 13:2, is all the more necessary in a world prone to explain human evil by any means except personal responsibility. To shift the blame of the action onto Satan or onto a malady or a scarred psyche serves only to add insult to the victim's injury and reduce the human agent of evil to the state of a senseless stone. Desirable though this might seem to some, it logically removes the possibility of attributing any good to the subject as well. This is particularly problematic in a world peopled by ordinary mortals, none of whom is entirely good or pure evil, but a mixture of both evil and good, constantly at war one with the other.

The Fate of Judas

> **Now no one at the table knew why he said this to him. Some thought that, because Judas had the money box, Jesus was**

telling him, "Buy what we need for the feast"; or, that he should give something to the poor (13:28–29).

Jesus' safeguarding of Judas' secret is a delicacy that can easily elude the comprehension of many today. Nevertheless, such discretion remains the mark of genuine love and respect in any circumstance. Of course, no one would wish to deny the enormity of Judas' imminent action. It is made all the more heinous when we consider the loving discretion of Jesus' dealing with Judas Iscariot, not just here, but up to the very end (see Mt 26:50).

What is more instructive in these verses (Jn 13:28–29), however, is the additional information about Judas' status among the twelve. We learn that he was the treasurer of the group, "had the money box" (13:29; 12:6), i.e., was in charge of providing for their needs and attending to the alms for the poor. Had it been otherwise, had Judas not been the "almoner," would the readers of the gospel not have been surprised? Had Judas emerged from the obscurity of Jesus' unnamed followers, or been just another Judas among the chosen twelve, one might well have wondered why he did what he did. Did his assigned task fan the fires of greed in him? Did he at some time wish he had been spared even that small distinction among Jesus' followers, which fired his ambition for more? Did he, at the end, reflect,

> Oh, had his powerful destiny ordained
> Me some inferior Angel, I had stood
> Then happy? (*Paradise Lost* 4.58)

Even without the hope of ever knowing, we do well ourselves to reflect on how easy the way and how wide the gate (cf. Mt 7:13) that lead into the night:

So, after receiving the morsel, he immediately went out; and it was night (13:30).

A work of genius is often known by many insignificant details. A small phrase like "it was night" bears witness to the evangelist's genius. In a gospel, where one of the principal themes is the coming of light into the world (1:9, 4–5; 8:12; 9:5; 11:10), to depart from him who is "the light of the world" is indeed to be in darkness (1:5; 8:12; 12:35, 46). Judas' departure from the light was a journey into the darkness. There it is perpetual night.

THE NEW COMMANDMENT (John 13:31–35)

Glory/Glorify

When he had gone out, Jesus said, "Now is the Son of man glorified, and in him God is glorified; if God is glorified in him, God will also glorify him in himself, and glorify him at once" (13:31–32).

It was remarked at the end of chapter 12 that, in the absence of the term "revelation" from the fourth gospel, a whole constellation of vocables is used to express this central concept which is so indispensable for understanding its message. Pride of place among such terms as prophet, light, Word, etc., must belong to "glory/glorify." Glory is the revelation of the person of God. It is the effulgence of his being; for, as 1 John says, "God is light" (1 Jn 1:5).

"Now is the Son of man glorified." He is "glorified" in his revelation as "the Son of man," the bearer of the revelation, who "descended from heaven" (Jn 3:13; cf. 6:62). To him the Father has given "authority to execute judgment" (5:27). His "hour" has now come to be "lifted up" (3:14; 12:34). It has come for his glory to become visible to the world. In his death on the cross he is "glorified," i.e., revealed to be who he really is: "When you have lifted up the Son of man, then you will know that I am [he]" (8:28). This is the reason why the hour of his approaching death is the "hour...for the Son of man to be glorified" (12:23).

Now, in the glorification of the Son, God himself is glorified. This is to say that, in his death on the cross, Jesus reveals who he truly is: the revealer of the Father. Thus, in him, in his death on the cross, "God is glorified," God is revealed as the Father. Of course, at that very instant, God, the author of the revelation, will also glorify the Revealer, his Son, "in himself" (13:32).

Christians do not perhaps sufficiently reflect upon God's choice of this moment for his supreme revelation. Of course, that the death of Jesus on the cross is the moment of his glorification neither negates the reality of the death nor attenuates the ignominy of the crucifixion. This is what many readers of John are tempted to overlook. It is precisely in the ignominious death on the cross that we come to know and recognize Jesus' "I AM": "then you will know that I am [he], and that I do nothing on my own authority but speak thus as the Father taught me" (8:28). Thus, in his death on the cross, in the totality of his obedience to the will of the one who sent him, he reveals his privileged identity as the only Son; and so, in that selfsame act and instant, he reveals God as the Father. The whole revelation he brings is therefore in obedience to the Father: "I... speak thus as the Father taught me" (8:28).

Jesus' Departure from the World

Little children, yet a little while I am with you. You will seek me; and as I said to the Jews so now I say to you, "Where I am going you cannot come" (13:33).

Though unique in the gospel, "little children" as a mode of address is quite frequent in 1 John (2:1, 12, 28; 3:7, 18; 4:4; 5:21). Needless to add, it is a term of genuine endearment, not of paternalistic condescension.

"Little children" here prefaces a theme that occurred frequently in the gospel–Jesus' departure from the world (7:33–34; 8:21; 12:35; 13:36; 14:19; 16:10, 16–19). "Where I am going you cannot come," is obviously another reminder of Jesus' imminent departure from them. Like Simon Peter (13:37), we are forever looking for means to circumvent this departure of Jesus from our world. We are at our most ingenious in inventing ways to negate the fact of Jesus' absence from our midst. We are stubbornly reluctant to accept his absence as the situation of the true believer in this world. Jesus is gone to where he came from, to where once he was.

We will have occasion to return to this point. What must be kept in mind for the moment, however, is that, in the context of the gospel, though Jesus speaks of his death, he does not speak of "Sheol," the abode of the dead in the Old Testament (see, e.g., Pss 18:4–5; 116:3; Prov 30:16; Is 38:10–11). This fact in itself constitutes a radically new element in our understanding of death within the Christian framework. Else, the "you cannot come" (13:33) makes no sense at all. A mortal is by definition one who can and does inevitably come to "Sheol," the abode of the dead. Sheol is where every mortal, not only can, but must descend. But Jesus' coming into the world and his departure from it, his going away, has made the descent into the abode of the dead not the sole destiny of mortals.

The New Commandment

A new commandment I give to you, that you love one another; even as I have loved you, that you also love one another (13:34).

To those that seek him and want to follow him where he is going, Jesus gives a "new commandment." Thus he answers their request to follow him and to be with him by turning their attention away from themselves and to "one another."

His new commandment that "you love one another" is new for many reasons. It is new, of course, because it belongs to the new age inaugurated by the incarnate Word coming into the world. It is, that is to say, eschatologically new, promulgated now that "the Son of man is glorified" (13:31). It is new with the newness of the dawning of the last times.

It is also new in contrast with the commandment in the old dispensation, "You shall love your neighbor as yourself" (Lev 19:18, 34), which the synoptics (Mt 19:19; 22:39; Mk 12:31, 33; Lk 10:27), Paul (Rom 13:9; Gal 5:14), and James (2:8) take up and enthrone at the heart of the New Testament. The extent and inclusiveness of "your neighbor" as compared with "one another" can be disputed and contrasted; but the primacy of the commandment, and hence its newness, resides in the love it enjoins.

If John insists on the "one another," if he singles out the members of the community of believers, then it is for the very evident reason that each member of this community is in fact one's immediate "neighbor." The Johannine community knew from bitter experience what we all too often choose to forget, that "charity" does indeed begin at home.

The evangelist's insistence on the "one another," moreover, has in view the community's role as a visible sign in the world, "By this all will know that you are my disciples" (Jn 13:35). A community that preaches love for the whole world and fails to manifest it to "one another" is scarcely more than an advertising agency.

It is remarkable how Christians in today's world, intent upon teaching and exemplifying in their boundless zeal the love for all the strangers, the aliens and those of remote lands, often use that very love to browbeat and oppress "one another," the brother and sister next door. One has the impression at times that their love of the world at large is but a means to lord it over one another, to find reason to despise one another.

"As I have loved"

But the principal reason why the commandment is "new" is, evidently, the "as I have loved you." To be sure, the coming of Jesus Christ upon the earth makes all things new (Rev 21:5). Saint Irenaeus understood this well when he said, "In offering himself, Christ brought all newness into the world" (*Adversus Haer.* 4.34.1). But when Jesus insists, "even as I have loved you...you also love one another" (Jn 13:34), he sets up the norm and measure of Christian love once and for all in this world. He himself loved "to the end" (13:1). So it is in this totality of self-donation that the new element in the commandment of love is to be found.

There are, therefore, in this new commandment no mensurables, no quantifiables. It admits no modification and is not susceptible of casuistic distinctions. To love one another as he loved is to give oneself wholly and fully here and now to the other. This might not be very much in a given instance. Even the object of my love might insist on more. Theological savants might decide my love is far inferior to another's. But my love of the other is not a virtue I can increase by dint of constant exercise. It could be lesser tomorrow and might have been greater yesterday. But, here and now, I give all I have to the other, for howsoever fleeting a moment, in the most insignificant and trivial of matters, in the only way I know how. There is and there can only be one love for me to give: the totality of my self to the other here and now.

If, as has been remarked, love is creative attention to the need of the other, then it is my creativity, my attention, my perception of the need here and now that determines the gift of my self. Others are free to judge the particular instance as they please; theologians and moralists can propose methods of progress and prescribe exercises for improvement. Others might judge me capable of more. But for me, here and now, this is all I have. It is the totality of my donation of self to the other that determines whether or not I do indeed love "as I have loved you" (13:34).

Finally, lest the "he loved them to the end" (13:1) be seen exclusively as dying for the other, we must keep in mind that Jesus' commandment is for life in the community, not for the rapid depletion of its numbers. Living for the other is infinitely more difficult than dying for her or for him. It takes much longer, lacks glamor, and has to fight boredom and the blight of familiarity. The coming of Christ into the world gives us life to live for others. Few of us are given the chance to die for one another; but all of us have a life to live for them.

True Discipleship

By this everyone will know that you are my disciples, if you have love for one another (13:35 NRSV).

Love for one another within the community of believers is the permanent sign of its belonging to Christ, of its members being truly his disciples. It is not, as scientific students of religion pretend, either its dogmas, its moral teachings or its rituals that determine and define the Christian community, but the love of its members for one another. Since loving one another is a demanding and never-ceasing task, the community itself is all too readily tempted to pretend that it is its dogmatic tenets, its moral teachings and its religious rites that set it apart from the rest of the world. It must therefore keep ever in the forefront of its preaching Jesus' reminder that "By this everyone will know that you are my disciples, if you have love for one another" (13:35).

It does little good to cite the early history of Christianity or to recall the wonderment of the pagans, "See how they love one another!" (Tertullian, *Apology* 39), or their astonishment that Christians did so even before they knew one another (Minucius Felix, *Octavius* 9). The little we know about the history of the Johannine community itself ought to temper our illusions in this regard. The history of early, as of later, Christianity can also witness to just how Christians did *not* love one another. If the world, then or now, failed to see in them "his disciples" and treated them as just another worldly institution hungry for power and domination even in their very exercise of love, then we have little reason to blame the world for its attitude.

Is this to say that there have been no believers that heeded the new commandment and manifested themselves as his disciples? Not at all! The number of such Christians is beyond count. In every age and every quarter of the globe they lived and do live lives of love for one another. The vast majority of them, in the words of George Eliot, "lived faithfully a hidden life, and rest in unvisited tombs." The totality of their self-donation to one another was and is as unself-conscious as unremarked. Those who have eyes to see can readily recognize them as indeed Jesus' true disciples because they "have love for one another."

PETER'S DENIAL FORETOLD (John 13:36–38)

Simon Peter said to him, "Lord, where are you going?" Jesus answered, "Where I am going you cannot follow me now; but you shall follow afterward" (13:36).

Understandable though his curiosity be, Simon Peter's question is more typical of him than of the other disciples. This is the same Peter who wanted to find out the identity of the betrayer (13:24). Being privy to that identity lent him power, power over others who remained ignorant of the fact (13:28), and power over the betrayer, even though in this instance it remained frustrate, except for a fleeting display of bravado in the garden (18:10–11).

In the present instance, Simon Peter's, "Lord, where are you going?" (13:36) might appear as ordinary curiosity, or it might even be regarded as laudable concern for the person of the Lord. But, given Peter's subsequent boast, "I will lay down my life for you" (13:37), neither is adequate to explain his question. The motive of his curiosity is self-interest, the desire to know his own fate and to have the security that comes from that knowledge. On the other hand, the response of Jesus, far from being a rebuke, shields him as it did Judas Iscariot (13:27–28).

Thus, "Where I am going you cannot follow me now" (13:36) has to be understood in its immediate context. The reference here, as in 13:33, is to death, but not to death as a descent into the abode of the dead. It is rather a reference to death as the gateway to a new life. This is what the "now" refers to in "You cannot follow me *now*" (13:36). This shift in the meaning of death is, moreover, another reason why the commandment to love is "new" (13:34).

Anybody and everybody can follow Jesus to death. After Jesus' death and resurrection, however, only those who are his own, who believe in him, can follow him: "You shall follow afterward!" It is no wonder then that Peter failed to grasp Jesus' meaning.

Following Jesus

Peter said to him, "Lord, why cannot I follow you now? I will lay down my life for you" (13:37).

There is nothing wrong with Peter's question. Without the hindsight of the evangelist and his readers, Jesus' response in 13:36 was a real poser. But what is wrong with Peter's added response, "I will lay down my life for you," is his blind impulsiveness. It is blind because Peter not only lacks self-knowledge but refuses to understand that following Jesus is not his own decision but Jesus' invitation (1:39, 41–42; 15:16 "You did not choose me, but I chose you").

Like so many of us, Simon Peter seems incapable of grasping one simple fact: following Jesus is not an act of heroism. Those who pretend that it is should be held responsible for the catastrophes that are bound to ensue when once this conviction takes hold of the life of any Christian. Anyone who thinks that following Jesus is an act of heroism is bound to end where Peter ended. To follow Jesus is to respond to his call and to recognize in the very act of following him that both the call and the response are his gift to us and not our prowess.

Peter's still worse error is to imagine that it is he who is doing Jesus a favor: "I will lay down my life for you." Everything Peter is or shall be, everything he does and will do, is directly attributable to Jesus' laying down his life for him, and not the other way around.

But worst of all is Peter's hubris in making such a boast. The sense of power his curiosity about the betrayer gave him is here displayed to its worst effect. His boast of loyalty and his protestation of fidelity are alike premature and, in his own case, quite ill-founded. Blindness to self is not the least mainspring of the quest for power. But the Jesus who knew "what was in man" (2:25) gently recalls the hapless Peter to reality and reminds him of the inanity of his boast:

> **Jesus answered, "Will you lay down your life for me? Amen, amen, I say to you, the cock will not crow, till you have denied me three times" (13:38).**

John 14

Jesus the Way to the Father: the way; the vision of God; Jesus and the Father; the "greater works"; answer to prayers.

The Promise of the Spirit: the Spirit and Jesus; the Paraclete; "you will see me"; the obedience of the Son; obedience to his commandments; word and commandment; the abiding of the revelation; the peace of Christ; the joy abiding; obedience to the Father.

JESUS THE WAY TO THE FATHER (John 14:1–14)

Let not your hearts be troubled; [you] believe in God, believe also in me (14:1).

The "troubled" heart of the disciples (see Jesus himself being "troubled" in 11:33; 12:27; 13:21, where the same Greek verb is used) is comprehensible enough, if only at the prospect of Jesus' impending departure. But the exhortation itself is valid for all times and under all circumstances.

Because of the way this exhortation is phrased in the original, it can be translated to read, "You believe in God" in the indicative mood, i.e., a statement of fact; or, "Believe in God" in the imperative, i.e., an exhortation. Whichever way one chooses to read it, the striking thing about it is the parity it establishes between faith in God and faith in Jesus Christ. Indeed, as Pascal has said, "We know God only through Jesus Christ" (*Pensées* 547).

The exhortation to "believe also in me" is consequent upon the disciples' belief in God. To believe truly in God is to believe in the one whom he has sent (see 12:44; 5:23, 37; 6:29, 57; 10:36; cf. 5:46–47). The proposition, of course, works both ways: If you really believe in God, you believe in Jesus Christ whom he has sent; and if you believe in Jesus Christ as the one sent by God, then you believe in God ("Who believes in me, believes not in me but in him who sent me" 12:44). This is why the transition from "God" to "my Father" in the following verse is barely perceptible:

> **In my Father's house are many rooms; if it were not so, would I have told you that I go to prepare a place for you? (14:2).**

Those who stop to speculate on the "many rooms" need not so much the study of Greek grammars and lexica as a passing acquaintance with human nature in a context only slightly different from their own. First of all, the "many rooms" do not refer either to a variety of grades or to distinctions in quality, but solely to multiplicity and abundance of space. Moreover, the "Father's house" is capacious, not by reason of its dimensions or architectural design, but because of the limitless love of the Father for all who come to him, without exception. In the Father's house, room is always available because it is a function of love, not of space.

Therefore, Jesus' going "to prepare a place" for his own should serve to remind us of the radically new destiny that awaits all those who believe in him. In Jesus' death and resurrection a new meaning is given to life both here and hereafter (see on "eternal life" under 3:16; 5:28–29; 11:25–26). With the proclamation of the resurrection, the disciples of Jesus know, as all who believe in him ought to know, that where the Lord is they also shall be:

> **And when I go and prepare a place for you, I will come again and will take you to myself, that where I am you may be also (14:3).**

Admittedly, this saying of Jesus has its grave problems. Its middle phrase, "I will come again and will take you to myself," is obscure to the point of incomprehensibility. In the context of the gospel narrative, the reference to coming *again* can only be to Jesus' resurrection from the dead and not to his "Parousia," his second coming at the end "to judge the living and the dead," as the creed puts it.

If, then, the reference in 14:3 is, in fact, to his resurrection, the meaning of "I will take you to myself" would be hard to grasp, unless you choose to read it as a statement of what will happen at the end of each disciple's life. Nevertheless, although the "I will take you to myself, that where I am you may be also" can still make sense in such a context, the "I will come *again*" remains difficult to comprehend.

A point, however, should be made here, if only for the consolation it ought to provide bereaved Christians in every age. The "where I am you may be also" applies not only to me individually but also to all those whose departure from the world I grieve. The where and the when of "you may be also" remain unknown and unknowable. But, to the faith of the believer, the fact of "where I am you may be also" itself remains incontestable. Therein lies our true consolation in the encounter with death and, as we shall see later, the dynamic of all our love as Christians.

And you know the way where I am going (14:4).

Added to the promise of the preceding verse, this statement seems to have no other purpose than to occasion Thomas' question. It is, of course, the Johannine literary device of misunderstanding being employed once more, and none too subtly at that. Nevertheless, Thomas' is not merely a misunderstanding but a confession of ignorance as well:

Thomas said to him, "Lord, we do not know where you are going; how can we know the way?" (14:5).

Even if it is evident, as it must be to the evangelist and his readers, that we in fact do know *where* Jesus is going, Thomas' question is not difficult to understand. If Jesus' return to the Father is taken for granted after his resurrection from the dead, it was by no means all that clear before it. However, the "how can we know the way?" is a genuine question both before and after the resurrection. That is to say, the answer to it can only be a revelation; and a revelation is what Jesus gives in his answer to Thomas.

The Way

Jesus said to him, "I am the way, and the truth, and the life; no one comes to the Father, but by me" (14:6).

The revelation comes in this triple "I AM" saying which is the perfect summary of Jesus' work as the Revealer. Henceforth, he alone is our way of access to the Father. He is "the way" to the Father precisely because he is the bearer of the revelation, the one who reveals "the truth." What he reveals is that he himself is "the truth," that is, both the Revealer and the revelation. To believe this "truth" is the sole condition for having "the life," eternal life. But, if we recall what was said of such "I AM" formulae above (on 6:35; 11:25), we realize that what this statement of Jesus says is: "The way is I; the truth is I; and the life is I."

Jesus is the way, moreover, not only because he is the Revealer of the truth, the one who brings the final and definitive revelation, but also because the revelation he brings gives life, and leads to eternal life. It is precisely because he brings the revelation which alone gives eternal life that he is "the way," the way to life (see Dt 8:6; 19:9; Pss 25:4; 119:14). The triple statement, therefore, is but one: Jesus is the way both to the truth of the revelation and to the life which it brings.

If you had known me, you would have known my Father also; henceforth you know him and have seen him (14:7).

The addition of these words is not just a Johannine device to evoke yet another misunderstanding that will lead to a further clarification of the revelation. It is of course that, but a great deal more. It makes explicit what the prologue stated: "No one has ever seen God; the only Son, who is in the bosom of the Father, he has made him known" (1:18); "Not that any one has seen the Father except him who is from God; he has seen the Father" (6:46). The verse (14:7) also makes explicit what the gospel has thus far insisted on: "He who sent me is true, and him you do not know. I know him, for I come from him, and he sent me" (7:28–29); "If you knew me, you would know my Father also" (8:19); "Who believes in me, believes not in me but in him who sent me" (12:44).

Throughout the first part of the gospel, Jesus reminded his hearers that "the Son can do nothing of his own accord, but only what he sees the Father doing; for whatever he does, that the Son does likewise" (5:19). He insisted that he never acts alone but "I and the Father who sent me" (8:16); "that I do nothing on my own authority but speak thus as the Father taught me" (8:28 and see 8:38, 42); and that "I and the Father are one" (10:30; cf. 17:11).

But Jesus' statement here in 14:7 goes well beyond the intellectual grasp of a fact, well beyond knowing Jesus and knowing the Father also (cf. 14:1). Jesus' statement here in 14:7 in fact identifies knowing one with knowing the other: to know Jesus is to know the Father. Therefore, he can state unequivocally, "henceforth you know him and have seen him." This is the very God whom "no one has ever seen" (1:18), whose "voice you have never heard, [whose] form you have never seen" (5:37). What the prologue said about beholding the glory of the Word who "was God" (1:1) and "became flesh and dwelt among us" (1:14) is here spelled out.

The Vision of God

Philip said to him, "Lord, show us the Father, and we shall be satisfied" (14:8).

Apart from his misunderstanding of Jesus' statement that "you have seen the Father," Philip's desire is neither singular nor uncommon. The vision of God has been the object of human desire from the dawn of human religious consciousness. Visions and dreams have been the stuff of religious lore and the object of aspiration in every age. Even after the plenitude of the revelation in Jesus Christ, Christians set the vision of God as the goal of their spiritual striving, and indeed continue to speak of the coming glory of eternal life as the "beatific *vision*." All this is done in perfect insouciance of the gospel of John and its message. Indeed, the gospel itself is perverted to serve the very end which has already been made futile by the coming of Jesus Christ into the world.

In a famous collection of anecdotes and sayings of the fathers of the Egyptian desert there is the story of a pagan priest who paid a visit to a group of Christian ascetics. After observing the monks' rigorous way of life, their continuous prayers and many austerities, he asked Abba Olympios, "Since you live like this, do you not receive any visions from God?" Olympios replied, "No." The pagan priest boasted, "When we make a sacrifice to our God, he hides nothing from us, but reveals his mysteries. Yet you say you see nothing?" "Nothing!" This has to be the answer of any believer that the Word indeed did become flesh and dwell among us.

Yet, neither in the fourth century nor after it has the gospel of John deterred Christians from their vain quest for visions or hindered their self-appointed guides from plying their trade. Indeed, innumerable manuals have been written, courses devised, and even academic degrees provided for the purpose. But the vast majority of Christians, who cannot indulge the luxury of the quest, must know, even if only instinctively, that their "we shall be satisfied" lies elsewhere than in "show us the Father." They can rest content with the truth of John's gospel:

Jesus said to him, "Have I been with you so long, and yet you do not know me, Philip? He who has seen me has seen the Father; how can you say, 'Show us the Father'?" (14:9).

Astonishing though this claim might have been then, and continues to be for many even now, it is the premise on which both the gospel and the first epistle of John rest: "We have beheld his glory, glory as of the only Son from the Father" (1:14b), which a modern commentator has singled out as the climax of the prologue, rather than the "Word became flesh" in 1:14a. Phrased differently in 1 John, the premise is stated no less boldly:

> That which was from the beginning, which we have heard, which we have seen with our eyes, which we have looked upon and touched with our hands, concerning the word of life—the life was made manifest, and we saw it, and testify to it, and proclaim to you the eternal life which was with the Father and was made manifest to us (1 Jn 1:1–2).

We must ever keep in mind that what their eyes in fact did see was none other and no more than Jesus of Nazareth. For the generations that followed them, not even Jesus of Nazareth was any longer available to behold. Nevertheless, for them, as for Christians in every age, the fourth gospel reserves a still more special beatitude: "Blessed are those who have not seen and yet believe" (Jn 20:29b).

Jesus' affirmation that "who has seen me has seen the Father" (14:9) defines the nature of the revelation he brings. The encounter with his person *is* the encounter with God the Father. Many, indeed most, of Jesus' contemporaries found the claim incredible and, even if credible, inadequate. Many of those who came after them find the claim of the gospel messengers both incredible and inadequate. They find Jesus' "Amen, amen, I say to you, he who receives any one whom I send receives me," even harder to swallow than "he who receives me receives him who sent me" (13:20). Yet the whole content of the revelation lies here. The only access available to anyone on the face of the earth is in and through the "flesh" which the Word became. There are no first-class means of access to God other than this lowly "flesh." Those who look for other means flatter themselves and slight the Revealer.

Jesus and the Father

Do you not believe that I am in the Father and the Father in me? The words that I say to you I do not speak on my own authority; but the Father who dwells in me does his works (14:10).

Philip's desire for the direct vision of God is met by turning his attention to the indirect vision of faith: "Do you not believe...?" "To believe" is all that any believer can have on this earth, and the gift is by no means to be despised. Those who pretend otherwise, who imagine there is a more privileged access to the Father other than through faith in Jesus Christ, deceive both themselves and their eager followers.

The intimacy of Jesus' relationship with the Father, "I am in the Father and the Father in me," (see 10:38; 10:30; 14:20; 17:21, 23) is the object of this faith. The revelation of this intimate union of Jesus with the Father ("I and the Father are one" 10:30) is the only response that Philip's request of "Show us the Father" has, or can ever have. Yet, while confessing faith in this mutual abiding of Jesus "in the Father and the Father in me," the believer cannot lose sight of the obedience which is at its very heart, which forms the basis of this relationship, of the mutual abiding. The only reason why Jesus can say, "I am in the Father and the Father in me," is the fact that, of and for himself, he is nothing but the executor of the Father's will: "The words I say to you I do not speak on my own authority; but the Father who dwells in me does his works" (14:10; see 5:19, 30; 7:16, 28; 8:28).

All that Jesus is for us, he is by reason of the totality of his obedience to the Father's will. He makes this explicit by adding, "the Father who dwells in me does his works." The whole "work" of the Son is to do the Father's will. Therefore, the works he does, the signs he performs, the words he utters, the revelation he brings, are all the work of the Father:

> **Believe me that I am in the Father and the Father in me; or else believe me for the sake of the works themselves (14:11).**

The farewell discourse can, in a sense, be regarded as Jesus' mission of the disciples and his instruction on discipleship. In other words, it is quite comparable to what we have in Matthew 10 and its parallels in Mark and Luke (see, e.g., Mk 6:7–13; Lk 9:1–6). But, on an even larger scale, the farewell discourse is more like the founding charter of the community of believers. In it this community can find the comprehensibility of its life in a hostile world, "Let not your hearts be troubled" (14:1); the courage to withstand the assaults of the world on it, "I have overcome the world" (16:33); and the assurance that their present sorrow will be turned into joy which no one can take away from them (16:22).

The "Greater Works"

Amen, amen, I say to you, he who believes in me will also do the work that I do; and greater works than these will he do, because I go to the Father (14:12).

The Jesus who is about to leave this world assures his disciples that his own work will be perpetuated in their life and ministry. All his work finds its reason and purpose in the glorification of the Father (11:4, 40; 12:28). So the work of his disciples down the ages will be "greater" because everything they do will be the work of him who sends them into the world, not any achievement of their own. Because Jesus goes to the Father, his own work will be magnified in them whom he will continue to send into the world.

To assure this "greater" work, Jesus will send "the Spirit of truth" (14:17) to be with them. It is this Spirit that will carry on the work of the Revealer through them. But to do this Jesus will have to leave them first. His absence from the world is the condition, not only of the sending of the Spirit, but of the "greater works" of the community through the centuries: "because I go to the Father" (14:12).

Should we find all this a bit baffling, we have to remind ourselves that we have been schooled for years to think of the history of the church as a pageant of triumphs both of heroic individuals and of the even more imposing institutions they served. We are not schooled to read church history as the "greater works" that glorify the Father, but rather as the accomplishments of administrative geniuses, great minds, social reformers and such; indeed, a whole calendar of saints, top-heavy with popes, bishops and religious founders. Even the inexhaustible elenchus of martyrs is laid under contribution for the glory of the institution, a telling argument in its triumphant apologetic with the world. Should we require any demonstration of this state of affairs, we have only to look at what popular preaching and the imagination of the faithful have made of the words that follow.

Answer to Prayers

Whatever you ask in my name, I will do it, that the Father may be glorified in the Son; if you ask anything in my name, I will do it (14:13–14).

Was there ever a Christian ignorant of these words of Jesus in one form or another? The destitute, the desperate and the ambitious dilettante, all grasp at this dominical saying. When–as it is bound to do–it fails to deliver what it promises, there are always those who make a living offering explanations, analyzing the technique of the petition, prescribing methods for improvement, and supplying their bemused clientele with tales of reassuring miracles. You need not be a devoted reader of the legends of the saints to garner the comforting samples. The religious and often even the secular press provide enough examples to satisfy the most avid seekers. Those in search of the miraculous at every juncture will, to be sure, find the proffered meaning of these verses in John not at all to their liking, and will therefore be inclined to dismiss it as false or fanciful innovation.

The promise of Jesus in these verses is unconditional ("*Whatever* you ask," "if you ask *anything*"), and unconditionally valid, "I will do it" (14:13–14). It is an unconditional and unconditionally valid promise because all that we can ever ask has in fact already been granted us by him. What Jesus has won for all of us is the gift of life, without which neither health nor riches nor success nor anything else on the face of the earth is of any use to us. Whatever we ask would be vain and idle without the gift of life, eternal life. This gift he has already conferred on us "abundantly" (10:10).

The reason why Jesus gave and continues to give this life to those who believe in him is "that the Father may be glorified in the Son" (14:13). This is why he says that whatever we ask he will do for us. All Christian prayer ought to be a reminder of this fact, the glorification of the Father in the Son, not a means of circumventing it.

"God's glory," Saint Irenaeus said, "is man alive!" (*gloria Dei vivens homo*) (*Adversus Haer.* 4.20.7). This making alive is what Jesus has done for us and, having done it in obedience to the Father who sent him, he has glorified and continues to glorify the Father forever. "If you ask anything in my name, I will do it." To ask for anything in his name is to ask that the Father be glorified. This is what we are reminded by the Lord's Prayer every time we say, "hallowed be thy name."

THE PROMISE OF THE SPIRIT (John 14:15–31)

If you love me, you will keep my commandments (14:15).

Much has been written to explain the use of the plural "commandments" here (cf. 14:21; 15:10) rather than the singular "commandment" (see 10:18 [NRSV]; 12:49; 13:34; 15:12). The explicit commandment he has given them is the "new commandment... that you love one another" (13:34). This love for one another is the only proof needed, and the only one available, of their love for him. The proof is not in following him where he goes, as Peter and Thomas imagined (13:37; 14:5); nor in direct vision of the Father, as Philip sought (14:8). Obedience to his "commandments" is the only means available to any of us to demonstrate our love for him. Nothing else will do, and anything else is an evasion.

Those who insist that the plural, "commandments," means more than one can seek the justification for it in Jesus' double imperative, "believe in God, believe also in me" (14:1). Thus, "commandments" can be read as a reference to "believe in me" as well as to "love one another." This would bring Jesus' teaching in the fourth gospel close to the "love commandment" in the synoptics. See, for instance, Mark 12:28–34, where the singular is used, "There is no other commandment," even though a "first" and a "second" have been cited (cf. Mt 22:35–40; Lk 10:25–28). But, whether in John or in the synoptics, faith in God and love of neighbor are inseparable. John indeed makes one conditional upon the other, "If you love me, you will keep my commandments" (14:15), "as I have loved you...you also love one another" (13:34). We show our faith in his having loved us by obeying what he commanded us, viz., to love one another.

The Spirit and Jesus

And I will pray the Father, and he will give you another [Paraclete], to be with you for ever, even the Spirit of truth, whom the world cannot receive, because it neither sees him nor knows him; you know him, for he dwells with you, and will be in you (14:16–17).

The choice of "Paraclete," a transliteration of the Greek term *(parakletos)* employed here and in the subsequent passages, is deliberate. It is in order to avoid slanting the meaning of the term which the RSV's "Counselor" and the NRSV's "Advocate" or "Helper" would inevitably involve. The term "Paraclete," whose origin remains problematic, is susceptible of all these meanings and others as well. Using a term which is by no means foreign to Christian ears seems advisable in this instance, if only to avoid the juridical and forensic connotations of synonyms like "advocate," "counselor" and "helper."

The evangelist identifies "the Paraclete" as "the Holy Spirit" (14:26) and uses practically all the terms he employs to describe Jesus' mission and activity to describe his (though "spirit" in Greek is a neuter noun, "Paraclete" is masculine): They both "come" from the Father (13:3; 15:26); are both "sent" by the Father (8:42 and 14:26); dwell with the believers (14:25 and 14:17); cannot be received by the world (1:11 and 14:17); both teach (18:20 and 14:26); and neither speaks on his own authority (12:49 and 16:13). Moreover, in John, Jesus declares, "I am the truth" (14:6); and 1 John affirms, "the Spirit is the truth" (1 Jn 5:7). Therefore, it is only natural that the fourth gospel should speak of "*another* Paraclete" (14:16).

Thus, to those who believe in him (14:1) and love him (14:15) and want him to be with them always, Jesus promises to send "another Paraclete." It is this Paraclete who will assure the permanence of the power of the community's faith in the risen Jesus. Of course, in doing so, the Paraclete assures the permanence of the revelation within the community of believers. This is why the Paraclete is "the Spirit of *truth*" (14:17). The way he will secure the permanence of this truth of the revelation in the world will be described later in 14:26.

The Paraclete

Here, in the first of the five statements about the Paraclete (14:16, 26; 15:26; 16:7, 8–11), two facts are stated: First, the world cannot receive him, any more than it could receive the Word made flesh (1:9–10, 11). The world cannot receive the "Spirit of truth" because it cannot tolerate the revelation. The revelation calls its values into question, inverts its hierarchies, and overturns its cherished idols. The world "neither sees him nor knows him" (14:17). This is its darkness ("men loved darkness" 3:19) and its abiding sin ("your sin remains" 9:41 NRSV).

The second fact about the Paraclete is that "he dwells with you, and will be in you," i.e., with and in the disciples of Jesus, with and in all those who believe in Jesus as the Revealer whom the Father has sent and, believing him, "have life in his name" (20:31). It is the Spirit, of course, that gives this life (6:63).

I will not leave you orphaned; I am coming to you (14:18 NRSV).

Jesus knows full well that his approaching departure from the world will trouble his disciples' hearts (14:1), that their loneliness in the world without him will "orphan" them. Hence, he reassures them with his promise to come to them. His immediate hearers had no way of knowing what the evangelist and his readers know: that Jesus will rise from the dead.

Yet, even the one risen from the dead had to leave this world and return to the Father (13:1). Therefore, those who believe in Jesus will come to understand that his resurrection and return to the Father is the indispensable condition for assuring the permanent mode of abiding that only the Paraclete can secure, "he dwells with you, and will be with you" (14:17). Thus, in truth, they are never "orphaned" (14:18).

"You will see me"

Yet a little while, and the world will see me no more, but you will see me (14:19a).

When once he has died, Jesus disappears from the world's field of vision. Those who do not believe in the resurrection cannot "see" the risen Jesus (see Acts 10:40–41, "God raised him on the third day and made him manifest; *not to all the people* but to us who were chosen by God as witnesses"). Seeing the risen Jesus is thus a function of believing in him, rather than the other way around.

To those who believe that the resurrection of Jesus from the dead was a phenomenon perceptible to other than the eyes of faith, John 14:19 can make no possible sense. Jesus' assurance "but you will see me" is made to his disciples, those who believe in him. What complicates matters, however, is that everything written in the gospel is written *after* the fact. We have therefore to keep attuning our ears constantly by keeping this in mind. After his death, "the world will see me no more" but "*you* will see me" (14:19).

...because I live, you will live also (14:19b).

This is the truth which undergirds the believers' faith in the resurrection. The life of Jesus, wherewith Jesus himself lives, is the reason why all who believe in him will live: "For as the Father raises the dead and gives them life, so also the Son gives life to whom he will" (5:21). The gift of eternal life which the Son confers on those who believe in him is, by the nature of things, conferred on *mortal* human beings. They are not and cannot be exempted from dying. But they can be assured of the resurrection from the dead, because he himself, the giver of the gift, lives: "*because* I live, you will live also."

Indeed, without the resurrection from the dead, talk of *eternal* life is meaningless. What guarantees its being "eternal" is the fact that Jesus himself lives; and the way we come to know this is by faith in his own resurrection from the dead. This is why we can say, as the evangelist does, "For the Father has life in himself, so he has granted the Son also to have life in himself" (5:26).

Thus, Jesus' saying "because I live" (14:18) echoes the prologue's "In him was life" (1:4). It finds its reason and explanation in that the Father who, having life in himself, i.e., being God–since God alone has life in himself–has conferred this exclusive privilege on the Son whom he sent into the world. This is why Jesus now adds:

> **In that day you will know that I am in my Father, and you in me, and I in you (14:20).**

The reference of "in that day" is to the time when he will come to them (14:18), the time, that is, of his resurrection from the dead. The resurrection of Jesus will reveal to the disciples the intimacy of his union with the Father, "that I am in my Father." He had already told them of this intimacy in the reciprocal indwelling of the Father and the Son: "that you may know and understand that the Father is in me and I am in the Father" (10:38; cf. 10:30; 14:10, 11; 17:21, 23). Here he reiterates the revelation and draws its corollary, "you in me and I in you."

The Obedience of the Son

This intimacy of the relationship between the Father and the Son is grounded in the life they share. It is revealed to us by the obedience of the Son, by the total conformity of his will to the will of the Father: "the Son can do nothing of his own accord, but only what he sees the Father doing" (5:19, 30; 7:17, 28; 8:28; 14:10). This is why, "When you have lifted up the Son of man, then you will know that I am (he)" (8:28). It is in the Son's death on the cross that we understand the true meaning of his obedience to the Father. It is then that we "will know" what "I am in my Father" (14:20) means.

The corollary that Jesus draws from this is that, "in that day," his disciples will also understand that they themselves are in him and he in them (14:20). Such intimacy of being between the believers and their risen Lord, however, is mutual and reciprocal in a special way. His being in them means that they live because he himself lives (14:19). But, though they live because of him, the "I in you," its inverse, the "you in me," evidently cannot and does not say that he lives because of them. It says rather that he is what he is because he is for them, because he is the Revealer of the Father to them. Only by believing in him, only by living their life in him, can they live at all. Of course, to live that life in him is to be obedient to the revelation he brings, obedient to his express will.

Obedience to His Commandments

> **He who has my commandments and keeps them, he it is who loves me; and he who loves me will be loved by my Father, and I will love him and manifest myself to him (14:21).**

Obedience to his commandments is indeed the only available means the believers have of manifesting their love for him. Nothing else can or will do. It is by obeying his commandments that the believers manifest to the world that he is in them and they in him (14:20): that they are his disciples (13:35). They will show the world that they truly live because he, their risen Lord, lives (14:19).

Those who want to cling to Jesus, who are forever desirous of "seeing" the Father (14:8), who devise ingenious means to perpetuate the presence of Jesus on this earth, are all referred to his commandment to love one another (13:34, 35). There is no other way, no other means, of having the Father's love ("will be loved by my Father") and of Jesus himself ("I will love him"). Only by obedience to Jesus' commandment can we grasp the revelation he brings: "I will manifest myself to him" (14:21).

This is the reason why Jesus reminded his disciples earlier that "men loved darkness rather than light, because their deeds were evil" (3:19). By contrast, the deeds of those who believe in him as the Revealer, those who have "the light of life" (8:12), are done in obedience to his commandment to love one another.

> **Judas (not Iscariot) said to him, "Lord, how is it that you will manifest yourself to us, and not to the world?" (14:22).**

Judas' is a true question, not a misunderstanding. It gives one the impression of having been a question actually posed by the Johannine community and is here woven into the account as part of the farewell discourse. This, of course, is a process that did not terminate on that particular day, nor is it confined to this one instance. The questions about the revelation that arise within the community and there receive the answer are all part of that promise whereby the Holy Spirit "will teach you all things, and bring to your remembrance all that I have said to you" (14:26).

The question itself of "Judas (not Iscariot)," "Lord, how is it that you will manifest yourself to us, and not to the world?" has to do with what can be visible ultimately only to the eyes of faith. It is, consequently, a question, which crops up in every generation of believers, about the blindness of the world (see 9:41; cf. 15:22, 24). This is, of course, what distinguishes the believers, who love him and keep his word, from the rest of the world:

> **Jesus answered him, "If a man loves me, he will keep my word, and my Father will love him, and we will come to him and make our home with him" (14:23).**

It all comes down to this: any love of Jesus can only be genuine if it is obedient to his word. This word is both the revelation of who he is, "I AM" (13:19; 14:29), and of his commandment to love one another (13:34, 35). There is no other means of demonstrating love for him, whether in ecstatic prayer, or in visions, or in scaling the ladder of perfection, or even in mystical union. Only the obedience to his word is valid demonstration of love for him. This obedience to his word is the sole condition for the indwelling of the Father and the Son in the believer: "We will come to him and make our home with him."

Word and Commandment

> **He who does not love me does not keep my words; and the word which you hear is not mine but the Father's who sent me (14:24).**

If in the previous verses (14:15, 21) the use of the plural "commandments" rather than the singular "commandment" poses a problem, then one has only to note the easy shift from "my words" to "the word" here in 14:24. There is but one revelation as there is only one commandment. Acceptance of this revelation, like the acceptance of its inseparable counterpart, the commandment to love, is what distinguishes the believers from "the world."

Thus, in his answer to the question of Judas (not Iscariot), Jesus reminds him that the division between the believers and the world is not the result of Jesus' manifesting himself to some but not to others. It is rather the inevitable consequence of each individual's choice. Those who love him keep his word; and those who do not love him do not keep his word. Indeed, they do not even hear it. This is the judgment spoken of above (3:19; 5:24; and see 1:10–11).

God loved the world, the whole world without exception (3:16). If the world remains plunged in darkness, it is because it rejects the light. It is "the world," in the pejorative sense of the term, because it freely chooses not to love Jesus, nor to keep his word (14:24a). It rejects the Revealer and his revelation. It does not keep his words because it refuses to hear him.

Yet again is it necessary to remind the hearers of the gospel message, those who keep Jesus' word, of that single fact which makes him who he is: "the word which you hear is not mine but the Father's who sent me" (14:24); "the Father himself loves you, because you have loved me and have believed that I came from the Father" (16:27). He is who he is because he is the Revealer of the Father to them.

These things I have spoken to you, while I am still with you (14:25).

The whole point of this verse, as in any writing of the New Testament, is that the Jesus they all proclaim is no longer with them. From the very beginning, believers have had to face this difficult fact; and, refusing stubbornly to accept it, have set about devising innumerable substitutes to mitigate it. Scarcely are they ever satisfied with demonstrating their pretended love for him by keeping his word. So Jesus reminds his disciples here that what he said to them, the revelation he brought them, does abide; but that he, the Revealer, must return to the Father whence he came. This is why this final discourse is a "farewell" discourse.

The Abiding of the Revelation

But, to assure the continuity of the Revealer's task, the abiding of the revelation, Jesus promises them the Paraclete:

But the Paraclete, the Holy Spirit, whom the Father will send in my name, he will teach you all things, and bring to your remembrance all that I have said to you (14:26).

This, the second of John's Paraclete sayings (see 14:16–17), begins by identifying the Paraclete with "the Holy Spirit." The Paraclete, like the Son, is sent by the Father, but in the name of Jesus, "whom the Father will send *in my name.*" He will take the place and carry out the role of Jesus toward the community of believers. It is the Paraclete who assures the permanence of the revelation in the world. The "Paraclete, the Holy Spirit" is the only answer available to those who want to cling to Jesus and to see the Father.

The Paraclete is sent by the Father in the name of Jesus in order to "teach...and bring to your remembrance *all* that I have said to you" (14:26). His role, then, is to continue the work of the Revealer by assuring the permanence of the revelation in the world. But this task is performed in the community of believers wherever and whenever the word of Jesus is both proclaimed and heard, whenever and wherever his commandment is both heard and obeyed.

This is the reason why the Paraclete is identified with "the Holy Spirit." He is the Spirit precisely because he is the power of the abiding presence of the risen Jesus in the community of those who believe in him. The community of believers is where the word of the Revealer is proclaimed. That proclamation is the work of the Paraclete, "the Holy Spirit, whom the Father will send in my name."

The reader of the gospel cannot, therefore, overlook the fact that this is precisely what the evangelist does when he writes his gospel. It is what every proclaimer of the gospel message does. It is what the community of believers does whenever it hears, hearkens and comes to understand the gospel. Teaching and bringing to remembrance is never a solitary act. Those who are taught, to whose remembrance is brought "all that I have said to you" (14:26), are every bit as much part of the operation as those who teach them and bring to their remembrance the words of the Revealer. This is why we refer to them as "the *community* of faith."

This joint operation of "teach...and bring to your remembrance" is the work of "the Paraclete, the Holy Spirit, whom the Father will send in my name" (14:25). The Paraclete is sent by the Father "in my name" because "he will take what is *mine* and declare it to you" (16:14). The task of the Paraclete is not to uncover novelties but to preserve the newness of the revelation within the community of believers.

The Peace of Christ

Peace I leave with you; my peace I give to you; not as the world gives do I give to you (14:27a–b).

The peace Christ gives them is inseparable from the gift of the Paraclete to them. Indeed, this peace is what Paul would call "the fruit" of this Spirit (Gal 5:22, "But the fruit of the Spirit is love, joy, peace..."). It is a manifestation of the love of the redeemer abiding in the community of the believers in him.

The peace that Jesus gives his disciples and leaves with them is a peace that only he as the risen Lord (cf. "Peace be with you" Jn 20:19), as the Revealer of the Father's love, can bring them. It is the peace that comes, not so much from the cessation of strife and the end of hostilities, as from the stable and inalienable possession of what one loves and desires.

To say this is to rob the verse and similar New Testament verses (e.g., "and on earth peace" Lk 2:14) of their sloganeering potential. A casual reading of any history of the world ought to dissuade us from purveying our customary irenic platitudes. A reading of church history could even turn us into skeptics on this score. This is not to say that peace among individuals and between nations is not desirable. But it is not what Jesus is talking about here. The "peace I leave you" (Jn 14:27) is *his* peace, the peace he alone brings to the world as the Revealer and its redeemer. Only those who believe in him as the Revealer and obey his word have this peace, because they in fact possess eternal life (3:15 and 16).

Of course, if they do believe in him and love him, if they do really possess eternal life because they believe in him, then they are bound to manifest his peace in their love for one another (13:34, 35). If any peace were ever to come to this world, it has to start here. It can never start elsewhere. All attempts to locate Christ's "peace" elsewhere are tacit admissions of failure to keep his word.

No spectacle is more laughable in today's world than that of the proclaimers of peace who hate one another. No spectacle, that is, unless it be that of the community of believers proclaiming peace and resolutely failing to love one another.

The peace that Christ gives is "not as the world gives" (14:27b). There could be no gainsaying this unequivocal statement, no getting around it. Yet Christians in all ages, with the connivance of the church, have strained every effort to stand the statement on its head whenever it suited their purpose. Christians individually, and the church at large, took the world's idle prating about peace, and pretended it was the peace promised by Christ. Christ's peace, unlike that which the world pretends to give, reigns in the heart. This is why Jesus goes on to say:

Let not your hearts be troubled, neither let them be afraid (14:27c).

By repeating the "Let not your hearts be troubled," with which this segment of the farewell discourse began (14:1), the evangelist signals its conclusion. If, as some scholars have argued, the farewell discourse is made up of a series of sermons preached by the "Johannine prophet" to his community, then this chapter could serve as a good example of just such a sermon, and chapter 15, a better one still.

Fear and the troubled heart are what the redeemer puts far from those who believe in him. His gift of eternal life, not so much because it is eternal life but because it is a gratuitous and unearnable gift, removes the root of fear and apprehension from the heart of all who believe in him. It is, therefore, not easy to comprehend how Christians have allowed their lives to be lived with so much fear, trepidation, and even despair. It is more incomprehensible still how the preachers of the "good news" have elevated that fear into the status of dogma, have perverted 1 John 4:18 to read, "perfect fear casts out love."

The Joy Abiding

Not only is Jesus' injunction, "Let not your hearts be troubled, neither let them be afraid" (Jn 14:27c), clear and without any qualification, but it bears within it the further promise of joy, which is the twin of genuine peace:

You heard me say to you, "I go away, and I will come to you." If you loved me, you would have rejoiced, because I go to the Father; for the Father is greater than I (14:28).

What those who believe in him are likely to overlook is that the whole good news of Jesus Christ consists in the revelation that "God so loved the world that he gave his only Son" for the salvation of the world, that those who believe in him whom he sent "should not perish but have eternal life" (3:16–17). This fact, however, is revealed only in the return of the Son to the Father. Its revelation, therefore, must be the cause of our true and abiding joy (see 15:11; 16:22; 17:13).

To forestall the difficulty that the sequence of verbs, "go away... will come... because I go" in 14:28 might raise, we should keep in mind the point of view of the evangelist, which is, of course, also ours. He wrote his gospel and we read it at a point in time when the Son has already come into the world, died on the cross, returned from the dead in his resurrection, and then gone back to the Father who sent him. His going away in his death on the cross and his coming back to them in his rising from the dead can receive their meaning only in his return to the Father who sent him. His disciples can believe he has come from the Father and returned to the Father only when they believe that he who died on the cross is indeed risen from the dead. Only when they understand that the entire life of Jesus of Nazareth is one whole uninterrupted act of obedience to the Father's will, can they comprehend how and why he could say, "the Father is greater than I" (14:28). For his entire coming from the Father and return to the Father, that is to say, the very fact of his being the Revealer of the Father, becomes manifest in his death and resurrection in obedience to the Father's will (10:17–18).

And now I have told you before it takes place, so that when it does take place, you may believe (14:29).

Only when "it does take place," only when he has died and risen from the dead, will his disciples believe in him, believe who he is in relation to the Father and for the salvation of the world.

His telling them "before it takes place" is what in Mark and the other synoptics is commonly referred to as the "passion predictions" (Mk 8:31–33 par; 9:31 par; 10:32–34 par). Though the passion predictions serve a different purpose in Matthew and in Luke, in Mark they instruct us in the meaning of discipleship. It is at least arguable that John, in his own fashion, uses the prediction of the passion in 14:29 for a similar purpose. This purpose will become clearer in the next chapter.

Obedience to the Father

I will no longer talk much with you, for the ruler of this world is coming. He has no power over me; but I do as the Father has commanded me, so that the world may know that I love the Father (14:30–31a).

His disciples have to be reconciled to his departure from them, reconciled to the fact that Jesus is not going to stay with them to talk with them and instruct them always. Shortly, he will have to leave them. This is an integral part of the mystery of "the Word became flesh" (1:14). At the instant of Jesus' departure from them, the "ruler of the world," the powers of evil will seem to triumph (cf. Lk 22:53, "But this is your hour, and the power of darkness").

When this takes place, when the "ruler of the world" seems to triumph, it is more necessary than ever to remind the disciples that what happens is the outcome of his own obedience to the will of the Father, not a result of the machinations of evil in this world. Jesus' disciples have to keep in mind that nowhere is his love for and obedience to the Father more manifest or better revealed than by his death on the cross. It will have seemed to the disciples, as it persists in seeming to believers in all ages, that the "ruler of the world" is the one who orchestrates the action and triumphs at the last. The constant temptation of believers is to forget that everything Jesus said or did is one uninterrupted act of loving obedience to the Father, i.e., to forget that precisely in his death on the cross is this loving obedience manifested: "that the world may know that I love the Father" (14:31a).

Rise, let us go hence (14:31b).

This has occasioned more discussion and given rise to more explanations of the composition of the fourth gospel than one can number. It is proof, if proof were really required, that the gospel in its present state calls for some explanation of its order. For, immediately after uttering these words, "Rise, let us go hence," Jesus goes on with his farewell discourse(s) for three more chapters. Yet, without any break in sequence, chapter 15 follows; and, if the observation above about the passion prediction and the instruction on discipleship is of any worth, the transition from chapter 14 to chapter 15 is almost natural.

John 15

The True Vine: the work of the Father; being made clean; bearing fruit; abiding in him; "ask whatever you will"; being loved and loving; joy; "Christian" love; no greater love; Jesus' friends.

The World's Hatred: reason for the hatred.

The Third Paraclete Saying.

THE TRUE VINE (John 15:1–17)

I am the true vine, and my Father is the vinedresser (15:1).

This opening "I AM" saying sounds much like a text introducing another sermon. What follows it is indeed a sermon about the essence of discipleship. The reader can approach the whole chapter as the elaboration of an already stated theme: "In that day you will know that I am in my Father, and you in me, and I in you" (14:20). It is, moreover, an exhortation to "abide" in him in order to bear "much fruit" (15:4–5). In both instances, whether as the elaboration of a theme or as an exhortation, John 15 is, or can be understood as, an instruction on true discipleship that follows upon the prediction of the passion in 14:29. You might even say that the instruction is made necessary by the prediction of the approaching passion.

Like the other "I AM" sayings, "I am the true vine" insists that in Jesus and in him alone are all our desires for true life fulfilled. He is the true source of our life. Thus the image of the vine employed here is one that serves the theme of union with Jesus as the necessary condition for life. Life is, in turn, the indispensable condition for his disciple's bearing fruit.

The Work of the Father

Every branch of mine that bears no fruit, he takes away, and every branch that does not bear fruit he prunes, that it may bear more fruit (15:2).

The vine with all its branches belongs to the Father and is therefore under his care. He does what every vinedresser has to do to maintain the life and the fruitfulness of the entire vine. The purpose of the branches on the vine is, of course, not ornamental. They are there to bear fruit, and the fruit they bear attests to the health and the life of the vine.

Unfortunately, it is this metaphoric "bear more fruit" that can, and often does, mislead the reader into imagining the life of faith as a marathon of meritorious works. As the rest of the chapter will show, this is far from being the meaning of Jesus' words. To "bear more fruit" is a reference to the vitality of faith in who Jesus is. Since such vitality embraces the whole of the believer's life, it is bound to manifest itself in bearing "more fruit." But the whole process is, from start to finish, the work of the vinedresser, the Father.

The image of the vine is, moreover, a metaphor for the intimacy of union with the Lord as a condition of life for the believer. Life, by definition, is not static. It is manifested in its purposeful dynamism, its continuous renewal ("he prunes") and growth ("that it may bear more fruit"). The life of faith can, therefore, brook no interruption, because the love to which it calls us (15:8–10) can never cease. Beyond this the metaphor should not and need not be pushed. The verses that follow will indicate the sense in which the image of the vine is to be interpreted.

Being Made Clean

You are already made clean by the word which I have spoken to you (15:3)

This harks back to Jesus' dialogue with Peter at the washing of feet, "If I do not wash you, you have no part in me" (13:8; and see 13:10). That the disciples, those who believe in him, are "clean," that is to say, are rid of their sins before God, is the result of "the word which I have spoken to you." In other words, it is the result of the revelation he brings. Faith in him as the Revealer is what gives true life, "I am the *true* vine."

It does so because it is he who brings salvation to the world, it is he who "cleanses" us from sin and offers us forgiveness. This is the purpose of his coming: "to save the world" (12:47; 3:17; 10:9).

Jesus' affirmation, "You are already made clean," together with his assurance that the sole cause of their being made clean is "the word which I have spoken to you," are the reason why those who believe in him are rid of their fear, and their hearts are not troubled (14:27, 1). Of course, the salvation he brings implants his peace ineradicably in the hearts of those who believe in him (14:27; 16:33). Any doubt about their having been made clean, any illusion about what and who is truly responsible for that cleanliness is bound to rob them of this peace, trouble their hearts, and fill them with fear.

If Christians manifest scant signs of life and yield sparse fruit in the world, it is because they have come to believe that their being "made clean" is a result of their penitential practices and self-abnegation, or that their "bearing fruit" is in direct proportion to their pious exertions and their incessant, restless activity. They are all too ready to be dissuaded from believing that everything they desire and need is already theirs, that everything they are and everything they do is, and can only be, the work of the Father in them and the result of the word his only Son has spoken to them.

Bearing Fruit

Abide in me, and I in you. As the branch cannot bear fruit by itself, unless it abides in the vine, neither can you, unless you abide in me (15:4).

The exhortation to abide in him is a call to abide in faith in him, to continue to believe in him. Faith in him is not and cannot be static, any more than it can be a once and for all act. The whole life of the believer is a constant act of faith in him who is "the true vine," the source of the true life that only God can give.

To abide in him, moreover, is to "bear fruit." Unless we continue in our faith in Jesus Christ, we cannot possibly "bear fruit." But this faith in him is also faith in what he has done for us. It is faith that we are "already made clean by the word" (15:3). This faith not only provides us with the assurance of abiding in him but also removes any anxiety we might have about "bearing fruit." It is neither our effort nor our achievement that bears fruit. Only abiding in him can do this and, even then, it is the Father, and no one else, who sees to it that we "bear more fruit" (15:2).

How reluctant believers are to keep all this in mind. To "bear fruit" is not their concern, nor is it the consequence of their exertions. It should not occupy them, nor rob them of their peace. Because it is his abiding in them that produces the fruit, not their zeal or cleverness or techniques or inventiveness. The main concern of the believer is to continue to abide in him. If we but keep this in mind, genuine freedom will be ours, the freedom that rids us of the crippling care for ourselves and thus truly frees us to "have love for one another" (13:35).

To "bear *more* fruit" really means that, in the life of the Christian, there is no such thing as enough. To realize this, however, cannot be the source of anxiety, but only of assurance. The life of the branch depends solely on its attachment to the vine, that is, on abiding in him who is "the life" (14:6). To "bear more fruit" is the natural function of the branch, not its concern. That concern belongs to the vine itself.

Abiding in Him

I am the vine, you are the branches. He who abides in me, and I in him, he it is that bears much fruit, for apart from me you can do nothing (15:5).

As an absolute condition for fruitful life, the image of the vine and the branches cannot be bettered. The "abiding" as the condition for bearing fruit is but the natural consequence of the union of the branches with the vine. The reciprocity of "abides in me and I in him" clarifies further the consequence of the relationship to Jesus. To abide in him (cf. 15:4) is to abide in faith in him, to continue to believe in him, and hence to allow oneself to be determined by faith in him in everything one is and does. Reciprocally, to let him abide in us is to let ourselves be determined by him, to live out the life he imparts to us.

It is this mutual abiding that is, of course, the cause and condition of bearing "much fruit." The fruit of abiding in him and of him in us is wholly his gift. The believer need neither fret nor "be troubled." It is sufficient to know that apart from him we can do nothing, absolutely nothing. This only enunciates the obvious fact that God alone "has life in himself" and "has granted the Son also to have life in himself" (5:26). Abiding in the Son is the only condition for having life. Only we, on the other hand, can sever this link with him; and, when we do, we, like a severed branch, die and can therefore do nothing.

These words of Jesus (15:5) are what puts the whole discourse under the comforting reassurance of, "Let not your hearts be troubled" (14:1), "Peace I leave you.... Let not your hearts be troubled, neither let them be afraid" (14:27). The whole life of the Christian stands under this exhortation, which is founded, not on any achievement of the believer, nor on the judgment and approval of anyone else on earth, but solely on the saving gift of God in the Son he sent into the world.

If absence of peace, a troubled heart and fear are the lot of Christians today, it is not because of the gospel message but of its perversion. Call into question the "You are *already* made clean" (15:3); imagine for a second that a branch can "bear fruit by itself" (15:4); or harbor the illusion that without him you can do something (15:5); and you are deader than any dead branch and of less worth than even kindle wood:

> **Whoever does not abide in me is thrown away like a branch and withers; such branches are gathered, thrown into the fire, and burned (15:6 NRSV).**

Carrying through the image of the vine and the branches, these words give a vivid picture of the consequence of refusal to abide in him. There is no reference here either to "excommunication," whether in "gathered" or in "cut off"; nor to hell's punishment in "thrown into the fire, and burned." The evangelist is doing no more than elaborating the initial metaphor, underscoring the inevitable catastrophe of the refusal to believe in him: death, definitive and irrevocable.

For, even if Christians often choose in practice to forget it, the evangelist knows that the believers in Jesus Christ are "*already* made clean," not by any decision or action of their own or of the institution, but solely and uniquely "by the word which I have spoken to you" (15:3). The evangelist also knows what we stubbornly refuse to acknowledge in practice, that bearing fruit is not any measurable achievement of the believer but only the gift consequent upon abiding in the Son. That we persist in our deafness to all this is evident in our persistence in interpreting John 15:6 as the basis for the practice of excommunication, or as part of the scriptural arsenal of texts to prove the existence of hell's fire.

"Ask whatever you will"

If you abide in me, and my words abide in you, ask whatever you will, and it shall be done for you (15:7).

This is the reverse of the previous statement. It expresses positively what 15:6 expressed negatively. The preceding verse described the consequence of not abiding in Jesus; this, of abiding in him. "Abide in me" means to have his word "abide in you," and the other way around. They are two phrases for describing the same reality of the believer's life: abiding in the faith and living out of it, in obedience to the revelation.

"Ask whatever you will, and it shall be done for you," has also fallen victim to our perverse passion to force the words of Jesus to conform with our cherished dogmas. As has been said in 14:13 (cf. 16:23–24, 26), the consequence of our abiding in the Revealer and of his words abiding in us is the firm assurance we have that whatever we will ask shall be done for us. This assurance is absolute, not because it discounts the infinite caprice of human desires, but because it recognizes what lies at the heart of all such desires without exception: life, the desire to live.

Since life is what the Revealer is ("I am the life" 14:6) and life is what he gives to those who believe in him (10:10; 6:40, 47), then whatever the believers in him desire and wish for is already theirs. What they seek has already been granted them. All that is required of them, all that remains for them to do, is to abide in him, to continue in their faith in him, to let his word, the revelation he brings, abide in them and shape and determine their entire life by its command. So long, therefore, as they believe in him and are obedient to his revelation they *live*.

If a true believer asks for anything, "whatever you will" (15:7), then he or she can only ask to abide in him, to have his word abide in them. This is the sole condition of their having life, eternal life. They ask, in the words of the psalmist, "that I may dwell in the house of the Lord all the days of my life" (Ps 27:4); or, in the words of the prayers before communion, "keep me faithful to your teaching, and never let me be parted from you." There is no other thing a believer could conceivably ask for. Is it an accident, one wonders, that even this prayer in the eucharistic liturgy is fast sinking into desuetude?

By this my Father is glorified, that you bear much fruit, and so prove to be my disciples (15:8).

Are there then two means of demonstrating to the world that we are truly his disciples: "By this will all know that you are my disciples, *if you have love for one another*" (13:35) and "that *you may bear much fruit,* and so prove to be my disciples" (15:8)? No! There is only one way to demonstrate that we belong to him: the love we have for one another. Since this, and this alone, is the fruit any believer can bear; since the life that is ours is a consequence of abiding in him; since his abiding in us determines our life by the words he has spoken; and since his words are a commandment to love one another, there is only one way of demonstrating to the world that we indeed are his disciples. Therefore, by loving one another we prove to be his disciples, bear much fruit, and glorify the Father.

In our bearing "much fruit" by loving one another, "the Father is glorified" (15:8). The glory of the Father, as we have already had occasion to quote St. Irenaeus (see above on 14:13–14), is that we live, that we be truly alive. We live and demonstrate to the world that we are alive only if we love one another. But we, who believe in him, can live and love only if we abide in him. To abide in him is to believe in the revelation of the Father's love for us, to believe in the love of the Son who took flesh and dwelt among us. We manifest this life of abiding in him by obeying his command of love. Thus, the object of our love will also live; and "by this my Father is glorified."

Being Loved and Loving

As the Father has loved me, so have I loved you; abide in my love (15:9).

Any doubt about the meaning of the preceding verse (15:8) is bound to evaporate before the unmistakable imperative of this one. First of all, we must cling firmly to a basic truth whose fate in Christian history has been worse than neglect. The truth is that only someone who is loved can love. How this could have been perverted into a way of life where those who have not been loved are sent forth to terrorize the world with their "charity," remains a puzzle. As a consequence, even the comely word of "charity" has assumed a pejorative, an almost pernicious, sense.

The reason why you cannot love unless you have been loved is simply that, without having been loved, there is really no "you," but only someone out in search of "affirmation," "support," "caring," "sharing," and that whole collection of the jargon of exploitation, which provides the plethora of second-hand slogans by which many Christians seek to live today. It was Plato who defined love as "birth in beauty." Love is a coming to be of the beautiful, at least to one pair of eyes, in this vast and impersonal universe. Once this conviction lays hold of you–and once is more than enough–then for you to believe that a God loved you enough to give his only Son for love of you would be almost a matter of course. Once you believe in the love of this God for you, then you know that the life you have now is nothing less than God's own gift of eternal life. Once you accept it, the only thing you can do with this extravagant gift is to squander it on others with prodigality, never counting the cost, nor ever weighing the burden.

Alas, two flies spoil this perfumer's ointment. One is the false conviction, assiduously implanted in the mind of believers, that being loved is like getting inoculated, that you are forever in need of booster shots. Of course, this undying thirst for the repeated assurance of being loved, of being "appreciated," "supported," "affirmed," etc., is the only proof you need of your own sad conviction that you have never been loved by any creature, let alone by the creator.

This would be lamentable, but quite harmless. What makes it such a problem in the Christian community is that those who have never let themselves be loved, lay exorbitant claims to the exclusive love of God for them at the same time that they grow in self-loathing. They demand the love of others as a right and reject it as an exploitation, pretending to find all their sufficiency in "the love of Jesus."

The other fly in the ointment is the widespread misapprehension that, somehow, it is more difficult to love than to be loved. Nothing could be farther from the truth. Hence the malaise just described in the stoic refusal to allow oneself to be loved, and in the accompanying ascesis of charity which regards love of the other as an exercise in mortification.

If loving the other is humbling, being loved by another is humiliating. It is humiliating because we recognize in the offer of love an undeserved gift, and realize in its acceptance a deeply concealed need. Indeed, being loved by another, whether by God or one of his creatures, is about the only genuine humility a Christian can experience. If you require proof of this, consider the lives of the saints who, as they grow older, grow more abject in the realization of their unworthiness and "sinfulness." They realize, that is, how utterly gratuitous is the gift of love given them.

The saying of Jesus, "As the Father has loved me, so have I loved you; abide in my love" (15:9), is there to call us to the reality of his gift to us, and to its basis in God. "As the Father has loved me" is the mystery he reveals. But we come to know this revelation only by knowing and believing the "so have I loved you." In other words, from the love of the Son for us, we come to know of the love of the Father for him. He has loved us "to the end" (13:1) precisely because the Father first loved him. It is in revealing this love that he revealed God as his

Father. Not even the Son is exempt from the need to be loved in order to love.

Therefore, his injunction to "abide in my love" is an invitation, not just to believe in him, but to continue to believe in him, which is much more difficult. To abide in his love is to believe God's love for us in sending his only Son into the world. What is called "the logic of the incarnation" demands that someone like us does indeed love us. Only then can we believe in God's love for us. This is why God "so loved the world" (3:16) and sent his only Son into it. This, too, is why the Son who is about to leave the world commands his disciples to "love one another" and so to abide in his love. Being loved is the indispensable condition for believing in God's love as well as for loving one another.

If you keep my commandments, you will abide in my love, just as I have kept my Father's commandments and abide in his love (15:10).

It cannot have escaped the reader's attention that what these verses (15:8–10) are doing is setting up a comparison of the relationship between the Father and the Son, on the one hand, and the Son and the disciples who believe in him, on the other. Thus, that the condition for our abiding in his love is obedience to his commandments is set in parallel with Jesus' own abiding in the Father's love and his obedience to the Father.

We have already seen how, throughout the gospel, it is Jesus' obedience and the total conformity of his will to the Father's will that shows him to be the Revealer of the Father and of the Father's love. Here in 15:10 we see how his keeping the "Father's commandments" is both linked to his abiding in the Father and grounded in the Father's love for the Son ("For this reason the Father loves me, because I lay down my life" 10:17; see 3:35; 5:20; 17:23).

Thus "just as I have kept my Father's commandments and abide in his love" sets up the parallel for the relationship that binds his disciples to Jesus. The obedience to Jesus' commandments is the demonstration of their abiding in him, i.e., of their continuing to believe in his love for them. To abide in his love is to abide in the faith that he loved us (15:9). And, just as the "Father's commandments" were obeyed in the Son's laying down his life for his own (cf. 10:17), so Jesus' commandments are obeyed in the disciples' loving one another (15:12).

Joy

These things I have spoken to you, that my joy may be in you, and that your joy may be full (15:11).

Who in Christendom would actually believe that the revelation of the coming of the Son into the world has been, or can be, characterized by joy? About all that remains of this saying is its faint echo in the French saying that a saint who is sad is a sad saint indeed! Yet, judged by the criterion of joy, many a litany of saints would seem a grim affair indeed.

The joy that the words of the Revealer brings is the joy that wells up from the secure possession of the heart's desire. His revelation not only grants this desire, but grants it inalienably (see 16:22, "no one will take your joy from you"). The believer in him can thus say with the beloved of the Canticle, "When I found him whom my soul loves, I held him, and would not let him go" (Song 3:4). This is the joy that is "full." Like all true joy, it is not something we possess but something which possesses us. When such joy possesses us, it cannot be kept hidden in the recesses of our hearts. It bursts out of its bounds to infect all around us.

How little all this has to do with that ersatz "joy" manufactured by the blighted ingenuity of liturgical innovators; how far removed the genuine item is from what the loveless are constantly demanding as their right in the assembly of worshipers; and how alien true joy is from the cacophonous hilarity of those who imagine their incapacity to love a rule of life. All this can furnish rich material for reflection whenever this gospel is proclaimed. Yet how many sermons does a Christian actually hear in a lifetime on "that my joy may be in you, and that your joy may be full"?

With this verse (15:11), the first part of the discourse on the true vine is concluded. That its two parts (15:1–11 and 12–17) parallel the two interpretations of the foot washing (13:1–11 and 12–20) has been remarked by commentators on this gospel. The foot washing was interpreted first as, "If I do not wash you, you have no part in me" (13:8); and then as "You also ought to wash one another's feet" (13:14). So too the true vine image is interpreted first as "Abide in me, and I in you" (15:4); and then as "Love one another, as I have loved you" (15:12). The two interpretations in each instance are, of course, intimately linked: the service of one another (13:14) is the consequence of having a part in Jesus (13:8); the love of one another (15:12), of abiding in him (15:4). Thus, the true vine discourse reinforces and further illumes the foot washing and its interpretation.

"Christian" Love

This is my commandment, that you love one another as I have loved you (15:12).

The words reiterate the "new commandment" Jesus gave his disciples in 13:34, "A new commandment I give to you, that you love one another; even as I have loved you, that you also love one another." It is necessary to recall that what makes the commandment of love new is that which makes it specifically Christian, i.e., the "as I have loved you" (15:12; 13:34). It is faith in his love for us "to the end" that makes our obedience to his commandment of love possible. Of course, the "as I have loved you" also sets the essential pattern for the totality of this donation of oneself to the other. In the response to his commandment, nothing short of the unconditional giving of oneself to the other will do.

Nevertheless, we need to be reminded that it is not the love in itself or in its self-sacrificing extent that marks the believer's response as specifically Christian. Jews, Moslems, pagans, even the so-called godless, not only can but often do love with utmost generosity and utter selflessness, even to the laying down of their lives. What distinguishes Christians is merely this: when they love, they love *as* Christ loved them and *because* he loved them. What makes their love "Christian" is neither its quantity nor its quality. What makes it "Christian" is their faith in the love of Jesus for them, their abiding in his love (15:9), and nothing else.

No Greater Love

No one has greater love than this, to lay down one's life for one's friend (15:13 NRSV).

Self-evident though this be, it can, and all too often does, distract us from its true import. There are more ways of "laying down one's life for one's friends" than by dying for them. Living for others in serving them without regard for oneself (cf. Mk 8:34–35 par), counting them better than oneself in every encounter with them (cf. Phil 2:3), loving them as they are and where they are, all these call for the laying down of "one's life for one's friend." Even a long day's dying for another can be easier to bear by comparison with the heavy price of loving the other day in and day out. Dying for another is soon over with; laying down your life by living for the other takes a whole lifetime longer.

Nor is the cost of this love lessened by the endemic fallacy which confuses loving others with liking them. To imagine those you love to be what they are not–which is in fact what we do when we try to "like" them–is to love a figment of your imagination. To turn your eyes from their evident faults and shortcomings is not charitable indulgence but unmitigated pride. To love them in order to "improve" them–to conform them to your own image and likeness–is arrant blasphemy.

This is not what Jesus' laying down his life for his friends was. He died for us as we were and not, to borrow St. Augustine's phrase, as his grace will make us. His love for us knew only too well "what was in man" (2:25). The life he laid down was for all, even for those who chose to know him not and refused to receive him. The Jesus who loved the beloved disciple, Martha and Mary and Lazarus, loved also Judas Iscariot, Simon Peter and the Samaritan at the well. To imagine he laid down his life for some more than for others is to misunderstand the meaning, not of redemption, but of love.

You are my friends if you do what I command you (15:14).

Only obedience to his command reveals the true identity of his friends. He is helpless to call friends those who reject him and refuse to obey his command. It is not his failure to love them but their rejection of his love that denies them the status of friends.

What we should keep in mind is that those whom he calls friends are commanded, not to keep their gaze amorously fixed on him, but to turn it on one another, "if you do what I command you." They show they are Jesus' friends only in their love for one another (15:12). Even if comprehensible, the dilemma of the mystic who complained, "Lord, you keep telling me to go to others, when all I want is to be with you!" is not, and cannot be, theirs.

Jesus' Friends

No longer do I call you slaves, for the slave does not know what his master is doing; but I have called you friends, for all that I have heard from my Father I have made known to you (15:15).

Those who derive a peculiar satisfaction from calling Jesus *their* friend can have no way of comprehending this and the verse which follows. The fact that nowadays their number is legion is neither a justification for their attitude nor a reasonable interpretation of these verses. But, to anyone who can manage to subsist without referring to Jesus as "my friend," these two verses, 15:15–16, have much to say.

First of all, when Jesus in John says, "You are my friends," he does not and cannot put himself on a par with them. The equality which marks friendship is in this instance absent. "You call me Teacher and Lord; and you are right, for so I am" (13:13). He is and remains forever the Lord and Master of all those he chooses to call his friends. It is his role as Revealer of the Father to them that makes him call them friends. Those who reverse the process and call him their friend do so, not out of love for Jesus, but out of a desire to grasp at power, to evade, or even to abolish, his Lordship over them. They labor under the vulgar misapprehension that assumed intimacy banishes degree. "Take but degree away, untune that string/And, hark! what discord follows" (*Troilus and Cressida* 1.3.)

The reason Jesus calls his disciples, all those who believe in him, "friends" is the revelation he himself brings them. His role as Revealer is unique. It is what enables him to address them as friends and, so addressing them, make them in fact his friends:

> **You did not choose me, but I chose you and appointed you that you should go and bear fruit and that your fruit should abide; so that whatever you ask the Father in my name, he may give it to you (15:16).**

The initiative, therefore, is exclusively his. He it is who chose them; not they him. One does not become his friend and disciple by a process of elimination, or by lengthy deliberation over equally qualified candidates for the post. Jesus is not one among many. We do not "choose" him. It is he who chooses us and, as the Revealer and redeemer, first finds us and calls us "friends."

Nevertheless, his choice does require a response. It is always addressed to human beings who remain free to accept or reject it. Those he chooses are the ones who gratefully accept the gift he brings, confess their faith in him, and obey his words. Thus it is that those he chooses are they who "bear fruit" which abides (15:16).

Their bearing fruit, which is an all-embracing term for being the Lord's disciples, can be and is the object of their prayer. It is prayer that recalls and recognizes the gift he has conferred, renders thanks for it, and earnestly begs never to be blind to it. The assurance of the Father's response to this prayer rests firmly on the fact that the Father has already granted us in him "whatever" we ask (15:7).

Therefore, to pray that we continue to bear fruit is to pray to continue to acknowledge and obey the gift which the Father has given us. This gift, on God's part, is "irrevocable" (see "no one will take your joy from you" 16:22; cf. Rom 11:29). It is we, the recipients, who can at any time refuse the gift, deny its gratuity, or fail to submit to its demand:

This I command you, to love one another (15:17).

Loving one another is the only means of knowing ourselves to be, or demonstrating to others that we indeed are, his disciples, his friends; that we abide in him and he in us; that we are indeed bearing "much fruit." There is no getting around the simplicity of the command, and no escaping its consequences. Any and all casuistry about the when, the where and the how of carrying it out is ultimately a refusal to obey it. All preoccupation with other "commandments" is a vain attempt to evade the "This I command you, to love one another."

THE WORLD'S HATRED (John 15:18–25)

If the world hates you, know that it has hated me before it hated you (15:18).

The love which Jesus commands his disciples to have for one another is bound to earn them the world's hatred. For the beleaguered members of the Johannine community, for the early Christians living in the shadow of persecution, for the members of a minority religion in a world of paganism, and even for such Christian churches as exist even now in hostile regions, these words of Jesus can be a source of deep comfort and even of courage in the face of implacable opposition. Under the circumstances, such Christians would scarcely need a reminder that "a slave is not greater than his master" (13:16; and see 15:20), or that "the world hated me before it hated you" (15:18). But, in the midst of their tribulations, they do need to be reminded that:

If you were of the world, the world would love its own; but because you are not of the world, but I chose you out of the world, therefore, the world hates you (15:19).

These, too, are words that hardly need comment, were it not for the situation we find ourselves in today. Having for so long been of the world, having courted and won its favor, having erected in its midst a formidable and numerically powerful institution, any talk of the world's hatred can be no more than oratorical ornamentation. Those who know in their daily lives that they are "not of the world" and that the world hates them must realize sooner or later that this "world" is not necessarily somewhere out there outside the confines of the community of believers. The hatred and opposition they experience is within the very community that proclaims the Word.

The world is comfortably ensconced within the church. This church has learned over centuries, not only to skirt the world's hatred, but to court and win its approval, adopt its views, espouse its causes, and embrace its values. It willingly seeks the seats of honor in its councils, tailors its teaching to fit its ambitions, shrouds in decent obscurity whatever embarrasses it. In its eagerness to accommodate the world and its powers, it turns the juggernaut of its authority on those who dare to depart from the received and sanctioned orthodoxies of the day. If it rarely seeks to please the world, it never ceases to avoid displeasing it. The world's approval becomes the norm of its creeds and the judge of their "relevance." Were the hatred of the world a criterion for discerning the true community of believers, which church today could lay claim to the honor?

Those to whom the following words of the Revealer describe a familiar situation require no exegesis. But to those who think, as does the quack in Molière, "We have changed all that!" no exegesis is possible.

> **Remember the words that I said to you, "A slave is not greater than his master." If they persecuted me, they will persecute you; if they kept my word, they will keep yours also (15:20).**

The repeated reminder of the obvious fact (see Mt 10:24; Lk 6:40; Jn 13:16) is all the more necessary because it is so readily forgotten. The slave or, as the RSV chooses to translate the word, "the servant," is not greater than the master. No workable system for human life together has yet been devised to rid us of this truth. Even in an amicable exchange between equals, Plato observed, one leads and the other follows.

In one's relationship with Jesus Christ, not only is the maintenance of this hierarchy of persons essential to the relation itself, but awareness of it is a source of great comfort. "For," as the author of Hebrews reminds us, "we have not a high priest who is unable to sympathize with our weakness, but one who in every respect has been tempted as we are, yet without sin" (Heb 4:15). But, not for one moment, does this fact either invert the order of hierarchy between the Lord and his disciple, or abolish it.

Reason for the Hatred

But all this they will do to you on my account, because they do not know him who sent me (15:21).

Whatever the ostensible reasons proffered by the world to justify its attitude, the hatred and opposition it unleashes against the community has its true reason in its being the community of Jesus Christ. But, Jesus reminds his followers, the world's implacable hatred of him and of them is ultimately rooted in the world's refusal to acknowledge God, "they do not know him who sent me." This is to call things by their proper name. Whatever excuse the world might have had for its refusal to acknowledge God prior to the coming of the Revealer, has now lost all validity:

If I had not come and spoken to them, they would not have sin, but now they have no excuse for their sin (15:22).

These words echo Jesus' response to the Pharisees after the healing of the man born blind: "If you were blind you would have no [sin]; but now that you say, 'We see,' your [sin] remains" (9:41). The opposition of the world to Christ and to his followers is called by its proper name, sin. The world rejects God and him whom he sent (15:21). Neither ingenuity of expression nor variety of disguise can hide or attenuate this fact about the world, whether it be "the world" outside or inside the community of believers. The realization of this fact is, for the believer, not so much a cudgel to browbeat the world, but a source of genuine comfort and courage in the wilderness solitude of hatred by the world.

He who hates me hates my Father also (15:23).

In its stark simplicity, Jesus' statement is an echo of what we have in Matthew, "He who receives you receives me, and he who receives me receives him who sent me" (Mt 10:40); in Luke, "He who hears you hears me, and he who rejects you rejects me, and he who rejects me rejects him who sent me" (Lk 10:16); and of course in John, "He who does not honor the Son does not honor the Father" (5:23b; 12:48). But the logic of, "He who hates me hates my Father also," is rooted in, "He who has seen me has seen the Father" (14:9); and both are in fact corollaries of "the Word was God.... And the Word became flesh and dwelt among us" (1:1, 14). The incarnational logic of the fourth gospel is nothing if not consistent.

If I had not done among them the works which no one ever did, they would not have sin; but now they have seen and hated both me and my Father. It is to fulfil the word that is written in their law, "They hated me without a cause" (15:24–25).

The incomprehensibility of his rejection by the world and by his own people cannot for long be far from the evangelist's mind. If Jesus is who he says he is and his "works" show him to be, how could anyone reject him? Whatever reasons are adduced and whatever explanations invented to explain such rejection of the Revealer and, therefore, of the life he brings, the mystery remains. To cite the scriptures' "They hated me without a cause" (Ps 35:19) is, in this instance, more a confession of ignorance than an explanation.

THE THIRD PARACLETE SAYING (John 15:26–27)

But when the Paraclete comes, whom I shall send to you from the Father, even the Spirit of truth, who proceeds from the Father, he will bear witness to me (15:26).

The Paraclete, who will be with Jesus' followers "forever" and will "dwell" with them (14:16–17), whose task it is to "teach you all things, and bring to your remembrance all that I have said to you" (14:26), is the only assured source of their consolation midst the hatred of the world. Since the Revealer must return to the Father who sent him, it is the Paraclete who will "bear witness" to him. Therefore, it is the Paraclete, "even the Spirit of *truth*," who assures the permanence of the revelation in the world by never ceasing to bear witness to the Revealer in the community of those who believe in him.

Two things should be noted in this verse (15:26). First, that the Spirit, sent by the Son "from the Father," "proceeds from the Father" (cf. 16:7, "I will send him to you"), was at the basis of the debate which eventually precipitated the schism between the Eastern and the Western churches. Of this event we have a constant reminder in our creed's confession of faith in the Holy Spirit, "who proceeds from the Father *and* the Son."

The second thing to be noted is that, though it is the Paraclete who "will bear witness to me" here (15:26), the evangelist will later claim the same task to himself: "He who saw it has borne witness–his testimony is true, and he knows that he tells the truth–that you also may believe" (19:35); and, "This is the disciple who is bearing witness to these things, and who has written these things; and we know that his testimony is true" (21:24). This claim, of course, is not limited to the evangelist. It extends to all the proclaimers of the gospel down the ages and, in doing so, lends even greater significance to the reminder that the Paraclete "will bear witness to me" (15:26).

In their despair to find a satisfactory explanation for the term "Paraclete" in the fourth gospel, some commentators have even suggested that the Paraclete is none other than the evangelist himself. But the evangelist knows only too well that the Paraclete is "the Holy Spirit" (14:26). Nevertheless, the Holy Spirit also, like the Son who sent him "from the Father" (15:26), must somehow take flesh in order to "dwell" with us (14:17). He, as it were, takes flesh in the community of those who hear the word and proclaim it as "the word of eternal life" (6:68). This is why Jesus goes on to add:

> **...and you also are witnesses, because you have been with me from the beginning (15:27).**

It is difficult to imagine the evangelist writing these words unselfconsciously. To be witnesses to the Word is just what he is doing and what those who follow him will continue to do to the end of time. The Paraclete, the Holy Spirit, will continually call to the minds of all believers down through the ages and keep alive in them all that the Revealer said to them (14:26). He will do so in the "flesh" of the proclaimers of this revelation. It is thus the Paraclete who guides all of them, proclaimers and hearers alike, "into all the truth" (16:13) of the revelation.

Of course, this promise of the Paraclete is not confined to the evangelist and the community of his generation. For, so long as there is a community of believers that hears the Word and believes and proclaims it in the world, the work of the Paraclete, the Holy Spirit, abides.

John 16

The Disciples in the World: expulsion from the synagogue; community and tradition.

The Fourth Paraclete Saying: the function of the Paraclete; the community's judgment on the world.

The Fifth Paraclete Saying: the truth of the revelation; the glorification of Jesus.

Your Sorrow Will Turn into Joy: the disciples' loneliness; the abiding joy; the loss of the joy; ask anything.

I Have Overcome the World: the process of the revelation; "docetism"; "in my name"; to have his peace.

THE DISCIPLES IN THE WORLD (John 16:1–4A)

I have said all this to you to keep you from falling away. They will put you out of the synagogues; indeed, the hour is coming when whoever kills you will think he is offering service to God. And they will do this because they have not known the Father, nor me. But I have said these things to you, that when the hour comes you may remember that I told you of them (16:1–4a).

The "I have said to you" in 16:1 and 4a bracket these verses by the rhetorical device of "inclusion," which makes of them a self-contained introductory unit to this part of the discourse. As earlier in the discourse ("Let not your hearts be troubled" 14:1) so too here, the accent is on reassuring the disciples. It is they who will have to brave the world in Jesus' absence. Thus, "to keep you from falling away" (16:1) is a variation on the theme of, "Let not your hearts be troubled" (14:1). But at the source of all the reassurance is the revelation Jesus brings them, what "I have said to you."

The danger facing his disciples in every age is the "falling away," the "stumbling," as the NRSV puts it. However, one may wish to translate what the original Greek calls literally "scandal," the threat of stumbling, of falling away, is perennial, and no generation of believers is spared it. Indeed, the very feeling of security within the world can be the undoing of Jesus' disciples in any generation.

Of course, not every generation faces the overt persecution which the Johannine community was evidently facing at the time of this gospel's composition. But whatever form the danger that threatens them may take, the believers in every age can find their security and assurance only in the word the Revealer has spoken to them, only in his revelation.

Expulsion from the Synagogue

"They will put you out of synagogues" (16:2; see 9:22; 12:42) reflects, of course, a situation in the evangelist's time, not in Jesus'. Yet, here and elsewhere throughout the gospel, the evangelist has no hesitation to repeat, as generations after him will have to do, the prophetic gesture of, "Thus says the Lord!" He encourages and consoles his timorous community as though Jesus himself were addressing them. Whether in the evangelist's time or in ours, the words of the revelation proclaimed in the community are the work of "the Paraclete, the Holy Spirit" who "will teach you all things, and bring to your remembrance all that I have said to you" (14:26). It is because of this constant action of the Spirit Paraclete that the evangelist does not hesitate to address his readers in the words of Jesus, as though Jesus himself addressed them.

Thus, a community expelled from the synagogue, which was their rightful home, facing the threat of death at the hand of their enemies, and suffering the loneliness of their faith within a hostile world, can only have recourse to the words which the Revealer spoke to them, and find in those words the true courage to stand firm in the face of all opposition. The community of believers knows that, every time this word is proclaimed in their midst, the Paraclete carries out the task of teaching them and bringing to their memory all that Jesus had spoken to them (14:26). Only what Jesus says to them can keep them "from falling away" (16:1).

Community and Tradition

A generation deprived of this memory, bereft of what we refer to as "tradition," has no means of coping with its present predicament, and can therefore only despair of its future. If in times of crisis the church turns to this tradition, it does so in obedience to the Lord's "that when their hour comes you may remember that I told you" (16:4a).

Only in remembering what Jesus said to them, in being mindful of the revelation he brought to this world, will the community of believers in him be kept from "falling away" (16:1). Only thus will they have the clarity of vision to perceive the real reason behind the persecution and the ostracizing they suffer. They realize that those who hate them "have not known the Father, nor me" (16:3). Ignorance of God and of him whom he has sent is at the root of the world's hatred for them. Indeed, so convinced are they of this, that they realize its inverse also has to be true: that the absence of this hatred of the world for them is the sign that they themselves have "fallen away."

THE FOURTH PARACLETE SAYING (John 16:4B–11)

> **I did not say these things to you from the beginning, because I was with you. But now I am going to him who sent me; yet none of you asks me, "Where are you going?" But because I have said these things to you, sorrow has filled your hearts (16:4b–6).**

The sorrow that fills the disciples' hearts is sorrow for themselves, for being left orphans (14:18) in this world after Jesus' departure. They, like the generations that followed them, have found this sorrow at Jesus' absence almost too much to bear. Thus, over the centuries, the community of believers grew adept at devising means to negate this absence, had recourse to ingenious ways of circumventing it, and stubbornly refused to believe him when he says:

> **Nevertheless I tell you the truth: it is to your advantage that I go away, for if I do not go away, the Paraclete will not come to you, but if I go, I will send him to you (16:7).**

Only after his departure from this world will his disciples come to believe in him as the Revealer. So long as he has not gone away from them, the Paraclete cannot come, for his work can only begin after the Revealer's departure from this world. The Son has to return to the Father who sent him before he can send the Paraclete (cf. 15:26) to be with those who believe in him and are his disciples. They will know and believe who Jesus of Nazareth really is only *after* he leaves them.

This, of course, puts the first disciples of Jesus and those who believe in him today at an equal distance from him. There is, as Kierkegaard insisted, no difference between the "disciples at first hand" and the "disciples at second hand." "There is no disciple at second hand. The first and the last are essentially on the same plane..." *(Philosophical Fragments)*. Both they and we are equidistant from the Revealer. The community of believers can be what it is only because Jesus has died, is risen from the dead, has returned to the Father and sent the Paraclete to them. The Paraclete he sends them will accomplish his work in and through them as the community of those who confess their faith in Jesus Christ.

The Function of the Paraclete

> **And when he comes, he will convict the world concerning sin and righteousness and judgment; concerning sin, because they do not believe in me; concerning righteousness, because I go to the Father, and you will see me no more; concerning judgment, because the ruler of this world is judged (16:8–11).**

However difficult it has proved to explain the phrases used in these verses to describe it, the triple function of the Paraclete does sum up the work of the Holy Spirit in the community of believers. Indeed, these verses can be said to describe equally well the role of the church in the world. What the Paraclete "convicts" (RSV marg.), brings to light and condemns the world for are not individual moral failings, but a whole cast of mind that refuses to accept the revelation, refuses to accept any criterion but its own for judging it, and imagines it has the means of ultimately taming and bringing the revelation to subjection.

The very presence of the community of believers in the world is a living condemnation, not only of the refusal of the world to believe, but also of the world's whole attitude to the revelation. This condemnation is not matter for apologetic, polemic, or denunciation. The very existence and life of the community in the world shows that the world does "not know the Father, nor me" (16:3).

Unbelief is the "sin" of which the world stands condemned. The world's sin is its self-sufficiency, its refusal to acknowledge the need for him "who takes away the sin of the world" (1:29). It is the claim of the world not only to have but also to offer true life. It is the world's claim to possess the knowledge and the competence to dismiss the revelation as irrelevant or meaningless. "They do not believe in me" (16:9).

The "righteousness" that will convict the world is the judicial act that determines who is "right." This prerogative belongs to him alone who, having suffered death on the cross at the hand of an obdurate and hating world, is now risen from the dead and has returned to the Father. In his "I go to the Father, and you will see me no more" (16:10) is his victory over the world (16:33). In his death and resurrection he passes judgment and convicts the world. What to the world seemed "right" he condemns. This judgment, of course, cannot take place until the world is able to see him "no more," the very world which refuses to accept anything but visible, tangible, verifiable–by its own standards–evidence.

That the Paraclete, in and through the community, will convict the world of "judgment" (16:11) is a statement about the eschatological judgment that has already taken place (see 3:5, 19; 5:28–29; 6:54; 12:31). The "ruler of the world is judged" and condemned in the very triumph of the one who has, by his death and resurrection (12:31), "overcome the world" (16:33). The world stands convicted of "judgment" because it believes it has the means of judging by its own standards–the only ones it accepts as valid–both its own history and the history of the community of believers within it.

However you choose to describe the evil of which the world stands convicted by its refusal to believe in the Revealer and by its hatred of those who do, you have to call it by its true name: sin. Whether you choose to call this evil the work of "the ruler of this world" (16:11; 12:31; 14:30), "the devil" (13:2; 6:70; 8:44), or "the father of lies" (8:44), the fact remains that the evil of the world, like the evil of every individual on the face of the earth, requires no explanation outside and beyond itself.

The Community's Judgment on the World

The judgment pronounced on the world takes place by the mere existence of the community of believers within it. The very presence of the community of those who believe in him who "for judgment came into this world" (9:39; 3:19; 5:24), "convicts" the world. This judgment is not the vociferous recriminations and threats, the ostentatious displays of punishment and power, the moral posturing and pontificating of authority, in which the institution indulges from time to time. It is, rather, a permanent judgment executed by the community of believers in the world by its very existence, by the very life it leads in the midst of the world, and by the witness it bears to him who alone is "the life" and "the light of men" (14:6; 1:4; 8:12). This living and witnessing of the community can only be the result of the work within it of the Paraclete, the Holy Spirit.

The reason Christians today are likely to find such sayings about the Paraclete incomprehensible or outmoded is perhaps another indication of the extent to which the world has succeeded in inverting the entire process. It is the world that judges, finds wanting and condemns the community of believers. We truckle to, and cower before, the world's pretended knowledge and vaunted might. We are all too ready to abandon the "word of life" (1 Jn 1:1) and to cling instead to all that the world presumes to call life. We do everything in our power to acquiesce in the world's judgment, to embrace its values and succumb to its standards. At times, so intimate is the alliance between them, so complete the identification between the church and the world, that no room for judgment is left.

THE FIFTH PARACLETE SAYING (John 16:12–15)

> **I have yet many things to say to you, but you cannot hear them now. When the Spirit of truth comes, he will guide you into all the truth; for he will not speak on his own authority, but whatever he hears he will speak, and he will declare to you the things that are to come (16:12–13).**

The role of the Spirit of truth is, of course, not confined to the judgment of the world ("he will convict the world" 16:8–11). The identification of the Paraclete as "the Spirit of truth" (14:16–17) underlines the role he plays in assuring the permanence of the Revealer's work after the latter's departure from this world. That the Revealer himself has "many things to say to you" (16:12) is not, however, an allusion to the "development of dogma," but a description of the nature of the revelation. This revelation is not "finished," consummated (19:30), until after the death and resurrection of Jesus. Therefore, the "many things" he has to say to them before that event, "they cannot hear them *now*" (16:12).

The Truth of the Revelation

Each new generation will hear the revelation within its own particular situation and within its own specific circumstances. New generations will hear it as a word addressed to them here and now and, hearing it, will come to understand the revelation which the Word who became flesh brought into the world. It is the task of the Spirit of truth to guide the community of believers in every generation "into all the truth" (16:13a). This is not a cumulative process where the "deposit of faith" grows by accretion. It is not necessarily a progressive process either, where the believers of the twentieth century become, as it were, richer and more privileged than those of the first. The guidance of the Spirit of truth is "into *all* the truth" in every generation and every age. This "all" refers to the integrality, the wholeness, not the extensiveness, of "the truth."

Therefore, Jesus goes on to remind his disciples that the Spirit of truth "will not speak on his own authority" (16:13). The Paraclete is the Spirit of truth whom Jesus will send after his departure from this world ("I will send him to you" 16:7). The task which the Paraclete performs is the preservation of the revelation in its entirety, integrally: "whatever he hears he will speak" (16:13).

But the revelation addressed to the believers in their present situation lays bare before them the future that lies ahead, not by filling their heads with spectacular things to come, but by securing their hope in what God has accomplished in the sending of his Son into the world. That the Spirit will "declare to you the things that are to come" (16:13) is a reminder to them of the eschatological nature of the revelation, not a promise of apocalyptic spectacles. With the advent of the Revealer into the world, the "end" is already here; and because it is already here, the future of the believers is secure and lies open before them. The security and the assurance about the future that is genuinely theirs is the constant task of the Paraclete: "to be with you for ever" (14:16).

The Glorification of Jesus

He will glorify me, for he will take what is mine and declare it to you. All that the Father has is mine; therefore I said that he will take what is mine and declare it to you (16:14–15).

These verses contain about as good a definition of "glorify" as one can find anywhere. The glorification of Jesus is the revelation of who he is and the manifestation of what he has done. To glorify him ("He will glorify me"), therefore, is "to declare" what he is to the disciples. Thus, what the Paraclete will ceaselessly declare to them is the identity of Jesus of Nazareth and the intimacy of his union with the Father. This, of course, is what the proclamation of the gospel must do in every age and to every generation. In this proclamation the Paraclete does his work.

In proclaiming, "All that the Father has is mine" (16:15), the Paraclete declares, not a community of shared goods between the

Father and the Son, but the divine identity of the Revealer: "I and the Father are one" (10:30; 14:11; 17:11); "who has seen me has seen the Father" (14:9). This, too, is what the evangelist himself is doing in writing his gospel. This is what all proclaimers of his gospel will do in ages to come.

Therefore, to speak thus of the Paraclete, the Spirit of truth, is to keep in mind that his work is carried out within the Christian community in its proclaiming and hearing, its preaching and teaching, its worshiping and obeying the word. The Lord is thus "glorified" (16:14) in the humblest catechetical instruction as in the most solemn of ecclesiastical pronouncements. The ever-present danger, of course, is to turn this work into a propaganda machine or a theatrical display. But the Spirit of truth too is "not mocked" (see Gal 6:7).

YOUR SORROW WILL TURN INTO JOY (John 16:16–24)

> **"A little while, and you will see me no more; again a little while, and you will see me." Some of his disciples said to one another, "What is this that he says to us, 'A little while, and you will not see me, and again a little while, and you will see me'; and 'because I go to the Father'?" They said, "What does he mean by 'a little while'? We do not know what he means." Jesus knew that they wanted to ask him; so he said to them, "Is this what you are asking yourselves, what I meant by saying, 'A little while, and you will not see me, and again a little while, and you will see me'?" (16:16–19)**

As has been noted above (13:33; 14:19; cf. 7:33–34; 12:35), the disciples' bewilderment is quite comprehensible. The evangelist and we have the advantage of hindsight. So we must keep in mind that no amount of instruction or prediction of the resurrection could have been truly grasped before the event itself. Even if Jesus did tell them he was going to rise from the dead, he would still need to reassure them when the event did take place, with "It is I; do not be afraid!" (6:20; cf. Mt 28:5, 10). We are not dealing with a meteorological forecast or a human prediction, however spectacular. What Jesus tells his disciples about is nothing less than the revelation of the mystery of his person.

The readers of this or any other gospel must never forget that the gospels were written *after* the event, by disciples who believed, not just in the resurrection of the dead in general, but in the resurrection of the crucified Jesus of Nazareth in particular. Keeping in mind the nature of our gospels, we do well to ask ourselves sometimes whether, if Jesus in fact did know he was going to rise shortly after his death, he could be said to have died like any mortal human being. If he did not die like any other mortal, then how could we say, "the Word became flesh"? How could the Word truly become flesh, when the distinguishing mark of "flesh" is death? The Word, in other words, could not become truly "flesh" and escape the mortality which defines all flesh.

In the farewell discourse, Jesus knows only too well that the questionings of his disciples arise out of their apprehensiveness at being left alone in the world.

The Disciples' Loneliness

Amen, amen, I say to you, you will weep and lament, but the world will rejoice; you will be sorrowful, but your sorrow will turn into joy. When a woman is in travail she has sorrow, because her hour has come, but when she is delivered of the child, she no longer remembers the anguish, for joy that a [human being] is born into the world (16:20–21).

The disciples' weeping and lamentation is not for the loss of a beloved, nor is their sorrow the sorrow of bereavement. It is their loneliness in the world, their being left alone in a world which hates them (15:18), that is at the source of their grief. The consolation Jesus offers them is, therefore, a genuine and abiding consolation, not such as we are wont–albeit helplessly–to extend to the bereaved.

If the disciples are disconsolate at the thought of Jesus' departure from them, the consolation he promises them will radically alter their grief. But it is only after his death and resurrection that their "sorrow will turn into joy" (16:20). This joy is not only the joy of Easter at the raising of Jesus from the dead, but the joy that the resurrection itself makes possible: the joy of not being "orphans" in the world (14:18) even after he leaves them to return to the Father. It is, moreover, the joy of knowing that "where I am, there shall my servant be also" (12:26; 14:3; 17:24).

The image of "the woman" who has sorrow because she is in labor and her subsequent joy that "a child," "a human being" (RSV marg. and NRSV), has come into the world (16:21) is true of Jesus' disciples' sorrow before and their joy after his resurrection. In this, of course, they differ from all those who come after them, who already know Jesus is risen from the dead. The image, therefore, is not quite applicable to us who live after the resurrection of Jesus.

The Abiding Joy

So you have sorrow now, but I will see you again, and your hearts will rejoice, and no one will take your joy from you (16:22).

The reason for the abiding joy of all Jesus' disciples in every age is not just the fact of his victory over death but also what it makes possible. After his death and resurrection, Jesus departs from this world to return to the Father, and only then can he send the Paraclete to be with his disciples forever. Thus, their sorrow at being left alone in the world is turned into the permanent joy of knowing they will never be alone in a world that hates them. The Spirit he sends them "from the Father" (15:26) is, therefore, the true source of their abiding joy (cf. Gal 5:22, "The fruit of the Spirit is...joy").

In Jesus' victory over death, the believers find the courage to be in the world. Even in a world that hates them, their sorrow is transformed into joy in the very realization that the gift they possess, the eternal life they have by believing in him, cannot be lost: "no one will take your joy from you" (16:22). The "no one" is all-exclusive. No one, whether in the community or out of it, can ever deprive the believers of their joy. The gift they have in Jesus Christ is not contingent upon the whims and caprice of others, nor on public consensus, nor on institutional approbation. His gift is not at the pleasure and disposition of any person, however mighty, or any institution, however sacred.

The Loss of the Joy

We can, of course, give up the gift; but that is not the same thing as "losing" it. To lose something is to lose it unintentionally, or to be forcefully deprived of it by another. Because this joy springs from the assured possession of eternal life, which only faith in the Word makes ours, no power on earth, whether religious or civil, can ever take it away from us. It is no more in the power of anyone to deprive us of the gift than it is to have granted it in the first place.

Whence, then, the inspissated gloom of Christians all around? Someone recently remarked that the Catholic students at an institution of learning were sad because they were so angry at the church. Ought they not, one wonders, to have been angry at themselves for being sad, for having let others rob them of their joy, for having bartered away their Christian joy for the counterfeits foisted on them whether by the world or by the church itself?

No one and nothing in the world can take away from Christians this true joy (16:22), any more than they can deprive them of the life which they have "abundantly" (10:10), or alter the fact of the "I have loved you" (15:9; 13:34). But we can, and we all too often do, willingly cast away that life and that love in exchange for the tawdry bagatelles proffered by a world which promises us both, but is impotent to grant us either.

Ask Anything

In that day you will ask nothing of me. Amen, amen, I say to you, if you ask anything of the Father, he will give it to you in my name (16:23).

First of all, the reader has to keep in mind that the use of "ask" in this verse is ambiguous. The Greek employs two different verbs: the first, "ask of me," for inquiry, and the second, "ask of the Father," for petition. Thus, Jesus' "you will ask nothing of me" says there will be no further questions to put to him "in that day."

This is a reference to the eschatological nature of the revelation. It is conclusively the last. With his death and resurrection, "in that day," Jesus' work of revelation will be complete. Thenceforth, the understanding of it by the believers can of course be deepened; but the revelation itself cannot be more extensive. "In that day" there will be no more questions to ask the Revealer; and, in any case, he won't be there to answer them. The Paraclete will, however, be there to teach them "all things" by bringing to their remembrance all that the Revealer said to his disciples, "all that *I have said* to you" (14:26).

This very fact, moreover, is at the basis of the believer's confidence in prayer. The assurance that "if you ask anything of the Father, he will give it to you in my name" (16:23) rests on the fact that the Father has *already* given us all things in him (see above on 14:13–14, and cf. Rom 8:32, "He who did not spare his own Son but gave him up for us all, will he not also give us all things with him?"). This is what Jesus means when he adds, "in my name." In sending his Son into the world, God has given us all things in him, "in his name." Henceforth, all God's gifts to us are given in the name of the only Son, who has indeed given us all things.

> **Hitherto you have asked nothing in my name; ask, and you will receive, that your joy may be full (16:24).**

Let it be said at the outset that asking in Jesus' name is not here a reference to a liturgical formula. The coming of the Son into the world has radically altered the meaning and the mode of prayer. The believer always prays in Jesus' name, i.e., out of faith in the Son. Henceforth, all prayers are made in the name of him whom the Father has sent into the world to grant eternal life to all those who believe in him. In their faith in the Revealer and in their obedience to his commandment, they will find their true and inexhaustible joy. "Ask, and you will receive, that your joy may be full" (16:24).

I HAVE OVERCOME THE WORLD (John 16:25–33)

> **I have said this to you in figures; the hour is coming when I shall no longer speak to you in figures but tell you plainly of the Father (16:25).**

That Jesus had spoken to them thus far in "figures" (i.e., figures of speech) rather than "plainly" and openly was inevitable before the coming of "the hour." It is only in that "hour," the hour of his death and resurrection, that he is revealed as who he really is: Jesus Christ the Lord, the Son sent by the Father into the world to give eternal life to all those who believe in him (3:15, 16; 10:10). But we have to keep in mind that the process of this revelation was, in fact, the inverse of that to which our catechism and religious instruction have accustomed us.

The Process of the Revelation

In our understanding of the mystery of God's love for us, we follow the progression of the articles in the creed we recite: God the creator sent into the world his only Son, who becomes man, suffers, dies on the cross, and is raised from the dead. The order of events in John, like that in any of the other gospels, reinforces this way of understanding the succession of events. Thus we can very easily forget that Jesus' disciples had to arrive at their understanding in exactly the inverse order.

Only after his resurrection from the dead did the disciples comprehend the meaning of Jesus' suffering and death on the cross. Only when they comprehended this did they come to see the significance of Jesus' words and deeds in the public ministry. Gradually and slowly it dawned on them that the Jesus who was revealed to them as the Lord in his resurrection had to have been so before his death and during his life. Indeed, he had to be the Lord from the very beginning.

"Docetism"

John's gospel takes this ascending line farther still to its, so to speak, logical conclusion. His gospel opens with, "In the beginning was the Word," and this Word who "was God" (1:1) "became flesh and dwelt among us" (1:14). It should not come as a surprise, therefore, that some scholars have detected in the fourth gospel traces of "docetism," which denied the humanity of Christ, one of the first Christian heresies. The "became flesh" can seem to be incidental to "the Word was God." The Jesus of John can sometimes give the impression of a "God striding the earth."

It could well be that the first epistle of John had to be written because of this very early suspicion of docetism in the gospel, the suspicion that it stressed the divinity at the expense of the humanity of Jesus. The opening line of the epistle, "That which was from the beginning, which we have heard, which we have seen with our eyes, which we have looked upon and touched with our hands" (1 Jn 1:1), seems designed expressly to remove any suspicion of docetism (see 1 Jn 4:2, "every spirit which confesses that Jesus Christ has come in the flesh is of God"). Some scholars even opine that the first epistle of John facilitated the acceptance of the gospel by the universal church. The gospel of John was, in fact, the last to gain admission to the ranks of the other three.

All this is by way of reminding the reader of the fourth gospel today that Jesus' disciples could have heard him tell them "plainly of the Father" only after "the hour" had come, only after his death and resurrection. That event not only revealed who he is to them but also, by reason of that revelation, altered the status of their own relation to the Father:

> **In that day you will ask in my name; and I do not say to you that I shall pray the Father for you; for the Father himself loves you, because you have loved me and have believed that I came from the Father (16:26–27).**

The faith of the disciples in Jesus as the one who "came from the Father" and their love for him show them that they themselves are loved by the Father, "the Father himself loves you," just as they are loved by the Son, "I have loved you" (13:34; 15:9). All this can dawn upon them only "in that day," only after the death and resurrection of Jesus.

"In my name"

"In that day" too, the believers will turn to the Father "in my name," i.e., in their faith in Jesus of Nazareth as the only Son of the Father. Their prayer, as indeed their whole life as Christians, will henceforth be determined by that relationship to "the Father himself" who loves them (16:27).

Their relationship to the Father is of course based on their faith in, love for, and obedience to the Son (14:15; 15:10). It is Jesus of Nazareth whom they believe and love and obey as the only Son whom the Father has sent. Only in the name of the Son ("in my name" 16:26) do they have this unhindered access of beloved children to the Father who loves them. This is why the church fathers spoke of the relation of the believers to the Father as of *filii in Filio*, "sons in the Son."

I came from the Father and have come into the world; again, I am leaving the world and going to the Father (16:28).

This only repeats the basic assertion of the gospel about the mission of the Son: that he had "come from God and was going to God" (13:3); that he "proceeded and came forth from the Father" (8:42).

Jesus' disciples have to reconcile themselves to the fact that he is "leaving the world and going to the Father" (16:28). Only when they contemplate his leaving the world can they begin to understand the meaning of his coming into it. It is the end of his mission in the world that reveals its true beginning and origin.

His disciples said, "Ah, now you are speaking plainly, not in any figure! Now we know that you know all things, and need none to question you; by this we believe that you came from God" (16:29–30).

Alas, they do not really "know," and they will not be able to know until "the hour" has come (16:25). Only in "that day" (16:26) will they understand (see 16:12); only "in that day" will they ask no more questions of him (16:23). But their eagerness to "jump the gun" is quite understandable. Their enthusiasm, though rash, is genuine. The Revealer in whom they believe will not cease to speak in "figures of speech" (NRSV 16:29 and cf. 16:25) until "that day" has come. He can speak to them "plainly" and openly only when that "hour" comes (16:25). Indeed, only in that "hour" of his death and resurrection, in his hour of glorification (see 12:16, 23; 13:31–32; 17:1), will they finally understand that he who returns to the Father is the Son whom the Father sent into the world to save it (3:17; 12:47). Only then will they really know what it is for him to be "speaking plainly, not in any figure" (16:29). Only then will they know who he is for them and for the world.

Jesus answered them, "Do you now believe? The hour is coming, indeed it has come, when you will be scattered every one to his home, and will leave me alone; yet I am not alone, for the Father is with me" (16:31–32).

Simon Peter was not singular in his presumption (see 13:37–38). All the disciples who are with him "will be scattered," every single one of them will run away and leave him alone. Yet they persist in thinking that their faith in him is the result of their own perspicacity, of their mental acumen and their native good will. We all do this, and like the disciples, require very little to make us turn tail and run. That over the centuries we have grown more adept at devising explanations and inventing excuses for our betrayal, cannot attenuate our failure or alter the fact that we usually fail when most sure of ourselves.

Jesus' words to his disciples, like his words to Simon Peter (13:37–38), are a warning. We tend to forget that the evangelist is writing after the facts from the vantage point of his faith in the risen Jesus. But we must not let his reiteration of Jesus' true relationship with the Father, "for the Father is with me" (16:32; cf. 10:30; 17:11), distract us from all which "you will leave me alone" must have truly meant for Jesus of Nazareth. Alone will he be in his trial, alone in his crucifixion and above all, like every mortal on this earth, alone in his death. But, in spite of that, Jesus' first thought is still for those whom he loves:

I have said this to you, that in me you may have peace (16:33a).

The reference of "this" is evidently to the words that Jesus has just addressed to his disciples. But the true import of Jesus' words lies in the revelation he brings in *all* that "I have said to you" (cf. 14:26). Therein lies the genuine peace he brings those who believe in him; for the only peace his disciples can have is that which comes from him as the Son of the Father, who grants eternal life to all who believe in him. It is in the assured possession of that gift of eternal life that their true peace lies.

To Have His Peace

Therefore, the peace which the believers can have is genuine only if they have it in him, "that *in me* you may have peace" (16:33a), and in no one else. It is his peace because he alone can confer it, and in him alone can it be had, "*my* peace I give you" (14:27).

One cannot help but reflect that part of the restlessness in the heart of believers today is attributable to the clouding of precisely this one simple fact. So many in this world pretend to give them peace. So many more take it upon themselves to tell them where it can be found. The very muddle of the vocabulary and the babel of meanings make this peace an illusion, just a part of the day's social amenities at best.

Yet the fact remains that the only peace to be had is that which "the world *cannot* give," that which only he who loved us "to the end" (13:1) and revealed the Father's love for us (16:27) can give. It is only in the secure possession of this love that the believer can come to know real surcease of the heart's troubles, and true repose from its restlessness (14:27; 16:33b). Only the Son can grant this secure possession of "the Father's love for us" and the genuine peace it confers:

> **In the world you face persecution. But take courage; I have conquered the world! (16:33b NRSV).**

That believers in him "face persecution" in the world is by no means incidental to their lot. The opposition, hatred, tribulation and even out-and-out persecution, which the disciples of Jesus face in the world, arise from what they are and what the world is. The world presumes to submit the revelation to its criteria of what it judges acceptable and what it deems credible. His disciples believe in him as the Son whom the Father has sent (6:69; 11:27; 12:44; 14:1; 20:31). The world rejects both the judge and the judgment he executes. His disciples know that their very presence in the world is a judgment upon it. The world arrogates to itself the power to determine what is opportune, to set the conditions for peace, to define the meaning of love, and to be forever on its way to conquering death. His disciples know that "it is the last hour" (1 Jn 2:18); that he gives peace "not as the world gives" (Jn 14:27); that they love "as he loved" and because he loved (13:34); and that there is no conquest of death save in the eternal life which is "to know you the only true God, and Jesus Christ whom you have sent" (17:3).

"But take courage, I have conquered the world!" His conquest of the world and of all the mechanisms of its slavery gives Jesus' disciples their true peace. This peace is what gives them the courage to withstand the hatred of the world.

Yet such words must seem almost otiose now that "godless communism" has been vanquished and Christian might has yet again proven right. That in the world "you face persecution" must sound remarkably vacuous in a church which has won out and established its secure place in this world. Christians know only too well that it is *our* world. Its values and norms are ours. We boast of our keeping up with it, tirelessly soliciting its approval and praise, ever striving to meet its standards. We change whenever the world alteration finds. We labor ceaselessly to purge our message of any element that the world finds "politically incorrect." What the world enacts as law we hasten to promulgate as gospel morality.

It is not the least irony of our times that the believers in the Christ who "conquered the world" can boast that they, too, have done so. And the last irony of all is–in the words of Horace–that the Rome which conquered the world has been led captive by it.

John 17

The Prayer of Jesus: human idiom about God; the gift of eternal life; human freedom and divine goodness; eternal life; knowledge and faith; creation and revelation; the Father's gift to the Son; the world; the believers in the world; ecumenism; the world's hatred; sanctified in the truth; the holiness of the community; "through their word"; the end of unity; the source of unity.

That the farewell discourse should culminate in a prayer is evident, but that the prayer with which it culminates is unique might not be. The prayer of Jesus is unique because his relation to the one he addresses in it is unique. There can be no doubt—certainly not in the mind of the evangelist—that Jesus addresses God as "Father" with the awareness of the singularity of the relationship between them: "*my* Father and *your* Father... *my* God and *your* God" (20:17). This relationship of Jesus of Nazareth to the Father, moreover, is not only unique but also determinative of every other relationship to God. In it, ultimately, is revealed the true source and meaning of any relationship to God which claims to be Christian.

THE PRAYER OF JESUS (John 17:1–26)

When Jesus had spoken these words, he lifted up his eyes to heaven and said, "Father, the hour has come; glorify your Son that the Son may glorify you" (17:1).

Jesus assumes an attitude of prayer which was common in his world (see 11:41). That heaven is the dwelling place of God is no less an anthropomorphism, a human way of speaking about God, than is the act of lifting up the eyes to heaven. Gestures are, of course, integral to prayer, cadaverous rigidity being as unconducive to prayer as to any other mode of communication. In Jesus' posture we recognize an attitude appropriate to addressing God.

The reference to "the hour" is, of course, a constant theme throughout the gospel. "My hour has not yet come" (2:4; 7:30) in its first part gives place to "his hour had come" (13:1) in the second. It is, as has already been pointed out, the hour of Jesus' departure from the world, the hour of his death, resurrection and return to the Father.

One important element in this prayer of Jesus is its insistence on the mutuality and reciprocity of the relationship between him and God the Father. His petition to "glorify your Son" has for its purpose "that your Son may glorify you." By sending him into the world, God reveals the identity of his Son to the world and thus glorifies him. The glory which the Son had "before the world was made" (17:5) thus becomes manifest in the work the Son accomplishes in and for the world.

Human Idiom about God

Our faith in the Trinity can often make us overlook a few elementary facts. Human beings live and act in a human way, and in no other. When they speak of God they can only do so from a human point of view, in human language and with human reason. Their confession of faith in God is an acknowledgment of their own creaturehood. To pretend to speak of the deity in and for itself is to pretend not only too much but falsely.

Moreover, if human beings speak of any deity in and of itself, they can do so only in reference to themselves and in language inextricably bound up with their human condition. Of course, no other language exists. The gods of the *Iliad* spoke in Homeric hexameters; the God of Israel, in the language of the psalmist and the prophets; the Father of Jesus Christ in the vocabulary of the Johannine community. To pretend there is another, more sublime or elevated idiom than the human for speaking about God, is to misconceive God and impugn the rational creature created by him. The limitations of our language when we speak of God stem, not from a defect in human intelligence nor from the unmetaphysical disposition of all but a few, but from the fact of our creaturehood. So, when "The heavens are telling the glory of God" (Ps 19:1), they tell it to creatures capable of raising their eyes to those heavens, just as Jesus "lifted up his eyes to heaven."

When Jesus prays the Father to glorify him, he prays that, in his redemptive work as the Son, the glory of the Father who sent him be manifested. He prays that, in the revelation he brings to the world, the glory of the God who "wondrously made and more wondrously still refashioned" be revealed to them whom he created and redeemed. In other words, Jesus prays that, in his loving "to the end" (13:1), the love of the creator for his own will become manifest; that, in his own obedience as Son to the will of the Father, the love of the Father for his own will be revealed.

The Gift of Eternal Life

...since you have given him power over all flesh, to give eternal life to all whom you have given him (17:2).

The Son glorifies the Father precisely in his giving "eternal life" to the world in obedience to the Father's saving will (3:16). This eternal life is the gift that only God the creator can give, and in giving it is glorified. The living God, the Father who "has life in himself" is he who has granted the Son "also to have life in himself" (5:26). This is the "power over all flesh," the power to make alive, that the Father has given the Son whom he sent into the world. Thus, by conferring this gift of eternal life on us, the Son not only glorifies the Father but is himself also glorified.

We must note, however, that even in this sublime statement, we are not allowed to forget that the glory of the Son is precisely in his obedience to the Father. It is the Father who has granted him the "power over all flesh," i.e., over every created being, therefore over all mortals, including those on whom the Son confers eternal life.

The reference therefore to "the hour" (17:1) is a reminder that he who came into the world that "they may have life, and have it abundantly" (10:10) is about to accomplish the purpose of his mission by the totality of his obedience to the Father in loving his own "to the end" (13:1). In this life-giving love for them, not only is the Son himself glorified, but he glorifies the Father also.

Human Freedom and Divine Goodness

A word here is again necessary to forestall the objection to divine arbitrariness and—perhaps more important still—to fend off the temptation to the glorification of the human. The power which the Son is given "over all flesh" extends to anyone born into the world, to everyone destined to die. That not every one of them chooses to accept the gift of the eternal life he brings, is proof of human freedom, not of divine partiality. Those who believe and have eternal life in him are, moreover, not paragons of human triumph and achievement, but merely manifestations of divine goodness. They reveal the glory of the Son and manifest the glory of the Father in their obedience to the gift, as well as in their acknowledgment of the utter gratuity both of the gift itself and of their acceptance of it. They are the ones whom the Father "has given him." To them the Son gives eternal life (17:2).

Eternal Life

And this is eternal life, that they know you the only true God, and Jesus Christ whom you have sent (17:3).

The "power over all flesh," which the Father has given his Son, is the power to "give eternal life" (17:2). This "eternal life" receives here its Johannine definition. To know "the only true God," to know that is the Father of Jesus Christ and, in one and the same instance, to know Jesus Christ himself as the Son whom the Father sent into the world, is to possess eternal life. This knowledge is indivisible. You cannot believe he is the Son without believing God is the Father. Nor can you believe that God sent him without acknowledging him to be the Son.

To say this is merely to encapsulate what has been consistently repeated throughout the gospel: "that whoever believes in him may have eternal life" (3:15, 16); "who believes in the Son has eternal life" (3:36); "who hears my word and believes him who sent me has eternal life" (5:24); "who believes has eternal life" (6:47 and see 6:40). Jesus himself reminds his hearers, "I came that they may have life, and have it abundantly" (10:10); "I give them eternal life, and they shall never perish" (10:28 and see 11:25–26). Indeed, the evangelist sums it all up by stating explicitly that the purpose of his gospel is "that you may believe that Jesus is the Christ, the Son of God, and that believing you may have life in his name" (20:31).

Jesus' words in 17:3 inverse the usual order, putting eternal life as subject, in order to remind us that the true life we all seek is ours to have, when we believe in Jesus Christ as the one sent by God, and so recognize "the only true God." The very phrasing of the saying, "And this is eternal life...," ought to be sufficient warning against imagining that by our faith in and knowledge of him as the Revealer and the Son of the Father we somehow merit or earn this eternal life, when in fact all we do is acknowledge it as the gift that only God can truly confer upon us. To believe in and to know the one whom God has sent does not lead to, or result in eternal life. It *is* eternal life.

Knowledge and Faith

Moreover, to misunderstand "that they *know* you" as setting a premium on intellectual excellence or on theological sophistication has already been forestalled. This "knowledge" of the truth of the revelation that the Revealer brings is what "sets us free" (8:32) from all the tyrannies of the stratification of faith by experts and savants. There is, of course, nothing wrong in constantly seeking to deepen the believers' grasp of the meaning of the revelation. Indeed, it is an obligation incumbent on all the proclaimers of the word, as on all those who hear it. The evangelist himself is, in fact, discharging just such an obligation in writing his gospel. The danger lies in setting up intellectual excellence as such–measured of course always by what I myself can attain–as the criterion of knowing "the only true God, and Jesus Christ whom you have sent."

I glorified you on earth, having accomplished the work which you gave me to do (17:4).

Lest we overlook what is at the basis of the conjunction in "that they may know you are the only true God, *and* Jesus Christ," we are given a reminder of the obedience that binds the one who is sent to the only true God who sent him. The entire life of Jesus of Nazareth is one uninterrupted act of obedience which reveals and bears witness to him as the Son, the Revealer of the Father. It is in his work of obedience that the Son "glorified" the "only true God" precisely by revealing him, in his obedience to him, as the Father.

Creation and Revelation

...and now, Father, glorify me in your own presence with the glory which I had with you before the world was made (17:5).

In accomplishing the work the Father gave him to do, the Son not only glorifies the Father but is himself also glorified (see 8:54 and cf. 8:50 and 7:18). The "glory which I had with you before the world was made" is in fact the glory which the Word had "in the beginning with God" (1:1). This is the glory that is revealed in the life and work of Jesus, the glory of "the only Son, who is in the bosom of the Father," the Revealer who "has made him known" (1:18).

From the very beginning God is a revealer of himself because, as the first letter of John says, "God is love" (1 Jn 4:8, 16); and love cannot but reveal itself. As one of Graham Greene's memorable characters says, "One can't love and do nothing." The creation of the world is an act of revelation of God's love, no less than the sending of his Son into it (see Jn 3:16). God is forever revealing himself as creator, whether in the creation of the world or in the gift of eternal life. This is the truth that the incarnate Word revealed and, revealing it, not only glorified "the only true God" as his Father but was himself also glorified as the only Son.

The Father's Gift to the Son

I have manifested your name to the men whom you gave me out of the world; they were yours, and you gave them to me, and they have kept your word (17:6).

The Son glorified the Father by revealing, by making known, his name to those whom the Father himself chose out of the world (cf. "all whom you have given him" 17:2; see 6:37, 39; 10:29 and also 17:6, 7, 8, 9, 12, 24). Those who choose to believe in him and to know the true God who sent him (17:3), those who accept the gift of eternal life which the Revealer brings to the entire world, are themselves the gift of the Father to the Son. They are the Father's handiwork (cf. "his workmanship [*poiema*, whence 'poem']" Eph 2:10).

Once again it is necessary to add here that the Father compels none of those whom he gives the Son "out of the world" (17:6). God cannot compel any one of them without denying her or him the essential freedom which constitutes any rational human being. A gift, even so august a divine gift as eternal life, cannot violate the recipient's freedom and still remain a gift.

By the very fact of their response to the revelation, those who believe in "the only true God, and Jesus Christ whom you have sent" (17:3) are set apart from the world. What sets them apart is not only their faith in the Revealer of the Father but their keeping his word, "they have kept your word," i.e., their obedience to the word of the revelation. But keeping the word of the Father is not merely to accept the revelation brought by Jesus of Nazareth ("If you continue in my word, you are truly my disciples" 8:31; 15:7, 14), but to submit to its commandment to love one another (13:34–35; 15:12, 17; 17:26). All revelation brings a commandment ("I am the Lord your God, you shall..." Ex 20:2–17; Deut 5:6–21), and the ultimate revelation of God in Jesus Christ is no exception.

> **Now they know that everything you have given me is from you; for I have given them the words which you gave me, and they have received them and know in truth that I came from you; and they have believed that you sent me (17:7–8).**

All prayer is acknowledgment of gift. The prayer of Jesus is no exception. In the very revelation he brings to his own, he acknowledges the Father as the author of the revelation. Thus, by believing in him as the Revealer, his disciples "know that everything you have given me is from you" (17:7). They know, that is, not only the fact that the mystery he brings is from God, but that "the only true God" is always the God who reveals himself, who speaks the mystery of his love to a world he "so loved" that "he gave his only Son" (3:16).

The words which the Word utters are those which the Father gave him. His disciples hear these words rightly only when they acknowledge their true source in the Father. Faith in Jesus Christ is faith in him as the Son whom the Father sent. It is faith in him as the Revealer who speaks the word which the Father gave him. To accept his words, "they have received them" (17:8b), is to recognize that he is the Son sent by God into the world and therefore to recognize that the God who sent him is indeed his Father: "they have believed that you have sent me" (17:8c).

> **I am praying for them; I am not praying for the world but for those whom you have given me, for they are yours; all mine are yours, and yours are mine, and I am glorified in them (17:9–10).**

If all prayer is acknowledgment of gift, then petition itself is a form of acknowledgment. It acknowledges the power of the God whom it addresses, and recognizes his work. When Jesus prayed before Lazarus' tomb, "I know that you hear me always" (11:42), he was but saying "all mine are yours, and yours are mine." When he now prays for those whom the Father has given him, he prays for all those who believe that "you have sent me" (17:8); for "No one can come to me unless the Father who sent me draws him" (6:44).

The World

There is no need for a misguided zeal to take the part of "the world" against the manifest injustice of its exclusion from the prayers of Jesus: "I am not praying for the world" (17:9). The God whom Jesus addresses loves the world (3:16). This is an immutable constant. Jesus himself came to save this world (3:17; 4:42; 12:47), to take away its sin (1:29). He does not pray for "the world" simply because he cannot. If he could, it would cease to be "the world," in its pejorative sense, and become his "own" for whom he prays in 17:9.

Here, of course, a reminder is again necessary. As elsewhere in the gospel, "the world" in this chapter can be used in its neutral denotation as the dwelling place of mortal human beings (e.g., "I am no more in the world, they are in the world" 17:11; see 6:14; 7:4; 8:12). But it can and is also used in its pejorative sense of all that is opposed to and rejects the revelation, as in, "I am not praying for the world" (17:11; see 17:16, 25; 15:18, 19; and cf. 7:7). The simple fact of the matter is: Jesus does not pray for the world because he cannot, since the world rejects him and "knows him not" (cf. 1:10).

In his prayer to the Father, Jesus acknowledges that all those who are his disciples, all those who believe in him as the one sent by God, are the gift of the Father to him. This God is always a revealer because he is always creating, ever redeeming out of chaos and death. All those who believe and have eternal life are therefore the work of his hands. Their faith in Jesus Christ glorifies him by acknowledging him as the Revealer of the Father, and thus recognizing that all that the Father possesses belongs to him, just as all that he himself possesses belongs to the Father: "all mine are yours, and yours are mine" (17:10). It is this mutuality of possession that enabled him to say, "He who has seen me has seen the Father" (14:9). The faith of the disciples in this revelation glorifies him: "I am glorified in them" (17:10).

The Believers in the World

> **And now I am no more in the world, but they are in the world, and I am coming to you. Holy Father, keep them in your name, which you have given me, that they may be one, even as we are one (17:11).**

The situation of the believers in the world is unintelligible without the fact that he in whom they believe is "no more in the world." Therefore, the persistent effort expended and the ingenuity exercised by so many well-meaning believers to circumvent this fact can only be cause for wonderment. To those, however, who are content to accept the truth not only that he is "no more in the world" but that he has returned to the Father, this prayer and the farewell discourse it brings to such an appropriate close can only be the source of great consolation, were it only because they make the life of the Christian in the world intelligible.

The believers' understanding of their loneliness in the world without him gives them, as it indeed must, the strength and the courage to withstand the world's hatred and opposition. The prayer of the departing Jesus to the Father, who always hears him (11:42), is further assurance that the strength and courage of believers are not illusory. Their true source is the "holy Father" who keeps them in his name, by his power.

Moreover, the believer, though lonely in a hostile and inimical world, is not alone. Jesus prays his heavenly Father "that they may be one, even as we are one." This oneness among the believers has for its paradigm the unity between the Son and the Father. It is not, and cannot be, patterned upon sociological, political, military or religious models; not because such models are necessarily defective or even inoperative, but because they are impotent to work the unity that only the Father can bring about. Jesus' prayer is that they be one "even as we are one" (17:11).

Ecumenism

This verse in John is of course one of the classical loci for ecumenism. It is rightly so if we but keep two things in mind. First, that the "they may be one" refers to those who "know you the only true God, and Jesus Christ whom you have sent" (17:3), i.e., to those who "believe that Jesus is the Christ, the Son of God" (20:31). It is his own disciples that Jesus addresses and for whom he prays. They can be his own only if they believe in him as the Son whom the Father has sent into the world. This is not an item on an agenda for future discussions. If you are intent on exploiting 17:11 for ecumenical purposes, then it is indispensable to begin with the "they" for whose oneness Jesus prays.

Secondly, the very fact of the prayer itself should alert us to the gravity of its object. That it is addressed to God the Father, "Holy Father" (17:11), should make it clear that it is not an end that can be achieved by political savvy, nor the desired outcome of human negotiating skills. The unity Jesus prays for is not, in other words, a unity attainable by compromise, barter or delicate adjustments in phraseology, not unless you conceive the revelation as merely a set of dogmatic statements and moral principles.

The unity Jesus prays for can only derive from faith in the revelation he utters and from obedience to the commandment he brings. If those who believe in him are to "be one, *even as* we are one," then his relationship to the Father is the only revealed truth in the light of which his prayer can be understood: "I glorified you on earth, having accomplished the work which you gave me to do" (17:4; see "My food is to do the will of him who sent me," 4:34; 5:30; 6:38). The unity Jesus prays for is the unity of the believers' obedience to the will and the commandment of the Father.

> **While I was with them, I kept them in your name, which you have given me; I have guarded them, and none of them is lost but the son of perdition, that the scripture might be fulfilled (17:12).**

That "your name, which you have given me" is here repeated from 17:11, "keep them in your name, which you have given me," should show us how important the revelation of this name is for the evangelist. The name that the Father has given him is Son, "the only Son of God" (3:18), he who reveals the Father in everything he says and does: "I have come in my Father's name" (5:43); "The works that I do in my Father's name" (10:25). The conferring of that name on him is what gives Jesus the power to carry out the work of salvation for which he was sent into the world by the Father. By the power of that name, he keeps and guards those who believe "in the name of the only Son of God" (3:18).

We must, however, reflect on the fact that, even among Jesus' own, there was an exception, "the son of perdition." For, however holy the prayer and powerful the name, the human being, even someone chosen by Jesus himself, remains free to the end. The Jesus who prayed for the oneness of his disciples in 17:11 has to admit in the very next verse that his prayer at least was not answered, not fully answered anyhow. The fragmentation of the unity for which he prayed took place even while he was still with them in the world, even while he was praying to the Father, who always hears him (11:42).

Those who urge Jesus' assurance that "if you ask anything of the Father, he will give it to you in my name" (16:23; 14:13; 15:16) as an argument that God grants all our prayers, have to reckon with the example of Jesus' prayers. They would be the first to insist on the holiness and worthiness of the petitioner. Nevertheless, they cannot get around the fact that the prayer of the only Son "that they may be one" is not really answered. In the synoptics, of course, Jesus' prayer to "remove this cup from me" (Mk 14:36 par) is not answered either. Any sophistry to get around this instance must come up against Jesus' cry on the cross: "My God, my God, why have you forsaken me?" (Mk 15:34).

But now I am coming to you; and these things I speak in the world, that they may have my joy fulfilled in themselves (17:13).

The whole purpose of the revelation, which he brings to the world and which becomes manifest only after his departure from it to return to the Father, is to fill those who believe in him with joy, to have his own joy take possession of them and transform them. Of course it is hard to make sense of these words of Jesus in a world where gloom is the aura of Christianity and doom the message of its prophets. Nevertheless, the present state of affairs cannot be allowed to blind us to the fact that the purpose of his revelation is to have his "joy fulfilled" in all who believe in him. His joy can be fulfilled in them only if they believe the "things I speak in the world," if they obey the commandment he brings. Only then can the true believers understand the meaning of his "my joy fulfilled in themselves."

The World's Hatred

I have given them your word; and the world has hated them because they are not of the world, even as I am not of the world. I do not pray that you take them out of the world, but that you keep them from the evil one (17:14–15).

The revelation that the Son brings into the world can only set those who believe in him at odds with those who reject both him and his revelation. Those who believe his word in a world that arrogates to itself the power to judge the worth and relevance of the revelation must, inevitably, earn the world's hatred. The message the Revealer brings is not only not of this world but passes judgment on it. He earned the world's hatred, and so will those who believe in him, "If the world hates you, know that it has hated me before it hated you..." (15:18, 19).

This, as has already been remarked, is a particularly difficult saying to comprehend in a church that is very much "of the world," a church that proclaims its being "not of the world" ever more loudly as it strives with all its might to take deeper and deeper roots in the world.

Nevertheless, the departing Jesus does not pray that his own be taken "out of the world" (17:15). For all its hatred and opposition, this world is still the world that God so loved that he gave his only Son (3:16), the same world that the Son has come to save (3:17). Jesus entrusts those who believe in him to the care of the Paraclete in order to carry on the task of bearing witness to him in this same world

(15:26–27). They can only do so, not by submitting to the world's norms, meeting its expectations, or embracing its principles, but by resolutely keeping the word that the Son has brought into the world and obeying his commandments.

The believers in him are not saviors of the world by ending its wars, preventing its calamities, minimizing its losses, or righting its injustices. The hubris of the present should not be allowed to blind us to the history of the past twenty centuries. Small and insignificant though it seems in their eyes or the eyes of the world, the task of the believers is to witness in and to the world to the eternal life that is theirs in their faith in the revelation. Their task is to obey the "new commandment" (13:34), and by their obedience to remind the world of its status of creaturehood in order that it, too, may live.

This, of course, is no facile task. It is all too easy to succumb to the lure of the world's power. This is why Jesus prays that his own be guarded against and preserved from "the evil one," or "from evil." Evil is all that sets itself up against the Revealer. Evil is whatever presumes to sit in judgment on the revelation. Everyone and everything that denies its own inalterable creaturehood, and presumes to set itself up as a creator and judge of all that lives and moves, is evil. Individuals in the world do this, nations do it, governments, institutions, even churches do it. The powerful incentive they all possess is the irresistible lure of the "glory from men" (5:41). Those who "receive glory from one another," wherever they be and in whatever walk of life, simply cannot believe (5:44). So they set about tailoring the revelation to meet the approval of the world and win its plaudits. They believe firmly that the world has it in its power to grant them or withhold from them "the glory from men." Against this Jesus prays, "keep them from evil" (17:15).

They are not of the world, even as I am not of the world (17:16).

There is of course a sense in which Jesus is "not of the world" that is unique to him. But here he speaks to his disciples as one of them. He had a work to accomplish in this world, so the Word became flesh and dwelt among us (1:14). But his work violated all the world's criteria of judgment, and the revelation he brought contradicted all its premises. This is why he is, in a unique sense, "not of the world" (17:16). Of course, those who continue his work after his departure and have the abiding Paraclete with them in their work of witness are also "not of the world." His followers, too, are "not of the world" because their faith in the revelation offends the world.

Sanctified in the Truth

Sanctify them in the truth; your word is truth (17:17).

Those who believe in him are "sanctified in the truth," that is, they are made holy in the revelation he brings. To say this is to say that the believers in him belong, no longer to themselves, but to God. Therefore their "sanctification," their status of holiness, is a status of appurtenance, of belonging to another, not of achievement. They are holy because of what they are, not as a consequence of what they do. They belong exclusively to the Father, and this constitutes their sanctification: "I have manifested your name to the men whom you gave me out of the world; yours they are, and you gave them to me" (17:6); "all mine are yours, and yours are mine" (17:10). To be "sanctified in the truth" is, therefore, to belong to the Father by faith in the Son who reveals him.

The Holiness of the Community

As you have sent me into the world, so I have sent them into the world. And for their sake I consecrate myself, that they may be consecrated in truth (17:18–19).

The hatred of the world is the criterion of the community's existence in it. By the hatred of the world the community is known for what it truly is. The same world that hated the Revealer hates all those who believe in him and carry out the work he himself was sent to accomplish. The revelation he brought consecrates, makes holy, those who believe in him by making them his own. It is their belonging to him and their believing the truth he reveals that makes the community a holy community.

This, of course, is what we mean every time we profess our faith in the "one, *holy,* catholic and apostolic church" in the creed. The holiness of this community of believers is the mark of their belonging to the Revealer, of their having been "consecrated in the truth" (17:19), the truth of his revelation, "your word is truth" (17:17). This holiness is not the consequence of the community's actions or the actions of its members. Rather the reverse is true. Whatever holiness is manifested in the life of the community and in the life of its individual members is directly attributable to the Revealer and to the revelation in which they believe: "they also may be consecrated *in truth.*" What is true of the holiness of the community is no less true, of course, of its unity (17:20–21).

"Through their word"

I do not pray for these only, but also for those who believe in me through their word (17:20).

This is the task for which he sends his disciples "into the world" (17:18). It is the task made necessary by Jesus' departure from the world, made necessary, that is, by the very logic of the incarnation. Because the Word became flesh, he had to die. All flesh is mortal. Therefore, he has to entrust to others the task of proclaiming to generations yet unborn the revelation he brings, so that they, too, may believe and have life "in his name" (20:31). Those to whom this task is entrusted are flesh, with all the limitations to which fallible flesh is heir.

The farewell prayer of Jesus embraces the disciples present with him as well as all "those who believe in me through their word" (17:20). The evangelist, like all those who believe through his word and proclaim its message in every generation, had to be aware of the significance of Jesus' prayer for his own undertaking ("these are written that you may believe" 20:31). This "you" in 20:31 refers to "those who believe through" the disciples' words. The Word always was and always will be proclaimed "through their word," the word of ordinary human beings, subject to the limitations of language, to the rules of its imperfectly mastered grammar and syntax. "Their word" will always be subject to their personal prejudices and narrowness of vision, to their imperfect knowledge, and the constraints and conditions of the particular time and place they inhabit.

God, who sent his only Son into the world "that the world might be saved through him" (3:17), did not disdain the flesh he created. His Word became flesh and sent into the world his disciples, those who believe in him, in order that others may come to believe in him "through *their word*" (17:20). He who knew "what was in man" (2:25) must have known only too well what was in human language; and yet he prays

...that they may all be one; even as you, Father, are in me, and I in you, that they may believe that you have sent me (17:21).

Jesus' prayer repeats the petition for the unity of those who "believe in me through their word" (17:20) The petition assumes added gravity from the fact that "their word" can cause divisions, occasion strife, and give reason for dissent. Not even the words of the evangelist are exempt from this risk. What little we know of the history of the Johannine community and its gospel can bear witness to this. Even the words of the Revealer himself are not spared this risk: "Do you also wish to go away?" (6:67).

The End of Unity

To Jesus' reiterated petition, "that they all may be one," there is added an important element: the finality of the unity, the desired result of what he prays for is "that the world may believe that you have sent me" (17:21). Even as the Father and the Son are one in their mutual abiding, "as you, Father, are in me, and I in you," so too all those who believe in him are to be one in their abiding in the Father and the Son, "that they also may be one in us." Only thus can the believers in him bear witness to the revelation so that the world can believe "that you have sent me." It is their life in unity that bears witness to the revelation in the world.

If we speak of the scandal of division in Christianity, we must recall its gravity, not for social intercourse, political harmony and the genteel civilities of ecclesiastical protocol, but for the essential task of the community of believers to bear witness to the Word. That the world is reluctant to believe the message we proclaim is not entirely the world's doing. All the churches, without a single exception, stand accused in their failure to "be one... be *in us,* so that the world may believe that you have sent me."

The Source of Unity

> **The glory which you have given me I have given to them, that they may be one even as we are one, I in them and you in me, that they may become perfectly one, so the world may know that you have sent me and have loved them as you have loved me (17:22–23).**

The petition for unity is once again elaborated, this time by specifying even further its source. To the unity of the Father and the Son, "even as we are one" (17:11, 21, 23), and to the mutuality of their indwelling, "I in them and you in me" (17:23 and see 17:21), are added "the glory" and "the love." The purpose for which the Father glorifies the Son by giving him "power over all flesh, to give eternal life to all" whom he has given him (17:2); the purpose for which the Son himself glorifies the Father by manifesting his "name to the men whom you gave me out of the world" (17:6), is that all those who believe in him "may be one... that they may be perfectly one," or, put perhaps better still, "that they may be perfected in unity."

Only in their unity can they carry out the task for which he sends them "into the world" (17:18). Only if they are "perfectly one" can the world come to know Jesus as the one whom the Father has sent out of love into the world (3:16). Only thus will the world know of the love of the Father for the Son and of the Son's love for all who are in the world. This surely must be something the world can finally come to understand, even if reluctantly. It was Sophocles who, in his indulgent philanthropy, said long ago that everyone finally comes to learn wisdom, willy-nilly. Will the world ever come to the wisdom of knowing God's love for it? Certainly not before the world can see those who proclaim this love loving one another before they speak to others of love: "By this [all] will know that you are my disciples, if you have love for one another" (13:35).

Father, I desire that they also, whom you have given me, may be with me where I am, to behold my glory which you have given me in your love for me before the foundation of the world (17:24).

We need little reminder from ancient philosophers or patristic and medieval writers to tell us that all love seeks union. This is the true nature of love: to desire to be with the beloved. In the assurance of the permanence of this state, love finds its ineffable joy.

Jesus' prayer for those whom the Father has given him, for all those who believe in him, is that they be with him where he is. This, of course, is what his resurrection from the dead, the work of the Father who loves him, makes possible. The eternal life which Christ himself confers on those who believe in him means: they will be where he is. This is why when he comes to them in his resurrection their hearts "will rejoice, and no one will take your joy from you" (16:22).

As he utters the words of his prayer in John's gospel, Jesus stands as the unique paradigm of all love. In his firm knowledge of the love of the Father for him, "before the foundation of the world" (cf. 1:1 and 18 "In the beginning...in the bosom of the Father"; 15:9; 3:35; 5:20; 10:17), Jesus finds the love with which he loves all of us. The Word had to become flesh in order to demonstrate this love for specific flesh-and-blood individuals dwelling in Palestine in the early part of the first century. Only if they accepted his love, if they let themselves be loved by him (13:8) and believed in his love, could they in turn love one another and, in their turn, make it possible for others to believe that the one sent by the Father loves them, indeed that "the Father himself loves" them (16:27). Only then can they believe the "glory which you have given me in your love for me before the foundation of the world" (17:24).

> **O righteous Father, the world has not known you, but I have known you; and these know that you have sent me (17:25).**

In these words the whole task of Jesus as the Revealer is encapsulated. They who "know you have sent me" believe in him as the one whom the "righteous Father" has sent to save the world. Only by their faith in Jesus of Nazareth can they come to know God. But "the world," which sees in Jesus no more than it sees in its revered heroes or its cherished *bêtes noires*, does not, and cannot know him. This does not say that the whole world is atheist; but it does say that, unless it acknowledges Jesus Christ as the Son of God and God as the Father of Jesus Christ, it does not know "the only true God" (17:3). For the evangelist, no knowledge of God is possible without knowing him whom God has sent, Jesus Christ.

> **I made known to them your name, and I will make it known, that the love with which you have loved me may be in them, and I in them (17:26).**

The task of the Revealer of the Father's name is drawing to a close, "I made known to them your name." Of course, given the double perspective from which these words are written, Jesus' and the evangelist's, it is necessary to add, "and I will make it known." The task of revelation is not accomplished except in the death and resurrection of Jesus. By his death on the cross he will show the true nature of his love for them and, by showing it, reveal the Father's name to them. In the totality of his obedience as Son, he reveals that the "only true God" (17:3) is his Father and our Father (20:17).

The purpose of this revelation is, of course, to show that the love of the Father for the Son "be in them," that the Son himself be "in them." This abiding within the believers shapes them, gives definition and meaning to their lives. It even shows them their own death in a new light. That love which created and moves the firmament, which sent the only Son into the world, was revealed to the whole world on the cross. It is this love that dwells in all those who believe in him whom the Father sent into the world. It gives them eternal life. By means of this love, the Father glorifies the Son in order "that the Son may glorify" the Father (17:1).

John 18

The Passion according to John.

The Betrayal and Arrest of Jesus: human evil; "I am he"; Simon Peter's impulsiveness; the will of the Father.

Jesus before the High Priest: Annas and Caiaphas; Caiaphas' prophecy.

Peter's Denial of Jesus.

The High Priest Questions Jesus: "I have spoken openly"; not turning the other cheek.

Peter Denies Jesus Again.

Jesus before Pilate: the Passover; history and faith; injustice; a kingdom not of this world.

THE PASSION ACCORDING TO JOHN

The only thing to do with an account of the passion is to read or hear it through, and then to do so again. But there is no better way of coming to comprehend what Jesus Christ is all about than to read the passion in Mark's gospel, unless it be to follow it with a reading of the passion in John. The two accounts complement each other admirably, for they reveal, Mark the abasement, and John the exaltation of the redeemer as no other gospel does.

Of course, the cross and the crucifixion of Jesus play a very prominent role both in Paul ("we preach Christ crucified," 1 Cor 1:23; "the word of the cross...is the power of God" 1 Cor 1:18; "the stumbling block of the cross," Gal 5:11; see Gal 3:1; 6:14; Phil 2:7–8) and in the synoptics (see Mk 8:31; 9:31; 10:33–34; Mt 16:21; 17:22–23; 20:18–19; Lk 9:22, 31, 44; 18:31–33). In John, however, neither the cross nor the crucifixion is mentioned outside chapter 19, the account of the event itself. John refers to the death on the cross in his gospel as the "lifting up" ("so must the Son of Man be lifted up" 3:14; 8:28; 12:32, 34) or the "glorification" (7:39; 12:16, 23; 13:31).

The Jesus of John has come as "light into the world, and men loved darkness rather than light" (3:19). "The true light that enlightens every man was coming into the world" (1:9). "The light shines in the darkness, and the darkness has not overcome it" (1:4). Thus, a major theme enunciated in the prologue finds its culmination in the drama of the passion. In the passion, the darkness seems to advance from triumph to triumph, yet it is at the very moment of its victory that its defeat is encompassed. The world and all its hatred seem to claim the day and emerge as the victors in the struggle, when in fact it is the world itself that is defeated and overcome ("I have overcome the world" 16:33). Even death itself seems to have the last word; yet, just at that very instant, Jesus proclaims his task of giving eternal life "accomplished" (19:30).

Nothing in the life of Jesus revealed that "in him was life, and the life was the light of men" (1:4) like the moment of his death on the cross. His light shone most clearly in the darkness of Good Friday. The resurrection narratives that follow only demonstrate how thorough his conquest of darkness and death really was. The resurrection appearances are the "signs" of his definitive victory over the darkness of death.

Nevertheless, when all is said and done, the passion of Jesus, like his crucifixion, is every bit as real in John as it is in the synoptics. No amount of theologizing about the glorification and the exaltation of Jesus can either obscure the determined malignity of his enemies or mitigate the suffering and humiliation they inflicted on him. No evangelist can find an antidote to the betrayal by friends, the mockery of the nameless crowd, the blatant miscarriage of justice, and the unspeakable agony of the death on the cross. If John shows Jesus as the undisputed master of the situation from start to finish, if he portrays him as taking the initiative at every turn, he does not for a moment pretend either that the suffering was any the less felt or that the death any less genuine. The evangelist's insistence on Jesus' deliberate advance to his death is not there to minimize the horror of the crucifixion but to underscore the totality of Jesus' obedience to the Father.

THE BETRAYAL AND ARREST OF JESUS (John 18:1–11)

> **When Jesus had spoken these words, he went forth with his disciples across the Kidron valley, where there was a garden, which he and his disciples entered. Now Judas, who betrayed him, also knew the place; for Jesus often met there with his disciples. So Judas, procuring a band of soldiers and some officers from the chief priests and the Pharisees, went there with lanterns and torches and weapons. Then Jesus, knowing all that was to befall him, came forward and said to them, "Whom do you seek?" They answered him, "Jesus of Nazareth." Jesus said to them, "I am he." Judas, who betrayed him, was standing with them. When he said to them, "I am he," they drew back and fell to the ground. Again he asked them, "Whom do you seek?" And they said, "Jesus of Nazareth." Jesus answered, "I told you that I am he; so, if you seek me, let these men go." This was to fulfil the word which he had spoken, "Of those whom you gave me I lost not one" (18:1–9).**

It is relatively easy to pick out in this narrative the features which demonstrate Jesus' mastery of the situation. He acts not so much the accused as the accuser, not so much the judged as the judge. The evangelist portrays Jesus as knowing right from the start "all that was to befall him" (18:4) by anticipating the bluster of a "band of soldiers and some officers" by a simple "Whom do you seek?" Jesus' dominating position in the incident is further underscored by adding that, "When he said to them, 'I am he,' they drew back and fell to the ground" (18:6).

Human Evil

None of these details, however, should obscure the painful and real drama as it unfolds. The role played by one of his own disciples cannot be minimized. There is a consistency and almost a logic about human evil that spares its doer the luxury of hesitation. Once Judas left the supper, "after receiving his morsel" (13:30), he stuck undeviatingly to his course. His evil–and there is no other description of his betrayal–would have been a bit more tolerable had it not been for the good that was in him. It was La Rochefoucauld who remarked that there are bad people who would be less dangerous if they had no good in them at all. To portray Judas as pure evil is almost to exculpate and dehumanize him. It is the good in each of us that makes the evil we do of such enormity.

But, whatever purpose the narrative of Judas' heinous betrayal might serve, it is most certainly not there to furnish preachers–as it has done for ages–with the salutary example of a flesh and blood person surely deserving of hell's fires. Rather, if there is a lesson to be learned from Judas' action, it is in the crime itself, not in its punishment. Judas' betrayal of his Master is all the more reprehensible for its utter gratuity. In John's account, it lacks even the express motive of pecuniary gain. John says nothing about "thirty pieces of silver" (Mt 26:15; see Mark 14:11 and Luke 22:5). The lesson to be learned from Judas is that neither proximity to, nor intimacy with Jesus can avail; that neither miracles nor revelations can compel or guarantee our response to Jesus of Nazareth.

Evil, human evil, ours no less than Judas Iscariot's, is the creature's rejection of the creator's gift. It remains always a mystery, an incomprehensible darkness. For, before such rejection, even the Revealer stands helpless. Neither love "to the end" nor the gift of eternal life can compel acceptance of the gift.

"I am he"

Two things call for comment in Jesus' response to the arrest. His repeated "I am [he]" (18:5, 6, 8) is, of course, different from most of the "I AM" formulae encountered in the gospel. Here the formula is a straightforward identification. To those who came to arrest "Jesus of Nazareth," he says very simply, "I AM [he]." Moreover, lest it escape notice amid all the multiple details surrounding it, we should keep in mind that the Jesus of Nazareth who is about to be arrested as a common criminal is someone whose father and mother were known (6:42), from whose place of origin scarcely any good could come (1:46). The band of soldiers arrested a flesh and blood person just like any one of themselves.

The other point calling for comment is Jesus' solicitude for his own disciples: "If you seek me, let these men go" (18:8). This is not inserted in the narrative to illustrate Jesus' altruism, or to teach the readers to think of others rather than of themselves in time of trouble. The purpose of this particular detail is made evident in the evangelist's addition, "This was to fulfil the word which he had spoken, 'Of those whom you gave me I lost not one'" (18:9; see "I have guarded them, and none of them is lost," 17:12; 10:28, 29; 6:37, 39).

But, surely, this is confusing. Jesus has just lost Judas, and no one would want to pretend that Judas was not, at some time or another, one "of those whom you gave me." Peter will soon follow suit, and so will the rest of them. But, if we keep in mind the dual perspective of the narrative, that of Jesus of Nazareth and that of the evangelist, then what the evangelist is doing becomes comprehensible.

With the hindsight of a post-resurrection community of believers, the evangelist exercises the prophetic function of re-reading past events as the unfolding of the divine will. He can do this, of course, because he is writing after the event. To his dying moment, Judas remained free not to be one of those whom the Father had given to his Son. Unless we keep this in mind, we can very easily misread the Jesus of Nazareth in the passion as a mere illusion. That is to say, we risk reading into the passion a "docetism," when in fact Jesus of Nazareth is throughout a man of flesh and blood, someone very much subject to death.

Simon Peter's Impulsiveness

> **Then Simon Peter, having a sword, drew it and struck the high priest's slave and cut off his right ear. The slave's name was Malchus. Jesus said to Peter, "Put your sword into its sheath; shall I not drink the cup which the Father has given me?" (18:10–11).**

Obtuse to the end, Simon Peter–and not for the last time in history–has recourse to arms. He cannot quite grasp the fact that this is not what Jesus of Nazareth is all about. Alas, in his obtuseness, Peter has had many and illustrious followers.

To inquire why Simon Peter had a sword with him in the first place, what he hoped to accomplish by ridding the hapless slave of his right ear, and why Malchus is identified as "the high priest's slave," though interesting questions, are idle. We really have no way of finding out, nor any truly compelling need to know.

Similarly, if it be true that saying something is not as important as the way it is said, then whether Jesus' words, "Put your sword into its sheath," were a command to, a rebuke of, or a mere weariness with Simon Peter, remains unclear. In the Johannine account as it stands, Jesus' response not only effectively puts an end to Peter's misguided impulsiveness, but also directs the reader's attention to an essential element in the narrative. "Shall I not drink the cup which the Father has given me?"

The setting of this scene in John 18 is, of course, a garden "across the Kidron valley" (18:1). It is what Matthew and Mark call "Gethsemane" (Mt 26:36; Mk 14:32). So, in a sense, the scene of the arrest in John has within it the familiar "agony in the garden" motif summed up in the, "Shall I not drink the cup which the Father has given me?" (18:11).

No one would wish to deny the marked difference between this verse and what we have in Mark 14:32–42 (Mt 26:36–46; Lk 22:39–46). There is a great difference between Jesus' repeated prayer in Mark, "Abba, Father, all things are possible to you; remove this cup from me; yet not what I will, but what you will" (Mk 14:36, 39) and his rhetorical question in John, "Shall I not drink the cup which the Father has given me?" (Jn 18:11; cf. 12:27).

In John, to be sure, Jesus is very much the master of the situation, who takes the initiative even when he is about to be arrested like a common criminal (18:3). His prior knowledge, "knowing all that was to befall him" (18:4), is something that has been stressed throughout the gospel (1:48; 4:29; 5:6; 6:6, 64, 70–71; 13:1, 11, 18). But such knowledge must not be allowed to diminish the reality of what he suffers throughout the passion.

The Will of the Father

Nevertheless, two essential elements bind the prayer in Gethsemane in the synoptics to the rhetorical question put to Simon Peter in John 18:11b. In Mark, Jesus expresses his submission to the will of the Father, "Yet not what I will, but what you will" (Mk 14:36); in John he embraces it. In both instances, it is the totality of Jesus' obedience that is to the fore. "And what shall I say, 'Father, save me from this hour'? No, for this purpose I have come to this hour" (12:27–28).

Furthermore, both in the synoptics and in John, Jesus speaks of "the cup," and that cup is the cup of his suffering. John has no more the desire or the intention to minimize, tone down or trivialize the suffering of Jesus than does Mark or any of the other evangelists. Indeed, the passion in John is no less an account of Jesus' suffering for being the culmination of the Son's glorification by the Father, whom he glorified throughout his life, but especially by his love for his own "to the end" (13:1; cf. 12:27–28).

JESUS BEFORE THE HIGH PRIEST (John 18:12–14)

So the band of soldiers and their captain and the officers of the Jews seized Jesus and bound him. First they led him to Annas; for he was the father-in-law of Caiaphas, who was high priest that year (18:12–13).

The Jesus seized and bound could not have looked, even to the most discerning eyes, anything like "the God striding the earth" he is supposed to be in John's gospel. The first place to which the "band of soldiers and their captain and the officers of the Jews" (18:12) lead him is the religious authorities of the day.

Annas and Caiaphas

John is the evangelist who informs us that Annas was the father-in-law of Caiaphas, "who was high priest that year" (18:13; and see 11:49, 51). Why, knowing this, he still calls Annas "high priest" (18:15, 16, 19, 22, cf. 24) is a moot question. Did he perhaps apply the title to Annas as a courtesy to a former holder of the office? Whatever the explanation, Annas doubtless possessed power, and clearly exercised some authority in the trial of Jesus—at least according to John, who is the only one to provide this bit of information.

Moreover, why those who arrested Jesus took him first to the father-in-law of the high priest Caiaphas is not very clear, unless one wishes to read the incident as some marginal comment on that hardy perennial of corrupt power: nepotism. Good and convincing explanations can doubtless be found for the tortuous path of injustice in Jesus' trial. But the order of events in John's gospel is hard enough to reconcile with the order in the synoptics without complicating it further with hieratic family trees. What is evident from all four gospel accounts, however, is that the corruption of power and its perversion of justice have changed very little over the ages.

The oppressors and the oppressed, the unjust rulers and their long-suffering subjects have retained their recognizable features throughout the centuries. Their names change from one generation to the next, but the evil they do remains singularly lacking in invention or novelty. What we always tend to forget is that the victims are not really nameless masses, but identifiable individuals, each of whom bears within himself or herself the suffering of a whole world.

Caiphas' Prophecy

It was Caiaphas who had given counsel to the Jews that it was expedient that one man should die for the people (18:14).

Aware of a larger scheme of events than even the vast wasteland of evil in the trial of Jesus, the evangelist reminds the readers that this Caiaphas the high priest was the one who, in his ignorance, had uttered a commonplace that far surpassed his comprehension. After the stir caused by the raising of Lazarus had made the "chief priests and the Pharisees" fear lest "the Romans will come and destroy both our holy place and our nation" (11:48), this same Caiaphas had unwittingly "prophesied that Jesus should die for the nation" (11:51). His political savvy told him what his religious sense refused to see, that "it was expedient that one man should die for the people, and that the whole nation should not perish" (11:50). Little did he know, and little did "the chief priests and the Pharisees know," that the Romans will indeed come and wreak destruction on the temple and the people, without Jesus of Nazareth having anything to do with it at all. Moreover, neither Caiaphas nor "the chief priests and the Pharisees" could have even begun to suspect that the death of Jesus "for the people" was, in fact, a death for the salvation, not just of their nation, but of the whole world.

PETER'S DENIAL OF JESUS (John 18:15–18)

Simon Peter followed Jesus, and so did another disciple. As this disciple was known to the high priest, he entered the court of the high priest with Jesus, while Peter stood outside at the door. So the other disciple, who was known to the high priest, went out and spoke to the maid who kept the door, and brought Peter in (18:15–16).

Whatever motivated Simon Peter's action, his following Jesus from the garden to the trial was surely not what Jesus had in mind when he said to his disciples, "Follow me" (1:43). It was certainly not what Jesus meant by "Come and see" (1:39). A characteristic impulsiveness (18:10), a trace of native loyalty (13:37), or an indomitable curiosity (13:24), might have prompted Peter's action. But, whatever its motive, it ended tragically.

Even at this stage of the unfolding drama, Simon Peter and that "other disciple," who was "known to the high priest" (18:16), and therefore no stranger to the corridors of power, set a familiar pattern for coming generations. It is not what you know but whom you know that matters. It is your social ties and political links that get you where you want to go. Even your acknowledged position within a community of believers can be ineffectual. High or low, you simply need to know the "right people."

In the arena of political reality, sanctity and learning count for naught. Those who choose to forget the world are "by the world forgot." Indeed, a contemporary writer has remarked that those who abandon the world will soon come to resemble those whom the world has abandoned. Even within the community of believers, the surest path to success is fidelity to the established norms and standards of the world.

The maid who kept the door said to Peter, "Are not you also one of this man's disciples?" He said, "I am not" (18:17).

Thanks solely, not to his position among the twelve, but to his companion's palace connections, Simon Peter gains admittance to the court of the high priest. Without the other disciple's intervention on his behalf, Peter would still be standing "outside at the door" (18:16).

What this other disciple said to the "maid who kept the door" (18:16) we are not told. But, from her question to Peter, "Are you not *also* one of this man's disciples?" one might deduce what Peter's fellow-disciple had said to her. If she indeed saw no harm in admitting one disciple of Jesus who happened to be known to the household, then Peter's reaction becomes doubly lamentable. In that case, one cannot even plead fear as an excusable motive for his denial. Nevertheless, Peter's precipitous "I am not" is, if regrettable, not really shocking. Only hypocrisy would be shocked by it.

Now the servants and officers had made a charcoal fire, because it was cold, and they were standing and warming themselves; Peter also was with them, standing and warming himself (18:18).

Commentators are wont to remark the symbolism of "it was cold" which follows Peter's chilling denial of the man he had just assured so wholeheartedly, "Lord...I will lay down my life for you" (13:37). The Jesus he now says he does not know is he to whom he had once protested, "Lord, to whom shall we go? You have the words of eternal life" (6:68). If commentators are sensitive to the symbolism of 18:18, it is because, like the rest of us, they know from experience the numbing chill that supervenes our betrayal of those we love.

THE HIGH PRIEST QUESTIONS JESUS (John 18:19–24)

The high priest then questioned Jesus about his disciples and his teaching (18:19).

The matter of the interrogation is straightforward enough. A criminal is brought before the authorities and certain preliminary questions have to be put to him. It is remarkable how intent any established authority is to follow protocol, to observe every legality, and to seem most deliberate about the workings of justice, just when it is resolved to carry out an injustice. The authorities' scruples about niceties and the quillets of the law is always in direct proportion to the enormity they seek to perpetrate.

"I have spoken openly"

Jesus answered him, "I have spoken openly to the world; I have always taught in synagogues and in the temple, where all Jews come together; I have said nothing secretly. Why do you ask me? Ask those who have heard me, what I said to them; they know what I said" (18:20–21).

In his autobiography, G. K. Chesterton cited the dictum, "Truth can understand error; but error cannot understand Truth." Something very like this is at play here. Jesus responds forthrightly to what appears a straightforward enough question. Unlike the Jesus of the synoptics, Jesus in John does not explain anything "privately to his own disciples" (Mk 4:34). He speaks quite openly to anyone who has ears to hear. There is no "Messianic Secret" in the fourth gospel, no injunction to the disciples to "tell no one" (Mk 7:36; 1:34; 5:43; 8:30; 9:9 and parallels). The Jesus in John speaks "openly to the world" (Jn 18:20). He proclaims to all who would hear, "I am the light of the world" (8:12; 9:5), and he acts accordingly. There was, therefore, no other honest answer to give the high priest.

But an honest answer always strands a dishonest question. Jesus' answer robs malignity of its purpose, and Annas' discomfiture becomes no more than the proof of his own evil intent. Therefore, to save the face of his thwarted master, a subordinate decides to seize his own opportunity:

> **When he had said this, one of the officers standing by struck Jesus with his hand, saying, "Is that how you answer the high priest?" (18:22).**

It is arguable that the officer's senseless action had nothing to do with his opinion of Jesus, that he neither knew the man nor had any prejudice of his own, one way or another. His action, unjust and cruel, is directed wholly toward pleasing his routed master. If this be a right reading of the officer's action, then it, too, is of a pattern quite familiar to us. The subordinates who, to please their masters, exaggerate their zeal, multiply their victims, and wreak the impotent vengeance of their frustrating inferiority on the innocent are, alas, not unknown to us. Like all those lacking common decencies, they are ever so punctilious about observing protocol, "Is that how you answer the high priest?"

Not Turning the Other Cheek

> **Jesus answered him, "If I have spoken wrongly, bear witness to the wrong; but if I have spoken rightly, why do you strike me?" (18:23).**

The Jesus who, in the Sermon on the Mount, instructed the crowds, "Do not resist one who is evil. But if any one strikes you on the right cheek, turn to him the other also" (Mt 5:39; Lk 6:29), fails to follow this evangelical counsel in John. He does "resist one who is evil." He does not turn the other cheek to be unjustly struck. The Jesus of John has come into the world "to bear witness to the truth" (18:37), and this is what he does in his trial, as he had done throughout his life (18:20–21).

The incident itself is, nevertheless, instructive. The discrepancy between what Jesus says in one gospel and what he says in another should serve to remind us that the New Testament is simply not the kind of a book we imagine it to be. It is not a manual of prescriptions for the way to act under this or that circumstance, in this or that situation. It is not a book of answers to our dogmatic questions, our moral quandaries, or our social dilemmas. This reminder, alas, has served little purpose in Christian life. For, at every opportunity, our spontaneous reaction to any situation remains, "What does the good book say?"

Annas then sent him bound to Caiaphas the high priest (18:24).

The officer who struck Jesus must have been of a particularly spineless variety. Others in his position would have redoubled their zeal at Jesus' rebuke, especially since the rebuke was more than merited. They would have taken Jesus' words as an effrontery to their own non-existent probity, and regarded his response as questioning their imagined authority. They would, in today's cant, have "resented" Jesus' answer.

But Annas, more schooled in the ways of the world, knows just how to act. He did not get to his position by indolence or miscalculation. He knew just when to "pass the buck." He stands as a monument to all those who claim most authority and share it least with subordinates but, at the least mishap, are readiest to shift responsibility onto others. Admirable diplomacy claims its victims in every generation.

PETER DENIES JESUS AGAIN (John 18:25–27)

Now Simon Peter was standing and warming himself. They said to him, "Are not you also one of his disciples?" He denied it and said, "I am not" (18:25).

Ordinary common sense ought to have warned Peter after his first denial (18:17) to be more cautious and to avoid notice. But nothing is more uncommon than common sense. The spontaneity with which he dissociated himself from Jesus the first time might well have blinded him to the gravity of his deed. So, oblivious of his recent failure, he exposes himself to graver danger still. What might have been excusable as an impetuous reaction is now a deliberate betrayal.

There is at work in this sad narrative something more instructive than the mechanism of sin and the avoidance of the occasion of sin. So, too, what symbolism there is in Peter's quest for warmth (cf. 18:18) must yield to a more important, if less obvious, point: This Peter is not just another disciple, but the one destined to occupy a special place among Jesus' followers (1:42; 6:68; 13:6–10; 21:3, 15–19). His betrayal is all the greater for the eminence of his position among the twelve. Even Jesus' prayers for his disciples, "Father, keep them in your name...keep them from the evil one" (17:11, 15), seem not to have reached Peter (cf. Jesus' words to him in Luke, "I have prayed for you that your faith may not fail; and when you have turned again, strengthen your brethren," Lk 22:32 with John 17:9, 11, 15).

Jesus' choice of his disciples was not, at least not to the eyes of the world, a happy or even an astute one. To be sure, the disciples he chose were not the ones the world would have chosen, nor such as would or could win the world's approval. In the illogic of that choice, very few of his followers have had the courage to follow his example.

> **One of the servants of the high priest, a kinsman of the man whose ear Peter had cut off, asked, "Did I not see you in the garden with him?" Peter again denied it; and at once the cock crowed (18:26–27).**

Thus Peter's triple denial, already foretold by Jesus (13:38), reaches its climax. So, at this point, the incident is terminated. Nothing is said of Peter going out and weeping "bitterly" (Mt 26:75; Mk 14:72; Lk 22:62). In the fourth gospel, the reader is left just with that numbing fact of the triple denial.

To deal with the hatred of his enemies must have been easier by far for Jesus to bear than to suffer the loneliness of betrayal at the hands of his loved ones. No amount of talk about the glorification of Jesus should minimize the very real suffering undergone by him in his passion, even in the gospel of John.

JESUS BEFORE PILATE (John 18:28–40)

> **Then they led Jesus from the house of Caiaphas to the praetorium. It was early. They themselves did not enter the praetorium so that they might not be defiled, but might eat the passover (18:28).**

The liturgy of Good Friday and the sermons on its gospel must have surely added "praetorium" to our vocabulary by now. The NRSV, taking no such chance, paraphrases the word as "Pilate's headquarters." Whichever one chooses to call it, the fact remains that, for Jews about to celebrate the Passover, it was pagan territory and thus off-limits: "that they might not be defiled" (18:28).

The Passover

The reference to the Passover here continues to present an obstacle to any attempt at harmonizing John's account of the passion with the synoptics'. In the synoptics, Jesus and his disciples had already eaten the Passover (Mt 26:2, 17–19 par). But in John we are reminded that Jesus's accusers did not want to be defiled so they can "eat the Passover" (18:28). Thus, in Luke, Jesus at the Last Supper says, "I have earnestly desired to eat this Passover with you *before* I suffer" (Lk 22:15). Though gospel commentaries bear ample witness to the great scholarly efforts expended to find some solution to this discrepancy in the different accounts, no solution proposed thus far can claim to have resolved the difficulty to everyone's satisfaction.

Whether or not a given solution ultimately wins credibility, the reader still has to come back to what the evangelist is doing when he narrates these events in his own fashion. Was chronological accuracy his prevailing concern? or was he, perhaps, more theologically intent on synchronizing the sacrifice of the Passover lamb with the death of the "Lamb of God" (Jn 1:29, 36) on the cross? If harmonization of his account with the data of the tradition was not the evangelist's main concern, why should it be the reader's?

History and Faith

To pose the question is, of course, not to dismiss the value of history for the Christian faith. History occupies its secure place right at the heart of the creed: "He suffered under Pontius Pilate." It was during that arctic night of the Modernist crisis that one of the protagonists declared his readiness to believe every article of the creed except the "under Pontius Pilate," which riveted the revelation to history. That phrase took the credal affirmations out of the realm of "religious myths" and set them firmly within human history (cf. Lk 3:1–2). When John's prologue says, "the Word became flesh and dwelt among us" (Jn 1:14), it says just that. The Word entered our human history and cannot, therefore, be intelligible without it. So, with this all-important fact firmly in possession, the evangelist can set about his elected task of providing theological comprehension to what in fact took place, not out of time, but in human history.

So Pilate went out to them and said, "What accusation do you bring against this man?" They answered him, "If this man were not an evildoer, we would not have handed him over." Pilate said to them, "Take him yourselves and judge him by your own law." The Jews said to him, "It is not lawful for us to put any man to death." This was to fulfil the word which Jesus had spoken to show by what death he was to die (18:29–32).

The readers need hardly be enlightened on all the implications of this deadly exchange. The evangelist is so parsimonious in detail as to render the narrative almost elliptical. Evidently, this is not the trial of an accused in any system of law. Mere legality, "It is not lawful for us to put any man to death" (18:31), is what comes between the accusers and the death of the accused. His guilt or innocence is irrelevant. Expediency is all: "It was expedient that one man should die for the people" (18:14; 11:50).

Injustice

They accuse Jesus of being "an evildoer" (18:30) who are themselves blind to the evil they do. The zeal of the unjust for the law, their scrupulous care to observe its every minute prescription in order to sanctify their injustice with legality, was by no means an invention of the Jews. They had notorious predecessors and were destined to have even more nefarious followers in a religion that claims to teach justice to the nations. The followers of Jesus went the Jews one better and raised gibbets and ignited pyres in the name of him who was crucified. They dug out dungeons, devised torments, and staged trials for "the salvation of souls." At least the accusers of Jesus were straightforward enough. They just wanted to crucify him, to be rid of a nuisance to them, and be spared a liability to their nation.

The evangelist's reference to Jesus' prediction of "what death he was to die" (18:32; see 3:14; 8:28; 12:32) is clearly to the crucifixion. This is what his accusers intended for Jesus: the death reserved for the worst of criminals. They appealed to the civil authority which alone possessed the power to execute this cruelest and most dreaded of sentences. Having decided upon this form of execution, they spared no ploy in compelling a timid and vacillating Roman governor to comply with their wishes (18:38b–40; 19:7–8, 12). Centuries of subjection to foreign rule had schooled them in the art of subjecting their rulers to their own will, while protesting their submission and loyalty (19:12, 15).

> **Pilate entered the praetorium again and called Jesus, and said to him, "Are you the King of the Jews?" Jesus answered, "Do you say this of your own accord, or did others say it to you about me?" (18:33–34).**

Jesus' question must be the reader's also. But what prompted Pilate's question? Nothing in what transpired thus far had alluded to Jesus' kingship. If the triumphal entry into Jerusalem (12:12–18) or the even earlier attempt to make Jesus king (6:15) lay behind Pilate's inquiry, Pilate himself leaves Jesus' own question unanswered. "Do you say this of your own accord, or did others say it to you about me?" (18:34).

A Kingdom Not of This World

Pilate answered, "Am I a Jew? Your own nation and the chief priests have handed you over to me; what have you done?" Jesus answered, "My kingship is not of this world; if my kingship were of this world, my servants would fight, that I might not be handed over to the Jews; but my kingship is not from the world" (18:35–36)

All non-answers to questions are inane. Ignorance is as prolix as dissimulation in responding to what we do not know or do not wish to admit knowing. We all seek evasion in multiplying inanities and responding to questions no one has put to us. The whole world knows Pilate is not a Jew; Jesus knows who handed him over to the Roman governor; and both Jesus and Pilate know that the simple answer to "What have you done?" is "Nothing!"

So Jesus brings Pilate back to the initial question, "Are you the King of the Jews?" (18:33). King that he in fact is, Jesus declares plainly, "My kingship is *not* of this world" (18:36). Had it been a kingship of this world, it would have met this world's powers on their own ground, answering force with force, lie with lie, injustice with greater injustice.

History and the contemporary life of his followers are there to witness how few have, in fact, heeded Jesus' repeated insistence that "My kingship is not of this world" (18:36). Indeed, at the first opportunity that presented itself, the community that proclaimed his unworldly kingship was only too eager to act as though that kingship were and always will be of this world. From the moment it triumphed as the religion of the Roman Empire, Christianity had recourse to John 18:36, "My kingship is not of this world...not from the world," as but a slogan to further its "kingship" precisely in this world.

Those of us who deem "king" and "kingship" unsuitable for our "democratic" Christianity will do well to reflect that the evil resides not in the word itself but in our lives, which are so enslaved to the dominant fashions of the world ("They loved the praise of men more than the glory of God" 12:43). Those who willingly embrace slavery are not very convincing arguments against tyranny in whatever form.

> **Pilate said to him, "So you are a king?" Jesus answered, "You say that I am a king. For this I was born, and for this I have come into the world, to bear witness to the truth. Every one who is of the truth hears my voice" (18:37).**

To Pilate's direct question, Jesus gives an unequivocal answer: "For this I was born, and for this I have come into the world" (18:37). His kingship, his lordship, all the claims to his titles of glory have to do with that one single aim and purpose of his coming into the world: "to bear witness to the truth," to be the Revealer of the Father. For this he was born, for this he came into the world. His Lordship, his conquest of the world (16:33c), his kingship, are all facets of his being the Revealer of the Father.

Such revelation by its nature is, however, accessible solely to those who believe. "Every one who is of the truth" (18:37), every one who believes in him as the Revealer, every one whose life is therefore shaped and fashioned by the revelation he brings into the world, believes Jesus of Nazareth to be the one sent by God, the Son, he who reveals the Father. In that mysterious circularity by which the believers in Jesus are drawn by the Father (6:44, 37), they become Jesus' disciples and show themselves to be "of the truth."

But the Pilate who put the question to Jesus in the first place does not heed the answer. Like all who would not listen, he was too busy formulating another question and, when he was dead and gone, then those who took his place did the same, another and another to the end of time.

> **Pilate said to him, "What is truth?" (18:38a)**

It is characteristic of those who put this question in whatever age that, like jesting Pilate, they "would not stay for an answer."

> **After he had said this, he went out to the Jews again, and told them, "I find no crime in him. But you have a custom that I should release one man for you at the Passover; will you have me release for you the King of the Jews?" They cried out again, "Not this man, but Barabbas!" Now Barabbas was a robber (18:38b–40).**

John 19

Jesus Sentenced to Die: corrupt authority; power and self-preservation; his own received him not.

The Crucifixion of Jesus: the title on the cross; the fulfilment of the scriptures; at the foot of the cross; failure; "behold your mother."

The Death of Jesus: the accomplishment of the revelation; the witness of the evangelist; the scriptures and the crucified.

JESUS SENTENCED TO DIE (John 19:1–16)

Then Pilate took Jesus and scourged him. And the soldiers plaited a crown of thorns, and put it on his head, and arrayed him in a purple robe; they came up to him, saying, "Hail, King of the Jews!" and struck him with their hands (19:1–3).

Injustice knows no logic, abides by no rule, and transgresses all limits. The gratuitous cruelty of a mob feeds on itself, and nothing stirs its appetite more than delight in its own evil. To attempt to make sense of the mob's preference of Barabbas over Jesus (18:39–40) is as futile as trying to fathom Pilate's motive in having him scourged (19:1). What remains always within our grasp, however, is some vague awareness of what the victim of this cruelty must have undergone.

It is by no means beyond our capacity to imagine what the innocent must feel when the guilty triumph over them. Few of us have escaped unscathed in this world. We cannot pretend to be ignorant of the sting of mockery at the hand of strangers, or of the agony of rejection by those to whom we timidly extend our goodwill. Such knowledge should spare us any facile misunderstanding of "Now is the Son of man glorified" (13:31; 12:23) at the cost of forgetting the suffering and bitterness of "the cup which the Father has given me" (18:11). The reality of Jesus' suffering in this gospel, no less than in the others, is surely comprehensible, at least to the majority of the world, the silent victims. Our comprehension ought to be all the greater if we but pause to reflect upon our own capacity to victimize others.

Pilate went out again, and said to them, "See, I am bringing him out to you, that you may know that I find no crime in him" (19:4).

But it is already too late. A Roman governor with just a hint of backbone would have refused to have any part of this judicial farce. Whatever Pilate's disdain for the rabble before him, it was no match for their contempt. He lost the match when once he tried to barter with them (18:30). A timorous mob grows bold, and their cruelty hardens at the first hint of weakness. And Pilate was far from strong.

We can, if we wish, sneer at Pilate and despise the crowd. But there is nothing unique in the process unfolding before us. Our century, like every century before it, can furnish like instances. The actors in that cruel drama of Jesus' trial did not do what they did because they were Jews or Romans. Like any one of us, they found the exercise of power attractive and the lure of gratuitous cruelty compelling.

So Jesus came out, wearing the crown of thorns and the purple robe. Pilate said to them, "Behold the man!" When the chief priests and officers saw him, they cried out, "Crucify him, crucify him!" Pilate said to them, "Take him yourselves and crucify him, for I find no crime in him" (19:5–6).

Where commentators and preachers left off, painters and sculptors vied with each other to reveal the majesty and the horror of the *Ecce homo*, "Behold the man!" Stirring though the emotions of such efforts be, they are really no match for the starkness of John's narrative. The fate of the innocent caught between a vacillating authority and a mob intent on evil needs no gloss.

Corrupt Authority

If Pilate found "no case against him" (19:4 NRSV), he should of course have let Jesus go, not handed him over to the crowd that clamored to see him crucified.

The Jews answered him, "We have a law, and by that law he ought to die, because he made himself the Son of God." When

Pilate heard these words, he was the more afraid; he entered the praetorium again and said to Jesus, "Where are you from?" But Jesus gave no answer. Pilate therefore said to him, "You will not speak to me? Do you not know that I have power to release you and power to crucify you?" Jesus answered him, "You would have no power over me unless it had been given you from above; therefore he who delivered me to you has the greater sin" (19:7–11).

Pilate is a showcase of corrupt authority. Like so many tyrants before and after him, he displays, not genuine fear of God, but superstition: "He was the more afraid" (19:8). His inquiry about Jesus' origin is almost pitiful. He would have found "Nazareth" (1:46) an irrelevance, and "from above" (8:23) an impertinence. So Jesus "gave no answer" (19:9).

In utter insouciance of what the gospel is all about, endless theories of civil and political power have battened on Jesus' response to Pilate's claim: "You would have no power over me unless it had been given you from above" (19:11). Jesus is no more furnishing premises for the theoreticians of power and for the moralists of its exercise than he was elaborating a theory in obstetrics to Nicodemus (3:3). Even the suffering Jesus must have known that "power" in that instance resided elsewhere than where heaven had ordained. It was in the hands of those "who delivered me to you" (19:11). But the evangelist penning Jesus' response was not unmindful of, "Shall I not drink the cup which the Father has given me?" (18:11).

Power and Self-Preservation

That "he who delivered me to you has the greater sin" (19:11) does not exculpate Pilate nor attenuate his sin. It is not an apportioning of guilt either. It merely states a fact.

Upon this Pilate sought to release him, but the Jews cried out, "If you release this man, you are not Caesar's friend; every one who makes himself a king sets himself against Caesar" (19:12).

With a deadly astuteness that must command admiration even if it fails to win approval, the Jews confront Pilate with a choice he cannot evade. His vaunted power (19:10) stopped exactly at Caesar's feet and no higher. As for so many of his tribe from the dawn of time, justice and equity, the law and morality, the very gods themselves took second place to self-preservation. The power wielded by subordinate officials, even the loftiest among them, is in direct proportion to their impotence before those above them.

The Caesars of the world, whatever the insignia of their power, the bay, the orb or the triple crown, take homage where they find it, even from those who hate them and execrate their name. On the other hand, those that seek glory from one another (5:44) and love "the praise of men more than the praise of God" (12:43) have scant regard for the source of their power. They remain in thrall to anyone disposed to recognize it. The chains of power's hierarchies are relentless. The innocent are not its only victims.

His Own Received Him Not

> **When Pilate heard these words, he brought Jesus out and sat down on the judgment seat at a place called The Pavement, and in Hebrew, Gabbatha. Now it was the day of Preparation of the Passover; it was about the sixth hour. He said to the Jews, "Behold your king!" They cried out, "Away with him, away with him, crucify him!" Pilate said to them, "Shall I crucify your king?" The chief priests answered, "We have no king but Caesar." Then he handed him over to them to be crucified (19:13–16).**

Enough circumstantial details are provided by these verses to have engaged archaeologists for years, and to continue to occupy commentators for ever. But what stands at the heart of this portion of the passion narrative is not Jerusalem topography nor Jewish festival chronology. What is at the heart of the narrative is the acting out of the prologue's "He came to his own home, and his own people received him not" (1:11). In the circumstances, even the reference to noon, "it was about the sixth hour" (19:14), might well contain a symbolic reference to the light which darkness cannot overcome (1:5).

To the pagan Pilate's "Behold your king!" the Jews gave one answer, "Away with him, away with him, crucify him!" (19:14–15). But the reader's task here is not to allot guilt or to sit in judgment on the Jews or the Romans for the death of Jesus. What clamors for their attention is the everlasting mystery, not merely of rejecting the light (1:5, 9–10), but of choosing the darkness in all its counterfeit forms: "We have no king but Caesar" (19:15). The Jews knew this was not true; Pilate knew only too well it could not be true; and even Caesar must have been less than willing to entertain the possibility of its truth. But, when once anyone is intent on rejecting the Revealer, credence in any substitute, even the most unlikely, becomes a foregone conclusion. To paraphrase Chesterton's celebrated remark, when people refuse to believe in Jesus Christ, they don't believe in nobody, they believe in anybody.

THE CRUCIFIXION OF JESUS (John 19:17–27)

> **So they took Jesus, and he went out, bearing his own cross, to the place called the place of a skull, which is called in Hebrew Golgotha. There they crucified him, and with him two others, one on either side, and Jesus between them (19:17–18).**

The stark simplicity of the statement and the economy of its detail, not only befit the subject, but lend it added solemnity. All the actors and scenes with which the synoptic passion accounts have acquainted us are omitted. Jesus' "way of the cross" is limited to "he went out, bearing his own cross" (19:17). There is no mention of Simon of Cyrene (Mt 27:32; Mk 15:21), no "daughters of Jerusalem" (Lk 23:28), not even an indication that the two malefactors between whom Jesus was crucified were robbers (Mt 27:38).

The Title on the Cross

> **Pilate also wrote a title and put it on the cross; it read, "Jesus of Nazareth, the King of the Jews." Many of the Jews read this title, for the place where Jesus was crucified was near the city; and it was written in Hebrew, in Latin, and in Greek. The chief priests of the Jews then said to Pilate, "Do not write, 'The King of the Jews,' but, 'This man said, I am King of the Jews.'" Pilate answered, "What I have written I have written" (19:19–22).**

All four gospels agree about the affixing of this famous inscription on the cross. One might have thought that, at long last, here we possess a solid bit of *written* evidence which can be copied by even a myopic, monolingual scribe, able to decipher either Hebrew or Greek or Latin. Posterity would then have had just one sentence in the tradition put beyond all cavil and dispute.

This, however, was not to be. To this day, scholars discuss the brief inscription's endless variety: Matthew has, "This is Jesus the King of the Jews" (Mt 27:37); Mark, "The King of the Jews" (Mk 15:26); Luke, "This is the King of the Jews" (Lk 23:38); and John, "Jesus of Nazareth, the King of the Jews" (19:19). John, who tells us the inscription was trilingual (19:20), mercifully spares us the Hebrew and Latin versions. They would have only provided fuel for more debates. This did not prevent John's inscription, in its Latin version, from being the winner in most artistic and pious representations of the crucifix. The "INRI" we often see affixed there is the acronym for the Latin of "Jesus of Nazareth, the King of the Jews."

The inscription occasioned another debate. To the very end, the authorities who sought to crucify Jesus persisted in their quibbles. They would have the last word. Their battle of wits with Pilate climaxed in his "Shall I crucify your king?" and their categoric response, "We have no king but Caesar" (19:15). Their remonstration was quite unnecessary. They must have known that the inscription was an accusation of the crucified, not a vindication of his claim. Yet they felt compelled to exploit the last tittle of the law and Pilate's weakness. "Do not write, 'The King of the Jews,' but 'This man said, I am King of the Jews'" (19:21).

But Pilate, like so many who share his weakness of character, had a limit, and that limit was trespassed. At last, he recoils with an unwonted show of strength, "What I have written I have written" (19:22). As is so often the case, his tragedy was that the limit of his endurance was reached too late either to confound his enemies or to spare the innocent victim.

The Fulfilment of the Scriptures

> **When the soldiers had crucified Jesus they took his garments and made four parts, one for each soldier; also his tunic. But the tunic was without seam, woven from top to bottom; so they said to one another, "Let us not tear it, but cast lots for it to see whose it shall be." This was to fulfil the scripture, "They parted my garments among them, and for my clothing they cast lots" (19:23–24).**

The "seamless tunic" of Jesus, far more famous than that of Nessus, fast became a Christian homiletic topos, a rich commonplace for preaching church unity and denouncing Christian division. That it is an apt symbol, no one would wish to deny. But, as it stands in the Johannine narrative of the passion, the whole incident of Jesus' garments has but one purpose in view: the fulfilment of the scripture (19:24).

John, of course, is not the only evangelist to exploit Psalm 22, the "My God, my God, why have you forsaken me" Psalm, in the account of the passion. The psalm itself, as is evident throughout the New Testament, is a cornerstone of Christology and a principal clue to understanding the suffering and death of Jesus of Nazareth. Therefore, to appreciate the significance of the citation of Psalm 22:18 in John 19:24, one must reflect upon the entire psalm. Upon such reflection, the reader will come to appreciate, even if imperfectly, the unique and indispensable role that the Old Testament plays in the revelation of Jesus Christ.

It is surely a clear, even if insufficiently remarked fact, that, without the Old Testament, the person of Jesus would be incomprehensible. Indeed, without the Old Testament, the New Testament itself would be unintelligible. For, without "the law...given through Moses," the "grace and truth" which came "through Jesus Christ" (1:17) would have defied understanding. One can readily understand why scholars have theorized that collections of Old Testament texts were among the very first written documents that accompanied the missionaries who proclaimed the gospel of Jesus Christ to the world. They were, and are, the indispensable means of comprehending the Christ event. The fourth evangelist, in having recourse to Psalm 22 here, is doing what he has done throughout his gospel, and what all other New Testament authors do naturally and regularly. Their only clue to understanding Jesus of Nazareth is "the law and the prophets."

At the Foot of the Cross

So the soldiers did this. But standing by the cross of Jesus were his mother, and his mother's sister, Mary the wife of Clopas, and Mary Magdalene. When Jesus saw his mother, and the disciple whom he loved standing near, he said to his mother, "Woman, behold, your son!" Then he said to the disciple, "Behold, your mother!" And from that hour the disciple took her to his own home (19:25–27).

It is not the very few who stood "by the cross of Jesus" (19:25) that call for comment, but all those who ought to have been there, all whom one might have expected to see there, and yet were not. From his cross Jesus sees what the reader of the gospel sees. In Mark, not even the mother of Jesus was there, and even the women who were there looked "from afar" (Mk 15:40 par). But, whether near or far, that sight must impress on the reader of any gospel the realization that the last act of Jesus' life was the inevitable recognition of its failure for all the world to see.

Whether "the disciple whom Jesus loved" was one of "the twelve" continues to be disputed by interpreters. The fact remains that, of those whom Jesus had chosen, who accompanied him throughout his public ministry, witnessed his signs and listened to his words, not one was there at the foot of the cross. Judged by any method of assessment the world can devise, the crucified Jesus had to reckon with failure.

Failure

Few mortals are unacquainted with failure. The reader needs but a minute's recollection to appreciate what Jesus' failure must have meant to him, to realize the enormity of the suffering it caused him. This is not for a moment to slight the presence of his mother, his aunt, Mary Magdalene and the beloved disciple. But the lesson of the genuineness of the suffering Jesus endured on the cross has to be driven home. The Word who became flesh assumed not only our mortality but also our failure, which is another form of dying.

One might have thought that Christians would have taken to heart by now the lesson of the cross, and discovered norms other than those of the world to assess success and failure. The lesson of the cross most necessary for the life of the community in the world is the one lesson that has to be repeatedly grasped. It will not do to bury it under a cascade of Easter alleluias. Yet worldly success and statistically measurable achievements are still the rule and norm of life in the community of believers, no less than it is in the world in which they live.

"Behold your mother"

The scene depicted by John, however, is not one of unrelieved gloom. That, to the very end, Jesus in his suffering thinks first of others is only fidelity to a whole life spent in loving them. "If you seek me, let these men go" (18:8). That he should think of providing for his mother after his death is–in any other world but ours–expected filial piety. But that he should entrust the disciple whom he loved as a son to his own mother, is a striking demonstration of his loving his own who were in the world "to the end" (13:1): "Woman, behold, your son!" (19:26).

If, as at least one famous commentator on John has maintained, the "beloved disciple" was only a symbol of all true believers, then the significance of Jesus' final action becomes even greater. By his "Woman, behold, your son!" Jesus entrusts every one of those who believe in him to his own mother; and one need be neither a Roman Catholic nor a Mariologist to appreciate the significance of what he does. From that moment on the cross, one can no more claim Jesus as brother without acknowledging Mary as mother, than claim Jesus as Revealer and refuse to confess God as Father.

THE DEATH OF JESUS (John 19:28–37)

> **After this Jesus, knowing that all was now finished, said (to fulfil the scripture), "I thirst." A bowl full of vinegar stood there, so they put a sponge full of the vinegar on hyssop and held it to his mouth. When Jesus had received the vinegar, he said, "It is finished"; and he bowed his head and gave up his spirit (19:28–30).**

The density of scriptural references in the passion narrative might well be an indication that the understanding of who Jesus is had its starting point for believers there. The cluster of Old Testament texts in the passion narratives can provide proof that the inception of Christology lies in some insight into those texts. Indeed, as remarked above (see on 12:12–15), Luke attributes such insight to the risen Jesus himself, who, "beginning with Moses and all the prophets, he interpreted to them *in all the scriptures* the things concerning himself" (Lk 24:26–27).

The Accomplishment of the Revelation

In John's account of the death of Jesus, the scriptural references are both implicit and explicit. Not only the "I thirst" but also the vinegar and perhaps even the hyssop (see Ps 69:21; 63:1; Ex 12:22) carry scriptural allusions. To speak of the fulfilment of the scriptures in 19:28, the evangelist uses a different word that means, not just "to fulfil" (as in 19:24 and 36), but "to bring to completion," which is used nowhere else in such a context. Jesus, in knowing "that all had now come to its appointed end" (Revised English Bible), brings all the scripture to its appointed end by saying, "I thirst." This is his role as the Revealer. This is what the Word, which was in the beginning, has come into the world to accomplish. The revelation in Jesus Christ brings all revelation to its appointed end.

Thus, the task for which Jesus came into the world is now "finished," fully accomplished. It has achieved its ordained end. Of course, the world judged, and continues to judge, otherwise. In its eyes, the end of Jesus' life had little to commend it. There was nothing there to sort and tabulate and chart. But, to the eyes of faith, Jesus came into the world to do one thing, and one thing only. He came to carry out the will of the Father, "I always do what is pleasing to him" (8:29; 5:30). His task was to reveal that "God so loved the world" (3:16). Now that he has done this and perfectly accomplished the Father's will, he can say, "It is finished" (19:30).

By his death on the cross, Jesus demonstrates the full extent of his obedience and thus reveals his true identity: "When you have lifted up the Son of Man, then you will know that I am he" (8:28). "For this reason the Father loves me, because I lay down my life, that I may take it again" (10:17).

Commentators in all ages have called attention, not just to the triumph of "It is finished," but also to the momentous implications of "he gave up his spirit" (19:30). They continue to remind us–and with good reason–that the crucifixion of Jesus is not only his own glorification but also a Pentecost as well, the giving of his Spirit to the world. Yet this cannot avert our gaze from the cross, even in the gospel of John. The man who hung on it, whatever the aftermath of Good Friday, did really suffer the agony of the crucified, did die the death that all the refined cruelty of his enemies devised for him. "Having loved his own who were in the world, he loved them to the end" (13:1). In that love he revealed just how much God the Father "loved the world" (3:16).

Since it was the day of Preparation, in order to prevent the bodies from remaining on the cross on the sabbath (for that sabbath was a high day), the Jews asked Pilate that their legs might be broken, and that they might be taken away. So the soldiers came and broke the legs of the first, and of the other who had been crucified with him; but when they came to Jesus and saw that he was already dead, they did not break his legs. But one of the soldiers pierced his side with a spear, and at once there came out blood and water (19:31–34).

These straightforward enough details have occasioned endless comment and even engendered controversy. Such will be the case whenever we approach the gospel for what it was not meant to convey. The narrative is not a postmortem on the causes of Jesus' death, nor is it a cipher to be decoded. Would the physiological details of death by crucifixion add anything to the one essential fact that Jesus "was already dead" (19:33)? Can the search for the causes of the "blood and water" that flowed out of the pierced side of the crucified (19:34) alter the quality of the faith it calls forth? Our faith in Jesus Christ is not a faith in historical facts. Historical facts are objects of knowledge, not of faith. What matters for the evangelist is the witness he bears to the significance of the facts for faith and their correlation with the scriptures.

The Witness of the Evangelist

> **He who saw it has borne witness–his testimony is true, and he knows that he tells the truth–that you also may believe. For these things took place that the scripture might be fulfilled, "Not a bone of him shall be broken." And again another scripture says, "They shall look on him whom they have pierced" (19:35–37).**

It is difficult to imagine the evangelist insisting on the truth of what he sets down and yet confining his statement to the details of the certification of Jesus' death. The insistence on the fact of Jesus' death is important because of what it reveals about the true identity of Jesus of Nazareth. But the witness borne by the evangelist embraces his entire gospel, not just its concluding drama.

Were the bare fact of death by crucifixion our principal concern, then we could just as well undertake the verification of the fate of the other two malefactors who were crucified with Jesus. We can bring all the apparatus of historical learning and medical science to bear on what the soldiers did to them and why (19:32); and, when we do, when all our researches are crowned with incontestable success, what have we but another entry in an ancient "police gazette"?

The witness which the evangelist bears (19:35) embraces all that has preceded the crucifixion and all that follows it: the entire gospel of Jesus Christ. That "you also may believe" (19:35) cannot be confined to the "blood and water" from Jesus' side (cf. 1 Jn 5:6–7), however rich the sacramental symbolism of the incident might be. The faith the evangelist has in view is faith in Jesus Christ as the Revealer of the Father, whose revelation reaches its appointed meridian at the hour of the cross.

The Scriptures and the Crucified

As is to be expected, the fulfilment of "the scripture" provides the explanation of all that took place on Golgotha: "For these things took place that the scripture might be fulfilled" (19:36). The reader cannot be unaware that the Exodus reference, "Not a bone of him shall be broken" (see Ex 12:46, 10; Num 9:12), is part of the instruction for the eating of the paschal lamb at the "Lord's passover." If symbolism there be in John's account of the crucifixion, then it is to be sought in the Exodus account of the paschal lamb (Ex 12). The one who hangs dead on the cross is the one whom John the Baptist proclaimed at the very beginning, "Behold, the Lamb of God, who takes away the sin of the world" (1:29). This is he whom the Father sent into the world "that the world might be saved through him" (3:17).

The true significance of the soldiers' decision that spared Jesus the *coup de grâce* of having his bones broken is also to be sought in the psalms. There, speaking of the Lord's care for "the afflictions of the righteous" (Ps 34:19), the psalmist says, "He keeps all his bones; not one of them is broken" (Ps 34:20). He who dies on the cross is "the righteous" one *par excellence*, the only Son who has fully accomplished the will of the Father ("I always do what is pleasing to him" 8:29) and thus brought to completion all the scriptures.

"They shall look on him whom they have pierced" (19:37) goes on to say in Zechariah, "they shall mourn for him, as one mourns for an only child, and weep bitterly over him, as one weeps over a first-born" (Zech 12:10). Could the evangelist have been unaware that he on whom "the inhabitants of Jerusalem" (Zech 12:10) gazed was indeed "an only child...a first-born" in a sense the former prophet could not have begun to conceive?

After this Joseph of Arimathea, who was a disciple of Jesus, but secretly, for fear of the Jews, asked Pilate that he might take away the body of Jesus, and Pilate gave him leave. So he came and took away his body. Nicodemus also, who had at first come to him by night, came bringing a mixture of myrrh and aloes, about a hundred pounds' weight. They took the body of Jesus, and bound it in linen cloths with the spices, as

is the burial custom of the Jews. Now in the place where he was crucified there was a garden, and in the garden a new tomb where no one had ever been laid. So because of the Jewish day of Preparation, as the tomb was close at hand, they laid Jesus there (19:38–42).

John 20

The Resurrection Narratives.

The Discovery of the Empty Tomb: Simon Peter; the race to the tomb; revelation and resurrection.

The Appearance to Mary Magdalene: the failure at recognition; "do not cling to me."

The Appearance to the Disciples: "receive the Holy Spirit"; the forgiveness of sins; the mission.

Jesus and Thomas: the beatitude.

The Purpose of the Book: inspiration; the Christ, the Son of God.

THE RESURRECTION NARRATIVES

More than it is in either Matthew or Luke, the resurrection narrative in John is integral to the account of the passion and the crucifixion of Jesus. Strictly speaking, Mark in its original form has no resurrection narrative. It concludes with, "And they went out and fled from the tomb; for trembling and astonishment had come upon them; and they said nothing to any one, for they were afraid" (Mark 16:8). Consequently, if Mark be taken as one of the sources for both Matthew and Luke, the resurrection narratives in these can be regarded as additions, much like their infancy narratives (Mt 1–2 and Lk 1–2).

The ending of Matthew's account of the passion has a ring of finality about it: "So they went and made the sepulchre secure by sealing the stone and setting a guard" (Mt 27:66). Luke ends with a marked pause: "On the sabbath they rested according to the commandment" (Lk 23:55b). But in John there is something almost provisional about the burial itself, the incident being but a stage in what is still an unfolding drama.

Nevertheless, unless we keep in mind what it is the resurrection narratives try to tell us, whether in John or in the synoptics, we risk missing the good news they all alike proclaim. First of all, the burial of Jesus is the definitive proof of the reality of his death, in John no less than in all three synoptics. For, without a real death, there can be no resurrection. Jesus was not resuscitated, nor was he revived. He was raised from the dead. Jesus of Nazareth had to die in order to rise from the dead.

Moreover, the one risen from the dead had to be identifiably the same Jesus of Nazareth whom the disciples knew and believed in and followed in his lifetime. The true purpose of the accounts of the resurrection appearances is to demonstrate this identity of the one risen from the dead with the Jesus of Nazareth who died on the cross. The accounts themselves are not, and cannot be, proofs of the resurrection, which, unlike the death on the cross, can only be the object of divine revelation, not of human reasoning upon the evidence.

THE DISCOVERY OF THE EMPTY TOMB (John 20:1–10)

Now on the first day of the week Mary Magdalene came to the tomb early, while it was still dark, and saw that the stone had been taken away from the tomb. So she ran, and went to Simon Peter and the other disciple, the one whom Jesus loved, and said to them, "They have taken the Lord out of the tomb, and we do not know where they have laid him." Peter then came out with the other disciple, and they went toward the tomb (20:1–3).

Mary Magdalene, who is first mentioned at the foot of the cross (19:25), is the first to come to the tomb: "Last at the cross and earliest at the grave," said a poet. The question of her identity (see above on 12:1–4) in the fourth gospel is therefore all the more intriguing for the singular role assigned her in this and the following scene (20:11–18).

Mary Magdalene's reaction at seeing that the stone had been taken away from the tomb (20:1) had nothing unusual about it. She reached a perfectly natural conclusion and thought that "they," whoever they might have been, "have taken the Lord out of the tomb, and we do not know where they have laid him" (20:2). To her, as to any reasonable observer who might have been with her, all that the empty tomb signified was that there was no one in it. The dead do not vacate their tombs at will.

Simon Peter

That she ran to "Simon Peter and the other disciple, the one whom Jesus loved" (20:2) is not surprising either. To her, at least, these two should have had some explanation, if any of the disciples did. The evangelist provides us here with the identification of "the other disciple" of the trial scene (18:15, 16) with the disciple "whom Jesus loved" (13:23). That Mary Magdalene sought him out is, therefore, easy to understand. He was with her at the crucifixion (19:25–26). But that she sought Simon Peter could well have been, to the mind of the evangelist at least, an indication of Peter's position among Jesus' disciples, which position, though severely compromised by his triple denial, was not forfeited. We should not forget that this is the first mention of Simon Peter since his denial of his discipleship at the trial of Jesus (18:27).

The consolation at the heart of this element in the narrative, both for those chosen to serve and for those whom they serve, is that Jesus knew whom he had chosen (13:18) and yet chose them nevertheless. Those given to despair at their own infidelity or driven to rage at the perfidy of others in the community will do well to reflect on Mary Magdalene's action, "So she ran and went to Simon Peter" (20:2).

The Race to the Tomb

> **They both ran, but the other disciple outran Peter and reached the tomb first; and stooping to look in, he saw the linen cloth lying there, but he did not go in. Then Simon Peter came, following him, and went into the tomb; he saw the linen cloths lying, and the napkin, which had been on his head, not lying with the linen cloths but rolled up in a place by itself. Then the other disciple, who reached the tomb first, also went in, and he saw and believed; for as yet they did not know the scripture, that he must rise from the dead. Then the disciples went back to their homes (20:4–10).**

There are those who wish to make the race to the tomb a lesson for some virtue or another, most often for the chastity of the beloved disciple. Without wishing to deny such a lesson, one must ask first how we come by it. Is it a presumption in the beloved disciple's favor? Then why not extend such presumption to Simon Peter? Is it because we infer from the other evangelists that Peter was married (Mk 1:30 par)? But that would be to confound—as is vulgarly done nowadays—celibacy with chastity. There are many married people who are chaste, and many celibates who are not.

Such an interpretation of the race between Peter and the beloved disciple, however hallowed by its permanence in the history of commentary on the fourth gospel, is just one of many instances of how not to read the gospel. The gospel is not elucidated by such interpretation, nor is the worth of chastity enhanced by it. Whatever the reason for the evangelist's insistence on the beloved disciple's winning the race to the tomb, his purported chastity could scarcely be one of them. Christian chastity is not embraced to win marathons.

Revelation and Resurrection

Many interpreters have similarly found the neat disposition of the napkin (20:7) significant. Yet, whatever it is that "the other disciple" saw and what he believed (20:8) remain puzzling. For the evangelist himself leaves no doubt about the reaction of both Simon Peter and the beloved disciple: "for as yet they did not know the scripture, that he must rise from the dead" (20:9). For them to believe "he must rise from the dead," the scriptures had first to be opened. To accomplish this, nothing short of divine revelation is needed. You do not *argue* to the resurrection from an empty tomb or from any observable fact, not from a scriptural text or several, nor even from an appearance of the risen Lord. Faith in the resurrection cannot be the argued conclusion from a syllogism, nor deduced from accumulated facts. It is and can only be a response to a revelation.

What the disciples "did not know" from the scriptures was that "he *must* rise from the dead" (20:9). The resurrection is not the happy ending to a sad story. It is the necessary manifestation of the true meaning of the story, without which there would be no story worth telling. The resurrection of Jesus is an integral part of his death on the cross, not a pleasing afterthought. The whole gospel of John is about Jesus of Nazareth as "the life" that was "the light of men" (1:4). That life cannot be manifest except in its victory over death; and that light can only shine out of the darkness of death. Without the resurrection there is no gospel. Whatever the life story of the other two malefactors crucified with Jesus, it is not and can never be the making of a gospel. "Christian faith is great, not because it believes that Christ died, but that he rose from the dead" (St. Augustine on Psalm 101.2).

THE APPEARANCE TO MARY MAGDALENE (John 20:11–18)

> **But Mary stood weeping outside the tomb, and as she wept she stooped to look into the tomb; and she saw two angels in white, sitting where the body of Jesus had lain, one at the head and one at the feet. They said to her, "Woman, why are you weeping?" She said to them, "Because they have taken away my Lord, and I do not know where they have laid him" (20:11–13).**

The reader cannot fail to remark the strangeness of the incident. There is no denying the fact that angels were part of the evangelist's world. Their mention in the gospel so far reflects this: they are part of the vision promised Nathanael, "You will see heaven opened, and the angels of God ascending and descending upon the Son of Man" (1:51). Some ancient manuscripts add to the account of the healing of the paralytic of Bethzatha (5:1–3, 5–9) verse 4, "For an angel of the Lord went down at certain seasons into the pool, and troubled the water..." (5:4). The evangelist's contemporaries quite evidently shared his belief in angels, as when some of them proposed an explanation for "the voice" they heard, "An angel has spoken to him" (12:29).

But here Mary Magdalene "saw two angels in white" (20:12). To the question, "What did Mary Magdalene actually see?" it is by no means easy to give an answer. Was Mark speaking of the same thing when he wrote, "a young man...dressed in a white robe" (Mk 16:5; cf. Mt 28:3)? In other words, are we given in the fourth gospel Mary Magdalene's interpretation of what she presumed she saw, "two angels," much as we are informed that what she supposed she saw later was "the gardener" (Jn 20:15)? Of course, a young man dressed in white and a gardener are visible in a way an angel simply is not and cannot be.

The Failure at Recognition

> **Saying this, she turned round and saw Jesus standing, but she did not know that it was Jesus (20:14).**

This, fittingly enough, is another strange incident. All the resurrection narratives necessarily share this strangeness, for they recount what is, strictly speaking, not of this world. The account here does not need to add that Mary Magdalene's "eyes were kept from recognizing him" as were those of the two disciples on the way to Emmaus (Lk 24:16). This detail needed to be stated clearly in Luke as it does not here in John. The reason Mary Magdalene "did not know that it was Jesus" is that she knew beyond the shadow of a doubt that Jesus was dead. Even if, like Martha, she certainly believed in "the resurrection *at the last day*" (Jn 11:24), that faith was not sufficient for her to conclude, from what she "saw" before her, either to the inbreaking of "the last day" or to the resurrection of Jesus of Nazareth from the dead. Both of these are objects of revelation, not of logical deduction.

All the encounters with the risen Jesus are susceptible of many explanations, none of which, of itself, postulates the resurrection from the dead of the one who was crucified. Indeed, without some prior faith in the resurrection of the dead, that explanation could not even be entertained as a possibility. You have to have some faith in the resurrection of the dead before you can believe that Jesus of Nazareth is risen (see Acts 10:41).

> **Jesus said to her, "Woman, why are you weeping? Whom do you seek?" Supposing him to be the gardener, she said to him, "Sir, if you have carried him away, tell me where you have laid him, and I will take him away" (20:15).**

This Jesus who addresses her is every bit the Jesus of Nazareth she will confess as Teacher (20:16) and risen Lord (20:18). Why then does she fail to recognize him and suppose him to be the gardener? The answer is that the resurrection is not a natural phenomenon subject to verification by sight. It is exclusively an object of faith. Therefore, it requires revelation. Nothing else can or will do. We, who have been so accustomed to "proving" the resurrection of Jesus by the historical verifiability of his appearances, should reflect on all those who saw him but failed to recognize him (Jn 20:15; Lk 24:16), no less than on all who did not see him at all "and yet believed" (Jn 20:29).

To have "seen" on Easter Sunday the Jesus who died on the cross on Good Friday is susceptible of many explanations. Matthew, for instance, cites one of them, perhaps because it was in vogue by the time he wrote his gospel: that his disciples "stole" Jesus from his tomb and told the people, "He has risen from the dead" (Mt 27:64). This is the "fraud" explanation in one of its many forms. Twenty centuries later, Renan would remark that anyone who observed the disciples on that Saturday could have told you Jesus would rise on Sunday. Their very anguish, in other words, gave birth to the fact. Their wish was "father to that thought." This is the "psychological" explanation in one of its forms. You can multiply such and similar explanations in any and all directions; but what you cannot do is rationally conclude from what we know by human means to the necessity of the resurrection. The resurrection is the object of revelation, and revelation always requires faith.

The situation, to cite a current example, is not unlike those who say they have seen UFOs. There are numberless possible explanations for their UFOria, but none of them necessarily, in and of itself, requires postulating the existence of creatures from outer space. Ignorance of what such people actually saw is neither a reason to doubt their claim to have seen something, nor justification for accepting their explanation of what it was they did see. Indeed, if we reflect a moment, it is their explanation that fails to win credence, and so renders even their initial claim questionable.

In Jesus' words to Mary Magdalene, two points should be singled out. His first question, it must be noted, is identical to that put to her by the "two angels": "Woman, why are you weeping?" (20:15 and cf. 20:13). Jesus now adds, "Whom do you seek?" (20:15) and thus echoes his very first words to his followers, "What do you seek?" (1:38). Of course, what the first disciples sought, and he for whom she now searches, are one and the same. Jesus of Nazareth is at once the revelation that the first disciples sought and the crucified Revealer for whom Mary Magdalene was now looking.

> **Jesus said to her, "Mary." She turned and said to him in Hebrew, "Rabboni!" (which means Teacher). Jesus said to her, "Do not hold me, for I have not yet ascended to the Father; but go to my brethren and say to them, I am ascending to my Father and your Father, to my God and your God." Mary Magdalene went and said to the disciples, "I have seen the Lord"; and she told them that he had said these things to her (20:16–18).**

The force of this rightly celebrated recognition scene lies in its simplicity. Of all the resurrection appearances, it alone rated celebration in the Sequence of the Easter liturgy. Any additional comment on the verses in John seems therefore doomed to fall far short of the muted dignity of the eleventh-century Burgundian hymn, the *Victimae paschali laudes*, our Easter Sunday Sequence. Nevertheless, an all-important theological implication of the Johannine narrative does require to be made explicit.

Commentators and preachers alike stress the fact of Mary Magdalene's failure to recognize the risen Lord. They offer a variety of explanations. What is of the utmost importance in this and all other failures at recognition, however, is the fact that the Jesus of Nazareth who is risen from the dead is finally recognized as the Lord: "I have seen *the Lord*," "We have seen *the Lord*" (20:18, 25).

To recognize Jesus of Nazareth as Lord, ocular vision alone is not enough. Divine revelation is required in each and all instances. The risen Lord is a reality that belongs to "the world to come," an eschatological reality. It is therefore not visible the way objects and persons are visible and recognizable in this world. Faith is as indispensable to see the risen Jesus as it is to recognize him as Lord. Mary Magdalene's "Rabboni!" is a cry of faith, not just a dramatic anagnorisis.

"Do not cling to me"

Jesus' saying to her, "Do not hold me," must be familiar to anyone who has been exposed, on however elementary a level, to the admirable efficacy of the moods and tenses of the Greek verb. The expressive discrimination of one language inevitably occasions debate in translating it into a less abundantly endowed other: "Do not hold me"; "Do not touch me"; "Do not cling to me" (RNEB); "Stop holding on to me" (NAB). But the importance of Jesus' words to Mary Magdalene (20:17) lies in the implication of his message, not in the force of the Greek imperative.

"I have not yet ascended to the Father...I am ascending to my Father" (20:17) quite naturally raises the question of the sequence in events that, of their very nature, are beyond time. We have had occasion to remark that in the fourth gospel the lifting up of the Son of man on the cross (3:14; 12:34) comprises in one indivisible moment his crucifixion and death, his glorification and ascension (12:32, 8; 13:31, 32; 17:1, 4), and his sending of the Holy Spirit (19:30; 16:7; 20:22). Nevertheless, the way the evangelist and his readers first come to apprehend this revealed truth is necessarily piecemeal, as distinct events in a sequence, before they can come to grasp their significance as an integral whole. In their confession of the Lordship of Jesus, therefore, the believers acknowledge the redemptive death, the glory of the resurrection, the return to the Father and the sending of the Holy Spirit, as one integral event. Their confession of faith is thus the confession of Jesus of Nazareth as the Revealer of the Father, as the Christ, the Son of God.

In his commission to Mary Magdalene, we have already encountered the distinction that Jesus maintains—and necessarily so—between "my Father and your Father," "my God and your God" (20:17). This distinction underlines, not only the uniqueness of his own relationship to God, but also the singular and indivisible position he occupies vis-à-vis his "brethren," all those who believe in him. His perfect obedience to God reveals God as his own Father. The revelation he thus brings to all who believe in him as the Son is that the God they believe in and worship is their Father. They demonstrate their own obedience to their Father when they confess his only Son as their Lord.

THE APPEARANCE TO THE DISCIPLES (John 20:19–23)

> **On the evening of that day, the first day of the week, the doors being shut where the disciples were, for fear of the Jews, Jesus came and stood among them and said to them, "Peace be with you." When he had said this, he showed them his hands and his side. Then the disciples were glad when they saw the Lord (20:19–20).**

It is a sign of the times that these verses should require a reminder of the obvious. The risen Lord had to be recognizably and identifiably the Jesus of Nazareth, the man whom the disciples knew and followed, whom they saw and heard, with whom they ate, and because of whom they now cowered behind closed doors for "fear of the Jews." For him to have risen as any other than the Jesus of Nazareth they knew would void the resurrection of all its meaning. The one they confessed as their risen Lord is the same Jesus of Nazareth they had known and followed. Showing them "his hands and side," which bore the marks of the crucifixion and the pierce by the lance, was not a theatrical gesture, but the necessary credentials of the identity of the risen Lord who stood before them with the crucified Jesus of Nazareth whom they knew.

The joy that is theirs at this event, "the disciples were glad when they saw the Lord" (20:20), harks back to his promise: "So you have sorrow now, but I will see you again and your hearts will rejoice, and no one will take your joy from you" (16:22, where the same Greek verb "to rejoice" is used as in 20:20). Easter joy is the permanent possession of the community of believers. It is a gift conferred by the risen Lord, not an achievement of the community or any of its members. Like all the gifts of the risen Lord, it has to be constantly guarded against all the "anointed sovereigns of sighs and groans" in their midst. This is why Jesus reiterates his "Peace be with you" (20:19, 21). It is the stable possession of this peace, which the risen Lord alone brings them, that is at the basis of the believers' inalienable joy.

"Receive the Holy Spirit"

Jesus said to them again, "Peace be with you. As the Father has sent me, even so I send you." And when he had said this, he breathed on them, and said to them, "Receive the Holy Spirit. If you forgive the sins of any, they are forgiven; if you retain the sins of any, they are retained" (20:21–23).

Once again the sequence of events can be puzzling. He who told his disciples, "If I do not go away, the Paraclete will not come to you; but if I go, I will send him to you" (16:7), and who told Mary Magdalene, "I have not yet ascended to the Father" (20:17), now breathes on his disciples this promised Holy Spirit (20:22). So this "Johannine Pentecost," already anticipated on the cross ("gave up his spirit" 19:30), precedes his return to the Father. But, once again, we must beware of isolating discrete moments in what is one integral event in the revelation. He who dies on the cross is he who rises from the dead, returns to the Father who sent him, and sends his Holy Spirit on all who confess him as Lord and Son of God.

Furthermore, our catechetical instruction has acquainted us with the Christian tradition that recognizes in these verses of John the institution of the sacrament of penance, which nowadays, lest the "unhealthful" shadow of sin fall athwart the sunny path of Christian existence, is spoken of as the sacrament of reconciliation. The pre-Vatican II rite of ordination to the priesthood also had recourse to these verses in John 20:22–23, which were recited verbatim at the final imposition of hands.

The Forgiveness of Sins

But what runs the risk of being overlooked in all this is the fact that the power to forgive sins is explicitly linked here to the Holy Spirit who, as our creed reminds us, "spoke through the prophets." The forgiveness of sins, in the prophets of old and in the Johannine prophet, expresses the significance of the redemption. "The Lamb of God" is he who "takes away the sin of the world" (1:29). Refusal to hear the word of the revelation is the sin. "But now you say, 'We see,' your *sin* remains" (9:41, the RSV here uses "guilt" to translate the Greek word for "sin"; cf. 8:47; 15:22, 24; 16:8, 9). The function of those whom Jesus sends into the world (20:21) is, therefore, to proclaim the revelation, not to promulgate an ever more refined *catalogue raisonné* of human foibles.

The Mission

"As the Father sent me, even so I send you" (20:21) confirms the meaning of the impartation of the Holy Spirit to his disciples. We cannot forget that they are sent into the world at the very moment their Lord is leaving it. In John's gospel there is no "mission of the twelve" before the resurrection, as there is in the synoptics (Mk 6:7–13; Mt 10:1, 5–15; Lk 9:1–6). We must also keep in mind the comparison Jesus establishes here: *as* the Father sent him into the world to be the bearer of the revelation *so too* he in turn sends his disciples for the same purpose (see 5:23; 15:20, 23; cf. Lk 10:16). Their forgiving and retaining sins is integral to their task of proclaiming the revelation to the world. It is in the response to the proclamation of this revelation that life or sin are operative.

The mission of Jesus' disciples, therefore, continues his task of bringing the revelation to the whole world. The Paraclete, the Holy Spirit, assures the truth of that message and its permanence in the world (see 16:13). Rejection of this message is what constitutes sin. The Paraclete's function is to "convict the world concerning sin...because they do not believe in me" (16:9–10 marg). What we usually speak of as "sins" come from the rejection of the revelation which Jesus' disciples are sent into the world to proclaim.

JESUS AND THOMAS (John 20:24–29)

Now Thomas, one of the twelve, called the Twin, was not with them when Jesus came. So the other disciples told him, "We have seen the Lord." But he said to them, "Unless I see in his hands the print of the nails, and place my finger in the mark of the nails, and place my hand in his side, I will not believe" (20:24–25).

The incident, so dear to the readers of John's Gospel, has this to distinguish it from many other equally instructive incidents in the life of Jesus: Those who are most disposed to cite the incident in order to "demonstrate" some point or other of the faith, are often the very ones who are most like Thomas in their attitude to the risen Jesus. They are the ones most eager to prove the "historicity" of the gospel narratives, most tireless in their quest of the "historical Jesus," and most determined to find his very words in the gospels. The value of their faith rests on the irrefutable proof of history. Not for them the "Jesus is the

Christ, the Son of God" (20:31) of the revelation. Unless they find every element in the gospel "historically verifiable," they "will not believe." They go even further than Thomas. For them anyone who does not share their concern with the verifiable historical fact is dismissed as unbelieving. Whatever else may be said about his attitude, Thomas at least did not explicitly dismiss out of hand the other disciples' confession, "We have seen the Lord" (20:25). He merely insisted on visible, tangible proof for his own faith, "Unless I see...I will not believe" (20:25). In that he has had innumerable followers.

> **Eight days later, his disciples were again in the house, and Thomas was with them. The doors were shut, but Jesus came and stood among them, and said, "Peace be with you." Then he said to Thomas, "Put your finger here, and see my hands; and put out your hand, and place it in my side; do not be faithless, but believing. Thomas answered him, "My Lord and my God!" (20:26–28).**

Every attempt to translate this scene into a stage presentation or a cinematic episode, not only misrepresents these verses, but misses their intent altogether. The very point this gospel incident tries to make risks being neutralized, if not altogether negated, by any attempt to translate it into a proof text of the resurrection. If Thomas' "My Lord and my God!" is to have any sense beyond that of a mere expletive of wonderment, then what called it forth could not have been anything less than an act of divine revelation. It is not a reaction to a conclusive and successful scientific experiment. Thomas did not believe *because* he saw with his own eyes and touched with his hands. Thomas saw precisely because he believed that the Jesus of Nazareth he knew all too well, the one whom he accompanied on many journeys and heard on innumerable occasions, with whom he sat at table and ate, the one who was crucified and died on the cross, that very same Jesus was his Lord and his God.

The Beatitude

This, of course, is just the point the writer wishes to make before he brings the gospel to a close:

> **Jesus said to him, "Have you believed because you have seen me? Blessed are those who have not seen and yet believe" (20:29).**

It is for those "who have not seen and yet believe," that the whole gospel is written. Neither this gospel nor any other is meant to be a substitute for actually being there. The gospel is not an album of snapshots, nor a log book, nor even a sworn deposition. It is the proclamation, not of assorted facts, but of the one essential truth that the Jesus of Nazareth of whom it speaks is indeed, "My Lord and my God!" (20:28).

The beatitude pronounced by Jesus, "Blessed are those who have not seen and yet believe," does not set up two echelons of believers, two classes of Christians. There is, in Kierkegaard's already cited words, no "disciple at second hand." We are all on a par when it comes to faith in who Jesus of Nazareth really is to us and for us. If blessedness there be in those "who have not seen," then it is the blessedness of their being spared the temptation which, not only Thomas, but all the contemporaries of Jesus, were subjected to. After all, of the thousands who saw and heard Jesus, only a few, a very few in all Palestine believed in him.

Thomas' "Unless I *see*... and place my finger" (20:25) echoes all too accurately Philip's "Lord, *show* us the Father, and we shall be satisfied" (14:8). But neither Thomas, nor Philip, nor any of the disciples of Jesus, past or present, can be exempt from the truth of the categorical statement in Hebrews: "Now faith is...the conviction of things *not seen*" (Heb 11:1). "Faith," as Paul reminds us, "comes from what is heard, and what is heard comes by the preaching of Christ" (Rom 10:17). This is equally true of the resurrection appearances as of all Jesus' words, deeds and miracles in this and any other gospel, as the following verses show.

THE PURPOSE OF THE BOOK (John 20:30–31)

> **Now Jesus did many other signs in the presence of the disciples, which are not written in this book (20:30).**

This verse reminds us of the obvious. It is not just that the reader is aware, from the other gospels, that there are indeed many other miracles of Jesus that are not recorded in this one. The statement reminds us of an even more obvious, and so more likely to be overlooked, fact. The author exercised his own judgment in selecting what signs to include and which to leave out. This is not only the prerogative of any intelligent author, but the mark of artistic genius.

Inspiration

This very obvious fact can so easily be forgotten when, "hot for certainties," we set out to exploit the content of the gospel. We risk forgetting this fact every time we allow our unbridled zeal to rob the human author of what is his due, in order to laud the divine. Those who believe in the divine inspiration of the scriptures should not forget that the God they so wish to praise is a God who will not rob his creatures of what they can do, any more than he will obliterate his own gifts in them in order to manifest his glory. Saint Augustine remarks at the start of his book on Christian Doctrine, "Our human condition would be sad indeed were God unwilling to communicate with us through human means." It were invidious to add here that such zeal to exaggerate the divine at the cost of the human springs more from an exaggerated self-importance than from enlightened concern for the glory of God. If revelation there be–the argument goes–then we want it to be a first-class revelation, meeting our standards of excellence.

The economy of choice exercised by John commands admiration. For all the difficulties that arise out of the sequence of events in the fourth gospel and in the order of the chapters within it, there is no denying the achievement in the narrative of the signs, the dynamics of the intermingled dialogues, and the revelatory discourses that crown them. Such achievement has not failed to capture the minds and the hearts of believers over the centuries, even of those most troubled by the problems and the dilemmas in John's gospel.

Those, however, who turn to the pages of this gospel for what it does not claim to possess or to give, can have only themselves to blame for failing to find there what they look for. The signs and sayings, the discourses and dialogues which the gospel sets down in its pages have a specific, well-defined and clearly stated purpose. It is hard to imagine anyone turning to the gospel of John with that purpose in mind and being disappointed:

> **...but these are written that you may believe that Jesus is the Christ, the Son of God, and that believing you may have life in his name (20:31).**

The purpose for which "these are written" cannot find clearer expression. To believe that this Jesus of Nazareth is the Christ is to believe that in him all God's promises find their fulfilment, that in him all that God spoke through Moses and the prophets finds its ultimate meaning (5:39; 1:17) and its perfect accomplishment (19:30).

The Christ, the Son of God

To believe that "Jesus is the Christ, the Son of God" is to believe that the flesh and blood Jesus of Nazareth is the Son and, therefore, the revealer of the Father. His entire life and its culmination on the cross is one uninterrupted act of filial obedience to the will of the Father who sent him. Jesus of Nazareth is what the Word, which was with God and was God (1:1), became when it "became flesh and dwelt among us" (1:14). Deny the reality of the flesh, and you have just another religious myth among so many; deny the reality of the Word, and all you have is an edifying tale.

Faith in Jesus as "the Christ, the Son of God" is, moreover, the sole necessary condition for having life, true and genuine life, eternal life "in his name" (20:31). This life can only be gratefully received by acknowledging its giver as "the Christ, the Son of God." It is the only gift that brings all human search for substitutes to an end, makes superfluous all struggle after ersatz means of survival. It is the gift that truly sets human beings free (8:32) because it is the only salvation of the world (3:17): "This is indeed the Savior of the world" (4:42). Life "in his name" offers everyone on the face of the earth all they ultimately seek in their searches, everything for which they truly look for in their quests.

This life is "in his name" because it is the gift which the Son made possible by his coming into the world. Because it is a true gift, it can only be gratefully received by acknowledging him who brings it as "the Christ, the Son of God." By bringing to an end all human strivings after illusory counterfeits, by rendering vain all struggles to attain it by one's own power, this gift sets the believer free to expend her or his own life in loving service of the other.

Therefore, the only valid and available sign of possessing this "life in his name" is the reckless prodigality with which it is expended by believers in loving one another. "By this all will know that you are my disciples, if you have love for one another" (13:35). Life "in his name" sets believers free *from* the world and its trumpery precisely in order that they be *for* the world, so that the world, "through their word" (17:20), may know that you have sent me and have loved them as you have loved me (17:23).

John 21

The Appearance to Seven Disciples: the dramatis personae; the Lukan parallel; the miraculous catch; the meal; the bearers of the revelation; God the Creator.

Jesus and Peter: Peter's love; Peter's position and function.

Jesus and the Beloved Disciple.

The Conclusion.

The gospel of John could very well have ended with chapter 20. Indeed John 20:30–31 is a fine conclusion to any gospel. But the gospel of John we now have, and have had as far back as our manuscript evidence takes us, does not end there. The addition of chapter 21–and there is no need to conceal that it is a later addition–is there to be reckoned with, not merely by finding an appropriate description for it, whether as epilogue or appendix or supplement, but by taking it for what it indeed is, the concluding chapter of the gospel according to John.

The case of chapter 21 is not the same as that of the story of the woman caught in adultery in John 7:53–8:11. It is not even the same as the disputed endings of Mark (Mk 16:9–20). The story of the adulterous woman was for centuries absent from the early manuscripts of John's gospel. John 21, on the other hand, was there in the oldest manuscript we possess of this or perhaps any other gospel. So the initial resolve to call "evangelist" the one who left us the gospel of John in its present state must include chapter 21 as well. We must, therefore, try to understand the purpose of this chapter accordingly, and not dismiss it as a superfluous adjunct by a well-meaning if misguided scribe.

To resolve to treat the chapter as integral to the gospel is not to deny the very genuine problems we run into when we consider the composition of the gospel. The presence of John 21 only aggravates them. It is difficult to refute evidence of successive stages of composition, perhaps even of a sequence of editions of the gospel we now have. To the various compositional problems that confront us throughout the gospel, chapter 21 adds the particularly knotty one of determining its intention and meaning.

THE APPEARANCE TO SEVEN DISCIPLES (John 21:1–14)

> **After this Jesus revealed himself again to the disciples by the Sea of Tiberias; and he revealed himself in this way (21:1).**

Whatever charge one may choose to level against the one responsible for the addition of this chapter to the finished gospel, deception is not one of them. The fact that this chapter is an addition stands there unconcealed. What is evident to the reader today must have been evident to the author of yesteryear. The author might have been gauche, but could not have been inept. The opening verse points unmistakably to a conscious addition after the admirable conclusion of the preceding chapter (20:30–31).

Given this fact, the question remains. Why? What purpose is this chapter intended to serve? What in it is so necessary that its omission was judged intolerable in the mind of the "final redactor" of the gospel of John?

The Dramatis Personae

> **Simon Peter, Thomas called the Twin, Nathanael of Cana in Galilee, the sons of Zebedee, and two others of his disciples were together. Simon Peter said to them, "I am going fishing." They said to him, "We will go with you." They went out and got into the boat; but that night they caught nothing (21:2–3).**

The list of the dramatis personae has rightly attracted the attention of commentators, not only because of the disciples who are named but also for the "two others" left anonymous (see 21:7). So, too, the identification of Nathanael as of "Cana in Galilee," where Jesus worked his first sign "and his disciples believed in him" (2:11, 1; 4:46), has piqued the attention of interpreters. Nevertheless, what is most striking of all, in this verse (21:2) and in the rest of the chapter, is the person of Simon Peter. In all likelihood, he provides some hint of a reason why John 21 was added to the rest of the gospel. The only other chapter where Peter is mentioned more frequently is John 18, where the story of his denial is told.

It is, therefore, not surprising that a salient feature in the introduction to this narrative of an added appearance of the risen Jesus "to the disciples by the Sea of Tiberias" (21:1) should be a definition of Peter's role vis-à-vis the other disciples. He not only heads the list and takes the initiative ("I am going fishing"), but quite evidently assumes the role of leader. The other disciples' reaction to his decision is, "We will go *with you*" (21:3).

The Lukan Parallel

From the first remark about the outcome of Peter's expedition, "but that night they caught nothing" (21:3), the reader senses a vague familiarity with the story. It is very like the incident Luke uses to describe the call of the first disciples (Lk 5:1–11, note 5:5a). The elements common to both narratives are too many to be describing two distinct events. The very nature of the event, moreover, precludes repetition.

It has been suggested by several scholars–and with good reason–that Luke took what was originally a narrative of the appearance of the risen Lord and masterfully transformed it into a vocation narrative at the start of Jesus' public ministry. This procedure ought to surprise only such as go to the gospels for what the gospels do not pretend to give: a chronicle, a biography, a historical narrative about Jesus of Nazareth. Only if you think that Luke's writing in order that "you may know the truth concerning the things of which you have been informed" (Lk 1:4), is not in order that "you may believe that Jesus is the Christ, the Son of God" (Jn 20:31), could you find such procedure unacceptable.

The Miraculous Catch

Just as day was breaking, Jesus stood on the beach; yet the disciples did not know that it was Jesus. Jesus said to them, "Children, have you any fish?" They answered him, "No." He said to them, "Cast the net on the right side of the boat, and you will find some." So they cast it, and now they were not able to haul it in, for the quantity of fish. That disciple whom Jesus loved said to Peter, "It is the Lord!" When Simon Peter heard that it was the Lord, he put on his clothes, for he was stripped for work, and sprang into the sea. But the other disciples came

in the boat, dragging the net full of fish, for they were not far from the land, but about a hundred yards off (21:4–8).

That "the disciples did not know that it was Jesus" (21:4) requires neither acquaintance with meteorological conditions on the Sea of Tiberias nor familiarity with optics. The disciples' failure to recognize Jesus is the failure of any attempt to recognize the risen Lord without the necessary revelation. Unlike the case of Mary Magdalene, to whom the risen Jesus revealed his identity by calling her name, "Mary" (20:16), the disciples here come to recognize him by the miraculous nature of his good deed: "They were not able to haul it in, for the quantity of fish" (21:6).

At this point, the narrative links the "disciple whom Jesus loved" with Simon Peter (21:7). It is by no means without significance that the same two were also linked in the account of the betrayal (18:16). Could this then have been an additional reason why chapter 21 came to be appended to the gospel? If, as some New Testament scholars suggest, the beloved disciple is the figure behind the traditions enshrined in the fourth gospel, if not directly the author of its earliest version, then what could be more natural than the desire to link the community of the beloved disciple to the greater community at large, to the community over which Peter himself presided? and what more appropriate moment than an appearance of the Risen Lord to his disciples?

The Meal

When they got out on land, they saw a charcoal fire there, with fish lying on it, and bread. Jesus said to them, "Bring some of the fish that you have caught." So Simon Peter went aboard and hauled the net ashore, full of large fish, a hundred and fifty-three of them; and although there were so many, the net was not torn. Jesus said to them, "Come and have breakfast." Now none of the disciples dared ask him, "Who are you?" They knew it was the Lord. Jesus came and took the bread and gave it to them, and so with the fish (21:9–13).

That the risen Jesus manifests himself to his disciples in the ordinary intimacy of daily life is of a piece with the mode of the revelation. The Word that became flesh literally "dwelt among us" (1:14). Those who would have it otherwise misunderstand the gospel and misconceive the revelation. The whole point of John's gospel is that God brings his revelation to us in the lowly habiliments of the human, and assures its permanence among us in the still lowlier garb of the humdrum everyday life of those who believe in his name. It never ceases to be a source of astonishment how reluctant we are to see in limited, fallible, narrow-minded, prejudiced, bungling human beings the bearers of God's revelation of love to the world. Yet, we must again recall Augustine's words that the human condition would be abject indeed had God not chosen to minister his word to us through other human beings.

The Bearers of the Revelation

Our reluctance to accept this fact is the reason why we expend so much energy in transmuting the life stories of the apostles into heroic tales crammed with the miraculous. This is why we have so effectively managed to give even hagiography a bad name. This is why we have invented cumbersome myths of, not merely infallible, but also sinless evangelists, New Testament authors, fathers of the church, popes and saints. We make them bigger than life, suprahuman, towering giants of the mind and models of every conceivable virtue. We want all bearers of the revelation to us to be high above the noisome and madding crowd, not because of any devotion to them in particular, but because we are convinced that we ourselves deserve the very best.

"Come and have breakfast," said the risen Jesus to them, and "none of the disciples dared ask him, 'Who are you?'" (21:12). His ministering the bread and fish to them was another reminder of what his disciples will always be reluctant to remember, "If I then, your Lord and Teacher, have washed your feet, you also ought to wash one another's feet" (13:14; cf. "I am among you as one who serves" in Luke 22:27).

This was now the third time that Jesus was revealed to the disciples after he was raised from the dead (Jn 21:14).

Whoever was responsible for the addition of this chapter to the gospel wanted to secure its links firmly to the preceding chapter. "This was now the third time" reckons the appearance to the group of disciples without Thomas (20:19–23) as the first, and to the group with Thomas (20:26–29) as the second. The author is, of course, counting only the appearances to the group, "to the disciples," and not to a single individual like Mary Magdalene (20:11–18).

God the Creator

What should be adverted to here, however, is the passive tense of the two verbs: "Jesus was revealed" and "he was raised from the dead." As frequently in the scriptures, the use of the passive in these instances implies that God is the unexpressed subject of both the raising and the revealing. The resurrection of the dead is exclusively an act of God the creator. It constitutes, therefore, as has already been remarked, an object of revelation. Only the creator, who alone can raise from the dead, can reveal to us the fact of this resurrection.

That the New Testament speaks also of Jesus as himself rising from the dead (Lk 24:34; Jn 20:9) does not in any way contradict the exclusivity of God's action. It does, however, make a christological claim for the person of Jesus (see Jn 5:17, "My Father is working still, and I am working"). Thus, to say "he must rise from the dead" (20:9) is to claim for Jesus of Nazareth a prerogative that belongs exclusively to God the creator.

We are so accustomed to some form or another of the so-called "proofs of God's existence" that we overlook too readily the fact that "God is the creator" is itself an article of faith and, therefore, an object of revelation. Were it just a scientifically or philosophically demonstrable truth, it would compel assent, not elicit faith. The resurrection of the dead is also an act of God the creator (5:21; cf. Rom 4:17). Therefore, the appearances of the risen Lord are acts of revelation calling forth faith, not cumulative evidence yielding conclusions that command assent.

JESUS AND PETER (John 21:15–19)

When they had finished breakfast, Jesus said to Simon Peter, "Simon, son of John, do you love me more than these?" He said to him, "Yes, Lord; you know that I love you." He said to him, "Feed my lambs." A second time he said to him, "Simon, son of John, do you love me?" He said to him, "Yes, Lord; you know that I love you." He said to him, "Tend my sheep." He said to him the third time, "Simon, son of John, do you love me?" Peter was grieved because he said to him the third time, "Do you love me?" And he said to him, "Lord, you know everything; you know that I love you." Jesus said to him, "Feed my sheep" (21:15–17).

No great literary acumen is needed to realize that the triple question and answer here corresponds to the triple denial of Peter, which was predicted by Jesus, "till you have denied me three times" (13:38), and perpetrated by Peter (18:17, 25, 27). That Peter "was grieved" when Jesus put the same question to him "the third time" is testimony both to his acknowledgment of his sin and his repentance. We must, in Peter's case no less than in our own, keep in mind what Saint Augustine said about sinners, "Many sins are committed by reason of pride but not at all proudly; some are committed from ignorance, others from weakness, and many with sighs and tears." Like Peter, Augustine knew whereof he spoke.

Peter's Love

Commentators are wont to remind us that "to love" in the original text is expressed not by one but by two different Greek verbs. Given the fortunes of these and the still other words for "to love" in Greek (see above on 13:1) it would be unwarranted to attach too much importance to the alternating sequence of the verbs, let alone to make a theological issue out of it. The RSV's consistent "Do you *love* me?" is not just a concession to the limitations of the English language, but fidelity to the true meaning of Jesus' triple question. The author of the account, of course, leaves no doubt that the same question was repeated: "Peter was grieved because he said to him the *third time*, 'Do you love me?'" (21:17).

That Peter loved Jesus, both Peter and Jesus knew only too well. Even Jesus' prediction of Peter's denial (13:38) does not for a moment invalidate the love that prompted the hapless disciple to exclaim, "Lord...I will lay down my life for you" (13:37). Only a genuine lover, or else an arrant hypocrite, could say this; and Peter, whatever else he might have been, was no hypocrite.

Thus, Jesus' "Simon, son of John, do you love me?" (21:15, 16, 17) is not a request for information. If Jesus did not know Peter loved him, nothing Peter says could alter the fact. This is true of course of all genuine love. "And Jove but laughs at lovers' perjury." To say "I love you" to another is either a superfluous statement of the obvious, however pleasant and desirable, or mere desperation. This is why Peter's response to the question is "*You know* that I love you" (21:15, 16, 17). The third time Peter feels compelled to add, "Lord, you know everything; you know that I love you" (21:17). Should the Lord, *per impossibile*, be ignorant of Peter's love, then he who knew "all things" (16:30) must surely have known it.

Peter's Position and Function

Jesus' triple question, however, has a wholly other purpose. It was very likely this purpose which necessitated the belated addition of John 21 to the gospel. There was a need to make explicit, particularly after Peter's triple denial of his Lord, what has hitherto been implicit throughout the gospel about Peter's position and function (1:42; 6:68; 13:6–9, 24, 36–38; 20:2–10; 21:3, 7). Of all the others, Peter is the one singled out to "Feed my lambs... Tend my sheep... Feed my sheep" (21:15, 16, 17) and that despite his evident shortcomings and lamentable betrayal.

One need not be a Roman Catholic to understand this. It is not politics or sociology but the very nature of the revelation that dictates the position and the function of Simon Peter in the community of believers. Nor need one be blind to Simon Peter's–or any other "Peter"'s–manifest sins, faults, limitations and shortcomings. Jesus did not choose a philosopher king to shepherd his flock. He knew all too well whom he had chosen (13:18), and whom he continues to choose.

Jesus was not unaware of Peter's sins nor insensitive to his betrayal, any more than Peter himself was ignorant of one or unrepentant of the other. Unlike those who followed Peter and their assorted sycophants down the ages, Jesus did not deny the reality of Peter's sin, nor seek to call it by another name, nor wish to transmute it into a virtue.

By any standard known to the world, Peter was unfit for the job. It is the tragedy of so many of his successors that they used precisely the world's standards to demonstrate their worthiness, prove their fitness for office and find holy and hollow terms to describe their past betrayals. Simon Peter sinned, knew he sinned, and repented his sin. His encounter with the risen Lord in John 21 is an account of his repentance.

In the community of believers, the only criterion, the sole required test for tending the flock and feeding the sheep is: "Simon, son of John, do you love me?"

> **"Amen, amen, I say to you, when you were young, you girded yourself and walked where you would; but when you are old, you will stretch out your hands and another will gird you and carry you where you do not wish to go." (This he said to show by what death he was to glorify God.) And after this he said to him, "Follow me" (21:18–19).**

The reference to the death by which "he was to glorify God" is most likely not just a reference to the, by then, well-known fact of Peter's martyrdom, but also a hint of the date at which these things were written (21:24). But the point of citing the words of Jesus is not so much to prophesy Peter's future martyrdom as to insist on that which gives all martyrdoms their true sense: "Follow me" (21:19).

Simon Peter's position among the group of the twelve and the rest of the disciples, no less than his function within the community of believers, is a vocation of the Lord to follow him who reminded his disciples, "I am the good shepherd. The good shepherd lays down his life for the sheep" (10:11, 15). Of course, to follow the good shepherd and to lay down one's life for the sheep are possible only in love: "Greater love has no one than to lay down his life for his friends" (15:13). "Follow me" can only be genuine as a response to "Do you love me?" Only genuine love can follow Jesus, shepherd his flock and lay down its life for the sheep. In the community of believers, nothing else is, or ever can be, acceptable currency.

JESUS AND THE BELOVED DISCIPLE (John 21:20–23)

Peter turned and saw following them the disciple whom Jesus loved, who had lain close to his breast at the supper and had said, "Lord, who is it that is going to betray you?" (21:20).

If this highly unusual and rather lengthy identification of the beloved disciple (see 13:23, 25; 19:26; 20:2; 21:7) serves any credible purpose, then it serves to stress the importance of this beloved disciple to the evangelist. This purpose will be made explicit in the closing two verses of the gospel (21:24–25). The real relevance of the narrative itself, however, lies elsewhere.

When Peter saw him, he said to Jesus, "Lord, what about this man?" (21:21).

As is evident, Peter's confirmation as the shepherd of the flock did nothing to change him. It hardly ever does. High positions, places of power and responsibility might call forth virtues and powers that are latent in an individual, but they cannot confer them. A fool sitting on Solomon's throne acquires no wisdom, all propaganda to the contrary notwithstanding. Peter's curiosity about others might come to be described as disinterested charity, but Peter was a Nosey Parker before (see 13:24) and remains one now (21:21).

> **Jesus said to him, "If it is my will that he remain until I come, what is that to you? Follow me!" The saying spread abroad among the brethren that this disciple was not to die; yet Jesus did not say to him that he was not to die, but, "If it is my will that he remain until I come, what is that to you?" (21:22–23).**

The Lord's response to Peter occasions a misunderstanding. This time, however, it is not a "Johannine" misunderstanding but obtuseness, plain and simple. It is consoling, though ultimately futile, to witness the evangelist's attempt to squelch a rumor, misunderstanding's wayward child. The reaction of the evangelist is consoling because it reminds us how common this human frailty was then and continues to be now "among the brethren." But it is also futile, for it is a reaction doomed to failure from the start. People in every age continue to read the scriptures and hear the words of Jesus as though tropes and figures of speech were non-existent, hyperbole only an "oriental" failing, the subjunctive mood a sophistry, and the only mode of discourse the unadorned indicative.

THE CONCLUSION (JOHN 21:24–25)

> **This is the disciple who is bearing witness to these things, and who has written these things; and we know that his testimony is true (21:24)**

Once again, we have yet another good example of how not to read a text. The verse identifies the "beloved disciple" with the one who is "bearing witness to these things" and who "has written these things." But it does not tell us any more about who that disciple was, or whether he was one of "the twelve" (6:67, 70, 71; 20:24). If it seems unlikely that this is indeed the "beloved disciple" himself who is actually writing these words, then you have to ask whether this is what the verse is, in fact, saying, or whether it is merely the author's way of affirming that the beloved disciple's witness stands behind and guarantees the truth of all that is contained in the gospel.

In other words, what the Paraclete continues to do in and for the community, "teach all things, and bring to your remembrance all that I have said to you" (14:26) and "guide you into all the truth" (16:13), what was carried out through the beloved disciple in his lifetime, is now carried through by the evangelist, and will be carried through by all who come after him to open these pages and proclaim "these things." When they do, they will come to realize how right the one who added the twenty-first chapter to John's gospel was to say:

> **But there are also many other things which Jesus did; were every one of them to be written, I suppose that the world itself could not contain the books that would be written (21:25).**

...quorum pars minima hic!

Index